Seventh Edition

American Sports

From the Age of Folk Games to the Age of Televised Sports

Pamela Grundy

Benjamin G. Rader

University of Nebraska, Lincoln

D1412019

Routledge
Taylor & Francis Group

LONDON AND NEW YORK

First published 2015, 2009, 2004 by Pearson Education, Inc.

Published 2016 by Routledge
2 Park Square, Milton Park, Abingdon, Oxon OX14 4RN
711 Third Avenue, New York, NY 10017, USA

Routledge is an imprint of the Taylor & Francis Group, an informa business

COVER DESIGNER: Lumina Datamatics

ISBN 9780205888603 (pbk)

Library of Congress Cataloging-in-Publication Data

Grundy, Pamela.
   American sports: from the age of folk games to the age of televised sports/Pamela Grundy, Benjamin G. Rader,
University of Nebraska, Lincoln.—Seventh Edition.
      pages cm
   Benjamin G. Rader is listed as the sole author of the previous sixth edition.
   Includes bibliographical references and index.
   ISBN 978-0-205-88860-3 (alk. paper)
   1. Sports—United States—History.   2. Sports—Social aspects—United States.   I. Rader, Benjamin G.   II. Title.
   GV583.R3 2015
   796.0973—dc23
                                                                                                    2014017970

CONTENTS

PREFACE

In more than three decades of existence, *American Sports* has grown and developed along with the field of sports history that it seeks to encapsulate. The blossoming of sports history, with intriguing and innovative works appearing every year, has made it quite a challenge to keep up.

In this seventh edition—my first as author—I have attempted to preserve the great strengths of the earlier editions, while reordering and recasting a number of the arguments and attempting to stay abreast of rapidly evolving developments in the field and in the sporting world at large. I have also worked to integrate the experiences of athletes and communities from the margins of mainstream athletic culture—African Americans, Native Americans, women, and Latinos—more fully into the overall narrative. It has been a delight to see scholarship grow in these areas, as well as to watch the growing diversity of athletes appearing on the national and international scenes.

I have continued Ben Radar's approach of tracing the development of a few major sports over time, rather than attempting to explore the full range of games that U.S. residents have played. As a result, *American Sports* continues to focus on broad themes raised by institutions, events, and individuals that have claimed the national spotlight, rather than the myriad, equally fascinating endeavors undertaken in local communities. I hope this narrative will provide a useful starting point for further explorations.

Sports continues to offer a profoundly illuminating lens through which to view U.S. history and culture—one that grows in value as sports literature expands. While sports has definite limits as a metaphor for American society, or for any other non-sporting endeavor, I am constantly astonished by the insights it can offer into issues such as gender, race, class, sexuality, family, nationalism, religion, political processes, grassroots activism, community identity, and democracy. While it can be disconcerting to explore the ways that social and cultural dilemmas affect a realm so many people view as a pleasurable escape from the thorny challenges of daily life, few arenas of American society have so much to teach.

New to This Edition:

- Comprehensive revision of the entire text that preserves the strengths of the original text while incorporating a broad range of new stories and ideas.
- More detailed account of Native American, African and European sport prior to colonization, as well as of the interaction of sporting cultures during the colonial era.
- Far greater attention given to the sporting activities of women, African Americans, Latinos and Native Americans throughout the text.
- Complete revision of the post-World War II section that incorporates recent scholarship and sporting developments into the narrative.
- Expanded treatment of the challenges and dilemmas of twenty-first century sports.
- Learning objectives for each chapter provide guidance on major themes and events.

Acknowledgments

My largest debt, of course, is to Ben Rader, who did me the honor of entrusting his work to me, and who told me I should make any and all changes I saw fit. I believe this edition reflects both of our strengths, and is a better book than it would have been had either of us attempted it alone. Thank you, Ben.

As Ben has always noted, this work rests on the scholarship of countless individuals, many of whom have been associated with the ongoing work of the North American Society of Sports History. My own understanding of sports history has been shaped by my interactions with Elva Bishop, Susan Cahn, Mary Jo Festle, Jerma Jackson, John Kasson, Rita Liberti, Patrick Miller, Daniel Nathan, Susan Shackelford, Jill Snider, David Wiggins, the indefatigable Larry Malley, and the great John McLendon. I have also leaned frequently on the works of Arthur Ashe, Nelson George, Elliot Gorn, Lawrence Levine, Michael Oriard, Robert Peterson, Randy Roberts, Murray Sperber, Pat Summitt, and Jules Tygel, among many others.

Thanks also to those people who helped with comments, suggestions, and support along the way, including Clark Baxter, Allison Campbell, Amy Carreiro, and of course my two P's, Parker and Peter, who I am glad to see can manage quite well without me, at least for relatively short periods of time.

CHAPTER 1

Sports in Early America

Choctaw athletes competing in the centuries-old Native American ball game, as depicted by artist George Catlin in the 1840s.

In September of 1889, at a spot high in the Appalachian Mountains, two groups of Cherokee Indians squared off against each other in a ball game. At the appointed time, young men representing the rival communities of Wolf Town and Big Cove lined up face-to-face, wielding elaborately carved ball sticks and wearing eagle feathers tightly bound into their hair. Hundreds of spectators ringed the ball ground, which ran beside a river and was marked at either end with a pair of upright poles that served as goals. To one side lay closely guarded piles of the goods that players and spectators had wagered on their teams. As the players eyed each other, an elder urged them to play with honor, and to keep their composure when faced with injuries or setbacks. Then he tossed out the ball, and the players exploded into action.

"Instantly twenty pairs of ball sticks clatter together in the air, as their owners spring to catch the ball in its descent," anthropologist James Mooney wrote in an appropriately breathless account of the contest. "In the scramble it usually happens that the ball falls to the ground, when it is picked up by one more active than the rest. Frequently, however, a man will succeed in catching it between his ball sticks as it falls, and, disengaging himself from the rest, starts to run with it to the goal; but before he has gone a dozen yards they are upon him, and the whole crowd goes down together, rolling and tumbling over each other in the dust, straining and tugging for possession of the ball, until one of the players manages to extricate himself from the struggling heap and starts off with the ball. At once the others spring to their feet and, throwing away their ball sticks, run to intercept him or to prevent his capture, their black hair streaming out behind and their naked bodies glistening in the sun as they run. The scene is constantly changing. Now the players are all together at the lower end of the field, when suddenly, with a powerful throw, a player sends the ball high over the heads of the spectators and into the bushes beyond. Before there is time to realize it, here they come with a grand sweep and a burst of short, sharp

Cherokee exclamations, charging right into the crowd, knocking men and women to right and left and stumbling over dogs and babies in their frantic efforts to get at the ball."[1]

The centuries-old Native American ball game, which the Cherokee called "anetso" and French missionaries gave the name "la crosse," touched on many aspects of Cherokee culture. The strength, speed, agility, and daring that the participants displayed were the same qualities required in hunting and warfare. The excitement of competition, as well as the elaborate ceremonies that preceded the games, drew communities together. The game was also intimately intertwined with Cherokee religion. Cherokee legends told of games played by animals and gods. Players prepared for a match both physically and spiritually, with the help of a conjuror who guided them through time-honored rituals and called on powerful spirits to assist them in the game. As a result, the games became far more than exciting distractions from everyday affairs; they also served as powerful affirmations of community, identity, and worldview.

Outside Cherokee lands, in the burgeoning cities that increasingly marked the North American landscape, a very different kind of game held sway. Like anetso, "base ball" was played with balls and sticks. It too was an exciting game that displayed strength, speed, and daring and drew communities together. But baseball was only a few decades old. Its rules had been shaped not by centuries of play, but by an official committee charged with standardizing the game. Most of the fans who flocked to the newly built ballparks had migrated to the city from the countryside, or immigrated from abroad, and they often had little to connect them besides their support for the local team. Perhaps most significant, at its top levels baseball had become a commercial enterprise, much like the countless other business endeavors that were rapidly turning the United States into one of the world's most industrialized nations. The ballparks to which urban dwellers so eagerly flocked had been built in anticipation of profits from ticket sales. The newspapers that published enthusiastic accounts of the games sought to draw readers and increase circulation. The players, most of whom had roots in Europe or Africa as well as North America, were professionals, tied to their teams not by kinship or community, but by salaries and contracts.

The new game spoke to the changes that had transformed the North American continent since the arrival of European explorers set off a massive, worldwide migration that left few corners of the globe untouched. Starting in the 1500s, a flood of Europeans and Africans—the latter generally brought against their will—overwhelmed the native populations of North and South America, as well as the islands that ringed the Caribbean Sea. Propelled by the imperatives of commerce and Christianity, the new arrivals established colonial societies across the continents. In the temperate southern regions, colonialism was fueled by the profits from large-scale agriculture—sugarcane in the Caribbean and South America; cattle ranching in South America and Mexico; and cotton, rice, and tobacco in the southernmost colonies of North America. Further north, colonists established family farms and a small-scale manufacturing sector that would eventually help spark the Industrial Revolution.

As the inhabitants of these new worlds built new societies, they also shaped new sports, drawing on the circumstances in which they found themselves, as well as on their rich range of sporting traditions. Considering the sporting traditions on which inhabitants of the future United States drew, as well as the processes by which they shaped their games, helps illustrate some of the many ways that sports can be linked to culture, as well as the broad range of cultures that contributed to the sports we know today.

The North American Ball Game

While natives of eastern North America enjoyed many different kinds of games and competitions, none held as much significance as the ball game. The game, played from Huron and Iroquois territory in the north to Creek and Choctaw lands in the south, varied from community to community, depending on tradition and circumstances. Players might wield one stick or two, teams might have fewer than a dozen members or more than a hundred, ball fields could vary from 300 yards to half a mile in length. But no matter what the rules, young men—and sometimes young women—grew up carving sticks, tossing balls, and dreaming of some day representing their communities. Stories of the game were woven throughout Native American legends: telling, for example, of the day a powerful spirit presented the Fox people with a stick and a buckskin ball and taught them how to play, or of the time that kindness to a bat and a flying squirrel helped the creatures of the air win a game from the creatures of the earth.

Ball games often took place at times of spiritual significance, such as the end of harvest, and were frequently held to honor or solicit the deities who had taught humans how to play. They were accompanied by elaborate rituals. Among the Cherokee, for example, preparations for a game began weeks in advance. Players linked themselves with speed, flight, and keen vision by weaving bat wings through their sticks and gathering eagle feathers to tie into their hair. Community members began to gather goods for wagers and plan the ceremonies that would precede the event. These preparations reached a peak the night before the game, when each town took part in an all-night dance, and the players embarked on a 24-hour fast. With fires burning, musicians playing, and babies sleeping in the bushes, men, women, and children danced and chanted. During the dance, and again the next morning, each team made several ceremonial journeys to a nearby river, where the conjurers performed their final rituals.

Most ball games were played between individual communities, which often nurtured longtime rivalries. But because of their close connections with natural and spiritual forces, games were also linked to larger events. Games could be used to formally mend relationships or settle disputes among feuding communities. Like ritual dances, they could also be employed in efforts to influence the weather, or help heal the sick. In the fall of 1636, for example, Huron communities living around Lake Huron were ravaged by influenza, one of the many deadly diseases that Europeans brought to the New World. French Jesuit missionaries reported that one renowned Huron conjurer "had declared that the whole country was sick; and he had prescribed a remedy, namely, a game of crosse, for its recovery. This order had been published throughout all the villages, the Captains had set about having it executed, and the young people had not spared their arms."[2]

The Mesoamerican Ball Game

Further to the south, in areas that would become known as Mexico and South America, traditional games and entertainments included a yet another kind of ball play. In a tradition thousands of years old, athletes of the Aztec, Mayan, and other Mesoamerican empires competed on specially built courts, striving to send a heavy rubber ball through a stone ring. As with other traditional games, rules varied from community to community, but players were generally forbidden to use their hands, feet, or head, and instead propelled the ball with their hips, thighs, and shoulders. The largest and wealthiest empires had created elaborate, urbanized societies, and these cultures gave rise to highly skilled corps of specialized athletes, who performed for royalty and other elites. These players could compete for hours without allowing the ball to touch the ground. The game required tremendous strength and ability, and idealized images of strong, young ballplayers appeared throughout Mesoamerican art, indicating the high regard in which these athletes were held.[3]

The Mesoamerican game was also closely tied to Mesoamerican religion. Ball games frequently appeared in legends: most notably in Mayan accounts of a pair of gods known as the Hero Twins. According to the legend, the Twins descended into the underworld, rescued the Lord of Corn by defeating the Lord of Death in a ball game, and then ascended to the sky. Mesoamerican religious beliefs cast the world as an ongoing struggle between the opposites of day and night, good and evil, and life and death—a contest neatly encapsulated by competition between two groups of ballplayers. This link between the games and the balance of cosmic forces could make the stakes for ball games especially high. Mesoamerican beliefs held that human sacrifices played a key role in keeping the gods happy and the cosmos in balance. As a result, players who lost a game might also lose their lives.

European Sporting Traditions

The Europeans who arrived in the Americas carried their own sporting traditions. European Christianity drew sharp distinctions between material and spiritual worlds, and European sports bore little religious significance. Many traditional games and entertainments had in fact emerged from the continent's pre-Christian era and were often frowned upon by Christian authorities. But sports and games played important roles in European societies, and many colonial-era migrants sought to reproduce European traditions in their new settings.

One function sports served in Europe was to distinguish the upper from the lower classes. Sports that required costly investments in land or animals became ways for elites to cement bonds among themselves and display their superior wealth and abilities to commoners, who were frequently prohibited from engaging in such exalted activities. In England, the limited forest land belonged to the landed gentry, and hunting stags or foxes was a favorite sport of kings and noblemen (common Englishmen rarely had the chance to hunt, and those who journeyed to the colonies generally had to learn hunting skills from Native Americans). Horse racing, another elite pursuit, took place at specially built tracks attended exclusively by wealthy patrons. In Spain, where many families earned their wealth from cattle raising, the well-to-do were also avid hunters, and public festivities frequently centered on the display of upper-class horsemanship (the Spanish word for "gentleman," *caballero*, translates literally as "horseman"). As part of these events, which often took place in a town's public square, elaborately garbed noblemen engaged in cattle-roping exhibitions, in mounted mock combat, and in bullfights—the original bullfighters were noblemen who fought on horseback.[4]

European commoners, on the other hand, pursued their sporting activities as part of what historian Richard Holt has termed a "festive culture" that prevailed across Europe during the medieval era.[5] This culture underscored the social bonds that organized communal life, and offered participants a brief means of escape from the hard work that dominated their daily activities. European villagers invariably concluded their harvest season with a festival of thanks accompanied by hearty eating, drinking, dancing, and game playing. In addition, the Christian calendar offered numerous opportunities for communities to stop work in order to honor patron saints, celebrate major events in the life of Christ, and commemorate numerous other saints and martyrs. Some of these festivals were organized by nobles as exhibitions of their wealth and power, but many others, such as Maypole festivities and the exchange of eggs at Easter, were arranged by villagers themselves, and incorporated elements of Europe's pre-Christian past.

Folk games formed an integral part of these festivities. In Britain, many parishes enjoyed stoolball, foot races, quoits (in which a contestant attempted to throw an iron ring over a peg), and skittles or ninepins (both forms of bowling). Versions of bowling were also popular in Germany and Holland, and the Dutch were especially fond of a club-and-ball game they called "colf." Games played into the flirtatious atmosphere that so often infused community celebrations, furnishing young men with opportunities to display their physiques and skills to marriageable young women. In some places, games such as foot races served a similar purpose for women. "Nothing is more usual than for a nimble-footed wench to get a husband at the same time as she wins a smock," observed Joseph Addison about one British festival in the early eighteenth century.[6]

Games and spectacles were often violent, affirming a masculine ethos of individual prowess and physical courage. Britons especially relished wrestling and cudgeling. In cudgeling, the combatants employed wicker shields for protection, while using a long stick to "break the head" or draw blood from opponents. The ancient "blood sport" of cockfighting—where roosters armed with metal spurs fought to the death—was practiced throughout Europe, and excited spectators usually wagered on the outcome. In many parts of Spain, commoners arranged their own bullfights (without horses) and Britons avidly engaged in bullbaiting, in which a group of dogs attempted to immobilize a tethered bull. Admiration for the characteristics of "bulldogs" eventually transformed them into a national symbol of Britain's tenacity.

European villagers also reveled in a game known as "football." Unlike modern soccer, rugby, or American football, all of which sprang from the medieval game, the village sport had no common rules. Some games were ad hoc affairs with an unspecified number of players. Others were regularly scheduled contests between rival villages. Depending upon local customs, the game might emphasize kicking, running, or throwing the ball. The football, which was normally an inflated animal bladder, was sometimes encased in leather. The ostensible purpose of the game was to move the ball across a previously defined goal line.

In some places, the game had sophisticated rules and strategies for deceiving the opposition. In Cornwall, for example, custom required that each player pair off with another, attempting to block his opponent's advance. This feature, along with an offside rule, made it similar to modern American football. On the other hand, in many places football seems to have been little less than an unregulated brawl. The players kicked, wrestled, and sometimes struck their opponents with their fists. Damaged property, torn clothing, bloodied bodies, and sometimes death accompanied these contests. Citing football's contribution to social disorder, English monarchs and local magistrates banned the game on at least 30 separate occasions between 1314 and 1617. None of these measures permanently impeded the game's popularity.

Games and revelries helped satisfy particular needs of seventeenth- and eighteenth-century Europeans. Festivities relieved some of the grimness of life, which routinely included early death from disease and famine (the day-to-day struggles of ordinary life were one reason many Europeans were willing to take the risk of emigrating to the Americas). They frequently provided a setting for courtship rituals. They could offer a symbolic and thereby safe expression of resentments arising from the inequalities in the social structure. Young men frequently engaged in a pageant of "misrule" that included public mockery of social superiors, married men, the church, and even the monarch. Games such as football also helped to promote village unity. "At the seasons of football and cockfighting" according to a 1712 writer, many parishes "reassume their...hatred of each other. My tenant in the country is verily persuaded that the parish of the enemy hath not one honest man in it."[7] Versions of these European sporting traditions became common features of colonial life throughout the Americas.

European Sport in the Americas

When Europeans arrived in the Americas, they frequently sought to replace native festivals and celebrations with their own. The Spanish, for example, banned all the events associated with Mesoamerican religion, including the ball game, and instituted their own calendar of Catholic holidays. As landowners and merchants grew wealthy from the resources of their newly acquired land, they sponsored elaborate celebrations of Christian saints, feast days, and important government events, complete with music, fireworks, games, and dancing. As in Spain, they emphasized their status and power through lavish public displays, which featured elaborate costumes and exhibitions of horsemanship. They imported Spanish bulls and fighting cocks, and built bull rings and cockpits.

One particularly popular event in Mexico was the *corrida*—a day-long festival that featured the horsemanship that had been so important in Spain. At first, as in Spain, the horse events were limited to the elite, and both natives and *mestizos* (people of mixed Spanish-native heritage) were forbidden to take part. But as time went on, most large landowners relocated to the cities, and *mestizos* took over both ranching duties and the *corridas*. The *corridas* took on a more indigenous character; organizers included more local games and dances, and turned events that honored Catholic saints and holy days into celebrations of indigenous deities as well. *Mestizos* developed their own distinctive style of riding, and added new, often more dangerous events such as subduing wild bulls, riding wild horses, and bringing down animals with elaborate roping techniques. These new horsemen became known as *charros*, and their sporting activities as *charreria*. *Charros* and their skills gained new status in the early 1800s, when they played central roles in Mexico's war for independence. In 1821, when the Spaniards withdrew from the country, *charros* became national icons, and *charreria* became the official Mexican sport. In the mid-1800s, when the United States extended its reach into Texas and California, *charreria* became an American sport as well, eventually giving rise to the modern-day rodeo.[8]

Sport in the Southern British Colonies

A similar transformation took place in the southern British colonies, driven by a powerful landed gentry that had arisen from generous royal land grants worked by indentured servants, as well as by growing numbers of imported Africans (British planters initially sought to enslave Native Americans, but with limited success). Southern planters did their best to emulate the lifestyle of the English country gentry. They built splendid mansions that often included special rooms for dancing and billiard playing; they ate with silver decorated with the family's coat of arms. They frequently sent their sons to England to acquire the culture, tastes, and skills of "gentlemen"—an education that often included athletics. When a young William Byrd II returned home to Virginia, he enthusiastically played all the games that he had encountered in the mother country, including billiards, bowls, ninepins, skittles, and even a version of cricket.

As in Britain, the southern gentry used sports as a mark of social status. In colonial Virginia, only the gentry could legally hunt deer. Southern elites also organized fox hunts, and when the indigenous grey foxes proved overly elusive, they imported red foxes from England. Horse racing was another elite preserve, as dramatically illustrated in the much cited case of Virginia tailor James Bullocke. In 1674, Bullocke entered his mare in a race against a horse owned by Dr. Matthew Slader, with 2,000 pounds of tobacco at stake. For such presumption, the county court fined Bullocke 200 pounds of tobacco and asserted that horse racing was "a sport for gentlemen only."[9]

No pastime ignited the passions of the southern gentry more than horse racing. Racing began as a largely impromptu affair, in which young planters would challenge one another to a race on Saturday afternoons, on court days, or after Sunday church services. Bets would be placed, the owners would mount, a gun would be fired, and the horses would sprint down a quarter mile dirt track. "If you happened to be looking the other way," Thomas Anburey wrote, "the race is terminated before you can turn your head."[10] Virginians bred a particularly wiry animal with powerful hindquarters, known as the quarter horse, for this kind of race.

In the last half of the eighteenth century, however, the great planters had turned from the quarter horse to the English thoroughbred. Thoroughbred racing tested "bottom," the ability to race over a mile or several miles. In contrast to their English counterparts, the colonial gentry encouraged thoroughbred racing as a public spectacle.

In England, straightaway courses permitted exciting perspectives only in the vicinity of the finish line and only the upper strata attended the races. But the colonial gentry raced their horses on mile-long oval tracks, which afforded a good view to all, and men of all ranks attended the races. Horse owners formed jockey clubs in Maryland, Virginia, and South Carolina, which built fenced tracks and charged for admission. The clubs kept careful records of bloodlines, and races and racers began to don colorful apparel that separated them from one another.

As racing became more organized, so did the training of horses and jockeys. Much of this work fell to slaves of African descent. Africans had brought their own sports with them across the ocean. Like Native Americans, most of the Africans brought to the Americas came from traditional societies where sports and religion were closely intermixed. Africans from the ancient kingdom of Angola, for example, practiced a dance-like martial art known as *engolo* that centered on kicks and acrobatics and was tied to traditional spiritual beliefs. Their descendants would engage in the sport for generations, calling it "knocking and kicking" in the American South, *danmyé* in French Martinique, and *jogo de capieira* in Brazil, where it would eventually become an integral part of Brazilian culture. But like many of the traditions that enslaved Africans carried to North America, especially those with spiritual significance, sports such as *engolo* were practiced largely in secret, along with traditional forms of dancing, singing, and drumming that helped participants to maintain independent identities and community cohesion despite the assaults of slavery.[11]

Still, as the rise of black jockeys indicated, Africans and their descendants also adapted to the demands of their new situations. One early star was Austin Curtis, who formed a particularly strong relationship with his iconoclastic owner, North Carolina planter Willie Jones. Working together, they developed a renowned group of race horses that made Jones the most successful stable owner and Curtis the most famous jockey in the South. In 1891, Jones freed Curtis and made him a partner in the stable. Such a show of respect, however, was rare. More often, the planters' lavish displays of games and gambling were directed toward reinforcing their dominance over southern society.[12]

Southern Festivals

As in Spanish America, festivals became key parts of life in the southern colonies. The Hanover County Fair in Virginia, established in 1737, included a great feast accompanied by the music of drums, trumpets, and oboes. The fair sponsored contests with various prizes: five pounds for a horse race, a hat for a cudgeling match, a violin for a fiddling contest, a pair of silver buckles for a wrestling match, and "a pair of handsome silk stockings…[to] be given to the handsomest young country maid that appears in the field."[13] Festival pursuits also included blood sports. Gander pulling was a favorite. Usually staged on Easter Monday, a day of boisterous celebration in the Chesapeake Bay region, the neck of a goose was liberally greased and the hapless animal was hung by its feet from a rope stretched between two trees or tied to a tree limb. The contestants mounted their horses and galloped by at full speed, while they attempted to jerk the goose's head off. The winner got the blood-soaked goose for his supper.

Men of both high and low status frequented the cockpits. One traveler's account described a cockpit as "surrounded by many genteel people, promiscuously mingled with the vulgar and the debased. Exceedingly beautiful cocks were produced, armed with long, sharp, steel-pointed gaffs." Men placed their bets. The cocks then went at each other furiously, "not the least disconcerted by the crowd or the shouting." Even after having been pierced repeatedly by the gaffs, the cocks continued to fight as long as they were able to crawl. After the middle of the eighteenth century, cockfighting increasingly came under the patronage of the gentry. Newspapers began to announce the greater matches, many of which were scheduled on major holidays.[14]

Tensions in New England

Such traditional European pastimes, however, found far less favor in the New England colonies, where the dominant Puritans frowned on what they viewed as idle or sinful recreation. During the late sixteenth and early seventeenth centuries, even before the first permanent British settlements in North America, Puritan reformers made recreation a focus of controversy in Britain. They campaigned to extend the Church of England's break with the Roman Catholic Church by wiping out all remnants of the holy days, rituals, pageantry, and symbols associated with Catholicism. They were especially enraged by Sunday merriments, and in the early years of the seventeenth century mounted campaigns throughout England to suppress public recreation on the Sabbath.

In the New World, where Puritans sought to build a society free from the worldly absorptions of the country they had left behind, recreation became one focus of conflict. On Christmas Day in 1621, for example, William Bradford, the doughty governor of the tiny Plymouth colony, called his able-bodied men to work just before dawn. Bradford's summons came as no surprise to most of the settlers, who joined Bradford in rejecting the idea of Christmas as a holiday. Yet a few recent arrivals from England objected to Bradford's order. Their consciences, they informed the governor, forbade them from toiling on Christmas Day. Bradford disagreed with the newcomers, but as daylight hours were precious he decided to wait until later to convince them of their errors. He departed with the remaining men to take up the work at hand.

When Bradford, along with his workmen, returned at noon, he found that the new arrivals were shouting, laughing, and running about in Plymouth's single street "openly at play." As he later wrote, "Some were pitching the bar, and some [were playing] at stool-ball."[15] Bradford was furious. He seized the players' "implements" and ordered them off the street. Just as work on Christmas Day violated the newcomers' consciences, he proclaimed, merrymaking on Christ's birthday violated the conscience of the governor. This conflict continued. In 1640, for example, Massachusetts levied a fine upon anyone who fasted, feasted, or refused to work on Christmas Day. Quakers, another group of Protestant reformers whose zeal at times outstripped that of the Puritans, adopted similar laws in Pennsylvania.

The New England colonies established an unusually stern Sabbath. Beginning on Saturday night and ending at sundown on Sunday, the colonies forbade work, recreation, travel, idle conversation, sexual intercourse, and even "unnecessary and unreasonable walking in the streets and fields." In 1656, a Captain Kemble of Boston had to sit in the stocks for two hours for "lewd and unseemly conduct." After having been at sea for three years, the indiscreet captain had publicly kissed his wife on the Sabbath. Even as late as the 1730s, when stringent control of personal behavior had noticeably relaxed in colonial Massachusetts, Joseph Bennett, an English traveler, observed that in Boston the Lord's Day was the "strictest kept that ever I yet saw anywhere."[16] The Sabbatarian legislation of colonial America left an enduring legacy, one that was reinforced periodically by religious revivals. It was not until the 1930s, for example, that Pennsylvania dropped state bans on Sunday baseball games.

"Lawful Sport" in New England and the Middle Colonies

In both Old and New England, the Puritans objected more to the overall tenor of the festive culture than to the specific games associated with that culture. Indeed, the Puritans extended their approval to what Richard Baxter, a prominent divine, called *lawful sport or recreation*. To be lawful, a sport had to be dissociated from traditional revelries. Furthermore, a lawful sport should refresh the participants so that they could better execute their worldly and spiritual "callings" or duties. "We daily need some respite and diversion, without which we dull our powers; a little intermission sharpens 'em again," noted one minister. "Recreation," wrote another, "must tend also to glorify God...the scope and end of all recreation is, that God may be honored in and by them."[17]

To meet the standards of lawful pastimes required constant vigilance, an undeviating attention to the consequences of engaging in diversions. If a pastime became an all-absorbing activity, an end in itself without thought of one's higher duties, then one should stop engaging in it. If the sport stimulated the passions, entailed deceit, or resulted in idleness, gambling, excessive drinking, or sexual immorality, then it should also be avoided. Puritans believed that all time was sacred; one's use of every moment was accountable to God. As a result, conscientious Puritans approached all forms of play with excruciating caution.

Consistent with their notions of lawful sport, seventeenth-century New England Puritans expressly condemned certain sports. They castigated animal baiting, fighting, and all games associated with gambling or immoderate drinking. Puritans viewed gambling as especially sinful; not only was it a form of idleness, it also mocked God, who controlled all things. The colonial assemblies specifically legislated against "unlawful games at cards, dice, etc." and fined innkeepers who permitted gambling of any kind. Horse racing became another target. In Ipswich, Connecticut, legislation mandated that anyone "convicted of running races upon horses...in the streets of Ipswich, or for abetting and encouraging others of laying wagers on any side should pay 40 shillings," an extraordinarily severe fine.[18] Such legal strictures did not completely suppress racing; later in the eighteenth century, Boston newspapers even openly advertised races held outside the city's environs. Yet, unlike in the southern colonies, horse racing occupied at most a marginal place in New England's recreational life.

Young people were sometimes able to escape some of these strictures. Children played with toys and were allowed to swim in the summer and skate in the winter. Boys and young men also played football and bat-and-ball games, sometimes in defiance of official bans. Boston's selectmen prohibited football in 1657, after "several persons...received hurt by boys and young men playing at football in the streets." But the ban must not have been completely effective, for it was republished in 1677 and again in 1701. An English traveler, John Dutton, reported witnessing "a great game of football" between young men on a Massachusetts beach in 1685, but given the paucity of evidence for similar contests elsewhere, this game was probably unusual.[19]

The colony that became New York, which was originally settled by the Dutch and boasted an especially heterogeneous population, offered some recreational respite. Dutch settlers bowled, held boat races, and played "colf." Despite condemnation by local Puritans, the royal governor, his entourage, and prosperous merchants patronized other diversions. In 1664, the governor established the first organized horse races at the Newmarket course on Hempstead Plains, Long Island. In 1736, wealthy New York sportsmen built America's first circular racing track. Cockfighting and animal baiting also became common pastimes.

Farther south and west, the dominant Quakers specifically banned "all prizes, stage plays, cards, dice, may games, masques, revels, bull-baiting, cock-fighting, bear-baitings and the like." On the other hand, they specifically encouraged "useful" and "needful" recreation. Quaker schools set aside times for physical exercises and both youngsters and adults swam in the summer and skated in the winter. Hunting and fishing, if engaged in for subsistence, also met with Quaker approval. William Penn, the colony's founder, summed up the Quaker attitude in an epigram. "The best recreation," he wrote, "is to do good."[20]

Like the Puritans in New York, the Quakers encountered difficulties in enforcing their notions of lawful sport. In the eighteenth century they had to contend with a huge influx of non-Quaker immigrants, including not only non-Quaker English but also Scots-Irish and Germans. Each ethnic group had its own recreational traditions. Furthermore, by the middle of the eighteenth century, the Quakers were losing political and cultural power to a new and more secular upper class. The new group had little or no sympathy with Penn's idea of a "Godly Commonwealth." Emulating counterparts in London, the local gentry in Philadelphia formed exclusive clubs—the Mount Regal Fishing Club, the Society of the Sons of St. Tammany, and the Hunting Club, for example—and shared a rich associative life that revolved around leisure activities.[21]

Quaker and Puritan notions of lawful sport would persist long after the colonies declared their independence from England in 1776. Even those who had rejected Puritan or Quaker theology were products of its culture, and engagement in uninhibited play was likely to feel somehow unseemly. "I was not sent into this world to spend my days in sports, diversions, and pleasures," wrote John Adams in the middle of the eighteenth century. "I was born for business; for both activity and study."[22] Heirs of the Puritan tradition rarely engaged in sport simply for pleasure. Rather, they sought larger justifications, such as glorifying God or renewing and strengthening the body for more important tasks.

The Great Awakening and Republican Ideology

Sports took another blow in the 1730s and 1740s, when a religious revival of unprecedented proportions, known as the Great Awakening, swept through the colonies. Evangelicals, as Great Awakening converts came to be known, were if anything more suspicious of sport than the first Puritans. They believed in searing conversion experiences and an absolute submission of the self to a demanding and omnipotent God. Spiritual rebirth launched evangelicals on crusades against the evils of the secular world, in which they demanded complete purity in the church and in individual behavior.

Everywhere the evangelicals tried to suppress or at the least restrain the more boisterous sporting ways. A typical instance occurred in 1739, when the Great Awakening's most renowned evangelist, George Whitefield, met with the governor, local ministers, and several gentlemen in Annapolis, Maryland. "Some of the company, I believe, thought I was too strict, and were very strenuous in defense of what they called innocent diversions," Whitefield reported, "but when I told them everything was sinful which was not done with a single eye to God's glory, and that such entertainment not only discovered [reflected] a levity of mind, but were contrary to the whole tenor of the Gospel of Christ, they seemed somewhat convinced."[23]

For the rest of the eighteenth century and into the nineteenth century, evangelical Protestants continued to mount campaigns for the reform of leisure activities. In 1774, a Virginia planter lamented the influence of an evangelical group whose members "are growing very numerous and…quite destroying pleasure in the country; for they encourage ardent pray'r; strong and constant faith & the entire banishment of gaming dancing & Sabbath-day diversions."[24] Sportsmen throughout the colonies voiced similar complaints.

Republicanism, the political belief that sparked the American Revolution (1775–1783), also tended to inhibit sports. According to this theory, a successful republic—a state with sovereignty residing in the citizenry rather than a hereditary aristocracy or a monarchy—could not be founded upon the idle amusements of the decadent monarchies of Europe. For the American republic to survive and prosper, its citizens needed to be especially virtuous and abstemious; they had to abstain from luxury, practice frugality, and avoid dissipation.

Adherents of republicanism joined evangelical Protestants in encouraging the revolutionary governments to suppress popular pastimes. The First Continental Congress called for the colonies to "discountenance and discourage every species of extravagance and dissipation, especially all horse-racing, and all kinds of gaming, cock fighting, exhibition of shows, plays, and other expensive diversions and amusements."[25] The Sons of Liberty, an extralegal citizen group that spread to most of the colonies, worked to impose such strictures on the population for the duration of the Revolution. The new states likewise adopted sumptuary laws designed to curtail personal extravagance. As Samuel Adams, both a product of Puritan New England and an ardent republican, put it, each state ought to strive to become a "Christian Sparta."

Thomas Jefferson, republicanism's leading champion, also worried about the effects of popular diversions on the new republic. "Games played with the ball and others of that nature, are too violent for the body and stamp no character on the mind," Jefferson flatly advised his nephew, Peter Carr. He blamed the English gentry for the tendency of young American "gentlemen" to gamble, drink excessively, engage in riotous sports, and patronize prostitutes. If the young American "goes to England," Jefferson wrote in another letter, "he learns drinking, horse racing, and boxing." In addition, "he is led, by the strongest of human passions, into a spirit of female intrigue...or a passion for whores, destructive of his health, and in both cases learns to consider fidelity to the marriage bed as an ungentlemanly practice."[26] In these letters Jefferson aptly spelled out a fundamental republican fear, namely that the indulgences of the European monarchies and upper classes threatened to spread like a cancer, destroying the virtue and simplicity essential to a republic's existence. Nothing haunted the imaginations of the republicans more than an idle, pleasure-loving aristocracy.

In the end, the republican goal of abstemious behavior fell short of its goals. Even during the revolution, many ignored the demands for frugality and self-denial. General George Washington himself instructed his officers to encourage innocent "games of exercise for amusement" among the troops in the Continental Army. Soldiers bowled (sometimes using cannonballs) and played wicket (a form of cricket), shinny (a game similar to field hockey), fives (a form of handball), base (a form of baseball), and football (the medieval version of the game). Washington's orders to suppress gambling were frequently ignored.

Indeed, during the last half of the eighteenth century, America increasingly became an integral part of a larger North Atlantic market of commercial leisure. After mid-century, itinerant theater troops from London began to stage plays in cities along the Atlantic coast from Boston to Charles Town. As early as the 1750s, English equestrians and acrobats regularly visited the colonies, including the "celebrated" Anthony Joseph Dugee, who performed "on a slack wire scarcely perceptible with and without the balance." During the last two decades of the eighteenth century, the incidence of cockfighting as well as other kinds of diversions apparently increased. Instead of implanting a new respect for simplicity, frugality, selflessness, and order, as many of the Revolution's leaders had hoped for, the Revolution and its accompanying ideology fostered at least an equal amount of disorder and extravagance.[27]

Conclusion

By the end of the eighteenth century, the continent that was home to the newly founded United States of America had become a remarkably diverse place, bringing together people from many backgrounds and traditions of many kinds. Some sporting traditions, such as the clandestine *engolo*, remained confined to specific communities. Others, such as horse racing, had begun to cross cultural boundaries, taking on new forms and serving new purposes. The stage was also being set for far greater changes. In the nineteenth century, economic expansion, urban growth, and great advances in both transportation and communication would give rise to a new set of sporting cultures suited to a transformed social and economic world.

Critical Thinking Questions

1. In what situations did religious belief encourage sporting competitions? In what situations did religion impede sports?
2. How can you use the development of colonial American sports to explore the ways that the colonial American society both resembled and diverged from European society?
3. To what extent do present-day sports include elements of "festive culture"? How do you account for this persistence (or lack thereof).

Notes

1. James Mooney, "The Cherokee Ball Play," *The American Anthropologist* III (April 1890), 130–31. See also Thomas Vennum, Jr., *American Indian Lacrosse: Little Brother of War* (Washington, DC: Smithsonian Institution Press, 1994); Joseph B. Oxendine, *American Indian Sports Heritage* (Lincoln: University of Nebraska Press, 1995); and Michael J. Zogry, *Anetso, the Cherokee Ball Game: At the Center of Ceremony and Identity* (Chapel Hill: University of North Carolina Press, 2010).
2. Quoted in *The Jesuit Relations and Allied Documents*, Vol. 13 (Cleveland: The Burrows Brothers, 1897), 130.
3. See E. Michael Whittington, ed., *The Sport of Life and Death: The Mesoamerican Ballgame* (Charlotte, NC: The Mint Museum of Art, 2001).
4. For an account of sport in Spain and the Spanish colonies, see Jorge Iber, et al., *Latinos in U.S. Sport: A History of Isolation, Cultural Identity and Acceptance* (Champaign, IL: Human Kinetics, 2011), chapter 1.
5. Richard Holt, *Sport and the British* (Oxford: Oxford University Press, 1989).
6. Quoted in ibid., 4.
7. Quoted in R.W. Malcolmson, *Popular Recreations in British Society, 1700–1850* (Cambridge: Cambridge University Press, 1975), 83.
8. See Mary Lou LeCompte, "The Hispanic Influence on the History of Rodeo, 1823–1922," *Journal of Sport History* 12 (Spring 1985), 21–38.
9. For recreation in the southern colonies, see T.H. Breen, "Horses and Gentlemen: The Cultural Significance of Gambling among the Gentry in Virginia," *William and Mary Quarterly* 34 (1977), 239–57; Jane Carson, *Colonial Virginians at Play* (Williamsburg, VA: Colonial Williamsburg, 1965); and C.R. Barnett, "Recreational Patterns of the Colonial Virginia Aristocrat," *Journal of the West Virginia Historical Association* 2 (1978), 1–11. For the contrast between southern and northern life, see C. Vann Woodward's classic essay, "The Southern Ethic in a Puritan World," in his *American Counterpoint* (Boston: Little, Brown, 1971). Quote is from Breen, "Horses and Gentlemen," 250.
10. Quoted in David H. Fischer, *Albion's Seed: Four British Folkways in America* (New York: Oxford University Press, 1989), 361.
11. T.J. Desch Obi, *Fighting for Honor: The History of African Martial Arts in the Atlantic World* (Columbia: University of South Carolina Press, 2008).
12. For an account of early African American jockeys, see Ed Hotaling, *Wink: The Incredible Life and Epic Journey of Jimmy Winkfield* (New York: McGraw Hill, 2005), chapter 1; and Hotaling, *The Great Black Jockeys* (Rocklin, CA: Forum, 1999).
13. Quoted in Edmund S. Morgan, *Virginians at Home* (New York: Holt, Rinehart and Winston, 1962), 88.
14. Quoted in Rhys Isaac, *The Transformation of Virginia* (Chapel Hill: University of North Carolina Press, 1982), 102.
15. William Bradford, *Of Plymouth Plantation, 1620–1647* (New York: Alfred A. Knopf, 1952), 97. For an indispensable collection of primary sources for early American sports,

see Thomas L. Altherr, ed., *Sports in North America: A Documentary History* Vols. I & II (Gulf Breeze, FL: Academic International Press, 1997). The most analytical treatment of sports in early Anglo-America is Nancy Struna, *People of Prowess: Sport, Leisure, and Labor in Early Anglo-America* (Urbana: University of Illinois Press, 1996).

16. Quoted in John C. Miller, *The First Frontier* (New York: Dell, 1966), 87.

17. Hans-Peter Wagner, *Puritan Attitudes Towards Recreation in Early Seventeenth-Century New England* (Frankfurt am Main, Germany: Lang, 1982), 48; Perry Miller and T.H. Johnson, eds., *The Puritans*, 2 vols. (New York: Harper, 1963), I, 392. See also Bruce C. Daniels, *Puritans at Play: Leisure and Recreation in Colonial New England* (New York: St. Martin's, 1995).

18. Quoted in Fischer, *Albion's Seed*, 148.

19. Wagner, *Puritan Attitudes*, 34; and A.B. Hart, *Commonwealth History of Massachusetts*, 5 vols. (New York: Historical Society, 1927–30), II, 280.

20. Quotations in Fischer, *Albion's Seed*, 552, 555. See J.T. Jable, "Pennsylvania's Blue Laws: A Quaker Experiment in the Suppression of Sport and Amusements," *Journal of Sport History* 1 (1974), 107–21.

21. See Stephen Brobeck, "Revolutionary Change in Colonial Philadelphia: The Brief Life of the Proprietary Gentry," *William and Mary Quarterly* 33 (1976), 410–34.

22. John Adams, *The Work of John Adams*, 5 vols. (Boston: Charles C. Little and James Brown, 1840), II, 125–26.

23. Quoted in Philip Greven, *The Protestant Temperament* (New York: A.A. Knopf, 1977), 145.

24. H.D. Farish, ed., *Journal & Letters of Philip Vickers Fithian* (Williamsburg, VA: Colonial Williamsburg, 1943), 96.

25. H.S. Commager, ed., *Documents in American History*, 2 vols. (Englewood Cliffs, NJ: Prentice Hall, 1973), I, 86.

26. Quotations in Altherr, ed., *Sports in North America*, Part II, 75; and H.S. Commager, ed., *Living Ideas in America*, new ed. (New York: Harper & Row, 1964), 555–56.

27. See especially Struna, *People of Prowess*, chapter 8, and the data in Struna, "Gender and Sporting Practices in Early America, 1750–1810," *Journal of Sport History* 18 (1991), 13ff, as well as R.E. Powell, "Sport, Social Relations and Animal Husbandry: Early Cockfighting in North America," *International Journal of Sport History* 5 (1993), 361–81.

CHAPTER 2

The Setting for Nineteenth-Century Sports

Spectators line the Long Island racecourse for a race between two regional rivals, Peytona, who hailed from Alabama, and Fashion, from New Jersey.

LEARNING OBJECTIVES

2.1 Describe how economic, cultural, and technological factors both facilitated and impeded the growth of nineteenth-century American sports.

2.2 Explain how technological developments aided the development of popular sports.

2.3 Analyze the ways that the dominant Victorian culture impeded the development of sports.

2.4 Outline the factors that contributed to the development of a sports-centered Victorian counterculture.

2.5 Discuss the changes in sports and society that helped make sports more respectable near the end of the nineteenth century.

2.6 Articulate the ways that people at the margins of American society used sports to try to improve their social standing.

On May 13, 1845, nearly 100,000 eager spectators made their way to the Union race course on Long Island, New York. Wagons and carriages clogged the roads, creating enormous traffic jams. Trains converged from all directions. The crowds came to a race between two celebrated mares: eight-year-old Fashion, from New Jersey, and the much younger Peytona, who hailed from Alabama. The contest was notable not only for the elevated stakes—the winner would take home $20,000—but also for the broader political issues it invoked. At a time when the country's western expansion and the question of slavery in the new territories were sparking rising tensions between North and South, a contest between northern and southern horses carried a special edge. Horse racing had become one way that Americans played out sectional conflicts, and southerners were aching to avenge two previous high-profile losses: the defeat of Sir Henry by Eclipse in 1823, and Fashion's triumph over the southern stallion Boston in 1842. The entire South rejoiced when Peytona crossed the finish line ahead of her more seasoned rival.

The Fashion-Peytona contest marked the end of an era. As North–South conflicts progressed toward war, emotions became too heated for intersectional sporting competitions. Interest in horse racing also dwindled. Still, the forces that had nurtured the 1845 extravaganza would continue to spur other forms of sport. The growth of industry and corporations, revolutions in communication and transportation, rising per capita incomes, and the rapid growth of cities, all created conditions suited to sporting competitions with mass appeal. In addition, radical changes in society and work undercut traditional sources of excitement, job satisfaction, and a sense of belonging, prompting a search for other forms of self-improvement and self-fulfillment. These conditions combined with the sporting ways of the past to produce a range of athletic contests that differed significantly from the folk games that had once dominated the continent.[1]

The panoply of new sporting endeavors often mirrored a society that was rapidly separating into different groups: captains of industry who directed mammoth enterprises; immigrant workers who filled an expanding range of low-wage industrial jobs; middle-class women beginning to enter politics and paid employment; and newly freed slaves trying to make their way in a world fraught with peril and possibility. Some Americans invested large amounts of time and money in competitive sports; others frowned upon such "frivolous" or "immoral" activities. Still, by the end of the century, sports had won over many of its critics, and organized competitive athletics was becoming a key facet of a common American culture.

Conquering Space and Time

Improvements in communication and transportation, combined with the growth of cities, played key roles in the explosion of American sports. In the United States of 1800, many of the routines of daily life still resembled those pursued by human beings for thousands of years. A mere hundred years later, a radically new world had emerged, particularly in the nation's ballooning cities. Not only could urban dwellers gather more easily to play and watch games, news of sporting events could also be conveyed far more quickly in cities than in the countryside. By preserving elements of the older, festive culture in a new urban setting, games helped to compensate for some of the growing impersonality of nineteenth-century economic life. By the end of the nineteenth century, sports teams and athletic heroes also exhibited remarkable capacities for bringing together the polyglot peoples of the nation's urban centers. As with great civic monuments, heroes and teams became part and parcel of urban identities. Furthermore, urban entrepreneurs quickly seized upon opportunities to profit from sports.[2]

Improvements in transportation played a role as well. First came the steamboat, which began to prove its value on western rivers and lakes early in the century. By 1860, more than a thousand paddle wheelers carried freight and passengers up and down the Mississippi River. Steamboat racing became a sport itself for a brief time, as steamboat captains tried to demonstrate the superiority of their boats and skills, but it proved a dangerous endeavor, since overheated engines frequently exploded, killing passengers and crew alike. Steamers carried horses and fans to racing tracks, and transported crowds to prizefight rings. In 1842, five steamers bore some 2,000 spectators to the New York Narrows to watch prizefighter Yankee Sullivan vanquish Tom Secor.

Railroads soon supplanted steamers in importance. In 1830, travel from Detroit to New York had taken at least two weeks; by 1857, the trip required only an overnight train ride. By tying nearly every hamlet in the nation into a giant transportation grid, railroads sharply reduced constraints of space and time. As early as 1842, the Long Island Railroad reportedly carried some 30,000 passengers to the Fashion-Peytona race. The infant sport of baseball especially benefited from the railway system. In the summer of 1860, the Excelsiors of Brooklyn toured upper New York State by rail and then made their way south to Philadelphia and Baltimore. Only a rapidly expanding railway network permitted the 1876 founding of the professional National League, which included franchises as far-flung as Boston and St. Louis. Major league teams continued to travel by train until they switched to air travel in the 1950s.

Equally rapid improvements in communication encouraged the sporting revolution. The mass production of watches in the early nineteenth century allowed organizers of sporting events to schedule and advertise precise starting times. The newly invented telegraph flashed almost-instant results around the country, causing ardent fans to crowd around telegraph and newspaper offices to learn the outcomes of important contests. Two kinds of print media also stimulated public interest in sports: the regular daily newspaper and the weekly specialized sheet devoted to all aspects of nineteenth-century leisure. At first aimed specifically at the wealthy, who sought to reproduce the upper-class pastimes of the English gentry, the weeklies carried news of the theater, odd happenings, and sporting contests. Modeled upon *Bell's Life in London*, William Trotter Porter's *Spirit of the Times*, a weekly that began publication in 1831, was, for a time, the nation's premier sporting sheet. By 1856 it claimed to have 40,000 subscribers scattered across the nation. Unpaid, largely untutored authors sent Porter reports of sports, games, and curiosities.

In the last half of the century, other specialized sporting sheets appeared. The *New York Clipper* (1853) and the *Sporting News* (1886) popularized baseball while Henry Kyle Fox's *National Police Gazette* (1845), which gaudily covered all forms of entertainment, became the nation's widest-selling weekly. Most sporting sheets appeared briefly and sporadically, but their sheer numbers increased from 3 in the 1840s to 48 in the 1890s.

Rising literacy rates, along with new printing technology, broadened the potential market for sporting journalism. A new kind of daily that cost merely a penny first appeared in the 1830s; papers like the Boston *Transcript*, the *Baltimore Sun*, and above all James Gordon Bennett's *New York Herald* ignored Victorian proprieties to report crime, gossip, scandals, and sports. By the 1880s, newspapers recognized the value of continuous sports reporting. In the 1880s and 1890s, the great circulation wars between the dailies, especially in New York City, encouraged "yellow journalism," the sensational reporting of both sports and crime.

The expanding arena of sporting also had its effect on the rules of many sports. When teams competed primarily in limited geographic areas, each could play by a different set of rules. But as horizons for competition expanded and stakes for victory grew, so did an interest in spelling out a uniform and "scientific" set of rules. In 1860, for example, Montreal dentist William George Beers proposed a set of written rules for lacrosse, which had become popular among European as well as native players, and which in 1867 would be named the national game of the newly formed Dominion of Canada. In the fall of 1867, Beers and a group of colleagues formed the National Lacrosse Association of Canada to administer rules and regulate competition, congratulating themselves on the "improvements" they had made to the native game. In the United States, the National Association of Base Ball Players, formed in New York in 1857, embarked on a similar project for the increasingly popular U.S. sport.[3]

The Rise of Middle-Class Victorian Culture

Ironically, many of these developments unfolded during an era when the dominant American culture frowned on most forms of sport.[4] In the early years of the nineteenth century, a rapidly growing economy sparked the formation of a large middle class, whose members came to dominate national culture. Occupationally, the class

included successful farmers, merchants, professionals, independent artisans or crafts-
men, and small manufacturers. Many of them were self-made men who resided in
the northern portion of the country. They urged upon the nation a new moral discipline, a regimen particularly antithetical to commercial sport. Sometimes labeled as
"Victorians" and sometimes as a "new middle class," these citizens drew on Puritan
and Quaker legacies of "lawful sports," on the ideas of republican austerity and on
an a growing interest in evangelical Protestantism and the idea of respectability.
Victorians sharply condemned those sports played purely for pleasure, as well as
those associated with drinking, gambling, and other uninhibited behavior. Not until
the end of the century, when Victorian strictures softened and sports themselves
became more regulated, did athletic competition take its first strides toward becoming an integral part of mainstream American culture.

Victorian culture centered on the ideas of hard work and self-restraint, which
were increasingly seen as the keys to material success. While eighteenth-century colonists had little reason to believe that the future would be very different from the
past, many nineteenth-century Americans came to expect a better standard of living
and improved status for themselves and their children. The opening of vast new territories in the West, the construction of a national system of transportation, and the
growth in agriculture, commerce, and industry fed these material aspirations. Alexis
de Tocqueville, the perceptive French aristocrat who visited the United States from
1831 to 1832, was astonished by the nation's materialism. "We are most certainly in
another world here," he exclaimed. "Political passions are only on the surface. The
profound passion, the only one which profoundly stirs the human heart, the passion
of all days, is the acquisition of riches."[5] Those who were caught up in the pursuit
of material gain recognized that the ceaseless practice of such traditional Protestant
virtues as self-control, frugality, and hard work might aid their cause. The marketplace, they further believed, would reward moral fitness while punishing those weak
in moral character.

Victorian culture received an additional transfusion of energy and ardor from
evangelical Protestantism. Building on the first Great Awakening of the eighteenth
century, great revivals (sometimes collectively called the Second Great Awakening)
regularly swept the country in the early decades of the nineteenth century. Between
1800 and the Civil War, the number of evangelical churches grew twice as fast as the
population. Membership in the Methodist and Baptist denominations shot far ahead
of the more moderate Anglicans (called Episcopalians after the Revolutionary War)
and the Congregationalists (originally the Puritans). Evangelical Protestants came to
dominate most of the nation's pulpits, voluntary societies, newspapers, magazines,
and public schoolhouses, extending their influence into small towns and the countryside as well as cities.

Whether driven mainly by religious convictions, the quest for wealth, the fear
of social unrest, or a combination of these factors, the middle class frowned on
impulsive behavior. Philip Schaff, a visiting theologian from Europe, explained that
the ideal American "holds his passion in check; is master of his sensual nature; obeys
natural laws, not under pressure from without, but from inward impulse, cheerfully
and joyfully."[6] Victorian moralists tried to instill an internal set of values in each
individual, believing that only an interior moral gyroscope could guide each person
through the bewildering changes that were transforming American society.

As part of this quest for wealth, respectability, and order, the growing middle class carefully cultivated good manners, dressed conservatively, and reined in impulses to talk loudly or laugh uproariously. Self-control included sex: Victorians prescribed an ideology of sexual restraint and repression in which men were asked to curb their "natural" passions while proper women were assumed to lack sexual desire. Although a considerable gap existed between official ideology and actual sexual behavior, the middle class succeeded in limiting family size. The birth rate of Northern middle-class urban families fell especially sharply during the period.

Adherents of the new moral discipline drew particularly sharp distinctions between men and women. Victorians urged women to retreat to a special, separate sphere—the home. Presumed to be more delicate and sensitive than men, women were expected to cultivate compassion, gentleness, piety, and benevolence. Serving as models of propriety, women were supposed to exercise a large but unobtrusive influence over the community. Women assumed the main responsibility for the moral nurturing of children and for restraining the impulsive tendencies of men. Men, on the other hand, occupied the public sphere; they worked outside the home and were supposed to be the visible leaders of the community. Until late in the nineteenth century, proper manliness for Victorians entailed hard work, good moral character, and self-control rather than virility, toughness, or aggression.[7]

"Rational Recreation"

Like the Puritans, Victorians also argued that one needed recreation in order to strengthen one's body for serious duties such as work. But they promoted "rational recreation," as opposed to the drinking, wagering, excitement, and physical indulgence that characterized much of nineteenth-century sport. Rational recreation involved leisure activities that could be pursued in the private sphere of family and close friends and which were designed to refresh the mind and body for more serious endeavors. Such pursuits allowed Victorians to avoid the rowdiness so frequently associated with public forms of recreation while enjoying, in the security of their homes, the increasing availability of inexpensive books, newspapers, periodicals, sheet music, musical instruments, and more exotic foods. For intimate social gatherings, the ubiquitous parlor served as a bastion of middle-class propriety and respectability. Consistent with the idea of the home as a special refuge and moral training ground, women became the main providers of middle-class leisure. Outside the home, middle-class men and women created respectable semipublic or public arenas of spare time activities: fraternal groups for men, church societies for women, and temperance organizations for both sexes.

Rational recreation included the possibility of a program of vigorous physical exercises, but emphatically excluded competitive sports.[8] Some even thought that noncompetitive exercise might offset the evil attractions of the day's growing commercial amusements. Frederick W. Sawyer, in *A Plea for Amusements* (1847), proposed supervised gymnastics as a substitute for theaters, circuses, dance halls, saloons, brothels, and sports. Every town and city in the nation, Sawyer wrote, should establish "athletic institutes," which would be devoted to noncompetitive exercises. We should "see to it," added Sawyer, "that we have enough healthy sources of recreation to empty the gambling rooms, the tippling shops, and the brothels."[9]

Reformers such as Catharine Beecher also advocated regular calisthenics for young women, although they faced an uphill battle. Constricted by an 18-inch corseted waist, "a sea of petticoats," and a floor-length dress, the ideal woman, according to mid-nineteenth century novels, magazines, and lithographs, was pale and fragile. Consistent with this ideal, an English visitor reported in 1855 that middle-class American women regarded "anyone who proposed vigorous exercise as a madman." Even walking was "suited only to such females as are compelled by necessity to labor for their bodily sustenance," wrote another observer.[10]

As a whole, "rational" exercise enjoyed only modest success among the ante-bellum middle class. An effort to introduce German gymnastics into New England schools in the 1820s and 1830s, for example, failed to take permanent root, as most educators believed that the schools should be concerned solely with the intellectual and moral development of their charges. Whatever sports took place were instigated and run by students in an informal manner.

Alternatives and Opposition

Nineteenth-century sports developed primarily in realms outside the sway of Victorian culture: most notably among working-class men. From the outset of the nineteenth century, substantial numbers of Americans continued to adhere to their traditional ways, frequently placing a higher value on play, sensual gratification, gusto, spontaneity, and display than on hard work, self-control, and punctuality. As participants in what may be called an *oppositional culture* or a *Victorian counterculture*, their amusements often consisted of talking, drinking, gambling, and commercial spectacles, activities tied directly to preindustrial, preurban patterns of life. While this culture focused largely on men and male activities, working-class culture rarely stressed female frailty and domesticity the way Victorians did, and a number of women found ways to participate as well.[11]

Apart from the desire to preserve traditional forms of leisure, new conditions of work encouraged opposition to Victorian culture by those at the bottom of the social order. At the beginning of the century, most goods had been made in the small shops of independent artisans. Customers simply asked an artisan to fashion a pair of shoes or a chair according to their special wishes. Using skills passed down through many generations, the typical artisan was in effect simultaneously both a small manufacturer and a tradesman. Completely responsible for the final product, artisans frequently took a fierce pride in the quality of their work.

Although the factory system did not suddenly or completely annihilate the handicraft mode of production, the long-term trend away from small shops was unmistakable. Master artisans with foresight and capital enlarged their work forces, employed more machinery, and broke down the work into simpler tasks. The resulting work required fewer skills, and sharply separated the roles of employer and employee. Masters, journeymen, and apprentices no longer worked side-by-side, and ancient customs of mutual obligations and rights no longer governed. No longer did young apprentices or journeymen live in the household of the master artisan; increasing numbers lived in boarding houses. In addition, the factory substituted a rigid discipline for more casual work patterns of the past.

The workplaces of white-collar workers, especially clerks, likewise underwent radical changes. In the first quarter of the nineteenth century, working as a clerk was in effect a training period for those sons of the upper classes who aspired to become business or professional men. Employed in thousands of small offices, they acted in multiple capacities; for instance, they served as copyists of correspondence and business documents, bookkeepers, and collectors of invoices and receipts. The typical clerk had opportunities to learn all aspects of the business. With only two or three clerks per office, each had frequent and intense personal interactions with his employer.

By mid-century, this system of apprenticeship-clerking had begun to falter. The rapid growth of the economy resulted in the expansion of the size of business and manufacturing concerns, and consequently the need for thousands of additional clerks. To meet the demand, businesses recruited clerks from the ranks of the educated classes in both the countryside and the city. At the same time business firms began to reorganize their offices, and subdivided the work of clerks. Rather than serving as jacks-of-all trades, clerks were employed for specific jobs such as copyist, bookkeeper, or simply retail salesperson. With little or no opportunity for advancement, clerking became a dead-end job for the overwhelming majority of young men. The division of labor into simpler tasks and the introduction of the typewriter in the 1880s eventually resulted in the replacement of many male clerks by young female office workers.

Substantial numbers of workers accepted the values of their Victorian employers. White-collar workers in particular sought to get ahead by working hard, restraining their emotions, and practicing frugality. "Bank clerks, young merchants, [and] mercantile aspirants," observed *Harper's Weekly* in 1859, "all seem to think time devoted to any exercise wasted, and the model clerk him who drudges six days every week at his desk without an hour of physical labor."[12] But other workers, especially blue-collar workingmen, turned to the pleasures and associations offered by the adversaries of Victorian culture. For them, leisure activities frequently provided far more excitement, fulfillment, and sense of belonging than their work.

The cities' growing ranks of bachelors were more likely to spurn Victorian values than were married men. There was no shortage of single men: far more men than women swarmed into the growing cities. At mid-century, nearly 40 percent of men between the ages of 25 and 35 were unmarried, a figure much higher than today. Bachelors spent most of their leisure time with other males, as did many of their married counterparts. Members of this bachelor subculture sought sensual gratification, friendship, and a sense of community at saloons, brothels, gambling halls, billiard rooms, boxing rings, and race tracks.

Immigrants gave added support to these cultural alternatives. In the nineteenth and early twentieth centuries, great waves of immigrants arrived in the United States from Europe, Canada, and Mexico. Newly arrived workers, many of whom came from rural communities, frequently brought with them attitudes toward time-thrift, self-control and temperance at odds with Victorian America. The new arrivals, along with many old-stock workingmen, were slow to acquiesce to the regimen of the new economy. They did their best to preserve traditional holidays, preindustrial work habits, and "grog" privileges (the right to drink light alcoholic beverages during the workday).

Irish Americans, who started arriving in large numbers in the 1820s, made up an especially prominent component of this bachelor subculture. A high percentage of bachelors, delayed marriages, rigorous norms of premarital chastity, and traditions of segregation by sex made all-male groups particularly important to Irish Americans. Whether married or unmarried, a male's standing within the larger Irish community often rested on his active participation in the bachelor subculture. Gathering in saloons to drink, gossip, tell stories, and engage in business or political transactions, Irish men conducted the rites of passage for countless Irish youths. They promoted a gay, carefree life, which included placing a high value on success in fighting, physical prowess, and sports.

The Sporting Fraternity

The "sporting fraternity," or "fancy," as it was known, formed the most dramatic component of the Victorian countercultures. Although never a formal organization, the term "fraternity" implied shared values and interests, a special solidarity and a surrogate brotherhood. In the promotion and viewing of sports as well as in such associated activities as drinking, gambling, and telling stories, the fraternity consummated intensely shared experiences and a sense of belonging. As within a family, the fraternity developed its own set of special understandings, its own argot, its own acceptable behaviors, and its own concept of honor—much of it focused on rough, bloody sports that were the polar opposite of Victorian self-restraint. The fraternity drew its membership from within the larger Victorian demimonde—hedonists in the upper class, workingmen, ethnics, bachelors, and those, like saloonkeepers, who sought to profit from the Victorian underworld.

The Base Ball Fraternity

A second "fraternity" of sportsmen, known as the "base ball fraternity," sought to win the support of Victorian America. Made up of young clerks, artisans, and petty businessmen, the ballplaying fraternity tried to reassure Victorians of their game's propriety. A ballplayer "must be sober and temperate," reported Porter's *Spirit of the Times* in 1857. "Patience, fortitude, self-denial, order, obedience, and good-humor, with an unruffled temper, are indispensable....Such a game...teaches a love of order, discipline, and fair play."[13] No one could have coined a more satisfactory list of Victorian virtues.

It would be some time, however, before baseball would fully win middle-class support. Mostly young and living away from family influences, early ballplayers frequently ignored the austerities of Victorian life. Porter's *Spirit*, the same sporting sheet that had identified baseball with Victorian values, noted in 1858 that a marked feature of postgame celebrations was "the indulgence of a prurient taste for indecent anecdotes and songs—a taste only to be gratified at the expense of true dignity and self-respect." After the Civil War, as baseball became more commercialized, wagering on ballgames became more common. Circus master P. T. Barnum went so far as to say that "Idleness, Base-Ball and Billiards" had caused the economic panic of 1873.[14]

The Elite Clubs

In addition to creating a new working class and a new middle class, nineteenth-century industrialism also created a new, wealthy elite of industrialists, land-owners, and financiers. Although they were never quite as successful in resisting Victorian hegemony as their English counterparts, these Americans sought to imitate the English gentry by preserving earlier pastimes, especially in horse racing and field sports.

Some of these men participated in the spectacles and commercial pleasures of the fancy. Pleasure-loving sons of the elite, like their English complements, engaged in sports slumming—participation in the low sports of the common people. In the latter half of the nineteenth century, a group of newly enriched men, the parvenu, became especially conspicuous for their involvement in various sorts of commercial leisure. For the most part, however, this new elite seized on sports and leisure activities as a way to distance themselves from the masses. The nineteenth century saw an explosion of private, leisure-oriented clubs, such as the New York Yacht Club, Philadelphia's many cricket clubs, and the first "country club"—the exclusive Brookline Country Club, founded in 1882. In these private, exclusive organizations, the new leaders of society indulged in costly sports such as golf and tennis and enforced strict notions of "amateurism" designed to restrict participation to the wealthy.

Sports Moves to the Center

Following the Civil War, as the middle-class stance on recreation slowly but perceptibly began to change, sports began to assume a more prominent role in American culture. A decline in religious intensity and a rising concern about the "effeminacy" of American males in the late nineteenth century sparked a call for a "vigorous, robust, muscular Christianity." Several New England intellectuals drew invidious comparisons between the alleged robustness of Englishmen and the frailty of their fellow Americans. "I am satisfied that such a set of…stiff-jointed, soft-muscled, paste-complexioned youth as we [Americans] can boast in our Atlantic cities never before sprang from the loins of Anglo-Saxon lineage," declared physician Oliver Wendell Holmes Sr. in 1858.[15]

At the same time, a tiny but growing band of "muscular Christians," influenced by the English writers Thomas Hughes and Charles Kingsley, brought together physicians, clerics, essayists, and newspaper editors to launch a crusade that linked spirituality to physical vigor. The tireless American champion of muscular moralism, Thomas Wentworth Higginson, invoked classical Greek ideals in calling for a symmetrical life that gave equal attention to physical and spiritual growth. "Physical health," Higginson said, was "a necessary condition of all permanent success."[16] The muscular Christians were joined by advocates of what became known as the "strenuous life," who argued that elite white Americans needed to develop greater physical and emotional vigor in order to maintain their position at the top of a rapidly changing society.

In response, increasing numbers of middle-class Americans began to shift from an unmitigated hostility to nearly all forms of competitive sports to a belief that well-regulated sports could aid in forming good personal character, including such traits as integrity, reliability, and responsibility. This shift led to greater support for physical contests for boys and young men, and sometimes even for young women, providing they were governed by the spirit of amateurism and played under controlled conditions.[17]

The growing acceptance of competitive sports showed clearly in the nation's colleges, where athletic competition—especially in the newly developed game of football—became a center of student and alumni life. While college football had many critics, it also sparked volumes of rhetoric that cast competitive sports as a valuable preparation for the challenges that young men would face once they left school. Unlike in Europe, where sports would remain separate from formal education, athletics would eventually become an integral part of the American education system, giving it an additional form of legitimacy.

Sports and Respect

The growing mainstream acceptance of sports gave sporting competition yet another social role. Once success in sports was linked to moral character, and to the qualities needed for economic and political success, sports became an arena where those on the margins of American society sought to challenge social inequalities.

The economic divisions that marked the nineteenth century gave rise to an elaborate set of racial, ethnic, and gender hierarchies that took shape as the American population diversified. Immigrants arrived from many parts of Europe, and included many Jews and Catholics. Once African Americans were freed from slavery, they began to migrate in greater numbers across the country. As the United States enlarged its territory, it took in more Native Americans and Latinos. Contacts with Latinos grew further by the end of the century, as the growing nation expanded its influence into the Caribbean, Latin America, and the Pacific.

For many of these groups of people, sports became a way to carry on cultural traditions and cement ethnic bonds within a new society. Scots organized "Caledonian" clubs across the country in order to perpetuate "the manners and customs, literature, the Highland costume and the athletic games of Scotland, as practiced by our forefathers." During their heyday, from the 1850s to the 1870s, the clubs were the nation's most prominent sponsors of track and field events.[18] German immigrants organized *Turnverein*, or Turner societies, that promoted gymnastic exercise. Latinos in the nation's newly acquired Southwestern territories continued to flock to rodeos, horse races, and other traditional sporting activities.

The nation's varied populations also adopted the nineteenth century's new sports. Beginning in the 1850s, for example, Irish and German residents took up baseball with enthusiasm. In New Orleans alone, the Germans founded the Schneiders, Laners, and Lanwehrs, and the Irish, the Fenian Baseball Club. Baseball invariably accompanied the ethnic picnics of the Germans, Irish, French, and later,

Italian immigrants to the city. There were enough African American teams in New Orleans to hold a citywide "Negro championship" series in the 1880s. The game also spread rapidly throughout the Spanish-speaking areas of the Southwest, sparking the establishment of many popular teams.[19]

Racially or ethnically based teams helped build solidarity and reinforce community. Athletes also eagerly anticipated opportunities to compete with or against teams made up of whites. As competitive team sports came to be seen as a template for industrial society, success in white-dominated sporting arenas could both boost ethnic pride and counter the race-based ideology that relegated some Americans to second-class status. Women also seized on sports—most notably bicycling and basketball—as part of their efforts to break free from the restrictions of Victorian domesticity and claim a larger role in public life.

Conclusion

Nineteenth-century America witnessed sudden and momentous changes in the nation's economy, society, and culture. It was a century of technological innovation, industrialization, rapid population growth, immigration, urbanization, geographic expansion, and the greatest armed conflict held on American soil. The dominant cultural system it produced—a set of beliefs, attitudes, and techniques that can be summed up as middle-class Victorian—generally frowned on athletics. Still, Americans nurtured a variety of new sports that played important roles in the rapidly changing society: roles that included strengthening bonds of class and community; providing relief from the stresses of daily life; preparing young people to contend with the demands of an urban, industrial economy; and demonstrating fitness for full inclusion in the new society. By the end of the century, these many efforts had helped move organized sports from the margins of society toward the heart of national culture.

Critical Thinking Questions

1. How did the development of varying approaches to nineteenth-century sports reflect the developing economic structure of American society?
2. Nineteenth-century changes in transportation and communication facilitated the development of spectator sports. Which of the two developments do you think was the most important and why?
3. To what degree to the concepts of "rational recreation," a male sporting fraternity, and the use of sports to build racial, ethnic, or gender respect exist today?

Notes

1. An emphasis on "modernization" informs Allen Guttmann's global work, *From Ritual to Record: The Nature of Modern Sports* (New York: Columbia University Press, 1978); and his *A Whole New Ball Game: An Interpretation of American Sports* (Chapel Hill: University of North Carolina Press, 1988). Melvin L. Adelman's *A Sporting Time: New York City and the Rise of Modern Athletics, 1820–1870* (Urbana: University of Illinois Press, 1986) is a premier study of the application of modernization theory to a specific city while Dale A. Somers,

The Rise of Sports in New Orleans, 1850–1900 (Baton Rouge: Louisiana State University Press, 1972); Stephen Hardy, *How Boston Played* (Boston: Northeastern University Press, 1982); Steven A. Riess, *City Games* (Urbana: University of Illinois Press, 1989); and Gerald R. Gems, *Windy City Wars: Labor, Leisure, and Sport in the Making of Chicago* (Lanham, MD: Scarecrow, 1997) stress the role of the city more generally in comprehending the rise of sports. For analyses that emphasize the rise of sport in terms of a contested territory between social groups, see especially Elliott J. Gorn, *The Manly Art* (Ithaca, NY: Cornell University Press, 1986); Scott C. Martin, *Killing Time: Leisure and Culture in Southwestern Pennsylvania, 1800–1850* (Pittsburgh: University of Pittsburgh Press, 1995); and S.W. Pope, *Patriotic Games* (New York: Oxford University Press, 1997).

2. Apart from the works cited in note 1, see J.R. Betts, "The Technological Revolution and the Rise of Sports, 1850–1900," *Mississippi Valley Historical Review* 40 (1953), 231–56; and Betts, "Sporting Journalism in Nineteenth Century America," *American Quarterly* 5 (1953), 39–56.

3. For an account of Beers and his efforts, see Thomas Vennum, Jr., *American Indian Lacrosse: Little Brother of War* (Washington, DC: Smithsonian Institution Press, 1994), chapters 15–16.

4. The literature relevant to middle-class Victorian culture is enormous, but one may begin with David W. Howe, ed., *Victorian America* (Philadelphia: University of Pennsylvania Press, 1976); William L. Barney, *The Passage of the Republic* (Lexington, MA: D.C. Heath, 1987); Benjamin G. Rader, *American Ways: A History of American Cultures* 2 vols. (Belmont, CA: Thomson/Wadsworth, 2006); and Burton J. Bledstein and Robert D. Johnston, *The Middling Sorts: Explorations in the History of the American Middle Class* (New York: Routledge, 2001).

5. Alexis de Tocqueville, *Democracy in America*, 2 vols. (New York: Vintage Books, 1951), I, 51.

6. Quoted in Lewis Perry, *Intellectual Life in America* (Chicago: University of Chicago Press, 1989), 230.

7. See especially Linda K. Kerber, "Separate Spheres, Female Worlds, Women's Place: The Rhetoric of Women's History," *Journal of American History* 75 (1988), 9–39, and for the growing body of gender literature as it relates to sport, Patricia A. Vertinsky, "Gender Relations, Women's History and Sport History: A Decade of Changing Enquiry, 1983–1993," *Journal of Sport History* 21 (1994), 1–24.

8. See Adelman, *A Sporting Time*, 269–89 for the development of an ideology of sport by the New York City press, and, 362n for citations of other works treating the Victorian quest for rational recreation. Apart from Adelman, see especially J.C. Whorton, *Crusaders for Fitness* (Princeton, NJ: Princeton University Press, 1982); Harvey Green, *Fit for America* (New York: Pantheon, 1986); Roberta J. Park, "A Decade of the Body: Researching and Writing About the History of Health, Fitness, Exercise and Sport, 1983–1993," *Journal of Sport History* 21 (1994), 59–82; and Martin, *Killing Time*, chapters 5–7. For relevant primary sources, see George B. Kirsch, ed. *Sports in North America: A Documentary History*, Vol. 3 (Gulf Breeze, FL: Academic Press International, 1992), chapter 1.

9. Quoted in Hardy, *How Boston Played*, 50.

10. Quoted in Lois Banner, *American Beauty* (New York: Knopf, 1983), 54.

11. See especially Morse Pecham, "Victorian Counterculture," *Victorian Studies* 18 (1975), 257–76; Gorn, *The Manly Art*; and R.B. Stott, *Workers in the Metropolis: Class, Ethnicity, and Youth in Antebellum New York City* (Ithaca, NY: Cornell University Press, 1990), chapters 8–9. There were numerous examples of physically active women within the oppositional culture. See Allen Guttmann, *Women's Sports* (New York: Columbia University Press, 1991), 96–98.

12. *Harper's Weekly* 3 (October 15, 1859), 658.
13. *Spirit of the Times* 2 (May 30, 1857), 10.
14. Quotations from *Spirit of the Times* 5 (October 9, 1858), 84; and Bryan D. Palmer, *A Culture of Conflict* (Montreal: Queens University Press, 1979), 26.
15. O.W. Holmes, "The Autocrat at the Breakfast Table," *Atlantic Monthly* 1 (1858), 881.
16. T.W. Higginson, "Saints and Their Bodies," *Atlantic Monthly* 1 (1858), 585–86.
17. For quote, see E. Anthony Rotundo, *American Manhood* (New York: Basic Books, 1993), 86. See also Clifford Putney, *Muscular Christianity: Manhood and Sports in Protestant America, 1880–1920* (Cambridge, MA: Harvard University Press, 2001); Mark Dyreson, "The Emergence of Consumer Culture and the Transformation of Physical Culture: American Sport in the 1920s," *Journal of Sport History* 16 (1989), 261–81; and Pope, *Patriotic Games*, chapters 2–3.
18. Quotations in Gerald Redmond, *The Caledonian Games* (Rutherford, NJ: Fairleigh Dickinson University Press, 1971), 39, 45.
19. Quoted in Somers, *The Rise of Sports in New Orleans*, 120.

CHAPTER 3

The Sporting Fraternity and Its Spectacles

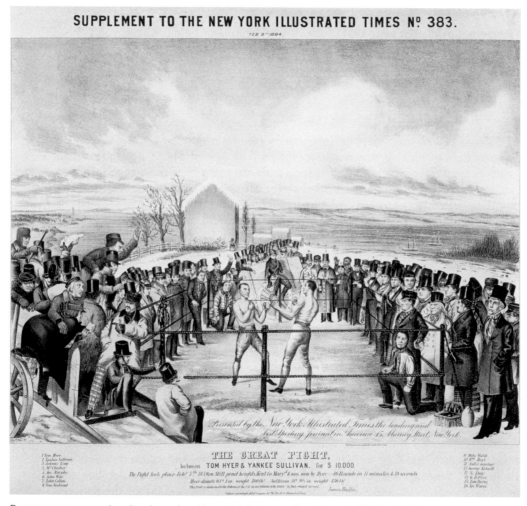

Poster commemorating the championship match between Tom Hyer and Yankee Sullivan.

LEARNING OBJECTIVES

3.1 Explain how nineteenth-century prizefighting embodied the values of working-class American men, and also offered them an escape from the stresses of an industrializing economy.

3.2 Describe the social classes that made up the American "sporting fraternity," along with their various motivations for patronizing less-than-respectable sporting events.

3.3 Analyze the different ways that prizefighting challenged dominant Victorian values.

3.4 Discuss the particular appeal that prizefighting held for American men of Irish descent.

3.5 Outline the developments that contributed to prizefighting's decline in the 1860s and 70s and then helped spark the sport's revival in the 1880s.

3.6 Articulate the social tensions embodied in the contrast between champions John L. Sullivan and James Corbett.

In February of 1849, supporters of prizefighters Tom Hyer and Yankee Sullivan set up an improvised boxing ring at a remote point on the coast of Maryland, and readied themselves for a fight. Several hundred spectators cheered the men on as they landed blows and struggled to throw each other to the ground. Seventeen minutes after the contest began, Sullivan's face was "clotted with gore" and Hyer bled heavily from a cut under his eye. Then Hyer threw Sullivan onto the ropes. Sullivan could not recover, and the fight was over.[1]

The importance of "The Great Fight," belied its short duration. For six months, a big-city public had followed the rivalry between the two fighters. They had devoured newspaper reports of training schedules, sparring exhibitions, and verbal challenges. Ethnic rivalry—Hyer was a native-born American and Sullivan an Irish immigrant—heightened interest in the match, reflecting growing tensions between native-born workingmen and a swelling number of Irish immigrants over jobs, turf, and political influence. Ten thousand dollars had been raised as a prize for the winner, and tens of thousands more had been bet on the outcome. Large crowds gathered at recently erected telegraph offices to hear news of the competition.

The Hyer–Sullivan match was the biggest sporting event the United States had ever seen. It was also illegal. Most states, including Maryland, had banned prizefighting in the 1830s. The bout took place only after the two combatants had repeatedly dodged police—saved at one point when the fighters' "seconds" managed to convince Maryland lawmen that they were in fact the two combatants, and allowed themselves to be arrested. While thousands of Americans eagerly read accounts of the combat, and others composed stories and poems celebrating Hyer's victory, many of the nation's most prominent citizens sharply condemned the contest and others like it.

As the illegality of the Hyer–Sullivan match suggests, prizefighting was the most dramatic example of an oppositional culture that challenged middle-class Victorian norms by championing often-brutal spectacles accompanied by drinking, wagering, and other forms of unrestrained behavior. Central to these contests was a group of men that became known as the sporting fraternity (or "the fancy"). The sporting fraternity scheduled and promoted sporting spectacles, those events that attracted crowds and public attention. These were often profit-focused ventures: money might be made by winning wagers, selling liquor at events, or charging gate fees. By winning side bets and competing for stakes—a sum set aside for the winner by the promoters—athletes could also profit from their skills. Still, sporting spectacles could mean far more than money to nineteenth-century men. The fraternity and its spectacles offered opportunities for male camaraderie and shared excitement, as well as a refuge from femininity, domesticity, and the demanding routines of the new economy.

The sporting fraternity extended to both sides of the Atlantic. The English contingent of the fraternity, who had begun to organize commercial sporting spectacles earlier than the Americans, exercised an especially large influence. While Americans had declared political independence in 1776, they continued long afterward to rely heavily upon Britain for cultural guidance. Americans conducted their horse races in strict accordance with the rules of Newmarket, ran their prizefights by the London prize-ring rules and copied the latest London modes of wagering on contests. England furnished much of the sporting equipment in the antebellum era, as well as sporting books, magazines, and images. All the American sporting sheets gave extensive coverage to the news from Great Britain, and by the 1820s a bevy of professional English and Irish athletes regularly visited the United States to demonstrate their skills and compete for stakes. American athletes soon began to reciprocate by visiting English shores.

Enclaves of the Fancy

Within cities, the fancy gathered in coffeehouses, the headquarters of volunteer fire companies, billiard parlors, and livery stables to talk, drink, and gamble. The grandest enclaves, however were the saloons, the nineteenth-century heir of colonial taverns. Saloons varied in the richness of their decor and the wealth of their clientele, but many offered workingmen some upper-class comforts. By mid-century, the more elegant saloons had brilliantly lighted windows flanked by wicker doors that swung open easily. Inside a patron might see variegated lampshades, frescoed ceilings, a gilded bar with a glittering mirror behind it, and paintings of famous race horses, prizefighters, and scantily clad women. Within, members of the fancy indulged themselves in distinctly non-Victorian pastimes, especially drinking and gambling.

An advertisement penned by saloon owner William Clark summarized some of the attractions of a major metropolitan saloon: "Ales, wines, liquors, segars, and refreshments. All the sporting news of the day to be learned here, where files of the *Clipper*, and other sporting papers are kept. Here also may be seen numberless portraits of English and American pugilists." In addition, Clark's saloon offered "a room of other facilities…at all times in readiness for giving lessons in sparring under the supervision of the proprietor. Drop in, and take a peep."[2] Saloonkeepers frequently arranged dog fights, ratbaitings, cockfights, and prizefights. They posted the odds on horse races and, after mid-century, on baseball matches. In the latter half of the century, saloons sometimes had telegraph hookups so they could report the latest sporting results instantly.

The betting that became an integral part of this sporting culture heightened the excitement of sporting events. Few experiences equaled the intensity of a bet. For spectator, promoter, and athlete alike, winning a bet might be far more important than the thrill of monetary gain. In wagering, one risked not only money but also one's self-esteem. By choosing to bet on a particular team or athlete, the bettor might make a statement of ethnic or occupational pride. Successful wagering also offered an occasion for men to display skills at a time when they increasingly found such opportunities denied in their workplaces. One might suddenly earn large amounts of money quickly with a minimum of physical exertion, and winning a bet might even signify a favorable dispensation from the fates.

By the 1850s, in New York City and other larger cities, both workingmen and upper-class hedonists could also gather at special halls that featured a regular fare of low sports. In 1860s New York, the best-known hall was Kit Burns's Sportsman Hall. Shaped as an amphitheater, the hall could seat up to 400 spectators. Apart from watching and wagering on how long it would take a dog to kill a pit full of rats, the patron might pay a quarter to see "Jack the Rat" decapitate a rat or a dime to witness him bite off the head of a mouse. Frederick Van Wyck, of a distinguished Knickerbocker family, suggested that patronizing such events served as a "rite of passage" for certain youth of the upper social ranks. At Tommy Norris's livery stable, he reported seeing a ratting, a cockfight, a goatfight, and a sparring match between two women who were nude above the waist. "Certainly for a lad of 17, such as I," reported Van Wyck, "a night with Tommy Norris and his attraction was quite a night."[3]

John Cox Stevens: Wealthy Sporting Patron

As American society became more segmented, sports became one arena where men from different classes still mingled. No single individual illuminates more fully the complex relationship between upper-class sportsmen, the sporting fraternity, and antebellum sporting spectacles than John Cox Stevens (1785–1857).[4] Heir to a steamboat fortune, Stevens at one time or another patronized, promoted, and wagered on horse, foot, and yacht racing. He also opened a large amusement park and furnished the playing grounds for some of the nation's first baseball matches. Like a substantial number of the landed and mercantile wealthy, Stevens cultivated an aristocratic lifestyle similar to his English counterparts; it was far more extravagant and expressive than the simplicity demanded by the republicans of the Revolutionary era but not as colossally ostentatious as that of the post–Civil War parvenus. Typical of many antebellum sports patrons, Stevens maintained a certain social distance between himself and the more ordinary sporting fancy. He never patronized prizefighting, for example, and though he loved the theater he did not associate with theater people. Even as he promoted popular spectacles, he also founded the exclusive New York Yacht Club.

Stevens's first passion was horse racing. During the Revolutionary era, horse racing had suffered a setback; indeed, fired by republican zeal, most of the states had banned the sport. But, in the 1820s and the 1830s wealthy landed and mercantile sportsmen led a nationwide turf revival. Regular racing circuits developed; the sheer number of thoroughbred races grew from 56 in 1830 to 130 in 1839. New sporting journals, in particular John Stuart Skinner's *American Turf Register and Sporting Magazine* (1829) and William T. Porter's *Spirit of the Times* (1831), helped plan the annual racing schedule, arrange for the payment of bets, fix rules of entry, and standardize handicaps. In a bid for respectability and to offset charges of corruption and chicanery, turf enthusiasts sometimes sought to discourage attendance at the track by ruffians and professional gamblers. They also argued speciously that the breeding and racing of thoroughbred horses improved the quality of horses for other kinds of work.[5]

In the 1820s Stevens established himself as the North's premier horseman. From his stables in Hoboken, Stevens raced horses frequently in New Jersey and New York and for 22 consecutive years he served as either the president or vice-president of the New York Jockey Club. Still, his interest was fleeting. He sold his stable in the 1830s, just before a severe economic downturn nearly destroyed the turf, and turned his energies to a large park, the Elysian Fields, which he set up with his brother on the family's waterfront estate in Hoboken, New Jersey. According to diarist Philip Hone, 200 "gentlemen," including New York's mayor and aldermen and members of the New York and Jersey City boat clubs, attended the grand opening, outfitted "in white jackets and trousers, round ship's hats, and checked shirts." They shared gourmet food and "abundant champagne."[6] Conveniently located across the river from New York City, the Elysian Fields (a place of perfect happiness in classical mythology) at one time or another served as the home of the New York Yacht Club, the St. George Cricket Club, the playing area of the New York Athletic Club, and grounds for some of the nation's first organized baseball matches.

Pedestrianism

Stevens also entered into more popular spectacles, most notably the phenomenon of pedestrianism. As early as the 1820s, a few sportsmen, taking their cues from England, had advanced small purses for long-distance runners and walkers. Stevens shocked the sporting fancy in 1835 by offering a $1,000 purse to any pedestrian who could run ten miles in less than one hour. If only one ped accomplished the feat he would receive an additional $300.

Stevens's "Great Race" generated almost as much excitement as earlier horse races. At least 20,000 fans watched an international field of peds compete at the Union Race track. Patrick Mahoney, a butcher from County Kerry, Ireland, who sported a green shirt and black slippers, set a torrid pace for the first five miles. Five of the nine peds reached the halfway mark in less than a half-hour. But to the delight of the spectators, Henry Stannard, a farmer from Connecticut who wore black pantaloons, pulled away from the others to finish in 59 minutes and 48 seconds. Stannard promptly mounted a horse, rode around the track to the cheers of the spectators, and made a short victory speech.[7]

The interest aroused by the Great Race of 1835, nationalistic rivalries with Britain, and the opportunities offered for wagering all catapulted footracing into one of the most popular sporting spectacles of the antebellum era. In 1844, a series of long-distance races at the Beacon Course in Hoboken attracted attention throughout the English-speaking world. Thirty-seven famed peds competed in the second race, including three Englishmen, three Irishmen, and John Steeprock, a Seneca Indian. The victory of John Gildersleeve, a New York chairbuilder, stoked the fires of white American ethnocentrism. "It was a trial of the Indian against the white man, on the point in which the red man boasts his superiority," reported an American newspaper. "It was a trial of the peculiar American *physique* against the long held supremacy of the English endurance."[8] (Unfortunately for this interpretation, English peds proceeded to win the next three Hoboken races.)

"During the next ten to fifteen years," noted a contemporary observer, "there were more athletes competing and more races than ever before. People in virtually every state in the union attended professional footraces."[9] Promoters devised an ingenious variety of competitions. Peds ran sprints, hurdles, and long distances against times and even against horses (with the human given a head start). The events generally took on a carnival-like atmosphere, rife with betting, drinking, and cursing, as well as occasional violence. Proper Victorians loathed it.

The Early History of American Prizefighting

The ultimate expression of the fancy, however, was prizefighting, which became a national obsession in the second half of the nineteenth century, despite being officially banned almost everywhere in the country. As with all the other popular antebellum spectacles, American prizefighting had close ties with Great Britain. When Americans first began to hear and read about the feats of English champions in the late eighteenth century, they showed little immediate enthusiasm. In the 1820s and 1830s, however, a small pugilistic fraternity began to emerge. Composed mostly of gamblers, saloon operators, and hustlers, the fraternity welcomed both English and Irish boxers to American shores. English and Irish "professors of pugilism" also offered (without many takers) sparring lessons to the nation's upper classes.

By the 1840s and 1850s, prizefighting became the nation's most prominent spectator sport. By the mid-1850s, reports of scores of fights appeared in the newspapers. In New York City, the capital of pugilism, the papers carried accounts of three or four local sparring matches each week. A series of sensational championship bouts—Tom Hyer vs. Yankee Sullivan (1849), Yankee Sullivan vs. John Morrissey (1853), John Morrissey vs. John C. Heenan (1857), and John C. Heenan vs. Tom Sayers (1860)—captivated millions. The 1850s became known as the "Age of Heroes."

No antebellum fighter exceeded the popularity of John "Old Smoke" Morrissey. Born in Ireland, Morrissey had come to America as a three-year-old lad with his impoverished family, part of an influx of Irish immigrants that would reach two million by the middle of the century. Morrissey combined fighting, gambling, and politics to ascend to fame and fortune. After acquiring a reputation as a brutal street brawler, in 1853 he defeated national champion Yankee Sullivan for the unofficial American championship. Four years later he bested John C. Heenan, another Irishman, to hold onto his title.

When Morrissey retired from the ring, he devoted his enormous energies to gambling and politics. Out of the earnings of his first fight he established a gaming house in New York that by 1860 had become the city's most celebrated parlor. Within five years he had acquired an interest in at least five other gambling halls and was the largest single shareholder in a million-dollar annual lottery business. Turning his interest to Saratoga, New York, he built the town's first horse race track in 1864 and in 1867 established a lavish gambling parlor and restaurant, helping to transform Saratoga from a fashionable spa into America's version of Monte Carlo. While he hobnobbed with some of New York's parvenu, his popularity among workingmen led to several political triumphs, including two terms in the U.S. House of Representatives. His feats gave a new meaning to the American gospel of success.

After Morrissey's retirement from fighting, John C. Heenan assumed the championship mantle. In 1860, Heenan met Tom Sayers, the English champion, in a bout outside London. On both sides of the Atlantic, the Heenan–Sayers bout excited far more interest than had any prior fight. In England, members of the English aristocracy joined the riffraff in watching the two-hour bloodbath. Americans anxiously awaited word of the outcome. While Sayers pulled a muscle in his right arm in the seventh round, he continued to stage a masterful defense. Finally, with both fighters bloody and exhausted, the crowd out of control, and the constables about to stop the bout, the referee called the match a draw. In the United States, interest in the fight overshadowed news about the sectional conflict that would soon culminate in the Civil War. Even respectable Victorians saw the bout as an opportunity to once again twist the British lion's tail, and citizens in both nations identified their respective fighters with national virility.

Meanings of Prizefighting

As exemplified by the career of Morrissey and the Heenan–Sayers fight, pugilism mirrored larger nineteenth-century cultural conflicts. Prizefighting played on ethnic divisions, especially tensions between American-born and Irish-born workers. As they lost both status and autonomy in their work, native workers began to turn on foreigners as scapegoats for their plight. Competition for jobs and political power as well as religious divides—most Irish were Catholic, most natives Protestant—further kindled ethnic hostilities. Prizefights dramatized these rivalries, creating symbolic contests for supremacy and honor.

Pugilism also manifestly mocked Victorian values, especially the cardinal virtue of self-restraint. The prevailing rules permitted a battle just short of unregulated combat. Under the Broughton (1743) and London (1838) prize-ring rules, fighters fought with their bare fists, and wrestling skills and brute strength were more important than finesse. A round ended only when a man was struck down by an opponent's fists, thrown to the turf with a wrestling hold, or deliberately fell to the ground to avoid further punishment. Once downed, a fighter had 30 seconds to recover before "toeing the mark," or "coming to scratch," terms that referred to a line drawn through the center of the ring. A fight ended only when a fighter was unable to come to scratch or conceded defeat. Under these rules fights could be savagely brutal, even fatal. In 1842, Thomas McCoy and Christopher Lilly pummeled one another for two hours and 40 minutes before McCoy, drowning in his own blood, fell dead.

The brutality stretched well beyond the ring itself. Since fights in the antebellum era were illegal, the fancy scheduled them in remote places—backrooms of saloons, on barges, or in remote rural spots. Fights attracted the roughest elements in American society—pickpockets, hustlers of various sorts, drunks, and bullies. Traditional ethnic animosities and abundant liquor added to the volatile mix. Those who sensed that their bets were in jeopardy or who felt that their favorite had been treated unfairly sometimes joined the fray, not only swinging their fists or trying to wrestle their foes to the ground but also flashing Bowie knives or brandishing pistols.

Prizefighting supporters thus celebrated a conception of manliness at odds with the Victorians. To Victorians, the ideal man labored diligently, kept a tight rein on his impulses, and supported family life. Workingmen more often confirmed their manliness in the company of other men, exhibiting toughness, physical prowess, and generosity. With his immense strength, muscular body, and swift, decisive answers, the successful prizefighter represented an appealing alternative to the more effeminate, self-effacing Victorian ideal of manhood. Prizefighting also spoke to male–female relationships. No other sport equaled prizefighting in suggesting that superior physical strength reflected and justified patriarchal power.

The ring also inverted Victorian ideals about money and success. For Victorians, the accumulation of money validated years of hard work and self-sacrifice by its possessor. The gambler and the prizefighter, on the other hand, might earn hundreds of dollars by simply winning a single bet or bout. The pugilistic fraternity valued money not as evidence of good character but as a means for enjoying the moment and the conviviality of their fellows. To some, prizefighting, saloonkeeping, and gambling, among other pursuits, were also highly valued alternative avenues to success. To succeed in the world of commercial entertainment carried as much—indeed, sometimes more—esteem within the sporting fraternity as success achieved in other sectors of the economy.

The entrepreneurial opportunities offered by the ring, as well as by other forms of nineteenth-century commercial entertainment, especially attracted Americans of Irish descent. As the numbers of Irish immigrants grew, so did prejudice against them. Finding opportunities frequently blocked in the more "respectable" occupations, many Irish turned to careers that satisfied the urban hunger for gambling, drink, and sport. Such pursuits required little education and could produce quick rewards in a society that placed a high value on material success.

Working-class Irish males held fighting ability in the highest esteem. Indeed, survival in the slums for a boy could depend as much on his fists as on his intelligence. Fighting was a common means of settling disputes and maintaining one's standing among fellow juveniles. Street fighting prepared youths for careers as pugilists, criminals, policemen, or even politicians. In antebellum New York City, for example, local political factions employed "shoulder hitters" to intimidate rivals on election day. Prizefighters were among the ranks of the shoulder hitters. When a youth became a successful prizefighter, he served as a role model for others. In part as a result, Irish boxers dominated the ring throughout the nineteenth century.[10]

Prizefighting in the Postbellum Era

Although the Civil War (1861–1865) brought to a close the Age of Heroes, it may have increased public interest in the ring as well as in other sports. By bringing together massive numbers of young men in military units, the war replicated conditions similar to those that existed among the young workingmen and clerks in the cities. Seeking to escape boredom and establish an identity in an all-male milieu, the soldiers frequently turned to baseball, running, wrestling, shooting matches, and boxing. They eagerly subscribed to the purses needed to stage in-camp matches between boxers-turned-soldiers. At least two reported instances of troops temporarily laying down their weapons to enjoy pugilistic encounters between their Union and Confederate comrades suggested the possibility of substituting nonlethal, individual combat for the carnage of actual warfare.

The popularity of boxing among soldiers failed to arrest a general decline in the ring during the 1860s and 1870s. Externally, the prizefight game suffered from the increased vigilance of legal authorities. In New York City, the center of postbellum boxing, the fancy could no longer take it for granted that they would be shielded from the law by local politicians. Internally, charges of fixes and failures of boxers to fight aggressively shattered the sporting fraternity's confidence in the integrity of the ring. Even so-called championships sometimes turned into farces. In 1871, before their bout was interrupted by authorities, Jem Mace and Joe Coburn "fought" for an hour and 17 minutes without landing a single blow.

In the 1880s, however, several circumstances joined to usher in a new era of prizefighting. One was Richard Kyle Fox, publisher and editor of the *National Police Gazette*. Printed on shockingly pink paper and distributed at discount rates to such all-male sanctuaries as barbershops, livery stables, private men's clubs, and volunteer fire departments, the notorious weekly *Gazette* exploited to the fullest the nation's interest in racial bigotry, sexual adventure, and sensational exploits of all kinds. "If not workplace democracy," concludes historian Elliott Gorn, "the ethos of the *Police Gazette* offered white working males a democracy of pleasure denied by Victorian culture."[11] Fox featured engravings of show girls in tights, printed stories of scandals and atrocities, advertisements for contraceptives, and bizarre contests. The *Gazette* awarded belts and other prizes for winners of championships in (among others) prizefighting, weight lifting, and one-legged clog dancing. But Fox's favorite sport was pugilism.

Key metropolitan saloons supplemented Fox's efforts to promote prizefighting. In the 1870s and 1880s one of the most important was Harry Hill's saloon, located on notorious Bleeker Street in New York City. While the saloon was described by a reformer as "the last resort of a low class of prostitutes, and the ruffians and idlers who support the prize ring," it became the headquarters for politicians and wealthy parvenus as well as gamblers, show people, and pugilists. "If you were anybody at all in New York night life in the seventies and eighties," wrote a contemporary, "you got into Harry Hill's as often as possible. Here boxing and wrestling were held and articles were signed for bigger matches elsewhere, shows were cast, [and] large bets were made."[12] In the early 1880s William Muldoon, the most renowned Greco-Roman wrestler of the day, and John L. Sullivan, the prizefighting champion, both worked out of Hill's saloon. Harry Hill himself was the best-known and most esteemed stakeholder and boxing referee in the country. Though usually less lavish, saloons in other cities served the sporting fraternity in a similar fashion.

"Athletic clubs" also contributed to the new era of the ring. A growing interest in boxing among the membership of elite athletic clubs, especially in New York, New Orleans, and San Francisco, improved the image of the fight game. Within the confines of the socially exclusive clubs, young men of high social standing took sparring lessons from "professors of pugilism." The New York Athletic Club, for example, hired Mike Donovan, the middleweight champion, to teach "gentlemen eminent in science, literature, art, social and commercial life" the finer principles of the "manly art."[13] The New York club also scheduled the first national amateur boxing championships. Sometimes wealthy men from the athletic clubs joined in an uneasy alliance with ethnic political leaders in campaigns to modify state laws or city ordinances that banned prizefighting.[14]

The entrance of athletic clubs into boxing also altered the nature of the sport. The clubs encouraged fighting for a specified number of rounds, though round limitations did not become a universal practice until the 1920s. The clubs joined Richard Kyle Fox in promoting weight divisions; by the mid-1880s, Fox was naming national champions, often with shadowy claims, for six distinct weight divisions. Finally, by bringing the matches indoors, charging admission and offering specific purses to the winners, the clubs altered the traditional mode of fight promotion.

The clubs prompted the growing acceptance of the Marquis of Queensberry rules. Drafted under the patronage of the English marquis in 1865, the rules required the use of gloves, limited rounds to three minutes, provided for ten-second knockouts and prohibited wrestling holds. The new rules may, as Elliott Gorn has argued, have made the sport even more brutal, since gloves protected the bones in the hands (thus permitting the fighter to hit harder with impunity) and added weight to each punch. But the use of gloves gave boxing the appearance of curbing brutality, thereby making the sport more acceptable. The banning of wrestling holds, the ten-second knockout rule, and the imposition of round limitations encouraged a faster-paced, more commercially appealing spectacle. A major breakthrough in the use of the Queensberry rules came in 1890, when New Orleans legalized gloved fights when sponsored by athletic clubs.

Enter John L. Sullivan

Into the new era of prizefighting stepped a new champion heavyweight whose contribution to boxing may have exceeded that of Fox, the saloons, the athletic clubs, and the use of the Queensberry rules. Born in Boston to Irish immigrant parents, John L. Sullivan achieved a celebrity status perhaps unequaled by any other public figure of his time.[15] After trying his hand at the various manual jobs available to an Irish youth in the 1870s, he discovered his talent for boxing. In exhibition matches in Boston theaters and music halls he soon developed a reputation as a slugger. In 1882, with a decisive knockout, he became national champion.

The American public adored Sullivan. Shortly after winning the title, he began the first of several nationwide tours in which he offered the astonishing sum (for that day) of $1,000 to anyone who could stand up to him for four rounds. Reportedly only one person performed the feat; scores of others succumbed to Sullivan's mighty blows. Sullivan used gloves in these exhibitions, thereby both saving his hands from damage and adhering to local ordinances against bare-knuckle fighting. When no local hero stepped forward for punishment (as frequently was the case), Sullivan sparred with a member of his own traveling troupe, which typically included other boxers as well as wrestlers, clowns, and jugglers. The tour, Sullivan's love of fighting, and his flamboyant lifestyle raised the "Boston Strong Boy" to the pinnacle of national popularity. Between 1884 and 1886 Sullivan added 14 official victories to his record, and Fox launched a worldwide search to find a worthy challenger.

In the late 1880s, Sullivan's fortunes turned sour. Suffering from alcoholism and poor health, he fought the English champion, Charlie Mitchell, to an embarrassing draw in 1888. The next year Sullivan met Jake Kilrain in the last bout of the bare-knuckle era. Public interest in the bout knew few bounds. "Never, during even a Presidential election, has there been so much excitement as there is here now," concluded the *New York Times*.[16] Whipped into tip-top shape for the match by wrestler-trainer William Muldoon, Sullivan dueled Kilrain under the blazing sun in Richburg, Mississippi, for 75 rounds before Kilrain's seconds finally threw in the sponge. During the bout, Sullivan's backers reportedly fortified him with copious drafts of tea mixed with whiskey. In the 45th round, Sullivan began to heave up the concoction, leading one wag to claim that the champion's stomach "rejected the tea but held the whiskey."

Exhilaration mounted even higher in 1892 when Sullivan defended his title against James J. Corbett in New Orleans. The Sullivan–Corbett match marked a series of important "firsts" in the history of prizefighting. Locked in circulation wars with one another, major daily newspapers switched from their usual condemnation to open support of the ring. Rather than signing the articles for the fight in a saloon or in the offices of the *National Police Gazette,* representatives of the two boxers met in the offices of Joseph Pulitzer's *New York World*. As a heavyweight championship bout, the fight was the first to be held indoors under electric lights, the first to use gloves, the first to employ the Marquis of Queensberry rules, and the first to be sponsored by an athletic club.

Corbett himself lent a new aura of respectability to the ring. Although of Irish extraction, Corbett had not fought his way up from the streets. Instead, he had attended college, held a white-collar job as a bank clerk, and learned his boxing skills in an elite athletic club, earning him the sobriquet "Gentleman Jim." These departures reflected boxing's transition away from its folk, countercultural origins to a form of mass, commercial entertainment. The sport that had become the ultimate symbolic test of masculinity had won the admiration of many Victorians. The fight's outcome underscored the change. Handicapped by age, and having relapsed into his old ways of drinking and eating too much, Sullivan put on a poor show. In the twenty-first round Corbett "shot his right across the jaw and Sullivan fell like an ox."[17]

"In 1892 I was reading aloud the news to my father," William Lyon Phelps, a professor at Yale, later reported. "My father was an orthodox Baptist minister... I had never heard him mention a prizefight and did not suppose he knew anything on the subject, or cared anything about it. So when I came to the headline CORBETT DEFEATS SULLIVAN, I read that aloud and turned the page. My father leaned forward and said earnestly, 'Read it by rounds!' "[18]

Sullivan, the first truly national sports hero, remained a celebrity long after his loss to Corbett. He performed in numerous vaudeville acts and plays (including the role of Simon Legree in a traveling production of *Uncle Tom's Cabin*) and even gave temperance lectures. Yet neither Sullivan's popularity, the Queensberry rules, nor the reforms instituted by the athletic clubs completely erased the traditional stigma associated with the prize-ring. The sport remained illegal almost everywhere and respectable women did not attend prizefights until the 1920s. Without a national regulatory body or a rational system for determining champions, boxing remained an unusually chaotic and disorderly sport. Champions invariably avoided challengers unless they could be assured of a large stake—"win or lose." Young fighters with dreams of reaching the top sought out "patsies" so they could leave their records unblemished. The bottom line for any fight was the anticipated profits of promoters. "Carrying" an opponent, "taking a dive," and "fixing records"— these and other fraudulent tactics were endemic to the fight game. Thus, despite the growing popularity of boxing among all social groups, the ambience of boxing remained working class and ethnic, and shrouded by the shady world of bookies, thugs, and racketeers.

Conclusion

Throughout most of the nineteenth century, American popular sports developed on the margins of "respectable" society, among groups of men who found greater satisfaction in the dramatic and combative masculinity of sports than in the drudgery of daily life. The sporting fraternity adapted and promoted traditional pastimes such as horse racing and prizefighting in ways that made them more engaging and also more profitable. In the case of prizefighting, these efforts helped a once-marginalized and frequently illegal sport gain a solid footing in American popular culture by the end of the century. In the twentieth century, prizefighting would retain its roots in the hard-bitten masculinity of working-class communities, and its ongoing association with gambling and gamblers would continue to raise eyebrows in some sectors of American society. But the heavyweight championship in particular would also be one of the most popular—and the most symbolic—of athletic contests.

Critical Thinking Questions

1. Prizefighting drew support from both upper- and working-class men, even as it was sharply condemned by middle-class Victorians. How do these divisions contribute to an understanding of the competing visions of manhood that characterized the nineteenth-century United States?

2. Historian Elliot Gorn distinguishes between "workplace democracy," which most nineteenth-century American workers failed to achieve, and a "democracy of pleasure" that proved easier to access. What does this distinction say about American democracy in general in the nineteenth century?

3. Do any present-day sporting events resemble early nineteenth-century prizefights? If so, what appeal does this kind of event hold today? If not, why might this interest have faded?

Notes

1. Elliott J. Gorn, *The Manly Art* (Ithaca, NY: Cornell University Press, 1986), 91–4.
2. Quoted in John R. Betts, *America's Sporting Heritage* (Reading, MA: Addison-Wesley, 1974), 162.
3. Quoted in Melvin L. Adelman, *A Sporting Time: New York City and the Rise of Modern Athletics, 1820–1870* (Urbana: University of Illinois Press, 1986), 242.
4. See John Dizikes, *Sportsmen and Gamesmen* (Boston: Houghton Mifflin, 1981), chapter 5.
5. See Adelman, *A Sporting Time,* chapter 4; and Nancy L. Struna, "The North-South Races: American Thoroughbred Racing in Transition, 1823–1850," *Journal of Sport History* 8 (1981), 28–57.
6. Allan Nevins, ed., *The Diary of Philip Hone, 1828–1851,* 2 Vols. (New York: Dodd, Mead, 1927), II, 861.
7. See George Moss, "The Long-Distance Runner in Ante-Bellum America," *Journal of Popular Culture* 8 (1974), 370–82.
8. Quotations from Adelman, *A Sporting Time,* 213, 214.
9. Quoted in Melvin Leonard Adelman, "The Development of Modern Athletics in New York City, 1820–1870," unpub. Ph.D. diss., University of Illinois, 1980, 535.
10. In addition to ibid.; see S.K. Weinberg and Henry Arond, "The Occupational Culture of the Boxer," *American Journal of Sociology* 57 (1952), 460–69.
11. Elliott J. Gorn, "The Wicked World: *The National Police Gazette* and Gilded Age Culture," *Media Studies Journal* 6 (Winter 1992), 14.
12. Quotations from Gorn, *The Manly Art,* 183; and D.B. Chidsey, *John the Great* (Garden City, NY: Doubleday, 1942), 13.
13. Quoted in Gorn, *The Manly Art,* 199.
14. See Steven A. Riess, "In the Ring and Out: Professional Boxing in New York, 1896–1920," in *Sport in America,* ed. Donald Spivey (Westport: CT: Greenwood, 1985), 95–128.
15. Apart from Gorn, *The Manly Art;* see Michael T. Isenberg, *John L. Sullivan and His America* (Urbana: University of Illinois Press, 1988).
16. Quoted in Gorn, *The Manly Art,* 235.
17. Quoted in Somers, *The Rise of Sports in New Orleans,* 184.
18. William Lyons Phelps, *Autobiography with Letters* (New York: Oxford University Press, 1939), 356.

CHAPTER 4

The Rise of America's National Game

The grand buildings and mixed gender crowd depicted at the New York Polo Grounds reflect baseball's growing respectability.

In 1842 and 1843, a group of young men—clerks, merchants, brokers, professionals, and assorted "gentlemen"—began playing a bat-and-ball game at the corner of 27th Street and 4th Avenue in Manhattan. According to legend, by 1845 bank clerk Alexander Cartwright had convinced the young men to organize themselves as the New York Knickerbockers Base Ball Club. They chose as a playing site a portion of John Cox Stephens' Elysian Fields in Hoboken, New Jersey, a most "picturesque and delightful" place that was easily accessible from Manhattan via the Barclay Street ferry. After a hard afternoon of play, the club members retreated to nearby McCarty's Hotel bar, where they regaled one another with manly talk and quenched their thirst with spirituous drink.

From these modest origins—not from the mythical creation by Abner Doubleday—developed what contemporaries called a *base ball fraternity*. The ballplaying fraternity organized clubs, adopted written rules, and initially placed a higher priority on playing for personal pleasure than for spectators and money. As early as the 1860s, however, baseball began to enter another stage of development, one in which the better teams played a commercial, spectator-centered sport. The formation of the National League in 1876 signified the sport's full arrival as a business enterprise.[1]

The Club-Based Fraternal Game

Today's fans would find the Knickerbockers game of the 1840s and 1850s both strange and familiar. Just as today, the game was played on a diamond-shaped infield. Three strikes swung at and missed retired the "striker" (batter), but the practice of having umpires call balls and strikes was unknown. The umpires, who at first wore tails and tall black top hats and sat at a table along the first base line, only gradually acquired this responsibility. On other matters, umpires rendered decisions only when controversies arose between the respective team captains. The fielders wore no gloves and the catcher stood several feet behind the "striker," hoping to catch the pitches on the first bounce. From a running start the "feeder" (pitcher) literally pitched the ball under-handed with a straight arm from a distance of 45 feet. In the early days, the pitcher was obligated to toss the ball gently, so the hitter could have a pitch to his liking.

Unlike the larger sporting fraternity that promoted prizefights, pedestrian races, and blood sports, the baseball fraternity's existence revolved around organized clubs. Like other voluntary associations of the day, the clubs drew up bylaws, elected officers, and held regular meetings. The club was both an athletic and a social organization. Initially, the Knickerbockers tried to restrict their membership to "gentleman amateurs"; one became a member by invitation only. Their shared interest in baseball, colorful uniforms similar to those of the era's volunteer fire departments, and a large array of social activities strengthened the fraternal bonds among the ballplayers.

The fraternity offered young men satisfactions missing in their work as well as in other parts of their lives. "We would forget business and everything else, on Tuesday afternoons, go out into the green fields, don our ball suits, and go at it with a perfect rush. At such times, we were boys again," recalled Frank Pidgeon, a former captain of the Eckford club in Brooklyn.[2] Often unmarried, less encumbered by concerns about the morality of competitive sport than stricter Victorians, and living away from home, the young men not only experienced emotional satisfaction in playing ball but also found in the game opportunities for companionship, a sense of belonging, and the development and display of physical skills.

Pageantry, rituals, and off-season social gatherings enhanced player fraternization. In a postgame ceremony, the winning team received the game ball as a prize; the ball was then ceremoniously inscribed with the date and outcome of the contest and retired to the club's trophy case. After interclub games, home clubs frequently provided visitors with a gala dinner. In 1858, for example, "the Excelsior Club was escorted to the Odd Fellows Hall, Hoboken, by the Knickerbockers Club, and entertained in splendid style....Dodsworth's band was in attendance to liven the scene."[3] Perhaps an extreme example of the effectiveness of postgame rituals in promoting amity within the fraternity occurred in 1860. According to the *New York Clipper*, after having shared a keg of lager, the players were unable to recall the score of the game that they had played earlier in the day.[4]

Clubs even scheduled formal dances; sometimes the players seemed to have been as busy and proficient on the dance floor as they were on the playing field. For example, in the winter of 1860–61, Brooklyn's Eckford club, composed of ship-building artisans, scheduled eight "hops" and an annual ball. A special treat at the ball was Captain Frank Pidgeon, who exhibited his talents in the "Parisian style" of dancing.

Enthusiasm for baseball soon spread beyond the ranks of petty shopkeepers, clerks, and artisans. Any group of men who enjoyed a work schedule that left a few daylight hours free and had the wherewithal to rent playing space might take up the game. In the greater New York area, clubs frequently organized along occupational, ethnic, and/or neighborhood lines. Boys played informal games on empty lots or in the streets. Special games and tours excited widespread interest in what was sometimes called the "New York game." In 1858, an "all-star" series between the best players from Brooklyn and the New York stars captured the attention of the entire city. Two years later, newspapers across the nation reported a tour by the Excelsiors of Brooklyn to upstate New York and then on to Philadelphia and Baltimore. The Civil War, far from impeding the growth of the sport, encouraged the introduction of baseball by veterans (especially the Union ones) to hamlets across the nation. Representation at the annual baseball convention of the National Association of Base Ball Players (founded in 1858) increased from 62 clubs in 1860 to 91 clubs in ten states at the war's conclusion in 1865.

The press encouraged baseball's growth. While the regular daily newspapers initially gave only cursory attention to the fraternity's activities, such sporting sheets as the *New York Clipper* and Porter's *Spirit of the Times* not only reported the results of matches and other baseball news but also provided direct aid to young men interested in forming clubs. No single journalist gave the sport greater assistance than Henry Chadwick, who because of his contributions later became known as "Father Chadwick." Chadwick edited baseball's first annual guidebook, which by the mid-1860s claimed to have a circulation of more than 65,000. Other guidebooks soon appeared; they enabled avid fans to keep abreast of the latest rules, clubs, and statistics, as well as other news of the diamond. Chadwick also invented the box score and batting averages, quantitative devices that enhanced baseball's appeal.

As early as the mid-1850s, the baseball fraternity began to promote their sport as "the national game." Such a strategy fitted perfectly the tense mood of the 1850s. In a decade that spawned the bitter divisions that culminated in the Civil War, yearnings for national unity spilled over into sports. Few public events captured the public imagination more than American challenges to English supremacy in horse racing, boxing, and even yachting. Made up largely of old-stock Americans, many of the first baseball clubs openly avowed their nationalism by taking on such patriotic names as Young America, Columbia, Union, Eagle, American, or National. As the English had their cricket and the Germans their *Turnvereins* (exercise clubs), Porter's *Spirit* declared in 1857, Americans needed "a game that could be termed a 'Native American Sport.'"[5] Baseball, its supporters agreed, filled that need. Not only had it evolved as a distinctive American sport, they argued, it also embodied more completely than any other sport the fast-paced nature of American life. In the twentieth century, along with such other icons as the national flag, the national anthem, and the Constitution itself, baseball would establish itself as a significant part of the nation's identity.

In the nineteenth century, however, baseball remained outside the boundaries of respectability for many Americans. Unlike the followers of prizefighting, whose activities explicitly challenged Victorian morals, the baseball fraternity sought respect and acceptance. But for Victorian America, plentiful instances of rowdy, uncontrolled behavior continued to cast suspicion on the game and its followers. While businesses in some places organized their workers into teams, others worried lest their employees neglect their work for the sake of the game. "The invariable question put to young men applying for situations in New York," according to the secretary of the Irvington, New Jersey, baseball club in 1867, "is, whether they are members of ball clubs. If they answer in the affirmative, they are told that their services will not be needed."[6]

The fraternity tried to counter such negative attitudes by insisting on the game's compatibility with Victorian values. Baseball encouraged manliness, or self-control, rather than boyishness, or impetuous behavior, its defenders argued. Play by boys, according to the *Brooklyn Eagle*, kept the youngsters "out of a great deal of mischief," preventing them "from hanging around [fire] engine houses, stables, and taverns."[7] But such assurances never fully allayed the fears of Victorian moralists.

Baseball as a Commercial Enterprise

At the very height of its success, the baseball fraternity began to disintegrate. Although features of the club-based, fraternal game lingered on, commercial considerations quickly engulfed the sport. Clubs began to encourage spectators to attend games in the 1850s, and in 1862 an ambitious Brooklynite, William H. Cammeyer, built a fence around some land that he owned and charged admission fees to spectators who watched games there. The "enclosure movement," as the drive to build fences around fields and charge a gate fee was called, introduced a new era of baseball history. It was, as Henry Chadwick wrote, "really the beginning of professional base ball playing."[8]

As fraternal bonds weakened and "nines" seized upon the opportunities presented by gate charges, teams began to play more games, practice more, embark on long summer tours, recruit athletes on the basis of their playing skills rather than their sociability and even extend sub *rosa* payments to outstanding players. By the mid-1860s, the postgame rituals of awarding the game ball to the winning team and hosting a dinner for visitors disappeared from the sport. Baseball's culture increasingly accepted the use of cunning tactics; indeed, the game's aficionados came to admire those players and teams who could successfully trick the umpire or their opponents. Unlike in the earliest days of the game, the "cranks" or "kranks," as the more rabid fans were called, cheered wildly for their heroes, heckled umpires and opposing players, and sometimes rioted. In the larger cities, more and more blue-collar youth, often of Irish or German extraction, found opportunities to profit from their skills.

As commercial baseball became more popular, charges of gambling and game dumping tainted its quest for respectability. Gamblers quickly seized upon the opportunities presented by baseball games, and fans began to suspect (justifiably) that some games were fixed. New York gamblers, for instance, apparently controlled the Troy, New York, Haymakers, a team that acquired a notorious reputation for game fixing. Because of the popularity of two-of-three game series, the Haymakers and other teams would deliberately lose one of the first two games in order to justify the playing of a third game. In California, just as a fielder was about to catch a fly ball, the gamblers who had placed bets on the side at bat would fire their six shooters. On several occasions, bettors even mobbed playing fields to prevent the completion of games in which they stood to lose money. "So common has betting become at baseball matches," complained a *Harper's Weekly* editor in 1867, "that the most respectable clubs in the country indulge in it to a highly culpable degree."[9]

The Victorian press condemned player behavior on other grounds as well. The typical professional player, according to the *New York Times* in 1872, was a "worthless, dissipated gladiator; not much above the professional pugilist in morality and respectability." The players spent their off-seasons, according to the *Times*, "in those quiet retreats connected with bars, and rat pits, where sporting men of the metropolis meet for social improvement and unpremeditated pugilism."[10]

Yet criticism for impropriety and commercialization hardly slowed baseball's burgeoning popularity. Indeed, the passing of each decade saw more young men taking up the sport. With opportunities for exhibitions of physical manliness limited by the radical changes in nineteenth-century work places and the prevailing Victorian restraints on self-expression, baseball offered an exciting arena for the display of physical prowess and aggressiveness in a controlled setting. On the diamond, young men could achieve reputations for their skills and experience, as well as a sense of participating in a common culture that revolved around ballplaying.

Intense rivalries among nineteenth-century cities encouraged the creation of professional baseball teams. "If we are ahead of the big city in nothing else," crowed the *Brooklyn Eagle* in 1862, "we can beat her in baseball."[11] Interurban rivalry was even more acute among the upstart cities of the West. Boosters tried to bolster extravagant claims on behalf of their city's superiority by founding suitable institutions, such as churches, hospitals, libraries, colleges, and representative baseball nines.

In 1869, the astonishing success of Cincinnati's Red Stockings, the nation's first publicly all-salaried team, vividly illustrated the possibilities of using baseball to advertise one's city. By vigorously pushing stock sales among local businessmen and politicians, Aaron B. Champion, the club's young president, raised enough money to employ star players from the East. Led by player-manager Harry Wright, a former professional cricket player, the Red Stockings swept through a season of 58 games with no losses and only one tie. Over 23,000 fans watched their six-game series in New York, previously considered the citadel of the baseball world. In Washington, D.C., President Ulysses S. Grant welcomed the "Cinderella" team and complimented the members on the excellence of their play. In September, the club crossed the United States on the newly completed transcontinental railroad to play a series of games in California. "Glory, they've advertised the city—advertised us, sir, and helped our business," exulted a delighted Cincinnati businessman.[12]

Cincinnati's success jarred other cities, including its longtime adversary, Chicago, into action. Chicago "could not see her commercial rival on the Ohio bearing off the honors of the national game," declared the *Lakeside Monthly* in 1870. "So Chicago went to work." Joseph Medill, owner of the *Chicago Tribune*, and Potter Palmer, owner of the famed Palmer House hotel, were among those who rose to the occasion by organizing the White Stockings baseball club as a joint-stock company. The $20,000 they raised for player salaries appeared destined, in the words of a jealous Boston newspaper, to "sweep the board."[13]

During the last three decades of the nineteenth century, small-time entrepreneurs, politicians, city boosters, and "traction" (transit) magnates formed dozens of joint-stock baseball clubs. Fortunately for them, the investors were frequently as interested in publicity as profits, for the clubs experienced staggering rates of failure. Even Cincinnati's storied Red Stockings closed down at the end of their second season, after apparently failing to earn a profit. Leagues of representative teams were equally fragile; franchises joined and dropped out with startling frequency. The National League, the most successful of the circuits, had franchises located in no fewer than 21 different cities at one time or another during the nineteenth century.

The National Association of Professional Base Ball Players (1871–1875), baseball's first professional league, was a loose confederation of clubs. Any team that mustered a mere ten-dollar entry fee could contend for the championship pennant, no matter what size of city they represented. Teams scheduled their own matches, and a team could qualify for the pennant by playing all other clubs at least five times during the season. Players were free to move from one team to another at the end of each season—another indication of the league's unbusinesslike character.

Harry Wright's Boston team dominated the new loop. After the 1870 season, Wright brought most of the Cincinnati team with him to Boston. Although narrowly losing the pennant to the Athletics of Philadelphia in 1871, the Boston team then won the next four consecutive championships. George Wright, Harry's brother, was the club's superb-fielding, hard-hitting shortstop. Young Albert Spalding was the most baffling pitcher in the league, and Roscoe Barnes was the perennial batting champion. In 1875 the Bostons had the four top hitters in the circuit and ran away with the league flag, winning 71 games while losing only eight.

The National League

In 1876, William A. Hulbert, president of the Chicago White Stockings, and Albert Spalding, Hulbert's recently acquired star pitcher and manager, led a coup against the National Association and founded a new professional baseball league, "The National League of Professional Base Ball Clubs." Significantly, the founders substituted the term "clubs" for "players." They refused to admit nines owned by the players, and instead restricted their new league to "regular [joint-] stock companies" located in cities of 75,000 or more residents. For the inaugural season of 1876, clubs in Boston, Chicago, Cincinnati, Louisville, Hartford, St. Louis, Philadelphia, and New York fielded teams. Any new club wishing to join the circuit had to have the approval of the existing clubs. The league also sought to obtain the patronage of stricter Victorians by banning Sunday games, prohibiting the sale of liquor at ball parks and charging a 50-cent admission fee.

Still, the National League often failed to function effectively. Major ownership and management decisions remained mostly with the individual franchises and restrictive agreements or decisions could not ultimately be enforced by the league or the courts. Consequently, each club owner usually placed his interest before that of the league. As Albert Spalding, a shrewd and longtime observer of professional baseball once put it: "The [baseball] magnate must be a strong man among strong men, else other club owners in the league will combine in their own interest against him and his interests."[14]

For its first six years, William Hulbert offered the National League strong, albeit sometimes questionable leadership. He cracked down on loose player behavior by dramatically expelling four Louisville players in 1877 for taking bribes. His other decisions were more debatable. When both the Philadelphia and New York teams refused to take their final season road tours in 1876, he led a movement to expel them from the league, even though they represented the nation's two largest cities. When the Cincinnati club persisted in selling beer at its park and playing Sunday games, Hulbert hounded them out of the league as well.

The expulsion of Cincinnati led to a direct challenge to the National League. In 1881, six clubs formed the American Association, or "Beer Ball League," as it was sneeringly called by its critics. Indeed, investors in four of the six clubs had investments in breweries. In an attempt to attract fans from the lower income ranks, the association authorized the sale of liquor at games, charged only 25 cents for admission and permitted play on Sunday. The association also invited National League players to jump their contracts, and several did. The success of the association forced the leaderless National League to call for a strategic retreat. In 1882, the presidents of the two leagues plus the head of the Northwestern League (a minor league) signed a tripartite National Agreement.

The American economy boomed in the 1880s, and interest in professional baseball reached unprecedented heights. On the playing field, the American Association clubs proved fully equal to the senior loop. The powerful St. Louis Brown Stockings, managed by young Charles Comiskey (later owner of the Chicago White Stockings), won four consecutive association pennants and two informal "World Championship Series" against the National League flagbearers. In the meantime, the truce between the circuits remained an uneasy one; from time to time clubs in both leagues violated the spirit if not the letter of the National Agreement of 1882.

Just as Chicago men had formed the National League and furnished the loop with its leadership, the Chicago White Stockings, under the leadership of Adrian C. "Cap" Anson, initially dominated National League play. Anson, who stood six feet two inches and weighed more than 200 pounds, was a veritable giant for his era. He played first base, won four batting crowns, and in 22 seasons failed to hit .300 only twice. Under Anson's capable guidance, Chicago won five pennants between 1880 and 1886.

Mike "King" Kelly competed with Anson for the adoration of Chicago's fans. "As Celtic as Mrs. Murphy's pig," Kelly inspired a host of legends. One story took place as the sun was setting on the bottom of a game's twelfth inning, with two outs, the bases full, and the score tied. Kelly, who was playing the outfield for the White Stockings, leapt into the twilight trying to catch a mighty drive. As he came down, he held his glove high in the air and jauntily jogged to the dugout. The umpire yelled, "Out number three! Game called on account of darkness!" "Nice catch, Kell," his teammates exclaimed. "Not at all, at all," the King responded. "Twent a mile above my head."[15]

The Players' Revolt

While the National League and the American Association fought fiercely with one another for profits and ultimately survival, an equally serious conflict raged between club management and the players.[16] In the first place, the players and owners collided over player behavior. Like the industrial magnates of the day, baseball's management sought a sober, well-rested, disciplined work force. But professional ballplayers were an unruly lot. Many of them came from working-class communities where drinking, brawling, and display were fundamental parts of male homosocial worlds. Young, usually unmarried and with large quantities of free time, the players frequented billiard halls, loitered in saloons, and consorted with gamblers and show people.

The owners saw player drinking as a special problem. While the National League campaigned against drinking throughout the 1880s, reports frequently surfaced of players abusing alcohol. Albert Spalding, who had become the president of the Chicago club, once hired a Pinkerton detective to secretly follow his players. Seven of them, the detective reported, spent almost every night going "up and down Clark Street, all over the tenderloin districts, through the whole roster of saloons and 'speakeasy' resorts." After Spalding had the report read to the team, King Kelly finally broke the long silence. "I have to offer only one amendment," he said. "In that place where the detective reports me as taking a lemonade at 3 A.M. he's off. It was straight whiskey; I never drank a lemonade at that hour in my life."[17]

Apart from admonishment and fines, the National League deployed other weapons against the players. From the outset, the owners had agreed to "blacklist"—refuse to hire—any player who had been dismissed by another club or the league for any reason. In 1879 the owners discovered an even more ingenious weapon, the reserve clause. The reserve clause, in effect, gave a team that first signed a player a lifetime option on that player's services. Unable to offer his skills to any other franchise, the individual player could only bargain for a salary increase from a weak position. If a player believed that he should be paid more, he had only two available options. He could "hold out"— refuse to play until promised a satisfactory salary. Or he could quit baseball. Neither alternative was attractive. Holding out meant losing income, and most players could not find jobs outside of baseball that paid equally well.

The owners quickly discovered another advantage in the reserve clause: They could "sell" players to other clubs. In 1887, Albert Spalding startled the baseball world by selling King Kelly's contract rights to Boston for the then-spectacular sum of $10,000. The sale angered the players: Why should the owners receive compensation for skills possessed by the players, they asked? To the players, the sale smacked of human slavery and dramatized their ultimate impotency when dealing with the owners.

The highly publicized sale of Kelly to Boston, clashes with the owners over drinking and a salary classification (salary cap) scheme, rising salary expectations stemming from baseball's growing prosperity, and the leadership of John Montgomery Ward triggered a full-scale players' revolt. In 1885, Ward, a lawyer and a star player, had founded the Brotherhood of Professional Base Ball Players. Initially a secret organization, the brotherhood had been little more than a fraternal lodge that assisted players suffering temporary hardships. But when the league tried to impose a $2,500 ceiling on salaries in 1887, the angry players first considered a strike and then decided to form a competing big league.

In 1890, an all-out war erupted between the newly created Players' League and the National League. The eight-team Players' League invaded seven of the senior circuit's cities and lured away its best players. In a novel departure from private enterprise, the players and investors assumed joint management of the new franchises. Albert Spalding, now a sporting goods entrepreneur and president of the Chicago club, headed a war committee to suppress the player uprising. Capitalizing on the fears of the day, Spalding described the players as "hot-headed anarchists," who were bent on a "terrorism" that was characteristic of "revolutionary movements." While most of the newspapers happily printed Spalding's scorching denunciations, he had no success in prosecuting the defecting players for violating the reserve clause. Efforts to bribe star players to stay in the loop were also, by and large, unsuccessful. Reputedly, Spalding offered King Kelly a "blank check" to remain in the league, but Kelly refused, saying "I can't go back on the boys."[18]

Yet the Players' League lasted only one season. Competing on the same day in the same city for the same customers cost both leagues heavily. The players had opted for Victorian respectability—refusing to permit Sunday games, barring beer at games, and charging a high gate fee—rather than a direct appeal to ethnic, working-class fans, a decision that reduced their appeal among those most likely to sympathize with them. At the end of the 1890 season, using a combination of complex deals with the Players' League's financial backers, Spalding brought down the League. In 1891 the American Association also folded, leaving only the National League as a major league circuit. The owners at once set about slashing player salaries. John Ward summed up the new position of the players. When William Joyce, a player seeking a $200 advance on his salary, approached Ward for assistance, the defeated leader informed him: "Your inning is over, my boy."[19]

Between the Foul Lines and in the Stands

As players and managers contended over power and profits, the game itself underwent a number of changes, many designed to make the game more attractive to fans. In the 1870s and 1880s, the rule governing how high the pitcher could raise his arm above his waist while delivering the ball had been gradually relaxed. Overhand pitching was fully legalized in 1884. In 1887 batters lost the privilege of calling for pitches above or below the waist. Two years later, rulemakers determined that four pitches thrown outside the strike zone entitled the runner to first base.

Managers gradually developed tactics familiar to modern fans. Infielders inched away from their respective bases and catchers moved closer to the plate. Fielders learned to back each other up in the event of wild throws or muffed balls. Players began to don gloves in the mid-1880s, a move that protected their hands from the sting of the ball, and carried the added benefit of improving fielding. During the era of underhanded pitching, pitchers typically worked a full nine-inning game and pitched day after day. Overhanded pitching and lengthening of the pitching distance to 60 feet and six inches in 1893 placed more stress on the pitcher's arm, and by the end of the 1890s most clubs rotated at least three hurlers.

Team captains and managers increasingly stressed offensive teamwork. Although the bunt was not yet widely used, clubs began to employ the "hit-and-run" play during the 1890s. Base stealing and "stretching" hits into extra bases became more commonplace. In sharp contrast to the conviviality of the early baseball fraternity, teams developed psychological warfare into an art form. Players and managers verbally harangued opposing players and the umpire. Violence or the threat of violence included the use of spiked shoes to intimidate or wound defensive players, tripping or blocking runners, and outright fistfights. John Heydler, an umpire in the 1890s (and later National League president) described the leading offenders, the Baltimore Orioles, as "mean, vicious, ready at any time to maim a rival player or an umpire."[20]

Baseball continued to grow in popularity, but not necessarily in respectability. The ballparks of the day were inexpensive, jerry-built, wooden structures that were doomed to become early victims of decay, termites, fire, or even collapse from the excessive weight of fans. Wooden fences kept out nonpaying fans, though some of them watched through cracks or knotholes in the boards (hence the origins of the term *knothole gangs*). A roof sheltered some fans from the sun while others sat on unprotected, sun-bleached boards (hence the term *bleachers*). At major games, fans continued to congregate along the foul lines and in front of outfield fences. Scorecards and refreshments could be purchased at the park, but the lack of a public address system or numbers on players' uniforms challenged the fans' ability to recognize players. Brass bands sometimes entertained fans between innings.

Professional baseball games attracted motley crowds. The *St. Louis Post-Dispatch* reported in 1883 that "a glance at the audience on any fine day at the ball park will reveal…telegraph operators, printers who work at night, travelling men [salesmen]…men of leisure…men of capital, bank clerks who get away at 3 P.M., real estate men…barkeepers…hotel clerks, actors and employees of the theater, policemen and firemen on their day off…butchers and bakers."[21] For the convenience of white-collar workers, clubs in several cities specifically started games in the afternoons. Steep ticket prices, the need to play during daylight hours, and bans on Sunday games restricted potential attendance by unskilled workingmen. Women were far less likely than men to attend games; early photographs show an overwhelming preponderance of men. In sum, most of the fans probably came from the ranks of the larger sporting fraternity, from show people and middle-income groups outside the reach of the strictest Victorian ideas.

Baseball continued to struggle for acceptance among proper Victorians, frequently driving a wedge between generations. Elders repeatedly warned their children about the moral perils arising from the game and discouraged them from pursuing baseball as a career. "You should never go to a ball game," Pittsburgh judge J.W.F. White lectured a defendant in an 1887 larceny case. "Baseball is one of the evils of the day." Suspicion even extended into New York City's Jewish neighborhoods. Future vaudevillian Eddie Cantor recalled hearing his grandmother shout at him as a child: " 'Stop! You-you-you baseball player you!'…That was the worst name she could call me. To the pious people of the ghetto a baseball player was the king of the loafers."[22]

Despite such widespread misgivings, however, baseball successfully invaded the nation's popular culture. During the nineteenth century, famed lithographers Currier and Ives released at least five baseball prints. As early as the 1880s, fans could purchase packages of cigarettes that included a small card with a picture of a player on it. Ballplayers frequently appeared on the vaudeville stage—some merely to be seen, others to sing, and a few to even dance and say a few lines. Baseball and music quickly developed a close union; more than 50 baseball songs were published before 1900.

Baseball Overseas

Baseball also began to win a foothold in other countries, where it served in part as an icon of American culture. This influence first surfaced in Cuba, where islanders began a struggle for independence from Spanish colonialism in the 1860s. During the ensuing social unrest, many Cuban elites immigrated to the United States, or sent their children to be educated at U.S. universities. Cubans quickly picked up the new game and brought it back to the island. The most storied pioneer, Esteban Bellán, became the first recorded Latino to become a U.S. professional player (the next

Latino major leaguer would be San Francisco-born Vincent Nava in 1882). A member of the Cuban elite, Bellán came to New York to attend Rose Hill College. He left school in 1868 to join the National League's Troy Haymakers. When he returned to Cuba in 1873, he immediately started to build the game there.

For Cubans who had their eyes on independence, playing the American game became not only an entertaining pastime, but a subtle protest against Spanish rule. In subsequent years, Cuban and American baseball players strengthened their ties through barnstorming tours, player exchanges, and newspaper reports. Cubans also actively encouraged the game in nearby Latin American countries, as did the growing number of Americans who were moving into the region on military, diplomatic, and economic missions. As the nineteenth century drew to a close, baseball had become popular in the Caribbean colonies of Puerto Rico and the Dominican Republic, as well as in Mexico, Venezuela, and parts of Central America.[23]

The Spanish–American War of 1898, in which the United States helped defeat Spanish armies and gained partial control over Cuba, Puerto Rico, and eventually the Philippine Islands, strengthened the determination of American leaders to spread their own version of enlightened "civilization" to areas beyond the U.S. borders. Advocates of baseball leaped quickly to associate themselves with this vision of a "superior" American culture. When A.G. Spalding penned his history of the sport, he waxed eloquent about the sport's spread. "Ever since its establishment in the hearts of the people as the foremost of field sports, Base Ball has 'followed the flag.'" Spalding wrote. "It has followed the flag to the Hawaiian Islands, and at once supplanted every other form of athletics in popularity. It has followed the flag to the Philippines, to Puerto Rico and to Cuba, and wherever a ship floating the Stars and Stripes finds anchorage to-day, somewhere on nearby shore the American National Game is in progress."[24]

Conclusion

For American men, no nineteenth-century sport exceeded baseball in popularity. Despite what many considered to be its tarnished associations, support for the game reached beyond the ranks of the urban sporting fraternity. During preadolescence, millions of boys—frequently against the wishes of their parents—learned the rudiments of the game. By 1900, semiprofessional and professional nines that represented towns or businesses could be found nearly everywhere. Millions of fans flocked to their games each summer. Baseball supporters were beginning to bill their sport as the true "American Game"—a claim that would solidify as the game continued to grow in popularity in the early twentieth century.

Critical Thinking Questions

1. What qualities helped make nineteenth-century baseball more respectable than prizefighting?
2. How might the game be different today if the Players' Revolt had succeeded?
3. Have the motives that animated baseball as a club sport disappeared, or have they moved to other social arenas?

Notes

1. A pioneering and still valuable book on nineteenth-century baseball is Albert Spalding's *America's National Game* (Lincoln: University of Nebraska Press, 1992). The standard multivolume histories are Harold Seymour, *Baseball*, 3 vols. (New York: Oxford University Press, 1960, 1970, 1990); David Voigt, *American Baseball*, 3 vols. (Norman: University of Oklahoma Press, vols. 1 and 2, 1966, and University Park: Penn State University Press, 1983); and Robert F. Burk, *Never Just a Game* and *Much More Than a Game* (Chapel Hill: University of North Carolina Press, 1994 and 2001). For an up-to-date, one-volume treatment, see Benjamin G. Rader, *Baseball: A History of America's Game*, 3rd ed. (Urbana: University of Illinois Press, 2008). For primary documents, consult Dean A. Sullivan, ed., *Early Innings: A Documentary History of Baseball, 1825–1908* (Lincoln: University of Nebraska Press, 1995), and for interpretive essays, John E. Dreifort, ed., *Baseball History from Outside the Lines* (Lincoln: University of Nebraska Press, 2001), and Jules Tygiel, *Past Time* (New York: Oxford University Press, 2000).
2. Quoted in George Kirsch, *The Creation of American Team Sports* (Urbana: University of Illinois Press, 1989), 116.
3. Quoted in Seymour, *Baseball*, I, 21.
4. Quoted in Warren Goldstein, "Playing for Keeps," unpub. Ph.D. diss, Yale University, 1983, 27. See also Goldstein, *Playing for Keeps* (Ithaca, NY: Cornell University Press, 1989) for a provocative interpretation of early baseball's history.
5. *Spirit of the Times*, 1 (January 31, 1857), 357.
6. Quoted in Adelman, *A Sporting Time*, 151.
7. Ibid., 173.
8. Quoted in Rader, *Baseball*, 20.
9. *Harper's Weekly*, October 26, 1867.
10. *New York Times*, March 8, 1872.
11. Quoted in Rader, *Baseball*, 32.
12. Ibid.
13. Ibid.
14. Quoted in Seymour, *Baseball*, I, 270.
15. Tristram P. Coffin, *The Old Ballgame* (New York: Herder and Herder, 1971), 36–37.
16. See in addition to the books cited in note 1, Lee Lowenfish, *The Imperfect Diamond: A History of Baseball's Labor Wars*, rev. ed. (New York: De Capro, 1991), part 1.
17. Quoted in Spalding, *America's National Game*, 184.
18. Ibid., 297.
19. Quoted in Seymour, *Baseball*, I, 270.
20. Quoted in Rader, *Baseball*, 75.
21. Ibid., 39.
22. Ibid., 102.
23. Adrian Burgos, Jr., *Playing America's Game: Baseball, Latinos and the Color Line* (Berkeley: University of California Press, 2007), 17–20; 30–33; Jorge Iber, et. al., *Latinos in U.S. Sport: A History of Isolation, Cultural Identity and Acceptance* (Champaign, IL: Human Kinetics, 2011), 79–80.
24. Quoted in Burgos, *Playing America's Game*, 71.

CHAPTER 5

Elite Sports

Members of the nation's expanding upper class relax with a game of tennis in a pastoral setting, 1887.

LEARNING OBJECTIVES

5.1 Describe the way that the founding of elite sporting institutions and the philosophy of amateurism helped to create an American upper class.

5.2 Outline the connections between the sports played by elite Americans and those played by their European counterparts.

5.3 Explain how the interests of elite sportsmen helped create a "Golden Age" of American horse racing.

5.4 Define the philosophy of amateurism and explain how it helped maintain certain sports as elite activities.

5.5 Analyze the reasons the philosophy of amateurism caused greater tensions among American sporting elites than among their British counterparts.

5.6 Discuss the origins of the American "country club" and how it differed from British institutions.

The first U.S. tennis championship tournament opened on August 31, 1881, at the posh Casino Club in Newport, Rhode Island. Fewer than 50 spectators, all wealthy vacationers who resided in their splendid stone "cottages" during the summer, milled around the court. The gentlemen, decked out in white flannels, striped jackets, and straw bowlers, stood. The ladies, who wore ankle-length petticoats and carried parasols to protect their delicate skin from the sun, sat on folding chairs or camp stools. The players themselves sported white flannels, long-sleeved shirts, and neckties, though they exchanged their bowlers for striped caps when playing. They played by the rules established by the All-England Croquet and Lawn Tennis Club, Wimbledon, England, when the first Wimbledon tournament was held in 1877. Richard D. "Dicky" Sears, a slight, bespectacled lad of 19 from a Boston Brahmin family, conquered a field of 22 players, all of whom came from wealthy families residing on the Eastern seaboard.

A deep chasm separated the sporting world of these Newport summer vacationers from the endeavors of the working classes. Only those in the highest social strata could watch or play in the tournament; the Casino Club was so exclusive that it had once turned away a president of the United States (Chester A. Arthur) for his inadequate social standing. The spectators paid no admission, and no one was paid to play. Only polite, whispered conversation punctuated the progress of the match. To the Newport crowd, winning or losing was of less importance than playing with proper grace, style, and etiquette. Following the match, players and spectators retired to the elegant Casino clubhouse where they could enjoy sumptuous food and drink. To most of the wealthy Newport residents, the tournament represented a pleasant interlude in their summer social season.

Yet the significance of tennis and other sports played by the rich in the last half of the nineteenth century extended far beyond the obvious. In a society characterized by an exceptionally fluid social structure, expensive sports provided a means by which the wealthy, especially the recently risen parvenu, could distinguish themselves from the masses. The wealthy, therefore, lavished their attention on thoroughbred horse racing, yachting, polo, track and field, cricket, tennis, and golf, games that required large amounts of free time, costly facilities, elaborate equipment, and sometimes travel to faraway places.[1]

Sports and the Forging of an American Upper Class

While there had always been Americans with aristocratic pretensions, the nation had never had a hereditary aristocracy in the European sense. But by the 1880s and 1890s, efforts to create what might be appropriately called an American aristocracy had, in the words of historian Robert Wiebe, "the look of a formidable enterprise."[2] Each city of any consequence had a fashionable residential area filled with the mansions of the superrich, who prided themselves on sending their sons to the most prestigious colleges.

Private clubs played a particularly significant role in the formation of a distinctive upper class. Before the Civil War, men of old wealth had formed metropolitan men's clubs, such as the Philadelphia (founded in 1835), the Union (1836) and the Century (1847) in New York, and the Somerset in Boston (1851). But these clubs rarely tolerated any physical activity more vigorous than napping in easy chairs, smoking cigars, sipping brandy, reading newspapers, or quiet conversations.

After the Civil War, the number of clubs patronizing the wealthy ballooned. Union Leagues (centers of Republican respectability) and University clubs (made up of the graduates of the nation's most prestigious colleges) ranked only slightly below the patrician metropolitan clubs. A variety of athletic, cricket, and country clubs came next in the urban club hierarchy. Unlike the clubs above them, these clubs usually welcomed women as guests or as auxiliary members, and they promoted a spirited, physically active club life. These clubs and their activities brought old and new wealth together, and experiences and values arising from the club nexus contributed to the formation of a distinctively American upper class.

Fascination with and efforts to imitate the European aristocracy, especially the English, often marked upper-class life in the United States. The nouveau riche frequently sent their children on European tours, married their daughters to sons of the European nobility, and took up the latest European pastimes with alacrity. As the century advanced, these pastimes included growing numbers of sports. In the middle decades of the nineteenth century, many members of the English upper class became avid sportsmen—forming hundreds of clubs for cricket, yachting, track and field, rowing, cycling, lawn tennis, and eventually golf. Americans soon followed.[3]

The Wealthy New York Sporting Community

New York became the leading center for wealthy sportsmen. Since colonial times the city's high society had been more tolerant of play than its counterparts in Philadelphia or Boston. New York's more flexible economy also played a role. In all three cities a residue of the colonial elite joined with newly wealthy men in the late eighteenth and nineteenth centuries to exploit the vast new opportunities presented in foreign trade, real estate, banking, law, and politics. But unlike New York, the Boston and

Philadelphia mercantile-Federalist elites founded virtual dynasties. Their descendants, the Boston Brahmin and Philadelphia Main Line families, managed for the most part to perpetuate their inherited status, continuing to dominate the industrial, financial, and cultural activities of their respective cities.

In New York, however, the rapid surge in population, commerce, railroad building, and the factory system fractured the older city elite in the latter half of the nineteenth century. "Separate enclaves dominated trade, politics, culture, and fashion, although some common membership existed among these groups," concluded a historian of New York's upper class.[4] The absence of a clear-cut dynasty or social arbitrator in New York gave rise to a *nouveau riche* who frequently defied Victorian restraints. The "smart set," or "Four Hundred," as the press dubbed them, splurged their wealth on highly publicized activities available only to the super-rich. Expensive sports promoted their consciousness as an elite social group and furnished them with a vehicle of self-advertisement.

The New York Yacht Club, established in 1844 by John Cox Stevens, became one of New York's first elite establishments. Membership in the club signified one's acceptance on the highest rungs of New York society. "A succession of gentlemen ranking high in the social and financial circles" of the city soon joined the club, wrote Charles Peverelly in 1866.[5] Stevens erected a handsome gothic clubhouse at the Elysian Fields; there the club held resplendent balls and festive dinners, with turtle as the favorite dish. The club took regular social cruises to Bar Harbor, Maine, Cape Hatteras, North Carolina, and other idyllic spots. In the postbellum era, the club's annual regatta at Newport became *the* social event of the summer season for the nation's upper class.

Yachting strengthened the bonds between upper-class American and British sportsmen. In 1851, Stevens organized a syndicate to build a special boat for the express purpose of challenging British yachtsmen to a race. Stevens' yacht, *America,* easily defeated 18 British yachts in a race around the Isle of Wight to win a coveted cup donated by the Royal Yacht Squadron. Queen Victoria visited the *America,* and congratulated the Yankees on their sterling performance. *America's* success encouraged the formation of other socially exclusive yachting clubs in cities along the Eastern seaboard. In 1857, the syndicate that owned *America* presented the cup to the New York Yacht Club on the condition that it should be contested for by yachtsmen from abroad.

One New Yorker who took advantage of the Yacht Club was James Gordon Bennett Jr., the colorful and eccentric owner of the *New York Herald.*[6] Bennett's father, a Scottish immigrant who had built the *Herald* into the world's most profitable newspaper, had been a social outsider. The younger Bennett, however, used his father's vast fortune to lift himself into fashionable circles. He became a member of the Yacht Club in 1857, at the tender age of 16. Nine years later, he captured the attention of the entire nation by winning the world's first transatlantic yacht race. The large purse of $60,000 won from side bets, as well as the loss of six members of his crew in a violent storm, added to Bennett's reputation for bravado. In the meantime, he sponsored Henry Stanley's exotic search for the explorer David Livingstone, who had been missing for several years in the African jungles. Both Europeans and Americans avidly followed Stanley's reports from the heart of Africa. His eventual success in locating Livingstone became the stuff of a monumental legend.

Bennett had a direct influence on several sports. Beginning in 1873, he awarded cups and medals to collegiate track and field champions. After having seen polo played by English Army officers, he introduced the game into the United States in 1876. Bennett and his wealthy friends formed the Westchester Polo Club in New York and took the sport to the Newport summer colony. Acutely concerned with staying current with the latest English sporting fashions, American polo enthusiasts even provided their ponies with upper-class comforts that included monogrammed linen sheets. In 1886, Newport hosted the first international match with the Hurlingham Club of England.

Bennett's assistance to the sport of lawn tennis had more bizarre origins. According to legend, in 1878 he secured for a British army officer a guest card to Newport's most exclusive club, the Reading Room. He then dared his friend to ride a horse up the steps of the club's front hall. When the man took up the challenge, the Reading Room immediately revoked Bennett's guest privileges. Miffed, Bennett retaliated by building a lavish sports complex, called the Casino, a few blocks away. The Casino subsequently became the site for the first 34 national tennis championships. While Bennett left New York to live in Paris in 1878, his *New York Herald* continued to lead the major dailies in reporting sporting news. Later in the century he contributed to the Olympic movement and promoted horse, auto, and air races.

Thoroughbred Horse Racing

No sport served the needs of New York City's parvenu sportsmen for conspicuous display more effectively than thoroughbred horse racing. Failing to obtain consistent patronage from the nation's wealthiest classes, wracked by the ricocheting business cycle, and confronted with persistent charges of gambling, chicanery, and commercialism, antebellum racing had never enjoyed sustained prosperity. But during the 1860s, a small group of newly made millionaires decided to place horse racing on a fresh footing. By building new tracks, providing large stakes, reducing corruption, substituting the dash for long-distance racing, and founding the New York Jockey Club as a central governing body, these men ushered horse racing into a new "golden age."

The main leader of the movement to transform the sport was New York City's Leonard W. Jerome, a man who had made a fortune selling short in the Panic of 1857. Blessed with enormous energy, Jerome was by day a calculating investor on Wall Street and by night a dashing man about town. The handsome financier engaged in scandalous love affairs, patronized the theater and the opera, and threw dazzling parties. At one of his parties, the fountains spouted champagne and eau de cologne. Infatuated by singer Jennie Lind, the Swedish Nightingale, he named a daughter after her—the daughter who would one day make Jerome the grandfather of Winston Churchill. But as much as he loved beautiful women, Jerome's special and lifelong passion was the turf.

In 1866, Jerome and his friends William R. Travers and August Belmont founded the American Jockey Club. Modeled after the socially exclusive Newmarket in England, the club purchased over 200 acres of land in Westchester County to build Jerome Park. The new park was by far the most lavish course in the nation. Located high on a bluff overlooking the backstretch, the luxurious clubhouse contained a spacious dining room, overnight sleeping quarters, and facilities for trap shooting, skating, and later, polo. Initially, only club members could sit in the grandstands. "From this sacred spot the respectable public are tabooed," noted the *New York Clipper* sarcastically, "and none but the sweet scented and kid glove subscribers can enter."[7] Led by the ostentatious display of the New Yorkers, men of new wealth across the nation took up horse racing. Other, less exclusive tracks—Monmouth Park (1870) in New Jersey, Pimlico (1870) in Baltimore, and Churchill Downs (1875) in Louisville—soon followed the construction of Jerome Park.

The golden age of horse racing entailed more than the opening of new tracks. To reverse the negative antebellum reputation of the turf, Jerome Park barred the sale of intoxicants, discouraged professional gamblers, and made a special effort to attract "the carriage trade." The wealth and social position of the club extended its influence far beyond New York. The New Yorkers led the movement to replace the old system of racing three- or four-mile heats with the modern dash system of racing. The dash placed more emphasis on speed rather than "bottom," or stamina, and permitted the running of several races on the same day. Large, permanent stakes, such as the Travers and the Belmont, added excitement and lent greater stability to the turf. In 1894, 50 giants in industry and finance founded the Jockey Club, which appointed officials, licensed jockeys, provided uniform national rules, and set national racing dates.

Despite its wealthy patronage, thoroughbred racing continued to operate outside of, or at best, on the fringes of Victorian respectability. As in the past, the centrality of gambling to horse racing continued to send shudders through the ranks of proper Victorians. Indeed, the introduction of bookmaking in the last quarter of the nineteenth century opened new opportunities for gambling; it allowed the small-time bettor to wager as little as two or three dollars on any horse at publicly posted odds. The horse racing fraternity was forced to turn to machine politicians to obtain the repeal (or exemption from enforcement) of laws restricting racing and gambling, which added to the suspicions of those who condemned the track for its unsavory character. As historian Steven Riess has documented, nearly every prominent Tammanyite had links to the track; the same was true of political leaders in Chicago, New Orleans, and other major racing centers.[8]

Athletic Clubs

Following the example of the English, elite Americans also began to form athletic clubs. Inspired by the formation of the London Athletic Club in 1863, the first English amateur championship meet in 1866 and the athletic activities of the New York Caledonian Club, three well-to-do young athletes founded the New York Athletic Club (NYAC) in 1866. Apparently the founders simply wanted an opportunity to engage in track and field with men of similar social standing and congenial interests. All three of the founders belonged to local boating clubs, and they induced several of their fellow rowers to join the NYAC. During inclement weather, the athletes worked out in the back parlor of a private residence. On fair days they went to the Elysian Fields or some other open space for running, vaulting, and shot-putting.

In 1868, the club incorporated with 14 members and sponsored the first open amateur track and field meet. A special invitation had been issued to the New York Caledonian Club, and the meet was hailed as "an international match—America against Scotland."[9]

Other clubs—among them the Staten Island, American, Manhattan, Pastime, University, and Crescent clubs, all of New York—soon organized on the NYAC model. By 1879, wealthy sportsmen in Baltimore, Buffalo, Chicago, Detroit, and St. Louis had also established athletic clubs. In the 1870s, the NYAC expanded its activities by building the first cinder track in the country, introducing the use of spiked shoes and sponsoring the first national amateur championships in track and field (1876), swimming (1877), boxing (1878), and wrestling (1878). In addition to the individual sports, many of the clubs eventually sponsored football, basketball, and sometimes baseball teams.

Beginning in 1882, the significance of the NYAC grew beyond athletics. That year, Alfred H. Curtis interested two of the city's wealthiest citizens, Herman Oelrichs and William R. Travers, in the club. Both Oelrichs and Travers were members of an exclusive upper-class social network that revolved around prestigious clubs; they were also prominent in the Four Hundred. Oelrichs, described by a contemporary as a "social leader" of the city, belonged to no fewer than 21 clubs, including the Union and New York Yacht clubs. A leading patron of "gentleman's sports," he was himself a capable swimmer, boxer, and polo player. Travers, a stockbroker, bon vivant and raconteur, was also a member of the Union Club and the Yacht Club as well as 24 other clubs. According to a contemporary, the decisions of Oelrichs and Travers to support the NYAC drew into the "club's ranks the most prominent and successful men in New York City and vicinity." By 1885, club membership had grown to 1,500.[10]

The NYAC acted as a gatekeeper for those seeking admission to even more socially exclusive clubs. It required a written application with pertinent personal information and the signatures of the members proposing and seconding the nominee for membership. With this information, the membership committee could seek to locate the applicant's standing within the city's social hierarchy. The initiation fee of $100 and annual dues of $50 also helped weed out undesirables. Athletic clubs could impose other strictures. The University Athletic Club, for example, required that all applicants possess a college degree, preferably from an Ivy League school. In short, membership in the metropolitan athletic clubs became an important link in a web of exclusive, upper-class associations.

With Oelrichs and Travers at the helm, the NYAC rapidly expanded its social activities. In 1885 it completed construction, at a cost of $150,000, of an elegant five-story, Venetian-style clubhouse that contained a gymnasium, swimming pool, dining rooms, club rooms, a bowling alley, a rifle range, a billiard room, a superb wine cellar, and sleeping rooms. In 1888, it acquired a country home at Travers Island where it built a track, clubhouse, boathouse, and clay tennis courts. Expanding the membership limit to 2,500 in 1892, the club constructed an even more lavish facility at the corner of 59th Street and 6th Avenue. Other clubs, attempting to emulate the NYAC, set up elaborate social calendars. "Wine, women, and song," according to the club's historians, "became more than a catch phrase—they were woven into the texture of NYAC activities."[11]

The 1880s and early 1890s marked the heyday of the athletic club. "Athletic clubs are now springing into existence in the United States in such profusion as to baffle the effort to enumerate them," an observer wrote in 1887. "Scarce a city can be found having a population of more than 30,000 inhabitants, in which there is not at least one club of this class."[12] While the clubs in smaller cities enjoyed far less commodious facilities than the metropolitan clubs, they were usually made up of the city's wealthiest citizens. In most cases they also sponsored annual track and field competition, although their athletes rarely competed successfully with those of the larger clubs.

Clubs in Boston, New Orleans, Chicago, and San Francisco soon rivaled the New York clubs in terms of facilities and membership. In 1893, the Chicago Club built a nine-story clubhouse costing nearly $1 million, a structure more costly than any of New York's clubs. Sometimes the clubs sponsored exotic and extravagant shows. In 1895, the Olympic Club in San Francisco put together a detailed reconstruction of Greek and Roman games, complete with a Caesar, courtiers, senators, gladiators, and vestal virgins. Over 4,000 persons attended the gala event, which cost $2.50 per seat.[13] But the 1890s also brought severe financial problems to many of the clubs. Some had overbuilt, and the economic depression of that decade brought about their collapse. While the metropolitan athletic club movement never fully recovered, the early twentieth century would witness the formation of many smaller, less pretentious, clubs whose energies were devoted primarily to sport.

Amateurism and Its Uses

Amateurism, which had its origins among upper-class English sportsmen, became a cardinal principle of American upper-class sporting ideology. In order to separate their pastimes from those of the ordinary people, the English amateur gentlemen insisted that play should not only be *without* pay, but also that it should be conducted in a *special* way. Ideally, amateur sportsmen always exhibited the principles of "fair play," never seeking unfair advantage of any kind. In principle, amateurs needed no officials to enforce the rules; they policed themselves. Those athletes who exhibited the greatest skills without apparent training and with the least visible physical exertion received the highest accolades. In quest of sanctions for their sporting ethos, the upper class also invented the myth of ancient Greek amateurism. The ancient Greeks never distinguished between professional and amateur athletes and did not have a concept of fair play. But the myth of Greek amateurism became a powerful idea in the world of modern sports.

Initially, the American athletic clubs raised no objections to pay for play. Members of the clubs sometimes ran in matches alongside professional pedestrians for bets one week and then in the following week competed in their club's closed games for a medal. But as the clubs became more concerned about social exclusion, they discovered the utility of British amateurism. As early as 1876, the New York Athletic Club restricted its fall games to "any person who has never competed... for public or admission money, or with professionals for a prize...nor has at any period in his life taught or assisted in the pursuit of athletic exercises as a means of livelihood."[14] In 1879, the National Association of Amateur Athletes of America, commonly known as the N4A and made up of the most exclusive athletic clubs, essentially copied the NYAC definition of amateurism.

The effect of these amateur rules was to prevent most lower-middle and working-class athletes from participating in club events as well as in other parts of club life. "The youths who participate in the health-giving competitions, as a rule, cannot afford the expense of membership in the so-called Athletic Clubs," complained Frederick Janssen in 1885, "and they retire in favor of the wealthy young man whose sole claim to fame to athletic distinction is his connection with a 'high-toned' club." Prohibiting the less privileged from competition served the larger purpose of building distinctive upper-class communities. As Will B. "Father Bill" Curtis, a founder of the NYAC, explained it: "There has grown up a system of clubs and associations whose best interests, pecuniary and social, would partially or wholly lose their value were the amateur fence to be taken down or materially lowered."[15]

In practice, however, the clubs fell short of fulfilling amateur ideals in one noticeable respect: Wealthy Americans often brought to sports the same winning-at-all-costs ethos that prevailed in the marketplace. In the 1880s the major metropolitan clubs embarked upon an era of intense rivalries for athletic supremacy. In order to field the strongest bevy of athletes possible, the clubs extended thinly disguised subsidies to superior performers. Many top athletes had little trouble finding clubs that would grant them a free membership and sometimes other valuable benefits as well.

The career of Lawrence E. "Lon" Myers, hailed as "the world's greatest runner," is a striking case in point.[16] Standing five feet seven and one-quarter inches tall and weighing a mere 114 pounds, Myers was not a wealthy man. Even had he been, his Jewish ancestry would have kept him out of many of the nation's more exclusive clubs. But in his running career he won 15 American amateur championships plus several English and Canadian titles. At one time or another, he held every American record in all distances from 50 yards to the mile run. When he died in 1899, he still held records in five distances. His talent won him a place at the prestigious Manhattan Athletic Club, where he spent most of his amateur career.

In 1884, charges surfaced that Myers had violated the N4A amateur code. According to a newspaper account, he had been paid for directing the construction of the Manhattan Club's new grounds, for serving as club secretary and for editing a portion of a sporting weekly. In addition, Myers had allegedly sold some of his medals. Without disproving or denying the validity of these charges, the executive committee of the N4A formally upheld Myers's amateur standing. In the next year the Manhattan Club even scheduled a benefit on his behalf, which netted the athlete some $4,000.

The passionate competition among the clubs (especially the NYAC and the Manhattan) and disputes over the eligibility of athletes resulted in the demise of the N4A. Amid bitter charges and countercharges, the New York Athletic Club withdrew from the association in 1886 and led a group of clubs in forming the Amateur Athletic Union (AAU) in 1888. The N4A collapsed the following year. While controversies revolving around the enforcement and meaning of amateurism would continue far into the twentieth century, the AAU seized effective control of U.S. track and field athletics, and the organization's definition of amateurism dominated that slice of American sport for decades.[17]

Cricket Clubs and Country Clubs

Cricket and golf also attracted elite Americans. In Philadelphia in particular, old-stock, upper-class Americans became enthusiastic cricketers. The popularity of cricket among Philadelphia's elite sprang partly from chance. In the 1840s, English textile workers employed at the Wakefield Mills introduced cricket to a group of young Philadelphians residing in the Manheim region. In the 1850s, Manheim youngsters organized three clubs; one, the Young America Cricket Club, explicitly excluded from membership anyone who was foreign-born. By so doing, the club helped dissociate itself from the "steak and ale" style of cricket played among the English workingmen.[18]

After the Civil War, men of old wealth built elaborate clubhouses and acquired spacious grounds. The top five clubs placed their grounds and built their club-houses in the city's most prestigious neighborhoods. By the 1890s, within a ten-mile radius, Philadelphia had four beautifully kept clubs, all with sumptuous grounds and lavish clubhouses. London, by comparison, had only two grounds of equal stature. Membership in the five "first-class" clubs ranged from 500 to 1,300 persons.

The clubs' cricketers even made a splash in international competition. In 1874, a team picked from the Philadelphia clubs accepted an invitation to play a series of matches against British and Canadian elevens at Halifax, Nova Scotia. After the Philadelphia eleven won the cup, cricket became the object of intense competition among the city's major clubs. By 1891, Philadelphia teams had played touring professional and amateur teams from the British Isles at least seven times, Australian clubs twice, and Canadian teams on numerous occasions. In both 1884 and 1889 the "Gentlemen of Philadelphia" visited England. They acquitted themselves well, winning four, losing three, and drawing five matches against top-flight English competition.

The cricket clubs were integral parts of Philadelphia's upper-class suburban life. Not only the expense of membership but also the time required to play cricket automatically excluded the ordinary workingman. As the "national game" of England, cricket also appealed to status-conscious Americans who sought to emulate the habits of English sportsmen. The clubs assumed a wide array of social functions similar to the metropolitan athletic clubs. The report of the Board of Governors of the Germantown Cricket Club in 1891 reveals the social character of the typical first-class club. "That the grounds are socially a success is now an undisputed fact, and too much credit cannot be given to the Ladies' Committee....Ladies' teas have been served every Tuesday; Thursday has been made music day, and Saturday match day, so that the entire week has been made attractive, and the attendance consequently large."[19]

The Germantown Club enjoyed a new clubhouse, designed by the distinguished New York architectural firm of McKim, Mead, and White. Like the other clubs, the Germantown Club also sponsored an elaborate program of cricket for juniors. Club leaders believed that playing cricket inculcated the young with gentlemanly values.

While the Philadelphia cricket clubs continued to thrive in the twentieth century, cricket as a sport declined rapidly. As the clubs became agencies of social exclusion, cricket tended to be only a by-product of the clubs' main function. Other diversions such as lawn tennis, golf, and swimming could serve the club membership equally well. Since tennis required less space and could be played much more quickly than cricket, it became, in time, the rage of the cricket clubs. Two members of the Merion club, William Jackson Clothier and Richard Norris Williams, were U.S. doubles champions in 1906, 1914, and 1916. William "Big Bill" Tilden, the country's greatest tennis player in the 1920s, learned his game on the courts of the Germantown Cricket Club. By the 1920s, the cricket clubs could hardly be distinguished from any other super-wealthy metropolitan country or golf club.

The country club was, in effect, a substitute for the English country home of the aristocracy or monied gentry. "It is a banding together for the purpose of making available to the group facilities which previously had been the privilege of the wealthy aristocrat," declared the official historians of the original Country Club at Brookline, Massachusetts.[20] While in England the aristocracy usually lived in the country and belonged to clubs located in the cities, rich Americans normally resided in the cities and sought outside their hurly-burly life an approximation of the English country home with its aristocratic privileges. The main activities of the early clubs centered on hunting, fishing, horseback riding, and other activities, which in England were reserved to those able to afford country estates.

Boston's Brookline Country Club, the first in the nation to call itself a "country" club, was far more socially exclusive than later imitators. Founded in 1882, it became one of the primary agencies for preserving the exclusivity of Boston "Society." "For many years after 1882 Boston had that of which it was very proud—its Society," wrote club historians. "Everybody was either in it or out of it; and those who were in it were proud of the fact and guarded its boundaries jealously. They played with each other, not with others; they competed with each other, not with others; above all, they married each other only, and so their children carried on the good(?) tradition."[21]

Historians of golf credit Joseph M. Fox, a member of Philadelphia's Merion Cricket Club, and John Reid, a transplanted Scot and an executive of an iron works in Yonkers, New York, with introducing modern golf into the United States. In 1887, Reid organized the first modern golf club, the St. Andrews Club, named after the historic club in Scotland. American clubs also sought to mimic the distinctive Scottish landscape. In the British Isles golf was often played on unoccupied links of land that bordered or stretched into the sea, and furnished natural hazards (hence the term "links" to describe golf courses). Having no equivalent physical features along the Atlantic seaboard, American clubs had to build inland courses. To approximate the hazards found in the British Isles, they constructed artificial bunkers, sandtraps and small lakes, and planted trees along the fairways.

In the early 1890s, golf caught the fancy of superrich tycoons in New York, Boston, Philadelphia, and Chicago. In 1891, William K. Vanderbilt brought over the famed Scottish golfer Willie Dunn to build the first professionally designed links, the Shinnecock Hills course, in Southampton, Long Island, where many wealthy New Yorkers had summer homes. The Shinnecock Hills Golf Club hired Stanford White, the noted architect, to design an opulent clubhouse. The clubhouse and course became models for wealthy men interested in forming clubs elsewhere. By 1900, rich golfers could follow the seasons. When the winter winds began to blow, they left their courses at Newport, Brookline, Yonkers, Long Island, and Chicago for sumptuous resorts built for them in Florida, Georgia, and North Carolina. In 1894, both the St. Andrew's Club and the Newport Golf Club scheduled national tournaments. With but few exceptions, a reporter concluded in 1898, golf "is a sport restricted to the richer classes of the country."[22]

The country clubs and summer resorts of the rich eased the process by which the wealthy shed lingering Victorian suspicions of play-for-play's-sake. At these private retreats, the rich could release inhibitions with far less fear of exposure than in public places. In sharp contrast to those middle-class Victorians who insisted that play could be justified only when it aided work, the upper strata frankly favored play for the pleasures it afforded participants. The Grafton Country Club of Worcester, Massachusetts adopted the motto "Each to His Pleasure"—a direct contradiction of the Victorian work ethic.[23]

Conclusion

The growth of nineteenth-century American industry created a new economic elite, based in the nation's largest cities. Like their British predecessors, wealthy American families began to use exclusive sports and recreation to cement ties with each other and to set themselves apart from less conspicuously successful citizens. Also like the British, they championed the principal of amateurism, which claimed to keep sport "pure" but which also conveniently limited serious pursuit of elite sports to those with ample time and money. But with the exception of amateurism, many of these distinctions would prove short-lived. Early in the twentieth century, the "country club" movement, along with the construction of public tennis courts and golf courses, would expand the popularity of these and other sports well beyond their elite origins.

Critical Thinking Questions

1. What factors might account for the differences between the "rational recreation" favored by the American middle class and the focus on recreational pleasure that marked the nation's upper classes?
2. Did the philosophy of amateurism mesh with or contradict American ideals of equal opportunity?
3. What roles do private sporting clubs play in present-day society?

Notes

1. See Donald J. Mrozek, *Sport and the American Mentality* (Knoxville: University of Tennessee Press, 1983).
2. Robert H. Wiebe, *Self-Rule: A Cultural History of American Democracy* (Chicago: University of Chicago Press, 1995), 87. For the making of an American upper class, see especially E. Digby Baltzell, *Philadelphia Gentlemen* (New York: Free Press, 1958); E. Digby Baltzell, *The Protestant Establishment* (New York: Random House, 1964); Frederic Cople Jaher, *The Urban Establishment* (Urbana: University of Illinois Press, 1982); Ronald Story, *The Forging of an Aristocracy: Harvard & the Boston Upper Class, 1800–1870* (Middletown, CT: Wesleyan University Press, 1980); and Sven Beckert, *The Monied Metropolis: New York City and the Consolidation of the American Bourgeoisie, 1850–1896* (New York: Cambridge University Press, 2001). Beckert equates "bourgeoisie" with what we have here described as the upper class.

3. See especially Richard Holt, *Sport and the British* (Oxford: Oxford University Press, 1989), and the discussion in chapter 2 of S.W. Pope, *Patriotic Games* (New York: Oxford University Press, 1997).

4. F.C. Jaher, "Style and Status: High Society in the Late Nineteenth-Century New York," in F.C. Jaher, ed., *The Rich, the Well Born, and the Powerful* (Urbana: University of Illinois Press, 1973), 259.

5. Charles Peverelly, *The Book of American Pastimes* (New York: author, 1866), 19.

6. See Donald Seitz, *The James Gordon Bennetts* (Indianapolis, IN: Bobbs-Merrill, 1928), and Richard O'Connor, *The Scandalous Mr. Bennett* (Garden City, NY: Doubleday, 1962).

7. Quoted in Allen Guttmann, *Sports Spectators* (New York: Columbia University Press, 1986), 99.

8. Steven A. Riess, *City Games* (Urbana: University of Illinois Press, 1989), 181–87.

9. F.W. Janssen, *History of Amateur Athletics* (New York: Charles R. Bourne, 1885), 35. See also Bob Considine and F.R. Jarvis, *The First Hundred Years: A Portrait of NYAC* (London: Macmillan, 1969); and J.D. Willis and R.G. Wettan, "Social Stratification in New York City Athletic Clubs, 1865–1915," *Journal of Sport History* 3 (1976), 45–63.

10. M.W. Ford, "The New York Athletic Club," *Outing* 33 (December 1898), 251.

11. Considine and Jarvis, *The First Hundred Years,* 43.

12. Henry Hall, ed., *The Tribune Book of Open-Air Sports* (New York: Tribune, 1888), 332.

13. J.W. Hinwell, "The Chicago Athletic Club," *Outing* 33 (November 1898), 145–52, and Arthur Inkersely, "Graeco-Roman Games in California," *Outing* 25 (February 1895), 93–111.

14. *Spirit of the Times,* September 2, 1876.

15. Janssen, *History of Amateur Athletics,* 103, and *Outing* 6 (May 1885), 251.

16. See J.D. Willis and R.G. Wettan, "L.E. Myers: 'World's Greatest Runner,'" *Journal of Sport History* 1 (1975), 93–111.

17. See Richard Wettan and J.D. Willis, "Effect of New York Athletic Clubs on Amateur Athletic Governance, 1870–1915," *Research Quarterly* 47 (1976), 499–505, and Eric Danhoff, "The Struggle for Control of Amateur Track and Field in the United States," *Canadian Journal of History of Sport and Physical Education* 6 (1975), 43–85.

18. See Melvin L. Adelman, *A Sporting Time: New York City and the Rise of Modern Athletics, 1820–1870* (Urbana: University of Illinois Press, 1986), chapter 5; George Kirsch, *The Creation of American Team Sports* (Urbana: University of Illinois Press, 1989); John A. Lester, ed., *A Century of Philadelphia Cricket* (Philadelphia: University of Pennsylvania Press, 1951); and J. Thomas Jable, "Cricket Clubs and Class in Philadelphia, 1850–1880," *Journal of Sport History* 18 (1991), 205–23.

19. Quoted in Lester, *A Century of Philadelphia Cricket,* 31.

20. F.H. Curtis and John Heard, *The Country Club* (Brookline, MA: The Country Club, 1932), 4. See Richard J. Moss, *Golf and the American Country Club* (Urbana: University of Illinois Press, 2001), chapter 1.

21. Curtis and Heard, *Country Club,* 139. The question mark appears in the original quotation.

22. H.L. Fitz Patrick, "Golf and the American Girl," *Outing* 32 (December 1898), 294–95.

23. Quoted in Roy Rosensweig, *Eight Hours for What We Will* (New York: Cambridge University Press, 1983), 140.

CHAPTER 6

The Rise of
Intercollegiate Sports

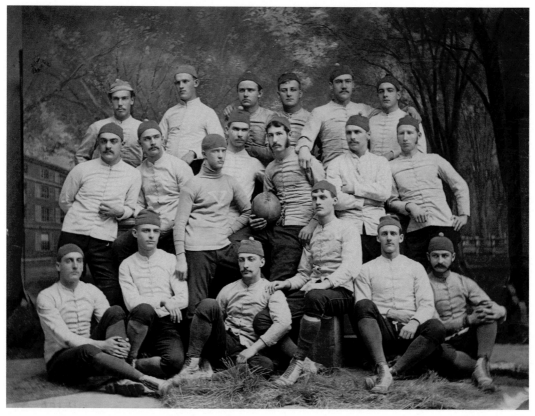

Yale University football team, 1879. Walter Camp is at the center, with the ball.

LEARNING OBJECTIVES

6.1 Explain the role played by college football in creating college communities and bolstering the confidence of their white, upper-class male students.

6.2 Outline Walter Camp's approach to football and the role he played in shaping the rules of modern American football.

6.3 Analyze how late nineteenth-century concerns about upper-class manhood facilitated the acceptance of a sport as violent as football.

6.4 Articulate the goals of late nineteenth-century college students and the role they saw for football in furthering those goals.

6.5 Summarize the advantages that football held for college officials.

6.6 Detail the way that developments in the popular press helped turn college football games into major sporting spectacles.

A jerky little train packed with students steamed out of Princeton, New Jersey, early on the morning of November 6, 1869. Upon arrival at the sleepy town of New Brunswick, New Jersey, Princeton's young men—white, Protestant, and mainly from the upper class—received a warm welcome from their counterparts at the College of Rutgers. During the morning, the Princeton lads strolled about the town with their hosts; a few played billiards at a local parlor. That afternoon at 3 o'clock some 200 students and assorted spectators gathered on the Rutgers Common. The milling fans paid nothing to watch the impending contest; there were no seats for comfort nor refreshments to satisfy hunger or thirst.

The students burst forth with a few college songs, and then the nation's first intercollegiate "football" contest got underway. Twenty-five young men lined up on each side. Rutgers soon demonstrated its superiority in "dribbling"—kicking the ball along the ground with short strokes—and won the game by six goals to four. (Though the students called it "football," the game resembled more closely what Americans today call "soccer.") That evening the Rutgers players treated their visitors to a festive supper and the guests joined their hosts in boisterous song and good humor.

Few if any of those present at this historic occasion dreamed that colleges would soon become, in the apt words of historian John Higham, "theaters of organized physical combat."[1] But within a short span of three decades, as nowhere else in the Western world, athletic competition emerged as a major enterprise on dozens of college campuses. College sports—most prominently football—helped to foster a new social institution, the college community. As with no other collegiate activity, sports forged and strengthened ties between students, faculty, college presidents, and alumni. The nation's upper class frequently saw special virtues in intercollegiate football; they believed that the sport nurtured personal character, manliness, and teamwork in their male children. With its emphasis on planning, cooperation, and rationality, football seemed especially suited to prepare young men for positions of leadership in industrial America—to become members of the nation's ruling class.

In those early years, involvement in football, as with track and field, golf, and tennis, also served as a class marker. By playing and patronizing the game, the wealthy could distance themselves from the hoi polloi. Football "is a gentleman's game," as Walter Camp, the game's foremost champion, bluntly put it. "[Just] as the 'Dandy' gentlemen regiments in the [Civil] war outmarched, out fought, and out plucked the 'bloody rebs,' so gentlemen teams and gentlemen players will always hold the foot ball field. Brutes haven't the pluck...."[2]

Rowing: The First Intercollegiate Sport

Before the rise of football, American collegians had dabbled in several sporting activities, including baseball, track, and rowing. True to the competitive spirit of the time, informal play in all these sports evolved into more serious, spectator-oriented competition. Rowing was a prime example. By 1844 students had formed small, informal rowing clubs at both Harvard and Yale. Initially the Harvard club used its boats mostly to transport members from Cambridge across the inlet to Boston drinking establishments, but the club also on occasion competed for cash prizes against noncollegiate clubs in Boston regattas.

Intercollegiate competition started with a small-scale Harvard–Yale matchup in 1852, and expanded in 1858 following widespread newspaper coverage of the Oxford–Cambridge crew race. Correspondents covering the race lauded the English students for their physical prowess while expressing dismay at "the entire disregard for exercise among Americans." Angered by such reports, the editor of Harvard's student magazine wrote: "What say ye, Yale, Dartmouth, Brown, Columbia, Harvard, shall we introduce a new institution in America?" Student representatives from four colleges responded to the challenge by forming the College Union Regatta Association in 1858. The association sponsored successful races in 1859 and 1860, each of which may have drawn as many as 20,000 spectators. Clubs hired coaches and began to train far more seriously.

The regattas became an important date on the social calendars of the northeastern elite. As *Outing* reported of the 1875 regatta: "The moneyed aristocracy... gilded the grand stand and the shore of the lake, outshown in turn by the kaleidoscopic ribbons of the intent, excited, uproarious mob which represented the thirteen colleges."[3] Newspapers frequently carried more than a page of special dispatches as well as extended discussions of the social leaders who graced the regattas with their presence. Even in the 1880s and 1890s, when football began to supplant rowing in popularity, intercollegiate rowing remained an important spectacle among the northeastern upper class.

Origins of Football

Football began as an internal affair. The first football games were medieval-like interclass matches, used as initiation rites for incoming freshmen. As with most other rites of passage, the game entailed the degradation of the initiates as a precondition for their acceptance into the group. Beginning in 1827, sophomores at Harvard subjected freshmen to a violent game on the first Monday of the school term. As early as 1840, Yale also took up the practice. These melees frequently resulted in black eyes, bloodied noses, sprained limbs, and shredded clothes. Postgame drinking, singing, and cheering signified the acceptance of the freshmen by upper-class men and the deepening of fraternal bonds among the participating students. Because of its disorderly character, university authorities periodically outlawed the rite.

During the 1860s and early 1870s two kinds of football began to achieve some prominence. One resembled "association football" (soccer) in Britain; it was a kicking game that prohibited picking up the ball with the hands. After the historic 1869 contest between Rutgers and Princeton, Columbia, Yale and Stevens also took up this version of the game. But in the Boston area, a hybrid of association football and rugby that permitted use of the hands was growing in popularity. More familiar with the rugby-style game, especially after an 1874 series of games with McGill University, Harvard students refused to play the association game popular on other campuses.

Given Harvard's esteemed position among the nation's colleges, within a few years the other elite northeastern schools followed suit. In 1876, student delegates from Princeton, Columbia, Yale, and Harvard founded the Intercollegiate Football Association. The delegates also decided to hold a championship game at the end of the season. Initially, the rules of the new organization closely resembled those of the Rugby Union in England. The association counted touchdowns as only one point and kicked goals as four. A modern observer would be especially surprised by the "drop kick," in which the kicker dropped the ball and kicked it through the goal as it bounced up. As the ball became more oblong in shape (at first, teams played with a large, almost round ball), and as the points for touchdowns increased, the drop kick disappeared.

Walter Camp: Father of American Football

Walter C. Camp, appropriately hailed as the "Father of Football," became the dominant figure of the game's early history. Frail as a youngster, Camp became an all-around athlete during his years at Yale. A member of Yale squads from 1875 to 1882, Camp participated in baseball, crew, track, lawn tennis, and football. After obtaining a bachelor's degree in 1880, he continued at Yale as a medical student and football player, eventually withdrawing from medicine because he could not tolerate the sight of blood. Camp became an executive with a New Haven watch manufacturing firm, and continued an active involvement in football until his death in 1925.

During the 1880s, Camp was responsible for a radical set of rule changes, each of which contributed to the evolution of the modern game of American football. Camp liked the physical roughness of rugby, but not the importance that the game assigned to chance. Play in rugby started with a scrum; the ball was set down in the midst of a huddle of players from both teams. Players then tried to drive the ball free with their feet so that a "back" could pick it up and run or kick it toward the opponent's goal line. Once a back had been downed with the ball, the players formed a new scrum. During the scrums, several minutes could transpire before the ball squirted out of a struggling mass of players.

In 1880, Camp persuaded the association rules committee to adopt a revolutionary way of putting the ball into play. The new rule provided for a line of scrimmage separating the offensive and defensive teams, and unless the ball was fumbled or kicked to the opposing team, the offensive team could retain possession. Much to the disgust of fans and players alike, the Yale–Princeton game of 1881 turned into a fiasco. Princeton repeatedly lost yardage while keeping possession of the ball in the first half and Yale employed the same strategy in the second half.

The next year, in 1881, Camp suggested an ingenious solution to this problem. If the offensive team failed to gain five yards in three attempts, it had to give up the ball. The down-yardage rule change led to the chalking of lines across the field at five-yard intervals (hence the origin of the term "gridiron"). The provisions for a down-yardage system, continuous possession by the offense, and a line of scrimmage initially spawned a wide-open, offensive-oriented game. The offensive line and backs typically lined up far apart, forcing the defense to do likewise. While players were forbidden to throw the ball across the line of scrimmage, the game featured sideline passes, open field running, and kicking.

In 1888, Camp came forward with another important departure from rugby—tackling below the waist. Legalization of the low tackle ended the wide-open, improvisational style of play. Already officials had allowed offensive players to run "interference" (i.e., block) between the ball carrier and potential tacklers, a violation of rugby conventions. As early as 1884, Pennsylvania had started its offensive action with the "V trick," a formation in which players formed a V with their arms encircling the players ahead of them. Breaking this fearsome formation required defensive men without much, if any, protective gear to hurl themselves directly into the V or try to crash its flanks. The new "mass momentum" style of offense encouraged by the legalization of the low tackle entailed massing players at a single point of attack. Fans were frequently treated to a spectacle of an incomprehensible mass of struggling bodies, shoving and pulling on one another in an effort to squeeze out five yards in three tries. Far less improvisational than rugby or the older style of football, the new game was intrinsically less exciting and far more brutal.[4]

In addition to the creativity of Camp, the evolution of American football rules arose from the prevalence of a winning-at-all-costs ethos among the collegians. Although American collegians of the late nineteenth century were nearly all from the upper social ranks, they were less inhibited by traditions of fair play than their upper-class English counterparts. Understood conventions rather than explicit rules governed much of the play of English "gentlemen." But when American students took up such games as rugby, they seized upon and exploited all the aspects of the game not covered by explicit rules. Rules had to be written and rewritten to encompass every possible contingency or ambiguity. Often a new rule resulted in unforeseen opportunities for a team to gain a new advantage, so that yet another rule had to be formulated. Rulemaking then (as today) became a major preoccupation of American football authorities.[5]

In the earliest years, students themselves organized clubs, scheduled games, managed finances (such as they were), and wrote the rules. Student-elected team captains determined who would play, player deployment, and the team's training regimen. With so much authority in their hands, football captains held esteemed positions on campuses. According to President Francis A. Walker of the Massachusetts Institute of Technology, the captains replaced those students renowned for "speech-making, debating, or fine writing" as campus heroes.

In their zeal to win, however, the students soon sought additional help. In the 1880s, they began to invite former players (called "graduate coaches") back to campus to assist them in preparing for key games. About 1885, Yale took this practice of informal coaching a step further, making Walter Camp the regular advisor to Yale captains and graduate coaches. Because of his full-time job, Camp could rarely attend practices. Instead, his wife, Alice, observed practices and carefully noted player progress. Camp met with the team leaders in the evenings to consider tactics and strategies. His dictatorial and centralized methods undercut student control of the game, and became known as the "czar system." But his teams' winning records inspired widespread admiration. "There is only one man in New Haven of more importance than Walter Camp," wrote Richard Harding Davis in 1893, "and I have forgotten his name. I think he is the president of the university."[6]

Camp's influence extended far beyond New Haven. Football men everywhere recognized him as the game's preeminent authority and spokesman. He flooded the newspapers and periodicals with stories of games, inside knowledge, and trivia. Altogether, he wrote 20 books on sports—boys' novels, histories, and coaching manuals. In 1889, he devised an ingenious promotional gimmick—the creation of a fictional "All-America" football team. Each year until 1924 Camp personally determined the composition of a hypothetical team of the nation's best players. Camp devoted an enormous amount of energy to advising those involved in football programs elsewhere. In addition, former Yale players and captains spread out across the country as football missionaries, teaching their mentor's ideas and methods at other campuses.

By the turn of the century, colleges everywhere were trying to emulate the Yale system. Yale's record from 1872 through 1909 has never been equaled; the Elis recorded 324 wins, only 17 losses, and 18 ties. From the final game of the 1890 season to the ninth game of the 1893 season, the famed eleven scored 1,265 points to none for its opponents. Yale so dominated archrival Harvard that, in the dry words of one historian, "Harvard felt a certain loss of manhood." Renowned Yale athletes included Amos Alonzo Stagg, the future longtime coach of the University of Chicago, W. W. "Pudge" Heffelfinger, who revolutionized line play, and Lee "Bum" McClung, who scored 500 points in four seasons. Famed illustrator Frederic W. Remington typified the Yale spirit when in preparation for the Harvard game of 1878, he took his football jacket to a local slaughterhouse and dipped it in blood to "make it look more businesslike."[7] Although Yale's dominance of college football ended in 1909, it was not until the 1920s that the elite northeastern men's colleges yielded football supremacy to more powerful teams from other regions.

Football and the Strenuous Life

Football drew some of its power from a broader belief that the nation was suffering from a massive malaise of the spirit. Frequently allied with other social reformers, the apostles of the sporting ideology concluded that the vitality of the nation depended upon the generation of higher purposes than merely making or spending money. As future president Theodore Roosevelt lamented: "No amount of commercial prosperity can supply the lack of the heroic virtues."[8]

Roosevelt and many of his peers linked this lack of "heroic virtues" directly to a drop in the nation's masculine force, produced when too many members of the old elite withdrew from an active involvement in the world to a "cloistered life" of ease and sloth. Ancient Rome had fallen, declared Alfred T. Mahan, "when the strong masculine impulse which first created it had degenerated into...worship of comfort, wealth, and general softness."[9] Intrigued by Darwinian analogies that depicted human society as a jungle in which only the "fittest" survived, the elite worried that their prized "Anglo-Saxon race" was losing ground in the contest for national and world supremacy.

Without a Civil War or a frontier to provide opportunities for the expression of heroism or nobility of character, the elite manifested its activism in an aggressive nationalism, an intense interest in untamed nature and an enthusiasm for organized sports. No one expressed the principles of "dangerous sport" more fully than Francis A. Walker, a Civil War veteran who became the president of Yale. In an address to the Phi Beta Kappa club at Harvard in 1893, he declared that the Civil War had fortunately produced "a vast change in popular sentiments and ideals," showing that the "strength of will, firmness of purpose, resolution to endure, and capacity for action" expressed in the war were far nobler than the soft intellectuality and sentimentalism prevalent in the antebellum era. He went on to say that "the competitive contests of our colleges" offered the best hope of preserving "something akin to patriotism and public spirit," which counteracted "the selfish, individualistic tendencies of the age." Sports not only instilled idealism in the youth, Walker concluded, it also toughened the "cultivated classes" for leadership roles.[10]

Experts on the human body gave added support to the turn-of-the century campaign for the strenuous life. Dozens of privileged young men, Roosevelt and Walker among them, passed through Dudley A. Sargent's famous physical fitness program (1879–1919) at Harvard. Sargent advocated exercises and the playing of sports primarily as a means of achieving general fitness rather than more esoteric social goals. But he also agreed that violent sports allowed young men to replicate the courage and hardiness that their fathers had experienced in Civil War combat.

No one exemplified the strenuous life in practice more fully than Theodore Roosevelt. Born into a family with old wealth, something of an intellectual, and unable to become enthusiastic about making money, Roosevelt rejected a life of ease for one of political and physical combat. He sought to embody the heroic virtues found in the soldier, the cowboy, and the prizefighter. Perhaps compensating for the asthma and physical weakness that plagued him as a youth, he began at the age of 14 to take boxing lessons (even in his forties, while occupying the White House, he occasionally sparred) and worked out regularly with dumbbells and horizontal bars. In his 20s, he left the safe confines of the East for the hazardous life of a cowboy in the Dakotas, where he relished the opportunity to help capture a band of cattle rustlers. When the Spanish-American War broke out in 1898, he created and led a cavalry unit of cowboys and college students who won national acclaim for their bravery. Succeeding to the presidency upon the assassination of William McKinley in 1901, Roosevelt enthralled the nation with his vigor. He preached to and bullied opponents both at home and abroad. "In life, as in a football game," he once advised the nation's boys, "the principle to follow is: Hit the line hard, don't foul, and don't shirk, but hit the line hard!"[11]

Football thus assisted the nation's colleges in developing a new, more aggressively masculine image, one that was more consonant with the values of late nineteenth-century culture. Through much of the nineteenth century, the popular media took delight in depicting the typical undergraduate male in effeminate terms—as a dyspeptic, shriveled up, and cowering scholar, only interested in gaining useless knowledge or cultivating an ineffectual spirituality. Football, on the other hand, projected the typical college man as rugged and fearless, as one who could hold his own in the world outside the walls of academe.

Football and the Making of College Communities

Perhaps more than any other aspect of higher education, football became a major force in bonding diverse groups into larger college communities. Although most college students came from families who were far better off than the national average, the fast-growing postbellum colleges attracted a heterogeneous student population. Few of them came to college in order to enhance their spirituality, hone their intellectual skills, or acquire a larger body of knowledge—all goals more likely to be closer to faculty than student hearts. Instead, the sons of the new rich frequently sought degrees as a means of achieving a social position commensurate with their family's wealth. Unlike in the antebellum era, a college degree, particularly from an Ivy League school, was increasingly perceived as a passport to high society. College training was also increasingly a prerequisite for becoming an engineer, accountant, doctor, or other professional.

Regardless of motives, late nineteenth-century students made extracurricular activities the center of their college experience. The sheer number of literary societies, debate clubs, Greek letter societies, and college athletic associations burgeoned. Student involvement in athletics had an especially strong effect on the spirit of college campuses. Student newspapers became major boosters of sport, roundly condemning "slackers" (those who failed to attend games or display adequate enthusiasm). "School spirit," expressed in terms of zeal for the success of the football team, could be a precondition for acceptance among one's peers. The average man at the English universities of Oxford or Cambridge, Caspar Whitney reported in 1895, evinced only a "lukewarm" interest in the football team's prospects "compared with the spirit with which a Harvard, Yale, or Princeton undergraduate will discuss his eleven, and grow eloquent over the brilliant rushes of the half-back, or sorrowfully deprecate the slowness with which an end rusher gets down the field under a kick."[12]

Football's supporters sang its praises. Student riots, rebellions, and drunkenness declined with the advent of football at Yale, according to Professor Eugene L. Richards. The sport nurtured "a sense of friendship among the students—not fellowship in mischief, but fellowship in pluck and manliness, in generous admiration of their mates." Students might be divided by social background, personal values, and the lack of a common curriculum, but football, in the words of Yale president Arthur Hadley, took "hold of the emotions of the student body in such a way as to make class distinctions relatively unimportant."[13] University of North Carolina professor (and future president) F.P. Venable focused on the sport's character-building components. "No half-way work will answer," he wrote in 1894. "A player must bring out every power, must develop to the utmost every faculty, must learn thorough self-control, must work for the team and not for himself, must make himself part of a perfectly working machine, must be full of nerve and pluck and strategy."[14]

Colleges also learned that football could aid them in recruiting students. Engaged in intense competition with other schools for students, college presidents extolled the strengths of their football teams. As early as 1878, President James McCosh of Princeton wrote an alumnus in Kentucky: "You will confer a great favor on us if you will get...the college noticed in the Louisville papers....We must persevere in our efforts to get students from your region....Mr. Brand Ballard has won us [a] great reputation as captain of the football team which has beaten both Harvard and Yale."[15] Football seemed an even more potent weapon in the battle for students among the land-grant institutions and numerous sectarian colleges of the West. Upon securing Princeton's Hector R. Cowan as a "coach" in 1895, University of Kansas president Frank Snow was ecstatic. "I repeat, this is an immense thing at U.K. and will tend to develop the green eyes rapidly of other Kansas institutions." Faculty, students, and townspeople in Lawrence enthusiastically joined in raising the money necessary to pay Cowan's salary.[16]

Upon assuming the presidency of John D. Rockefeller's newly endowed University of Chicago in 1892, William Rainey Harper set out to publicize the university by establishing a winning football team. Harper hired famed Yale player Amos Alonzo Stagg as coach, making Stagg the first coach with professorial rank in the country. Harper gave Stagg unambiguous instructions: "I want you to develop teams which we can send around the country and knock out all the [other] colleges. We will give [the players] a palace car and a vacation too."[17] Stagg responded with enthusiasm: "If Chicago university places a team in the field it must *be a winning team* or one which will bring honor to the University."[18] Fielding a successful football team might also generate private donations to a college. According to Stagg, during the halftime of a game in which Chicago trailed Wisconsin 12–0, Harper delivered an impassioned and blunt plea to the players. "Boys, Mr. Rockefeller has just announced a gift of $3,000,000 to the University. He believed that the university is to be great. The way you played in the first half leads me to wonder whether we really have the spirit of greatness....I wish you would make up your minds to win the game and show that we have it."[19] Chicago's players responded accordingly; they won 22–12.

College authorities found that football nurtured an alumni loyalty that was far more profound than fond memories of chapels, classrooms, pranks, or professors. "You do not remember whether Thorpwright was valedictorian or not," wrote a young college alumnus in 1890, "but you can never forget that glorious run of his in the football game." The alumni continued to identify with the football team long after their official connection with the college had been severed. Alumni in cities far removed from their college campuses organized chapters, sponsored elaborate homecoming events, and printed bulletins listing the achievements of their classmates and the latest exploits of the football team. "The feeling of solidarity and loyalty in the student body that intercollegiate contests develop is a good thing," ex-U.S. President William Howard Taft explained in 1915. "It outlasts every contest and it continues in the heart and soul of every graduate as long as he lives."[20]

Football as a Sporting Spectacle

Initially, the general public all but ignored intercollegiate football games. Until the mid-1880s only a few students and alumni watched the contests, and attendance rarely exceeded a few hundred fans. With few exceptions, the nation's wealthy paid no attention to the games. The students struggled to get the newspapers to publish even the shortest notices about their gridiron wars. But within a decade, all that changed. By the mid-1890s, the daily papers in New York, Philadelphia, and Boston were devoting a staggering amount of space to college football, and more than 40,000 fans attended major contests.

A revolution in the newspaper industry during the 1880s and 1890s, as Michael Oriard has detailed, contributed substantially to transforming college football into a major sporting spectacle, one that extended well beyond the exclusive patronage of the upper class.[21] Locked in circulation wars, the New York dailies, especially the *Herald*, the *World*, and the *Journal*, sought additional readers by expanding their coverage of sports. Football stories in October and November helped fill a void left in the sports calendar by the conclusion of the baseball and horse racing seasons. To grab the attention of readers, the papers employed banner headlines, exaggerated the heroics of individual players, filled their pages with lavish illustrations and devoted as much space to the spectators and their behavior as they did to descriptions of the games themselves. The newspapers gave particular attention to the "Social Set," or those who aspired to become members of upper-class "Society." In the 1890s, 30,000–40,000 spectators attended the Thanksgiving Day games in New York City, and nearly two million could read about the game in the metropolitan area's dailies.

Football gave a classic American holiday new meaning. "Thanksgiving day is no longer a solemn festival to God for mercies given," declared the *Herald* in 1893. "It is a holiday granted by the State and the Nation to see a game of football."[22] By the mid-1890s, according to Ronald Smith's estimate, some 120,000 athletes belonging to colleges, athletic clubs, and high schools, played in some 5,000 Thanksgiving Day football games. Until disbanded in the mid-1890s, few spectacles equaled the theatrics of the Thanksgiving Day contest held in New York City between the nation's two top college elevens. On Wednesday, an advance contingent of collegians arrived in the city to begin the festivities. The next morning a parade of horsedrawn coaches slowly made its way through the heart of the city to Manhattan Field. From atop their coaches, wealthy fans ate their lunches and drank champagne. After the game, fans boarded their coaches or the elevated trains for the return trip downtown. Happy parties crowded into restaurants for bacchanalian Thanksgiving Day feasts. During the evening, celebrants attended the theaters where they sometimes interrupted the performances with raucous displays of school spirit.

By the 1890s many colleges were already playing what later became known as "The Big Game." No other game on a team's schedule was as significant as the Big Game with a traditional rival; the success of the entire season hinged on winning the contest. The Big Game sometimes entailed winning or losing a traditional trophy. Stanford and California struggled to win the Axe; Minnesota and Michigan to possess the Little Brown Jug; and Purdue and Indiana to hold the Old Oaken Bucket. Enterprising undergraduates regularly devised schemes to steal such trophies from their rightful owners.

The invention of colorful pageantry not only helped give colleges distinctive identities it also helped intercollegiate football become not just a game but a sporting spectacle as well. Like nineteenth-century militia units, volunteer fire departments, and baseball teams, college students adopted special colors to differentiate their enterprise from others. As early as 1854 Yale rowers donned blue flannel. Apparently crimson was first identified with Harvard when the crew purchased China red bandannas to distinguish themselves from the Irish green of other rowers in a Boston regatta. Georgetown's blue and grey arose from the divided loyalties of students during the Civil War. Rochester students rejected goldenrod yellow, the recommendation of an alumni committee, because of its association with the women's suffrage movement.

Mascots and nicknames offered even more room for the imagination. Sometimes students named their teams after their institution's founder. Thus, Yale became the Elis, after Eli Yale, and Williams College became the Ephs, after its founder Ephraim Williams. Nicknames sometimes evoked humorous images. For a time Washington College's team was known as the Shoo Flies and the University of Nebraska as the Bugeaters. After Yale students paid the princely sum of $300 for a prize English bulldog as a mascot, their team became known as the Bulldogs in addition to the Elis. When Texas students discovered that Bevo, their first longhorn mascot, had been branded with the score of the 1915 Texas A&M victory, they unceremoniously slaughtered and ate the steer.

College football had its detractors. Football games were brutal, spectators could descend into drinking and revelry, and some teams began to recruit players whose physical abilities far outshone their academic inclinations. Some college authorities saw an athletic culture overwhelming the academic culture. "Colleges are presenting themselves to the public, educated and uneducated alike, as places of mere physical sport and not as educational training institutions," lamented President Charles W. Eliot of Harvard.[23] College trustees could also frown on the sport. At North Carolina's Trinity College, which would later become Duke University, football became the focus of a dispute between the school's Methodist governors and President John Franklin Crowell, a Yale graduate who had introduced football to the school as part of his efforts to modernize the curriculum. In 1892, the Western Conference of North Carolina's Methodists informed Trinity's trustees that football was "a source of evil, and of no little evil, and ought to be stopped." When Crowell ignored the warning and pressed on with his program, the trustees presented him with a stark rebuke and demanded that the game be stopped immediately. Crowell resigned shortly afterward, becoming perhaps the first college president in U.S. history to lose his job over football. But Trinity was an exception. Nationally, the game continued to grow.[24]

Conclusion

Unlike anywhere else in the Western world, intercollegiate sports and the pageantry accompanying them became a major feature of the American educational system in the nineteenth century. Sports helped to bind students, faculties, administrators, alumni, and social climbers into a single college community. The growth of college sports also helped to solidify the idea that competitive athletics helped young men build valuable qualities such as strength, discipline, and leadership. While a range of critics charged that sports such as football undermined the academic goals of higher education, such concerns would do little to slow the athletic expansion. Eventually, intercollegiate sports would become one of the most powerful forces in defining American college identities, and giving them emotional depth.

Critical Thinking Questions

1. Why do you think that organized athletic competition became a more important institution at American colleges and universities than it did in British ones?
2. From the information that this chapter provides, does it seem possible to use rules to reduce sporting violence, or does culture need to change as well?
3. Football's ascension to a major spectator sport sprang from several different interests, including those of players, college administrators, and newspaper publishers. Which of these do you think was most significant and why?

Notes

1. John Higham, "The Reorientation of American Culture in the 1890s," in John Higham, ed., *Writing American History* (Bloomington: Indiana University Press, 1970), 79. For all intercollegiate sports in this era, see especially Ronald A. Smith, *Sports and Freedom: The Rise of Big Time College Athletics* (New York: Oxford University Press, 1988), and Patrick B. Miller, "Athletes in Academe: College Sports and American Culture, 1850–1920," unpub. Ph.D. diss., University of California, Berkeley, 1987. For football, see also Parke H. Davis, *Football* (New York: Scribner's, 1912); Michael Oriard, *Reading Football: How the Popular Press Created an American Sporting Spectacle* (Chapel Hill: University of North Carolina Press, 1993); John Sayle Watterson, *College Football: History, Spectacle, Controversy* (Baltimore, MD: Johns Hopkins University Press, 2000); Gerald R. Gems, *For Pride, Profit, and Patriarchy: Football and the Incorporation of American Cultural Values* (Lanham, MD: Scarecrow, 2000); Mark F. Bernstein, *Football: The Ivy League Origins of an American Obsession* (Philadelphia: University of Pennsylvania Press, 2001); Guy M. Lewis, "The American Intercollegiate Football Spectacle, 1869–1917," unpub. Ph.D. diss, University of Maryland, 1965; and the provocative interpretation offered by A.S. Markovits in "The Other 'American Exceptionalism'; Why Is There No Soccer in the United States?" *International Journal of the History of Sport* 7 (1990), 230–64. Also see the review essay by John Nauright, "Writing and Reading American Football: Culture, Identities, and Sports Studies," *Sporting Traditions* 13 (November 1996), 109–27.
2. As quoted in Gems, *For Pride, Profit, and Patriarchy,* 112.
3. J.R.W. Hitchcock, "The Harvard-Yale Races," *Outing* 6 (1885), 393.
4. The V also led briefly to another interesting variation, known as the "flying wedge." See S.A. McQuilkin and R.A. Smith, "The Rise and Fall of the Flying Wedge, Football's Most Controversial Play," *Journal of Sport History* 20 (1993), 57–64.
5. See David Riesman and Reuel Denney, "Football in America: A Study in Cultural Diffusion," *American Quarterly* 3 (1951), 309–25.
6. Walter Harding Davis, "A Day with the Yale Team," *Harper's Weekly* 37 (1893), 1110.
7. Quoted in Bernstein, *Football,* 12.
8. Theodore Roosevelt, *American Ideals and Other Essays* (New York: Review of Reviews, 1897), 11.

9. Alfred Mahan, *The Interest of America in Sea Power* (Boston: Little, Brown, 1903), 121.

10. G.M. Frederickson, *The Inner Civil War* (New York: Harper & Row, 1965), 223–24.

11. Roosevelt, "What We Can Expect of the American Boy," *St. Nicholas* 27 (1900), 574. The other book recommended by Roosevelt was Nelson Aldrich's *Story of a Bad Boy.*

12. Caspar Whitney, *A Sporting Pilgrimage* (New York: Harper & Bros., 1895), 90.

13. E.L. Richards, "Athletic Sports at Yale," *Outing* 6 (1885), 453, and A.T. Hadley, "Wealth and Democracy in American Colleges," *Harper's Weekly* 93 (1906), 452.

14. *University of North Carolina Alumni Quarterly* 1 (October 1894), 28.

15. Quoted in Frederick Rudolph, *The American College and University* (New York: Vintage Books, 1962), 385.

16. Quoted in Lewis, "The American Intercollegiate Football Spectacle," 158–59.

17. Quoted in ibid., 141.

18. As cited in Kooman Boycheff, "Intercollegiate Athletics and Physical Education at the University of Chicago, 1892–1952," unpub. Ph.D. diss., University of Michigan, 1954, 19. For football at the University of Chicago, see Robin Lester, *Stagg's University* (Urbana: University of Illinois Press, 1995).

19. Amos Alonzo Stagg and Wesley Winans Sterit, *Touchdown!* (New York: Longmen's Green, 1927), 203.

20. William H. Taft, "College Athletics," *Proceedings of the Tenth Annual Convention of the National Collegiate Athletic Association* (1915), 67.

21. See esp. Oriard, *Reading Football,* chapter 2.

22. As quoted in Smith, *Sports and Freedom,* 181. For the estimates that follow, see ibid.

23. Quoted in Andrew Zimbalist, *Unpaid Professionals: Commercialism and Conflict in Big-Time College Sports* (Princeton: Princeton University Press, 1999), 7.

24. Pamela Grundy, *Learning to Win: Sports, Education and Social Change in Twentieth-Century North Carolina* (Chapel Hill: University of North Carolina Press, 2001), 23–6. Quote from Earl W. Porter, *Trinity and Duke, 1892-1924: Foundations of Duke University* (Durham, N.C.: Duke University Press, 1964), 38.

CHAPTER 7

Broader Horizons

Biddle University football team, 1913.

Senda Berenson in the Smith College gymnasium.

In December of 1892, in the midst of a rare North Carolina snowstorm, the football teams from Livingstone College and Biddle University took part in a historic event—the first-ever football game between black colleges. Athletic interest ran high at both schools. Livingstone students had chipped in to buy a football, fitted their shoes with temporary cleats, and padded their clothes with rags for practice sessions. Female classmates sewed their uniforms. Biddle players made similar preparations. The snowstorm sparked some controversy regarding lines and scoring, but Biddle eventually claimed victory, 4–0 (under the rules of the day, touchdowns counted 4 points, field goals counted 5, and there were no extra-point kicks). Livingstone students took the loss in stride. "The game between Biddle University and Livingstone College was played and very much enjoyed Tuesday, December 27th," students wrote in the *Living Stone* magazine. "Our boys played well, as did the Biddle boys. It was a great game."[1]

Barely three years later, at the other end of the country, basketball teams from Stanford University and the University of California staged the nation's first interscholastic contest between college women's teams. While the game was far from an offensive showcase—Stanford triumphed 2–1—the large and noisy crowd that packed the San Francisco Armory saw a fine show. The play, reported *San Francisco Chronicle* correspondent Mabel Craft, was "snappy" from the start, with "many calls for time and some disputes. Enthusiastic captains claimed fouls, and some were allowed… Sometimes with a slump and a slide three girls would dive for the ball, and end in an inextricable heap of red, white and blue. In less time than it takes to read it they were all planted firmly on their two feet, flushed, perspiring, intensely in earnest and oblivious of everything except that ball."[2]

Craft, a vigorous and respected advocate for women's rights, devoted particular attention to the way the contest challenged common assumptions about young women's abilities. Basketball "wasn't invented for girls, and there isn't anything effeminate about it," she noted. "It was made for men to play indoors and it is a game that would send the physician who thinks the feminine organization 'so delicate,' into the hysterics he tries so hard to perpetuate."

For players from colleges like Livingstone and Stanford, as well as Native Americans attending institutions such as the Carlisle Indian Industrial School, athletic contests held especially broad meanings. Like the white, male members of more celebrated teams, they were eager to develop abilities suited to the competitive society that was taking shape around them. In addition, however, they also looked at sports as a way to demonstrate their fitness for more equal status in American society. As discussions around the rising status of college football indicated, the nation's elites had reacted to changing economic and demographic circumstances with a new justification for Anglo–Saxon male supremacy, one that drew on old assumptions, new "scientific" theories derived from Charles Darwin's work on evolution, and a reformulation of the concept of civilization. Because athletic prowess served as one cornerstone of this new ideology, it also became an arena within which such ideas could be challenged.[3]

The Carlisle Indians

One of the first concerted efforts to use athletics to gain racial respect was mounted by students and faculty at the Carlisle Indian Industrial School in Carlisle, Pennsylvania. Founded in 1879, Carlisle was the most famous of hundreds of Native American boarding schools that removed young Indians from their traditional communities in an effort to "modernize" and "civilize" them. As college football gained in popularity, Carlisle head R.H. Pratt began to see the sport as a way to demonstrate the success of his endeavor. In a time when Native Americans were cast as "violent," "savage," and "uncivilized," the display of strategy and self-control amid the excitement of a sporting contest could dramatically challenge such stereotypes.

In his memoirs, Pratt stated that he urged his students to conduct themselves with rigorous self-control, requiring them to promise "that you will never, under any circumstances, slug. That you will play fair straight through, and if the other fellows slug you will in no case return it. Can't you see that if you slug, people who are looking on will say, 'There, that's the Indian of it. Just see them. They are savages and you can't get it out of them.' Our white fellows may do a lot of slugging and it causes little or no remark, but you have to make a record for your race. If the other fellows slug and you do not return it, very soon you will be the most famous football team in the country. If you can set an example of that kind for the white race, you will do a work in the highest interests of your people."[4]

The Carlisle team secured matches with many of the nation's top college squads, becoming a significant force on the national football scene. Players conducted themselves with distinction, and their own remarks suggested that many read their achievements in terms of self-discipline and intelligence, often inverting conventional distinctions between "civilized" whites and "savage" Indians. Renowned Carlisle coach Glen "Pop" Warner recalled one player who responded to an illegal hit by asking his opponent "Who's the savage now?" Another wrote home after a victory that while white men might be "better with cannon and guns," Indians were "just as good in brains."[5] Students reveled in beating white opponents at their own game. Warner noted that his players "believed the armed contests between red man and white had never been waged on equal terms." On the football field, in contrast, "they felt that the Indian had his first even break, and the record proves that they took full advantage of it."[6]

Observers of the Carlisle team did not always concur—underscoring the challenge involved in any effort to use a complex game with an uncertain outcome to make a political point. At times the popular press treated the Carlisle team with respect; at times reporters fell back on stereotypes. In 1896, for example, the *New York World* described a Carlisle–Brown match in thoroughly stereotypical terms, writing that "there was fought yesterday the bloodiest, the most savage contest between brawn and brain that modern athletic days have seen. The contestants were eleven young football players from Brown University, at Providence, R.I., representing the highest type of New England culture, and eleven young Indians from the Government school at Carlisle, Pa., drawn from the uncivilized sections of the far West and trained into the ways of the white man." When the game ended in a Brown victory, the reporter drew a predictable conclusion: "Brains won in the contest, as they always do in the long run. Science triumphed with her mysterious tricks and ways that are dark and puzzling to the untutored mind." Still, the team gained respect and numerous admirers, and Carlisle continued to compete at high levels until the school closed in 1917.[7]

Doors Close on African American Athletes

African American athletes, in contrast, found fewer opportunities to demonstrate their skills in competition with whites. Before and immediately after the Civil War, African American athletes could take advantage of a range of sporting opportunities—many of the nation's top jockeys and some of its best prizefighters were black, and African Americans secured places on both college and professional teams. By the end of the century, however, most of those opportunities had disappeared. A resurgent white South began to institute strict racial segregation, bolstered by the Supreme Court's 1896 *Plessy v. Ferguson* decision, which held that providing separate accommodations for the races did not violate the Constitution. Elsewhere in the country, an interest in reconciling South and North after the Civil War, in concert with widespread racial prejudice, began to squeeze African Americans out of many realms of American society, including athletic contests. While African American athletes had some white fans and supporters, they faced increasingly hostile crowds as well as sabotage and harassment from white competitors and sometimes white teammates. New regulations—written in some cases, unwritten in many others—began to exclude them from many contests altogether.[8]

Professional baseball players were among the first to see the doors close. African Americans had played baseball from the game's earliest days, and by the 1860s black clubs were traveling between U.S. cities to compete with one another. Some players also began to find places on integrated college and professional teams. In 1881, Moses Fleetwood ("Fleet") Walker, an Ohio native and a student at Oberlin College, became the catcher for Oberlin's first baseball team. Walker's talents eventually won him a spot on the professional Toledo (Ohio) Blue Stockings, where he was joined several years later by his younger brother, Weldy. The Blue Stockings became part of the major league American Association in 1884, making Fleet Walker the first African American to play for a major league team. By 1887, more than a dozen African Americans played for predominantly white professional teams, and the League of Colored Base Ball Clubs gained official minor league status under the prevailing national professional agreements.[9]

But as national race relations became more polarized, and the number of black baseball players grew, hostility toward them increased. Black players frequently faced slurs and threats from fans in southern cities such as Louisville, Kentucky, and Richmond, Virginia—during one trip to Richmond an anonymous letter warned Walker's manager not to play Walker, in order to "prevent much bloodshed." Opposition also grew among white players, some of whom began to refuse to play with or against African Americans. In the summer of 1887, for example, *Sporting Life* reported of the International League that "Several representatives declared that many of the best players in the League were anxious to leave on account of the colored element, and the board finally directed Secretary White to approve no more contracts with colored men." The *Syracuse Standard* called the decision "shameful," and Weldy Walker wrote directly to the league's president, terming the new rule "a disgrace to the present age," which "casts derision at the laws of Ohio—the voice of the people—that say all men are equal." But the outrage had little effect. By the turn of the century, no major league club fielded any black players, and African American athletes had been pushed out of most other mainstream sporting institutions.[10]

In response, some black athletes began to turn their eyes beyond the nation's boundaries. One of the most prominent was cyclist Marshall "Major" Taylor, who won the title "fastest bicycle racer in the world" after triumphing in the national sprint championships in 1898, 1899, and 1900. Taylor's talents and conduct—he held tight to the tenets of middle-class respectability and refused to race on Sundays for religious reasons—won him many fans. But from the beginning of his career as a "scorcher," the Indianapolis-born athlete struggled with discrimination. White competitors colluded to throw him from his cycle or "box" him in, and in at least one instance he was physically attacked by a white rider after the completion of a race. Promoters prohibited Taylor from racing on all southern and several northern tracks. By 1902, Taylor had seen enough. He left the United States for Europe and Australia, where his skills, conduct, and skin color commanded greater respect.[11]

Jockey Jimmy Winkfield, who won back-to-back victories in the Kentucky Derby in 1901 and 1902, endured similar harassment from white jockeys and fans. He left the United States for Europe in 1904. While Fleet Walker remained in the country, establishing himself as a newspaper publisher and owner of multiple other businesses, he was far from satisfied with his experiences. In 1908 he published a pamphlet entitled *Our Home Colony*. In it, he highlighted the many forms of prejudice against African Americans, including the escalation of lynching and other forms of racial violence in the late nineteenth and early twentieth centuries. Because of such overwhelming prejudice, Walker wrote, "We believe that the Negro race can find superior advantages, and better opportunities on the shores of old Africa, among people of their own race, for developing the innate powers of mind and body [than] anywhere else upon the face of the earth."[12]

Because baseball was largely an American sport, however, baseball players who wanted to keep playing their game had to look for opportunities for themselves within the United States. A few light-skinned players attempted to pass as Latinos or Native Americans—in 1901, for example, second baseman Charles Grant conspired unsuccessfully with Baltimore Orioles manager John McGraw to sign with the club as a Cherokee Indian named "Charlie Tokohama." Most black players, however, looked for spots on all-black teams. The low wages earned by African Americans meant that black communities were not able to provide African American teams with the same financial support that white teams enjoyed. But entrepreneurial individuals developed a number of strong teams, including the Cuban X Giants, the Chicago American Giants, and the Philadelphia Giants, that would eventually form the basis of the Negro Leagues. Players also found or created opportunities as barnstormers—teams that traveled from town to town, taking on local competition for a share of gate receipts. After being dropped from the International League following the exclusionary decision of 1887, John W. "Bud" Fowler became a particularly active organizer of barnstorming teams, often devising showy gimmicks that increased interest in his team's play (and also underscored their skills). In 1899, for example, Fowler's All-American Black Tourists paraded through towns across the Midwest in top hats and tails, offering to play in their finery should any team request it.[13]

College sports remained one arena where a handful of African Americans were able to make an athletic mark while competing with or against whites. Despite the nationwide expansion of racial discrimination, colleges outside the South continued to admit a few African American students, some of whom played sports. Black leaders kept close tabs on these athletes, and were quick to broadcast their accomplishments. They paid particular attention to William Henry Lewis, who played football for both Amherst and Harvard, and who in 1893 earned the honor of being the nation's first black All-American football player. After finishing his Harvard career, Lewis became a successful lawyer and a respected part-time coach. His coaching accomplishments were especially meaningful for African Americans, because they highlighted his formidable intellectual abilities. In 1900, the official publication of the A.M.E. Zion church took time from its focus on religious matters to make this point, publishing a lengthy description of a football game between Harvard and the University of Pennsylvania.

"The betting was ten to seven in favor of Pennsylvania," the *A.M.E. Quarterly Review* explained. "And yet with a weak and crippled team Harvard was overwhelmingly victorious. And why? because W.H. Lewis, the colored coach had studied the methods of the Pennsylvania system and mastered them. He devised a system of defense which completely blocked Pennsylvania's team and made it almost impossible for them to score." The article went on to probe the meanings of Lewis's feat. "The civilized world holds in high respect the trained and successful athlete," it noted. "The best of the colleges of the world encourage athletics as a means of strengthening and adding to the health of students and of stimulating their mental powers at the same time." It then concluded with a prediction about the wider effects of Lewis's accomplishments. "The proud Anglo-Saxon admits that his superior has not appeared on the athletic field....Our race is proud of him because in all his success he stands for us, and the higher he goes in the physical field of athletics or the mental field of law or literature, he must necessarily open the way for others, and lift us all up at the same time."[14]

Women Join the Game

American women also seized eagerly on new sporting opportunities. Like their male counterparts, they reveled in the energy of physical activity and the excitement of competitive games. Many also joined with Mabel Craft in viewing sports as a way to step beyond the constraints American society had imposed on women, and to prepare themselves for broader roles in an energetic, competitive world. Female athletes would, however, have to walk a fine line. During the course of the nineteenth century, as athletic prowess became an increasingly prominent cornerstone of male identity, links between sports and masculinity increased. While female physical activity caused little consternation in working-class communities, where demanding physical labor was a given for women as well as men, middle- and upper-class women faced greater challenges. For these women to compete without seeming to threaten fundamental gender relationships, proponents of women's athletics had to pay careful attention not only to the conduct of female athletes, but also to the games they played, the rules they followed, and the outfits they wore.

Most early women's sports took place in private enclaves. Within the boundaries of exclusive social clubs, upper-class women began to take up sports that included archery, croquet, tennis, and golf. In 1877, women in Staten Island, New York, formed their own athletic club under the aegis of the men's Staten Island Cricket and Base Ball Club. The Ladies' Club, founded in 1875, focused on lawn tennis and sponsored early women's tournaments. Within a decade, it had grown to more than 200 members. Similar circles of elite sporting women emerged in other major northeastern cities. The first women's national archery championship was held in 1879, the first tennis championship in 1887, and the first golf championship in 1895.[15]

Elsewhere, other women had begun pushing at Victorian boundaries. Many started with education. In 1837, Oberlin became the first college in the nation to admit women to its regular college programs. While some schools remained staunchly male well into the twentieth century, others began to admit women as well. In addition, numerous women's colleges sprang up, including Vassar College, founded in 1865, Scotia Seminary, founded in 1867, and Smith College, founded in 1875. While schools for women had once focused on genteel, home-centered activities such as literature and music, these new institutions expanded into a broader range of academic and scientific subjects. In 1870, 11,000 women were attending college. By 1900, there were 85,000. Many of these new collegians looked to a future that involved not simply marriage, but also some kind of career. By the end of the nineteenth century, many women were beginning to move into schoolteaching, clerical positions, and social work. A few set their sights on professions such as law and medicine.[16]

Women also moved into the political arena, advocating first for others and then for themselves. In the early 1800s, women began to fill the ranks of social movements such as temperance (getting people to swear off alcohol) and the abolition of slavery. In the 1840s, a group of women that included Elizabeth Cady Stanton, Lucretia Mott, Amelia Bloomer, and Susan B. Anthony began a movement to change laws that discriminated against women, as well as to win women the vote. Thousands of women across the country joined political activities, and figures such as temperance leader Frances Willard and crusading newspaper writer

Ida B. Wells-Barnett became well-known political figures. In the nation's burgeoning cities, pioneering women such as Jane Addams launched innovative social and cultural programs designed to assist working-class immigrant and migrant families.

As middle-class women moved into new fields, educators, health reformers, and early feminists began to see exercise as one way women could prepare themselves for their new endeavors. In the years after the Civil War, the growing number of women who entered colleges presented exercise advocates with additional opportunities to advance their cause. Prevailing, supposedly "scientific" theories held that intellectual activity robbed women of the energy they needed to bear healthy children. College-based advocates of women's exercise countered that properly regulated physical training restored energy and reduced anxiety, warding off such harmful effects. This argument helped wedge open academic doors for female physical educators, who eventually established themselves as a distinct profession. The Sargent School (opened in 1881) and the Boston Normal School of Gymnastics (founded in 1889) led the way. Within a decade, dozens of their graduates fanned out across the country. In school after school, these energetic women set up independent departments for women's physical education, granted degrees to majors, and created elaborate exercise routines for female students.

One of the most prominent of these women, Smith College's Senda Berenson, vividly described her dedication to her profession. Berenson was ill throughout much of her youth—to the point that she was unable to attend school for several years. When she took the advice of friends and enrolled in the Boston Normal School of Gymnastics, she spent the first months of her schooling lying across three chairs, in order to strengthen her back muscles. "I hated it," she later explained. By the time she graduated, however she was a changed woman. "It is impossible to tell how my life had altered," she continued. "I had changed an aching body to a free and strong mechanism, ready and eager for whatever might come. My indifference had changed to deep conviction and I wanted to work only in physical education so that I might help others as I had been helped."[17]

Women's enthusiasm for exercise burst into public view in the 1890s, when the nation was consumed by the "bicycle craze," the result of technical and manufacturing improvements that made bicycles less expensive and far easier to ride. American roads began to fill with female cyclists. For many of these women, bicycling fostered not only physical strength, but also an empowering sense of independence and self-confidence. Temperance activist Frances Willard, who took up the "wheel" at the age of 53, was so inspired by her experience that she wrote a short book describing it. "Just as a strong and skillful swimmer takes the waves," Willard explained, "so the bicycler must learn to take such waves of mental impression as the passing of a gigantic haywagon, the sudden obtrusion of black cattle with wide-branching horns, the rattling pace of high-stepping steeds, or even the swift transit of a railway train. At first she will be upset by the apparition of the smallest poodle, and not until she has attained a wide experience will she hold herself steady in [the] presence of a coach with four horses. But all this is a part of that equilibration of thought and action by which we conquer the universe in conquering ourselves."[18]

Fellow political activist Susan B. Anthony concurred, asserting that bicycling did "more to emancipate woman than anything else in the world" because of the way it gave them "a feeling of freedom and self-reliance."[19]

Bicycling and other forms of exercise also helped to free women, at least temporarily, from the clothing that constrained their daily movements. Proper Victorian women laced themselves into tight corsets that inhibited breathing and cramped internal organs, and they donned long, heavy skirts that made walking a chore. Such constraining garments reflected the idea of female frailty—some "scientists" actually argued that women needed corsets in order to stand up—and also contributed to that frailty by preventing healthy movement. Escaping from the restraints of Victorian clothing had been an issue for the emerging women's rights movement for decades. In 1851, for example, activist Amelia Bloomer had caused a national sensation when she appeared in public in a pair of wide Turkish trousers covered by a short skirt. Bloomer and other women's rights activists eventually abandoned the "Bloomer Costume" for everyday wear, because of the sensation it caused. But the outfit gained greater acceptance as athletic dress. While bloomers, which were made from yards of dark wool, remained hot and heavy garments, they were a tremendous improvement over corsets and long skirts.

By the turn of the century, young women's enthusiasm for vigorous activity had replaced the image of the prim and proper Victorian matron with the "athletic girl," whose popularity cut across age, class, and regional lines. Witty, sophisticated, and at ease on the golf course, at the tennis court or on horseback, athletic women expanded the acceptable boundaries of physical freedom for women. Indeed, advertisers, the popular press, and health and beauty authorities began to establish the modern linkage between physical activity and female beauty. Dudley Sargent, founder of the Sargent school, claimed that "good form in figure and good form in motion…tend to inspire admiration in the opposite sex and therefore play an important part in what is termed 'sexual selection.'"[20]

Some enterprising young women even found ways to make a living from athletics. The 1890s saw the establishment of numerous "Bloomer Girl" baseball teams, which barnstormed around the country challenging local male squads. Pitcher Maud Nelson, who had come to the United States from northern Italy as a child, was especially active in the sport—she would play and coach baseball for nearly four decades. In addition to offering a show that was "clean, moral and refined," Nelson's players took the game seriously—her Boston Bloomer Girls once played and won 28 games in 26 days. In 1897, when the team traveled to Oregon, the local paper noted that "the girls from Beantown put up a clean game and play like professionals, asking for no favors, but playing a hard snappy game on its merits."[21]

Fending Off Critics

This new version of womanhood, however, sparked consternation among some Americans, who believed that female participation in a "male" activity threatened the fabric of American society. Athletic women were often accused of seeking to usurp the social status of men, upending traditional hierarchies and placing men in subservient roles. A turn-of-the-century pamphlet called *The Taint of the Bicycle* painted a portrait of bicycle-riding women which mixed satire with a clear condemnation of female assertiveness and the assumption that such presumption sprang from male weakness. "Then, sad regret—woman went 'a coasting,' and 'a scorching,'" the pamphlet ran.

"For a time she rode her brother's bicycle—when he would let her; she rode her son's 'bike,' if she were larger and stronger than he; on her lovers 'safety,' if he loved her better than she loved him; and finally on her husband's 'wheel,' if he were a hen-pecked husband....[With] stiff hat, laundried shirt, high collar, four-in-hand tie, low cut vest, cutaway coat, plus a substitution for pantaloons, she rode and pretended to be happy in her new role."[22]

Alternately, women's athletics could turn into sexual spectacle, as men crowded to see bloomer-clad young women run, jump, and tumble to the ground. In 1903, when students at two North Carolina women's colleges scheduled an outdoor basketball game between their squads, school administrators barred male spectators and announced that "a close watch will be kept to see that none enter in disguise." Local newspapers reveled in the episode, asserting that if men had been allowed to buy tickets to the game "it would take an expert mathematician to figure out the amount of the gate receipts," as "business would have been suspended and the populace would have turned out en masse." The game's attractions gained further public attention when a group of young men defied the ban by scaling the buildings around the field to catch glimpses of the action.[23]

Promoters of women's sport were keenly aware that female athletes could be criticized both for usurping male prerogatives, and for putting their bodies on display in unladylike fashion. Administrators at women's colleges were especially sensitive to such critiques. Although the female college population was rapidly expanding, higher education for women remained a controversial subject, especially in cases where colleges were seen as preparing young women to step outside traditional social roles. College administrators were determined to turn out graduates with both the intellectual training and the physical stamina to make a difference in their communities. Physical educators pursued that work with particular zeal— Clara Baer, who taught at Newcomb College in New Orleans, became famous for compelling her students to "sweat off" their corsets. But physical educators also sought to mute the implications of their efforts by shaping programs that were clearly different from men's. To that end, they fashioned a philosophy of "moderation" that downplayed competition and drew explicit distinctions between men's and women's play. Basketball, the first competitive team sport that women took up in large numbers, became their first project.

In many ways, basketball was an ideal game for women. YMCA instructor James Naismith had drawn up the game's first rules in late 1891, and women began playing almost immediately. Since basketball was a new game, female players were not intruding on already-established male turf. Naismith had also designed the game specifically to avoid rough physical contact. In his original rules, players passed the ball rather than running with it, tossed it upward over defenders rather than trying to force it through them, and were barred from "shouldering, holding, pushing, tripping, or striking in any way the person of an opponent." While early participants quickly demonstrated that rough play was possible even within those restrictions, the limits on physical contact led some critics to term basketball a "sissy" game, especially when compared with the more "masculine" brutality of football. While such a reputation at times deterred male players, it proved an advantage for women.

Senda Berenson, who took a job at Smith College in January of 1892, was one of the first female physical educators to see promise in the game. She introduced it to a physical education class that spring, sparking immediate enthusiasm. For men, basketball offered an indoor alternative to the more established sports of football and baseball. For many women, it was their first opportunity at a vigorous, competitive team sport, and Berenson waxed eloquent about its effects. "Many of our young women are well enough in a way, yet never know the joy of mere living, are lazy, listless and lack vitality," she wrote. "Let such a person try this game, she will forget herself at the first throw of the ball, will take deep draughts of air with the unaccustomed exercise and 'tingle and throb with the joy of the game.' "[24]

Basketball spread rapidly. At colleges across the country, female students eagerly organized intramural competitions that pitted juniors against seniors, freshmen against sophomores. They combined heated clashes on the court with vigorous cheers and singing in the stands. Students wrote their own chants and cheers, such as a turn-of-the-century effort from the State Normal College in Greensboro, North Carolina.

Sing a song of tournament!
A week full of care,
Colors waving, rooters raving
Balls in the air!
When the game is over,
The winning class goes wild!
They yell and squall like savages.
But the losers all are riled.[25]

Students at schools like Stanford ventured even further, scheduling interscholastic games that would allow them to defend the honor of their school as well as their class.

Before long, however, physical educators began to rein in their students' enthusiasm. According to Victorian views of women as naturally gentle, women's games should have been calm and orderly, no matter what the context. But Senda Berenson, who had struggled to control her own fiery temper, knew better. She also received a convincing demonstration during some of Smith's early games, which featured turned ankles, fingernail scratches, and pulled hair. Along with colleagues across the country, Berenson used changes in basketball rules, curbs on emotional expression, and a focus on intra- rather than interscholastic competition to shape a distinctly female approach to athletics. These endeavors helped head off potential accusations that female athletes were stepping into male territory. As an added benefit, they also helped women avoid the very visible troubles that were beginning to plague male college sport.

Physical educators started with basketball's rules, adding modifications that limited players' movements and further restricted physical contact. Berenson's rules divided the court into three equal sections and assigned each player to one. Forwards played under a team's home basket, centers roamed the middle section, and guards patrolled the opposing team's goal. Teams could have anywhere from five to 10 players, but no one could venture outside her assigned section. The rules also banned physical contact of any kind. In New Orleans, Clara Baer divided the court into nine sections, with one player from each team assigned to each section. Players could not dribble, and any player who fell down was charged with a foul. In 1899, a committee of educators led by Berenson persuaded the A.G. Spalding

Company to publish Berenson's rules as the "Official Rules" of women's basketball. Several other sets of rules competed with Berenson's, and as late as 1914 as many as half the female players in the country still played by boys' rules. But modified "girls' rules" eventually became the norm.

Female physical educators also opposed varsity competition. Some restricted play to intramural games, which avoided the emotion of interschool rivalry, and also kept contests out of the public realm, reducing the possibility that they might turn into sexual spectacles. Others sought to end competition altogether, arguing that it was far more important to encourage cooperation. These physical educators focused on the "play day," an institution that would define female physical education for half a century. Play days involved intercampus visits by groups of physical education students. Rather than pitting one school against another, organizers frequently chose teams that mixed players from the different institutions. The ensuing games were played for fun, rather than to win, they were often followed by teas or dances.

These careful efforts to shape a distinctly female form of athletics deflected many potential critics. But they could not fully obscure the revolution that women's sports represented. Even the most modest athletic program challenged the idea that sports was a strictly masculine preserve. Like other women's rights activists, physical educators found that their claims on independence and physical confidence were frequently viewed not as expanding the bounds of womanhood, but as invading territory that belonged to men. Such tensions were particularly evident at coeducational schools, where men and women came into closest contact, and at times competed to use the same facilities. When Mabel Lee was hired to teach physical education at Beloit College in Wisconsin, for example, it took a full semester of negotiation for her students to gain access to the school's swimming pool—and then for only four hours a week.[26]

Faced with these challenges, female physical educators focused on charting their own, independent paths. They built a powerful professional network revolving around shared experiences in colleges, participation in physical education associations, and personal friendships. They also banded together in several state and national associations that came to wield considerable influence over educational policy. This power would hold both advantages and disadvantages for female athletes. It made women's athletics a national institution, providing training and careers for countless sports-minded women. But female athletes who sought to step beyond the physical educators' carefully drawn boundaries could find that they faced powerful female as well as male opponents.

Conclusion

As competitive sports gained greater social acceptance, they became one way that Americans relegated to the margins of the new industrial society sought to demonstrate their fitness for broader social roles. Native Americans, African Americans, women, and others seized on sports as a path both to individual fulfillment and broader social advancement. While progress was slow, these efforts helped make sports an arena for debating issues far larger than simply victory or loss.

Critical Thinking Questions

1. African Americans, Native Americans, and women all saw sports as a way to challenge a set of ideas that denied them full participation in American society. Which group faced the greatest obstacles and why?
2. In what ways did sports serve as a force for challenging social hierarchies in the late nineteenth century?
3. In what ways did sports serve as a force for reinforcing social hierarchies in the late nineteenth century?

Notes

1. William F. Foneville, *Reminiscences of College Days*, (Raleigh, NC: privately printed, 1904), 67. For more about the development of early athletic programs at Livingstone, Biddle and other historically black colleges, see Pamela Grundy, *Learning to Win: Sports, Education and Social Change in Twentieth-Century North Carolina* (Chapel Hill: University of North Carolina Press, 2001), chapter 1.
2. *San Francisco Chronicle*, 5 April 1896, 25. For more details on the game and on Mabel Craft, see Pamela Grundy and Susan Shackelford, *Shattering the Glass: The Remarkable History of Women's Basketball* (New York: The New Press, 2005), 19–23.
3. For a description of this reformulation, see Gail Bederman, *Manliness and Civilization: A Cultural History of Gender and Race in the United States 1880–1917* (Chicago: University of Chicago Press, 1995), chapter 1.
4. Richard Henry Pratt, *Battlefield and Classroom: Four Decades with the American Indian, 1867–1904* (New Haven: Yale University Press, 1964), 317–18.
5. David Wallace Adams, *Education for Extinction: American Indians and the Boarding School Experience, 1875–1928* (Lawrence: University Press of Kansas, 1995), 181–90.
6. Quoted in Kate Buford, *Native American Son: The Life and Sporting Legend of Jim Thorpe* (New York: Alfred A. Knopf, 2010), 61–2.
7. Michael Oriard, *Reading Football: How the Popular Press Created an American Sporting Spectacle* (Chapel Hill: University of North Carolina Press, 1993), 237. For an illuminating account of the Carlisle team's experiences, see ibid., 233–47.
8. The national shift in race relations is chronicled in numerous accounts. One particularly thoughtful work, which examines the ways that reimagining Southern culture and the Civil War helped Northerners to deal with postwar shifts in class and gender roles, is Nina Silber, *The Romance of Reunion: Northerners and the South, 1865–1900* (Chapel Hill: University of North Carolina Press, 1997).
9. For a detailed and thoughtful account of Fleet Walker's life, see David Zang, *Fleet Walker's Divided Heart: The Life of Baseball's First Black Major Leaguer* (Lincoln: University of Nebraska Press, 1995).
10. Robert Peterson, *Only the Ball Was White: A History of Legendary Black Players and All-Black Professional Teams* (New York: Oxford University Press, 1991), 23, 28, 31–2.
11. See Marshall W. "Major" Taylor, *The Fastest Bicycle Rider in the World* (Brattleboro, VT: Green-Stephen, 1972); Andrew Ritchie, "Marshall "Major" Taylor: The Fastest Bicycle Rider in the World," in David K. Wiggins, ed., *Out of the Shadows: A Biographical History of African American Athletes* (Fayetteville: University of Arkansas Press, 2006).
12. Ed Hotaling, *Wink: The Incredible Life and Epic Journey of Jimmy Winkfield* (New York: McGraw Hill, 2005); Susan Hamburger, "Jimmy Winkfield: The 'Black Maestro' of the Racetrack," in Wiggins, ed., *Out of the Shadows*; M.F. Walker, *Our Home Colony: A Treatise on the Past, Present and Future of the Negro Race in America* (Steubenville, OH: Herald Printing Company, 1908), 31.

13. Peterson, *Only the Ball Was White*, 54, 146.

14. *A.M.E. Zion Quarterly Review* 10 (October–December 1900), 64–5. For more about William Henry Lewis, see Gregory Bond, "The Strange Career of William Henry Lewis," in Wiggins, ed., *Out of the Shadows*. For an account of the career of another pioneering African American college football player, see John M. Carroll, *Fritz Pollard: Pioneer in Racial Advancement* (Urbana: University of Illinois Press, 1998).

15. See especially Cindy Himes, *The Female Athlete in American Society, 1860–1940* (Ph.D. dissertation, University of Pennsylvania, 1986), chapter 1, and Donald J. Mrozek, *Sport and the American Mentality* (Knoxville: University of Tennessee Press, 1983), chapter 5.

16. The following analysis is drawn from Susan Cahn, *Coming on Strong: Gender and Sexuality in Twentieth-Century Women's Sport* (New York: The Free Press, 1994), chapter 1; Grundy, *Learning to Win*, chapter 2, and Grundy and Shackelford, *Shattering the Glass*, chapter 1.

17. Edith Naomi Hill, "Senda Berenson: Director of Physical Education at Smith College, 1892–1911," in *Pioneer Women in Physical Education*, supplement to *The Research Quarterly* (American Association for Health, Physical Education, and Recreation, October 1941), 659.

18. Frances E. Willard, *A Wheel Within a Wheel: How I Learned to Ride the Bicycle* (Bedford, Mass., Applewood Books, 1997), 25–6.

19. Quoted in Lisa Larrabee, "Women and Cycling: The Early Years," in Willard, ed., *How I Learned to Ride the Bicycle*, 90.

20. Quoted in Cahn, *Coming on Strong*, 20–1.

21. Quoted in Barbara Gregorich, *Women at Play: The Story of Women in Baseball* (New York: Harcourt, 1993), 36, 7.

22. William F. Foneville, *The Taint of the Bicycle* (Goldsboro, NC: privately printed, 1902), 10–11.

23. *Charlotte Observer*, April 7 and 9, 1907.

24. Berenson, "Basketball for Women," draft 1 [transcript], 98. Smith College Archives, Senda Berenson Papers, Series 6, "Speeches." URL: http://clio.fivecolleges.edu/smith/berenson/6speeches/.

25. *Carolinian*, 1911, 66. Copy located in Walter Clinton Jackson Library, University of North Carolina at Greensboro.

26. Lee, Mabel, *Memories of a Bloomer Girl, 1894–1924* (Washington DC: American Alliance for Health, Physical Education, and Recreation, 1977), 348.

CHAPTER 8

Sports, Culture, and Nation: 1900–1945

Football star Red Grange gives a group of boys some pointers.

LEARNING OBJECTIVES

8.1 Describe the economic, technological, and cultural factors that helped make competitive sports an integral part of twentieth-century American culture.

8.2 Outline the reasons behind the expansion of organized youth sports at the turn of the twentieth century.

8.3 Describe the ways that a new generation of sportswriters and sportscasters helped increase interest in sports.

8.4 Summarize the economic shifts that gave a growing middle class more time and money for leisure activities such as sports.

8.5 Explain how cultural and political changes reshaped opportunities for female and African American athletes.

8.6 Detail the growing tensions between the drive for excellence and the concept of amateurism, as well as the different ways that different sports dealt with the challenge.

From the fall of 1923 through the fall of 1925, the flickering, elusive figure of a football player darted across moving picture screens around the nation, cutting deftly past defender after defender, scoring touchdown after touchdown after touchdown. Sports had become a staple feature of American newsreels, and University of Illinois tailback Red Grange, dubbed the "Galloping Ghost," quickly became one of its star performers.

Grange's rise to stardom illustrated the many inroads that sports made into American culture in the early decades of the twentieth century. Although Grange came from modest circumstances, he found plenty of outlets for his athletic talent. Competing for Wheaton High, in Wheaton, Illinois, Grange became the Illinois sprints and hurdles champion. He put his speed and flexibility to even more dramatic use on the football field, scoring 72 touchdowns in three seasons of high school play. The heavily recruited player chose to attend the University of Illinois, where he amazed the entire country with his explosive speed and open field dexterity. Newspapers, magazines, radio, and newsreels all sang his praises. After his junior season, he contracted with emerging sports agent Charles C. "Cash and Carry" Pyle to join the Chicago Bears of the fledgling National Football Association. He helped build pro football's foundations, reaped the gains of movie appearances and product endorsements, and eventually became a radio and television sportscaster.

Grange's opportunities were created by tremendous growth in sports at all levels of American society, from the smallest communities to the highest reaches of national popular culture. "Ball matches, football games, tennis tournaments, bicycle races, [and] regattas, have become part of our national life," concluded a writer in *Harper's Weekly* in 1895, "and are watched with eagerness and discussed with enthusiasm and understanding by all manner of people, from the day-laborer to the millionaire."[1] In this new era, organized sports achieved an institutional permanency and prominence in American life in some ways equal to those of business, politics, ethnicity, and religion.

Like other mass cultural institutions, sports achieved this hallowed status because it was able to encompass multiple social meanings, and thus appeal to a wide range of Americans. The discipline and hard work required for sustained athletic success made organized athletics seem an ideal way to develop the traits essential for good citizenship and success in a highly competitive society. In addition, the joy and beauty of physical movement, combined with the excitement of competition, made sports an exciting alternative to the humdrum of everyday life. And even as sports offered some Americans an escape from daily life, others tied them tightly to the issues of the day, addressing questions that ranged from racial identity to female abilities to the merits of different political systems.

Sports in Daily Life

During his climb to fame, Red Grange benefited from the spread of sporting institutions into the everyday life of young Americans. Throughout the nineteenth century, most young people competed largely on teams and in games that they themselves had organized. But around the turn of the century, a range of institutions began to sponsor organized youth sports, including the Young Men's Christian Association, private preparatory schools, churches, Public Schools Athletic Leagues, city playground associations, and public high schools. While adults often focused most of their attention on boys, girls found ways to participate as well, especially as sports moved into the growing ranks of comprehensive public high schools.

This drive for adult-directed sports was an integral component of a larger movement to organize and manage the spare time activities of the nation's youth.[2] As the nation grew, diversified, and urbanized, the members of the old-line Protestant middle class began to worry about young people's behavior. In their minds, the disappearance of the household economy, the absence of early work experience, the weakened authority of religion, and the breakdown of the small geographic community had left young people adrift. Adults looked to organized, competitive sports as one way to fill that void, by teaching teamwork, sportsmanship, and other components of what they called individual *character*.

Competitive sports spread quickly into the nation's rapidly growing secondary school system, in part because of its potential for character-building and in part because high school teams became a focus for community activity and community identity. This interest in youth sports stretched throughout the country, and across ethnic and gender lines. In 1903, for example, the Fort Shaw Indian Industrial School, located in Fort Shaw, Montana, was invited to send a delegation to the 1904 World's Fair in St. Louis. The director chose to send the girls' basketball team. Along with demonstrating traditional Indian culture, the Fort Shaw students gave twice-weekly basketball demonstrations and successfully defended their school's honor against an all-star lineup of St. Louis's best female high school players. As young people left high school, they found other opportunities on a burgeoning number of community teams, or on "industrial" teams that many companies began to sponsor for their workers, seeking to build both individual discipline and company loyalty.[3]

World War I (1914–1918) intensified the enthusiasm for sports. Before America joined the allied war effort in 1917, sports became an important component of a national preparedness campaign. Shortly after American entry, General John J. Pershing asked the YMCA to manage Army cantonments; the YMCA, employing 300 trained physical directors, also took charge of the athletics of the American Expeditionary Forces in France. The YMCA established comprehensive sporting programs everywhere. The campaign to tie sports to the military reached a dramatic climax in 1919 with the scheduling of the Inter-Allied Games in Paris. The Army invited 29 of the victorious nations to participate in "keen rivalry, a free field, and fair play."[4]

The Media and Sports

Like their predecessors, twentieth-century athletes benefitted from new technology and new forms of communication. An expanding national media made a particularly large impact, with improvements in newspapers, telegraphs and telephones, and eventually the development of radio and television. The sports page of the daily newspaper, mass-circulation periodicals, movie newsreels, and the broadcasting of sports on radio encouraged public interest in sports, and helped shape reactions to athletes and events. This expanding coverage elevated top athletes into national heroes, brought new sports into the public eye, and vastly expanded the appeal of established sports such as college football and professional baseball.

Joseph Pulitzer's New York World helped start the trend by creating a separate sports section in 1887. The other leading New York dailies quickly followed suit. By the 1920s, the sports page had become a standard feature in all major daily newspapers, and the percentage of total newspaper space allocated to sports was more than double that of three decades earlier. Even the New York Times gave front-page coverage to major prizefights and baseball World Series. With the exception of two columns on page 1, the Times devoted the entire first 13 pages of its issue of July 3, 1921, to the Jack Dempsey–Georges Carpentier heavyweight championship fight.[5]

The twentieth century also brought to the fore a new generation of writers specializing in sports. Some converted the sporting experience into poetry; only poetry, they believed, could reduce the wonder of sports to human comprehension. Grantland Rice, the dean of early twentieth-century sportswriters, had a gift for writing verse a cut above the popular commercial jingles of the day. Youngsters memorized his lines and coaches used them to inspire their teams. His most famous: "When the one Great Scorer comes to write against your name, he marks—not whether you won or lost—but how you played the game." After Knute Rockne's 1924 Notre Dame team defeated powerful Army, Rice composed the best-known opening lines in sportswriting history: "Outlined against a blue-grey October sky, the Four Horsemen rode again. In dramatic lore they are known as Famine, Pestilence, Destruction, and Death. These are only aliases. Their real names are Stuhldreher, Miller, Crowley, and Layden." Sportswriters frequently dispensed on-the-spot immortality to athletes. Even the racehorse Man O'War was immortal; he was dubbed the "horse of eternity."[6]

Despite Rice's continuing popularity, by the 1920s his form of sportswriting had begun to wane. Paul Gallico, Frank Graham, Damon Runyan, Ring Lardner, Westbrook Pegler, Heywood Broun, and Arch Ward (among others) tried to construct an interesting, lively, interpretive, and not infrequently exaggerated story of what had happened or was likely to happen. The best of them could weave a story as terse and tight as the strands of a steel cable. Apart from presenting a coherent narrative, they employed powerful, often onomatopoeic verbs, colorful figures of speech, and alliterative nicknames. Nicknames came in a virtual flood: the Galloping Ghost (Red Grange), the Fordham Flash (Frankie Frisch), the Sultan of Swat (Babe Ruth). They also delighted in using all three names of people involved in sports, such as Grover Cleveland Alexander, Kenesaw Mountain Landis, or George Herman Ruth, thereby conferring upon them a kind of tongue-in-cheek grandeur.

Radio began to have an impact on sports in the 1920s, although it did not reach the apogee of its influence until the 1940s and 1950s. Initially, radio aired only the more spectacular events rather than regularly scheduled contests. As early as 1923, an estimated two million fans listened to the broadcast of the Louis Firpo–Jess Willard heavyweight fight. The *New York Times* deemed the 23-station network established to carry the 1926 World Series to be such a pioneering venture that it printed the entire narrative of the broadcasts in its sports section. As early as 1934, the three major networks of the day paid $100,000 for the privilege of carrying the series. Radio executives soon discovered that sports fans liked announcers who were something more than disembodied voices objectively and dispassionately describing the action. The fans wanted announcers capable of becoming celebrities in their own right. Graham McNamee emerged as the new medium's first star. As the chief announcer of the National Broadcasting Company in the 1920s, McNamee enjoyed a remarkable capacity for using his voice to convey the gamut of emotions. Hailed as the "world's most popular announcer," McNamee covered the World Series, prizefights, major college football games, national political conventions, and important live news developments.

For many decades, millions of Americans found in the radio coverage of sports both an escape from the routines of everyday life and an entry into the wonderland of the imagination. "Radio—mysterious, disembodied, vivid as a dream—screamed for a fantasy response," wrote Bil Gilbert about his experiences listening to the games of the Detroit Tigers while a youngster in the 1930s. Even when not listening to the games, Gilbert imitated the Detroit broadcaster's voice as he described to himself his own tossing of a ball on the roof or throwing stones at a target. In his private world, where Gilbert always had his beloved Tigers crush rivals, he never suffered from the humiliation of defeat. To Gilbert and millions like him, the introduction of television in the 1940s and 1950s destroyed the magic. "Thereafter baseball was never again serious," Gilbert concluded.[7]

Consumer Culture and a New Middle Class

Twentieth-century sports drew particular support from a fast-growing middle class that was increasingly less evangelical, more impatient with demands for self-control, and more focused on leisure and excitement. The rapid growth of corporate capitalism in the late nineteenth and twentieth centuries vastly expanded the nation's middle class, as shopkeepers and skilled craft workers were joined by growing numbers of middle managers, salespeople, secretaries, and others.[8] Between 1870 and 1930 these corporate-based jobs grew twice as fast as the work force as a whole. Often possessing specialized skills acquired through formal education, members of this new class shared an enthusiasm for rationality and what they frequently called "science." Rather than emphasizing personal character, they took pride in specialized knowledge, and stressed the importance of personality. Away from their workplaces, members of the new class relaxed the traditional middle-class concern for self-control and embraced new, more expressive forms of behavior. Their leisure activities generally revolved around consumption, commercial amusements, informality, spontaneity, and intense feelings.

The new middle class became enthusiastic patrons of modern consumer culture. By the 1890s, the nation's economy had begun to shift from one organized around production to one organized around mass consumption and leisure. In the Industrial Revolution's first phase, the main catalyst for rapid economic expansion had been the growing demand for "producer goods," those made for other producers rather than for individual consumers. A classic example in the nineteenth century was the steel industry, which had grown up primarily to meet the demands of the nation's burgeoning railway network. Although producer goods remained important to the nation's prosperity in the twentieth century, manufacturing and sales targeted at millions of individuals became the hallmark of a new phase of the Industrial Revolution.

By the 1920s, industrial technology had transformed the United States into a consumers' paradise. The automobile, the most prized of all the new consumer goods, emancipated millions of Americans from a network restricted to home, neighborhood, and workplace. Electricity revolutionized the home; by 1940, four out of five Americans could, if they had the financial means, plug in electric lamps, washing machines, vacuum cleaners, refrigerators, toasters, and radios. The Great Depression of the 1930s and World War II temporarily set back the national buying spree, but in the postwar era, plastics, aluminum, and transistors became the staples of a new round of consumption. The consumer cornucopia extended to commercial leisure. As early as 1909, the A.G. Spalding and Brothers catalog contained more than 200 pages of advertisements for sporting goods and exercise devices. Overall, the first half of the twentieth century witnessed a 12-fold increase in recreation expenditures.

The changing nature of work, rising real incomes, a shorter work week, and paid vacations abetted the development of consumer culture. Although workers were subject to cycles of unemployment, an expanding economy and the achievements of a growing trade union movement meant that manufacturing wages nearly quadrupled between the Civil War and 1929. Although the Great Depression of the 1930s set back worker gains, earnings rebounded in the 1940s. At the same time, the average work week for those engaged in manufacturing followed a descending curve from 60 hours in 1890 to 47 in 1920 and 40 at mid-twentieth century. A week's paid vacation first became the norm for white-collar workers in the 1920s and then for blue-collar laborers in the 1940s. As income and leisure time increased, and factories and bureaucracies gnawed away at job satisfaction, consumption became the centerpiece of more and more people's lives.

Newspapers, mass circulation magazines, movies, and radio encouraged Americans to seek fulfillment in consumption. The media bombarded the public with new models of "the good life" that had been only furtively glimpsed by earlier generations. To encourage buying, salesmen and advertisers unrelentingly assaulted the older Victorian virtues of thrift and prudence. They urged consumers to "buy now, pay later" and to "live for the moment." "Life is meant to live and enjoy as you go along," insisted Bruce Barton, a leading apostle of the consumer culture in the 1920s. "If self-denial is necessary I'll practice some of it when I'm old and not try to do all of it now."[9] The suggestions made by advertisers and the media that consumption could solve personal problems such as loneliness, weariness, lack of sexual gratification, and lack of meaning in the workplace won increasing favor.

Although the consumer culture by no means obliterated traditional Victorian values or behaviors, it spawned an alternative set of powerful dreams and expectations. Growing numbers of Americans became more interested in obtaining the immediate pleasures arising from devotion to fun, play, sensual experiences, and less inhibited behavior generally. Consistent with the new attitudes, states and municipalities across the nation relaxed legal restrictions on amusements. Many states repealed or neglected to enforce their Sabbatarian laws. New York City, for example, finally obtained legal approval of Sunday baseball in 1919, though Philadelphia and Pittsburgh did not succumb until 1934. In the 1920s several states dropped their bans on working-class, ethnic sports such as prizefighting.

The rise of the new middle class could be seen in the way in which sports that had once belonged to the upper classes, such as tennis and golf, gained broader popularity. The shift in golf was especially noticeable. Popular hostility to the sport in the first decade of the twentieth century impelled Theodore Roosevelt to warn William Howard Taft of the political dangers of playing the game. "It would seem incredible that anyone would care one way or the other about your playing golf, but I have received literally hundreds of letters from the West protesting it," Roosevelt wrote. He further cautioned: "I myself play tennis, but the game is a little more familiar; besides you never saw a photograph of me playing tennis. I am careful about that; photographs on horseback, yes; tennis, no. And golf is fatal."[10] Ignoring Roosevelt's warnings, Taft became the nation's first golf-playing president, and the rapid growth of country clubs in the 1920s spread the game (as one wag put it) from the upper "Four Hundred" to the upper "Four Million." Membership in a country club became a salient badge of distinction, obligatory for families seeking higher status in large and small communities. Entire families usually participated in club life. Wealthier clubs erected large, Mediterranean-style clubhouses, sometimes valued at more than a million dollars, while at the other extreme, avid golfers in small towns sometimes built clubhouses of unadorned pine at a cost of only a few hundred dollars. Regardless of the cost of their clubs, in their isolated playgrounds, the nation's Protestant upper strata partook of hedonistic pleasures that had earlier been frowned upon. The lifestyle of the materially successful eased the transition of many Americans from a production to a consumption ethic.[11]

Golf's status as a spectator sport was boosted by charismatic players such as Francis Ouimet, a 20-year-old amateur golfer who upset Britain's two leading professional golfers in a rain-soaked playoff in the 1913 U.S. Open tournament, by the elegant and energetic Walter Hagan, and by the incomparable Bobby Jones, who ruled the sport from 1923 to his retirement in 1930 at the age of 28. Known as "The Emperor," Jones became one of the most popular athletes in an era known for its athletic heroes.[12]

Flappers and Female Athletes

Changing expectations for women also gave a boost to women's sports. When women won the right to vote in 1920, they expanded their claim on the public realm. Young women, known as "flappers," also came to symbolize many of the cultural changes of the 1920s. Flappers bobbed their hair short, smoked and drank in public, mingled freely with men, danced the fast steps of the Charleston, abandoned corsets, and donned shortened skirts. The quantity of cloth in a typical woman's outfit shrank from more than 19 yards in 1913 to 7 yards in 1925, causing consternation in the textile industry but delight among makers of silk stockings. The popular Kellerman bathing suit of the 1920s completely bared legs and arms while clinging closely to the body. These new styles of dress and manners helped free female athletes from some of the constraints faced by their nineteenth-century predecessors.[13]

Some athletes took full advantage of the new feminine norms, most notably Frenchwoman Suzanne Lenglen, who dominated women's international tennis in the years after World War I. Tennis meshed more neatly with conventional femininity than sports such as basketball, as female tennis players wore dresses, engaged in no physical contact, and moved about the court with a fluidity that could be compared to dancing. While Lenglen was a fierce competitor, she became better known for her remarkable grace on the court, and for her fashionable, short-skirted, outfits, some made from material thin enough to show the outlines of her body as she played. She played with passionate intensity: "I just throw dignity to the winds," she reportedly said, "and think of nothing but the game." Her combination of intense play and sexual appeal helped lift women's tennis into the international sporting spotlight.[14]

For other athletes, however, expectations that women should embody attractive sexuality caused problems. Women who did not fit the mold—or who competed in less "feminine" sports like basketball or track—could come in for harsh criticism from the all-male sports reporting fraternity. Mildred "Babe" Didrickson, a phenomenal athletic talent who began her career with a determined rejection of feminine norms, became one such target. After her dominating performance at the 1932 Olympics, reporters suggested that her competitive drive was little more than compensation for her lack of feminine appeal. "She knows she is not pretty, that she cannot compete with other girls in the very ancient and honored sport of man-trapping," renowned sportswriter Paul Gallico wrote. "She uses no cosmetics, creams or powders. But she competes with girls, fiercely and hungrily, at everything else."[15]

The new focus on sex and sexuality also raised another set of suspicions: that athletes such as Didrikson did not seek to attract men because they were not interested in them. In the nineteenth century, the charge of "mannishness" had implied that athletic women sought to take on "manly" qualities such as aggressiveness and competitive zeal. In the twentieth century, as sexuality and eroticism became more prominent components of American popular culture, critiques of female athletes were increasingly associated with suspicions of homosexuality. As a result female athletes who sought public acceptance often had to walk a very fine line.

Race and International Competition

As sports grew in popularity, so did efforts to use sporting success for racial advancement. The early years of the twentieth century marked a low point for many African American communities. Jim Crow segregation and black voter disfranchisement had solidified in the South, often enforced by the extralegal violence of lynching. Black America's first great athletic champion, boxer Jack Johnson, was hounded out of the country by the federal government. Conditions in the South would lead millions of African Americans to head North in what became known as the "Great Migration." But while the new migrants could exercise more rights outside the South, ongoing discrimination meant that they remained on the lower rungs of the occupational ladder. In Chicago in 1920, only a tenth of black men worked at skilled jobs, as opposed to more than one-quarter of white men. The nation's growing numbers of Asians and Latinos faced similar challenges. Yet, despite financial limitations, all these groups fashioned broad and varied community structures, of which sports became a vital component.

In the South, racially segregated schools offered an alternate arena for athletic development. Within these protected spaces, sports could become a powerful means of self-discovery and individual expression for both male and female students. The self-discipline that athletics required could also help give young African Americans the inner strength needed to endure and sometimes challenge the indignities of segregation and inequality.[16]

The growth of international sports also aided African Americans in ongoing efforts to use athletics to build racial respect. International sports, and the nationalistic fervor that they often sparked, expanded enormously in the first half of the twentieth century, with significant effects in the United States. American sports had nationalistic overtones from its inception—most games had roots in British sport, and Americans delighted in seeing American champions defeat British ones, whether in boxing, golf, horse racing, or other games. The revived Olympic Games, which debuted in Athens, Greece in 1896, expanded the scope of international competition. Americans also lionized games that they could call their own, and baseball's promoters in particular sought to spread the "American Game" around the world.

As the nation's international horizons expanded, so did the links Americans drew between sports and international politics. These connections reached a peak in the years leading up to World War II, as Adolph Hitler and his Nazi party began to cast their shadow over Europe, proclaiming their doctrine of Aryan superiority. In this new political context, African American athletes such as Jesse Owens and Joe Louis, who defeated German opponents, became heroes not simply to African Americans, but to the entire nation.

Challenges

Despite sports' exploding popularity, the growing levels of competition and commercialism also spurred detractors. A small but growing band of literary and artistic rebels registered a loud dissent. By giving precedence to the physical over the mental, these "modernist" intellectuals argued, sports represented a misplaced value. Historians

Charles and Mary Beard added another concern: At best, they said, sports provided only a momentary respite from the oppressions of modern society; at worst, sports were an opiate that promoted acquiescence to the status quo. A few sportswriters poked fun at the ballyhoo of sports promoters; others, like John R. Tunis, rued the capitulation of the joy of sports to commercial considerations. To Tunis, the new consumer society, of which sport had become an integral part, was destroying the pure spirit of play that he imagined had once prevailed. Unlike the opening decades of the twentieth century, an era in which Theodore Roosevelt led intellectuals in their enthusiasm for sports, these and similar refrains reverberated forcefully through the nation's major intellectual and artistic circles throughout much of the twentieth century.[17]

The Challenge of Amateurism

Continuing adherence to amateurism—the idea that sports should be pursued purely for the love of play—caused problems within sports as well, as participants and organizers wrestled with the growing gap between the amateur ideal and the commercial enterprise that sports had become. Athletic amateurism worked well enough when applied to the leisure activities of the wealthier classes, and it had the added benefit of neatly excluding members of the working class, who had little time or money to spare for purely recreational activities. But as competition mounted, and financial prospects grew, the amateur ideal began to cause more problems than it solved.

Some sports resolved the problem through professionalizing. Baseball and boxing had been professional sports since the nineteenth century, and golf joined them soon afterward. Those that did not, among them tennis and track and field, faced ongoing challenges. On the surface, the rules of amateurism could be quite strict: for example, the International Olympic Committee decreed that to be considered an amateur, an athlete should never have been paid for anything even remotely sports-related. But as the level of competition rose, top athletes needed growing amounts of support for training and for travel to competition. Those who were not independently wealthy usually financed their activities through sponsorships and expense reimbursement—sponsors of the U.S. National Tennis Championship, for example, might ensure the participation of popular players by offering specific sums for "travel expenses."

This conundrum made the finances of "amateur" athletics an extremely murky realm, frequently referred to as "shamateurism." It also gave governing bodies a great deal of power over athletes. If an athlete in an amateur sport, such as track and field, displeased an organization, for example the Amateur Athletic Union, it was usually easy for officials to find a "violation" of the amateur code that allowed the organization to strip the athlete of amateur status and bar him or her from further competition.

Colleges with big-time athletic programs faced their own challenges. Although the jackpot of television revenues lay in the future, by the 1920s, college football was big business: filling huge stadiums with ticket-buying customers. But most schools, sticking to the scholar–athlete ideal, did not offer full-fledged athletic scholarships until the 1960s. College athletes, most of whom were not independently wealthy, had to finance their way through school with on-campus jobs, or with the help of interested alumni, a practice that created its own shadowy realm. When the Carnegie Foundation financed a report on college athletics in 1929, for example, the author concluded that only a quarter of the schools he investigated operated "ethical" programs.

Conclusion

During the first half of the twentieth century, the ideology of sports reached deep into the very fabric of American life. It shaped the contents of a large body of juvenile literature and was a core ingredient in programs designed to manage the spare-time activities of adolescents. The rising profession of physical education used it to convince reluctant school boards and state legislatures across the nation to require physical training in the schools. To nearly the entire nation, the idea that organized sports could be an unusually powerful tool in building personal character became virtually a truism. Businessmen increasingly saw sports as a training ground for success in the marketplace, and even evangelicals began to use sports to recruit converts. But sports still remained a focus of considerable debate, particularly when it failed to live up to the appealing promises its supporters made.

Critical Thinking Questions

1. The authors make the claim that athletic competition became a major American institution "because it was able to encompass multiple social meanings, and thus appeal to a wide range of Americans." Do you agree with this statement? If so, why? If not, why not?
2. While nineteenth-century sports were often sharply divided by economic class, in the twentieth century many sports began to cross class lines. What might these shifts have meant for the way Americans viewed class differences?
3. Critics of the growing roles of sports in American society cited several reasons for their concern. Which of these criticisms do you find most insightful and why?

Notes

1. Henry S. Williams, "The Educational Value and Health-Giving Value of Athletics," *Harper's Weekly* 39 (February 16, 1895), 165. For a similar conclusion, see Charles D. Lanier, "The World's Sporting Impulse," *Review of Reviews* 14 (July 1896), 58. For overviews of several of the subjects covered in this chapter, see Steven A. Riess, *City Games* (Urbana: University of Illinois Press, 1989), and Gerald M. Gems, *Windy City Wars: Labor, Leisure, and Sport in the Making of Chicago* (Lanham, MD: Scarecrow, 1997).
2. For the larger movement to organize and manage the spare-time activities of youth, see Joseph F. Kett, *Rites of Passage: Adolescence in America, 1790 to the Present* (New York: Basic Books, 1979); and for historiography, Stephen Hardy and A.G. Ingham, "Games, Structures and Agencies: Historians and the American Play Movement," *Journal of Social History* 17 (1983), 285–301.
3. Linda Perry and Ursula Smith, *Full-Court Quest: The Girls from Fort Shaw Indian School, Basketball Champions of the World* (Norman: University of Oklahoma Press, 2008).

4. See especially S.W. Pope, *Patriotic Games* (New York: Oxford University Press, 1997), chapters 7 and 8, and Wanda Ellen Wakefield, *Playing to Win: Sports and the American Military, 1898–1945* (Albany: State University of New York Press, 1997), chapters 1 and 2.

5. For a superb overview of sports and the media between the 1920s and 1960s, see Michael Oriard, *King Football: Sport and Spectacle in the Golden Age of Radio and Newsreels, Movies and Magazines, the Weekly & the Daily Press* (Chapel Hill: University of North Carolina Press, 2001), chapter 1. For content analysis of sport coverage in the 1890s and 1920s, see R.S. Lynd and H.M. Lynd, *Middletown* (New York: Columbia University Press, 1929), 473, and H.J. Savage et al., *American College Athletics* (New York: Carnegie Foundation, 1929), 267–72. For the predominance of male readership, see J.H. Slusser, "The Sports Page in American Life in the Nineteen-Twenties," unpub. M.A. thesis, (Berkeley: University of California, 1952), 4; James L. Baughman, *The Republic of Mass Culture* (Baltimore, MD: Johns Hopkins University Press, 1992), 11; and Oriard, *King Football*, 28.

6. *New York Herald Tribune,* October 19, 1924.

7. Quoted in B.G. Rader, *In Its Own Image: How Television Has Transformed Sports* (New York: Free Press, 1984), 28. On radio sports, see especially Curt Smith, *Voices of the Game* (South Bend, IN: Diamond Communications, 1987).

8. See Benjamin G. Rader, *American Ways* (Dallas: Harcourt Publishers, 2001), 190–92.

9. Quoted in Richard W. Fox and T.J. Jackson Lears, eds., *The Culture of Consumption* (New York: Pantheon, 1983), 32.

10. Quoted in Harold Seymour, *Baseball,* II (New York: Oxford University Press, 1970), 45–6.

11. Richard J. Moss, *Golf and the Country Club* (Urbana: University of Illinois Press, 2001), and J.F. Steiner, *Americans at Play* (New York: Arno, 1933). For a study of upper-class life in Westchester, New York, in the 1930s, see G.S. Lundberg et al., *Leisure* (New York: Macmillan, 1934).

12. H.W. Wind, *The Story of American Golf,* 3d rev. ed. (New York: Knopf, 1975), 85. See also Stephen Hardy, *How Boston Played* (Boston: Northeastern University Press, 1982), 179–85, and *Sports Illustrated,* April 11, 1994.

13. See Susan Cahn, *Coming on Strong: Gender and Sexuality in Twentieth-Century Women's Sport* (New York: The Free Press, 1994), chapter 2; Pamela Grundy and Susan Shackelford, *Shattering the Glass: The Remarkable History of Women's Basketball* (New York: The New Press, 2005), chapter 2.

14. Quoted in "Decidedly Unconquerable is Mlle. Lenglen Tennis Champion," *Literary Digest* 62 (September 13, 1919), 80.

15. *Vanity Fair,* October 1932, 71.

16. See especially Pamela Grundy, *Learning to Win: Sports, Education and Social Change in Twentieth-Century North Carolina* (Chapel Hill: University of North Carolina Press, 2001), chapter 6, and Patrick Miller, ed., *The Sporting World of the Modern South* (Urbana: University of Illinois Press, 2002), chapters 5 and 6.

17. See Mark Dyreson, "The Emergence of Consumer Culture and the Transformation of Physical Culture: American Sport in the 1920s," *Journal of Sport History* 16 (1989), 268–81.

CHAPTER 9

The Rise of Organized Youth Sports

The girls' basketball team representing Central High School, Charlotte, N.C., 1923.

LEARNING OBJECTIVES

9.1 Describe how the interests of adults, young people, and communities converged to create a thriving culture of organized youth sports throughout the United States.

9.2 Summarize the cultural and legal shifts in the work done by children and youth that led to a new focus on organized youth sports.

9.3 Explain how the concept of "muscular Christianity" led the YMCA to play a major role in the early development of youth sports programs.

9.4 Outline G. Stanley Hall's evolutionary theory of play and detail its effect on the development of youth sports.

9.5 Analyze how concerns about the moral qualities of immigrant youth helped spur the development of competitive high school sports and of the "playground movement" in major American cities.

9.6 Articulate the benefits that high school officials outside major cities found in both boys' and girls' sports.

1926 was a banner year in Hampton, Iowa—at least where school athletics was concerned. That season, Hampton's prized girls' high school basketball team played its way to the state championship, winning the first-ever state title bestowed by the Iowa High School Girls' Athletic Union. According to the school yearbook, they triumphed in dramatic fashion. "Leaving overwhelming disaster in their wake, their record unblemished by defeat, the Hampton Sextet—the demons in red—swept to a state championship," the copy read. "Handling the apple with an adroitness never seen before in girls' basketball, sacrificing personal aggrandizement for cooperative play yet playing colorfully and brilliantly, battling from the initial tip-off to the final gun, pivoting, double passing, guarding mercilessly, darting and flashing about the waxed floor like streaks of red…a greater team than this has never been assembled."[1]

By the 1920s, teams such as the Hampton High squad had made organized, competitive sports an integral part of growing up in the United States. From the playgrounds of the nation's largest cities to the fields of its most rural communities, a plethora of athletic programs introduced young people to rules, coaching, teamwork, sportsmanship, the sting of defeat, and the pleasures of victory.

An interest in using sports to mold young people into useful citizens sprang from the social shifts of the mid-nineteenth century, as the United States became a more urban, industrial society, and the circumstances of childhood changed drastically. Earlier in the nineteenth century, children had grown up almost exclusively within their family circle, passing their time by helping their parents farm, spin thread, weave cloth, make garments, fabricate tools, construct furniture, bake bread, and pursue trades. But by 1890, all save the most wretched families purchased many of their essential items in the marketplace. Fathers and sometimes mothers worked away from home, and the children were left at best with dull, routine chores, "make-work" that in the view of reformers failed to exercise their "constructive impulses in a wholesome way."

Relieving the children of productive work in the home, most youth observers believed, had fatal consequences for healthy moral growth. Habits of good conduct could best be nurtured not through moral instruction, but within a family jointly engaged in creative, essential work. "The transmission of morals is no longer safe in the family," Luther Gulick, a leading proponent of youth sports, glumly concluded, "because the activities out of which morals arise have been taken away."[2]

Increasingly, the new society also segregated teenagers from the general work force. In the early nineteenth century, children 14 or younger had been expected to leave the family and strike out on their own. Sometimes they became apprentices learning a skill, sometimes they experimented with a variety of jobs, sometimes they attended local academies. But the growing reliance on machinery gradually undermined the apprenticeship system. Countless youths were left with dead-end jobs that required few if any skills and offered even fewer opportunities for a better future. While the children of workers had no choice but to continue taking jobs in industry at a young age, middle- and upper-income parents began to direct their offspring toward the growing white-collar sector of the economy. The key to becoming a lawyer, doctor, accountant, engineer, secretary, or business manager seemed to be an extended education, lasting until age 16 or even longer. Parents who could afford to do so began to withdraw their children from the job market and send them to school.

The push by middle- and upper-class parents for longer periods of formal education coincided with the passage of state laws that had the effect of barring younger adolescents from the work force. In the first two decades of the twentieth century, most of the states, as part of the "Progressive" reform impulse, increased the length of the school term from four months to nine months, extended compulsory school attendance to the age of 14 or older, and prohibited children from working at full-time jobs until they were 14 or even 16.

The separation of teenagers from the general work force undermined a traditional source of socialization. Instead of numerous casual contacts with adults through early work experience, youths now spent most of their time in school with other youngsters or in leisure activities that were unsupervised by adults. The school tended to restrict youth–adult interaction to the highly formal student–teacher relationship. The abundance of unmanaged spare time that younger adolescents increasingly enjoyed was a cause of deep concern for parents and youth observers alike.

Profound suspicions of the burgeoning cities likewise shaped the attitudes and values of workers in the Young Men's Christian Association (YMCA) on playgrounds and in schools. Traditional social restraints seemed to evaporate in the cities. Urban children, declared one youth worker, "watch the drunken people, listen to the leader of the gang, hear the shady story, smoke cigarettes, and acquire…vicious habits, knowledge, and vocabulary."[3] Furthermore, many of these workers saw cities as the home of alien peoples who held strange beliefs and often violated the behavioral codes of old-stock Americans. Young people were thus vulnerable to a host of perversions, including "the mad rush for sudden wealth," emulation of the "reckless fashions set by gilded youth," gang membership, the "secret vice" (masturbation), and sex.

The countryside, in contrast, appeared an academy of virtue. "The country boy roams the hills and has free access to 'God's first temples,'" waxed F. D. Bonyton, the superintendent of Ithaca, New York schools in 1904. "What can we offer to the city boy in exchange for paradise lost? His only road to paradise regained is thru the gymnasium, the athletic field, and the playground."[4] Sports, many came to believe, could serve as an effective substitute for the lost rural experience.

Efforts to build character through sports began in the name of the "muscular Christianity" that had taken shape late in the nineteenth century, most notably in the YMCA. Founded by laymen in England in 1851 and subsequently transplanted to the United States, the original purpose of the YMCA had been to offer spiritual guidance and practical assistance to the young men who were flooding into nineteenth-century cities. But after the Civil War, the local YMCAs began to broaden their programs. To attract young men and boys to their spiritual work, they offered classes in "physical culture," largely in the form of gymnastics and calisthenics. Instead of young displaced males, the main clientele of the YMCAs became young men from the clerical classes (bookkeepers, stenographers, clerks, and salesmen), businessmen, a few skilled workingmen, and boys from the middle- and upper-income ranks. By 1892 the YMCA membership had grown to nearly a quarter of a million, and the organization had 348 gymnasiums directed by 144 full-time physical leaders. The Young Women's Christian Association (YWCA) provided similar services to young women.[5]

Luther Halsey Gulick Jr.

Luther Halsey Gulick Jr., who began his career with the YMCA, played a preeminent role in all phases of the adult-directed sport movement. Born of missionary parents, Gulick waged a "determined war" against the "subjective type of religion" fostered by pietistic Protestants. While he rejected the formal religious doctrines of his parents, he retained a zest for embarking on crusades. He discovered his equivalent of a spiritual calling by becoming, in turn, the champion of muscular Christianity within the YMCA, a major proponent of a new theory of play, the founder of the Public Schools Athletic League in New York City, an organizer and the first president of the Playground Association of America, a leader of the American Boy Scout movement, and the cofounder, with his wife, of the American Campfire Girls.

According to Gulick, he turned to the strenuous life partly as a way of compensating for his personal feelings of physical and psychical inadequacy. Throughout his life he suffered from severe migraine headaches, periods of dark depression, and a weak physical constitution, all of which he attributed to his father, who had been the victim of a nervous breakdown. Although Gulick obtained a medical degree, he discovered far more exciting work than medicine in 1887, when he became an instructor in the physical department of the International Young Men's Christian Association Training School (later renamed Springfield College) in Springfield, Massachusetts. Since most of the general secretaries and physical directors of local YMCAs passed through the training school's regular two-year curriculum or summer school, Gulick had found an ideal position for reaching a national and even international audience.

In the classroom, in journals he edited for the training school, in numerous articles and books, and in speeches delivered throughout the country, Gulick unrelentingly preached the same gospel: A strong spiritual life rests on the equal development of the mind and the body. Gulick invented the famous emblem of the YMCA, the inverted triangle which symbolized the spirit supported by the mind and the body. Unlike previous YMCA leaders, Gulick welcomed the introduction of sport into YMCA programs. "We can use the drawing power of athletics a great deal more than we are doing at present," he wrote in 1892, although he cautioned that "we must work along our own lines and not ape the athletic organizations, whose object is the development of specialists and the breaking of records."[6]

Under Gulick's aegis, competitive sport began to supplant gymnastics in YMCA programs. The Springfield training school itself became a model of athletic activism. Throughout the 1890s, the school fielded a baseball team. From time to time the college sponsored competition with outside institutions in track and field, swimming, gymnastics, basketball, and volleyball. Amos Alonzo Stagg, the famed Yale football player and future University of Chicago coach, enrolled at Springfield in 1890. He promptly gathered a team of faculty and students, about half of whom had never played football before, and challenged all the prominent Northeastern colleges to games. That fall, "Stagg's Stubby Christians" almost upset mighty Yale before succumbing 16 to 10 in the country's first indoor football game, played in Madison Square Garden. The vigorous sports program at Springfield and the experience of the students there inspired YMCAs everywhere to organize their own athletic teams.

While the physical curriculum of the training school continued to center on such subjects as anatomy and motor development, Gulick added a pioneering course in the psychology of play as well as training in specific sport skills. In his psychology of play course, he asked students to experiment with new games and sports that could be played in the confined space of gymnasiums and that would be appropriate to each level of maturity. Gulick's inspiration and suggestions led to James Naismith's invention of basketball in 1891, and to the invention of volleyball in 1895.

The unbridled enthusiasm of young men and adolescent boys for basketball and other forms of athletic competition soon presented the YMCA leadership with a trying dilemma. On the one hand, organized games obviously increased membership, interest, and the physical prowess of the participants. On the other hand, basketball threatened to convert the YMCAs into full-fledged athletic clubs. As early as 1892, Gulick had warned the association of the dangers of a spectator-centered orientation. Yet, by the mid-1890s, in one local YMCA after another, basketball threatened to drive all other forms of physical activity off the gymnasium floor. "In several places," Gulick reported in 1895, "the game was played with such fierceness last year, the crowds who looked on became so boisterous and rowdyish, and the bad feeling developed between teams so extreme that the game has been abolished in toto."[7] Yet most YMCAs took far less drastic steps. In 1895, the YMCA formed the Athletic League of North America with Gulick as secretary. To curtail excesses, the league joined the Amateur Athletic Union, published a monthly newsletter, and developed an extensive body of rules and sanctions.

Ultimately, the league failed to ensure the "purity" of YMCA athletic programs. By 1905, YMCA teams regularly played more than 2,000 games with outside competitors. In their contests with the collegians and athletic clubs, the Y athletes enjoyed remarkable success. For example, for more than a dozen years the Buffalo German YMCA team dominated championship basketball. They won the Buffalo Exposition tournament in 1901 and took the gold medal at the 1904 Olympic Games in St. Louis. Eventually, much to the relief of YMCA officials, the Buffalo "five" became an avowed professional team.

The spirit of rivalry, athletic specialization, and professional tendencies of YMCA athletics equaled those of the athletic clubs and the colleges. Local Ys, despite the repeated admonitions of the Athletic League officials, were guilty of extending to star athletes special privileges such as free memberships, room and board, and generous traveling allowances to compete away from home. Many of the local secretaries and physical directors tried to resist "excessive" athleticism, but others capitulated to the demands of their membership.

In 1911, several years after Gulick had left the YMCA, the association changed the entire focus of its athletic programs. Henry F. Kallenberg, the new physical director at Springfield, recommended a radical break from past practices. The Y, Kallenberg argued, should promote a comprehensive sport program that would reach the "mass of young men and boys, [and] discourage prize winning and over-training."[8] Competition should be restricted to males of a similar age and weight and focus on local teams. At Kallenberg's initiative, the league severed its relationship with the AAU and began to organize local amateur athletic federations composed of Ys, high schools, churches, Turners, and other groups. By 1920, the YMCA had essentially completed Kallenberg's reform agenda. Never again would the Ys attempt to compete at championship levels in athletics.

The Evolutionary Theory of Play

In the 1890s, G. Stanley Hall, a pioneer in genetic psychology at Clark University, began to work with Gulick, once a student at Hall's summer school, to develop an evolutionary theory of play that would exercise an immense influence on every phase of early twentieth-century youth work, especially for boys. Hall and Gulick believed that humans had acquired the fundamental impulse to play during the evolution of the "race." Each person, as he or she passed from birth to adulthood, recapitulated or rehearsed in an approximate way each epoch or stage of human evolution. The play activities of early childhood—spontaneous kicking and squirming in infancy and running and throwing when a bit older—corresponded to the play of primal ancestors. The track, field, and tag games common to children between the ages of seven and 12 sprang from the hunting instinct acquired during the "presavage" stage of evolution. Games at this stage were individualistic. Finally, complex group games—baseball, basketball, football, and cricket—rested on a combination of the earlier hunting instinct and the new instinct of cooperation, the latter having emerged during the "savage" epoch of evolution, when savages hunted and fought in groups while subordinating themselves to the leadership of a chief.

Hall and Gulick postulated that each person had to recapitulate the history of the race through sports in order to promote proper physical, moral, and neural growth. Complex motor behavior became "reflexive" through repetition. Bountiful physical activity in childhood not only developed muscles but also spurred the growth of neural centers in spinal cord and brain. Directed motor behavior was also the primary agency in shaping what Gulick called moral "reflexes," or what might be viewed more popularly as the conscience. When young people repeated the evolution of the race via games, they engaged in physical activities that embodied moral principles and encouraged their development. Too often, however, the instincts from which group games sprang could result in the ripening of wicked reflexes. It could encourage the formation of juvenile gangs—"the most perilous force in modern civilization"—rather than team contests supervised by adults.[9] Team sport thus offered an unparalleled opportunity for adults to encourage the healthy growth of moral and religious reflexes. Stemming from the instinct for cooperation, team sports required the highest moral principles—teamwork, self-sacrifice, obedience, self-control, and loyalty.

In one version or another, the evolutionary theory of play became part of the conventional wisdom of youth workers in the first two decades of the twentieth century. G. Stanley Hall repeated it almost verbatim in his classic two-volume work on adolescence published in 1905. Joseph Lee, a prolific writer on play, took as his major premise the notion that play arose from an earlier stage of man's evolution, from the "barbaric and predatory society to which the boy naturally belongs." Henry S. Curtis, a pioneer in both the playground and Boy Scout movements, wrote that athletics "are the activities of our ancestors conventionalized and adapted to present conditions. They are reminiscent of the physical age, of the struggle for survival, of the hunt, of the chase, and of war." William Forbush, an ardent disciple of Gulick and Hall, a Congregationalist minister, and a leader in the Boy Scout movement, may have reached the largest audience of all in his advice manual *The Boy Problem*, reprinted eight times between 1901 and 1912. Each boy, Forbush wrote, repeated the "history of his race-life from savagery unto civilization."[10]

The acceptance of an evolutionary theory of play had important implications for the use of sport as a socializing agency. First, it seemed to require the creation of special institutions that would be closely supervised by adults. Unregulated activity would fail to encourage desirable social traits. Second, the theory encouraged workers to relinquish the extreme forms of piety associated with the evangelical temperament and emphasize activity at the expense of spirituality or intellectuality. Accordingly, the YMCA became increasingly secular in its programs. Many of the "institutional" or "social gospel" Protestant churches in the larger cities abandoned explicitly spiritual programs in favor of organized activities ranging from dances to baseball matches. Beginning in Brooklyn in 1904, one city after another organized Sunday School athletic leagues. In 1916, through the creation of the Boys' Brigade, Catholics also joined the movement.[11] Third, the play theory permitted workers to subordinate ethnic, religious, and social class differences to a presumably universal experience of maturation. They saw no need to fashion special programs for distinctive social or cultural groups.

Finally, evolutionary theory furnished a rationale for the sexual segregation of organized play, a rationale that would influence youth workers and physical educators until the middle of the twentieth century. They assumed that males and females had acquired distinct instincts or propensities over the course of human evolution. Of utmost importance to survival for males had been an adeptness in fighting, hunting, and running—activities recapitulated in the games of boys. Those females, on the other hand, who had become most adept in caring for the home were more likely to survive and produce offspring. "So it is clear," wrote Gulick in 1920, "that athletics have never been either a test or a large factor in the survival of women; athletics do not test womanliness as they test manliness." Hall opined that a woman "performs her best service in her true role of sympathetic spectator rather than as a fellow player."[12]

The Public Schools Athletic League

In the first two decades of the twentieth century, Gulick, Hall, and their followers found ample opportunities to put their theory of play into practice. After leaving the YMCA training school in 1900 and serving for three years as principal of Pratt Institute High School in Brooklyn, Gulick became the director of physical training of the public schools of Greater New York City in 1903. Rather than relying exclusively on traditional gymnastics and calisthenics to nurture physical and moral growth, Gulick quickly determined that "*all* the boys in the city needed the physical benefits and moral and social lessons afforded by properly conducted games and sport."[13] Consequently, he formed the Public Schools Athletic League (PSAL) in 1903. Although the PSAL was financially independent of the school system, it depended upon the city's 630 schools for implementing its program. It won the immediate plaudits of the city's press and the endorsement of such czars of industry and finance as Andrew Carnegie, John D. Rockefeller, J. Pierpont Morgan, S. R. Guggenheim, and Henry Payne Whitney, who contributed generously to the league's finances.

Underlying the enthusiastic reception of the league was a manifest fear of the city's foreign-born population. The founders were not only concerned with the absence of play experience for immigrant youths, recalled General George W. Wingate, the long-time president of the league, but they "also found the morals of the boys were deteriorating even more than their bodies."[14] School boys often joined street gangs and defied the authority of their teachers. Above all, ethnic youngsters seemed not to understand American values and institutions. A carefully managed sport program, the founders believed, would reduce juvenile delinquency and "Americanize" the ethnic youth of the ghettos. By 1910, the PSAL was hailed as the "world's greatest athletic organization," and had at least 17 imitators in other large American cities. In 1905, the league added a Girls' Branch, although unlike the boys' division, it did not permit public interschool competition.[15]

"Duty," "Thoroughness," "Patriotism," "Honor," and "Obedience"—these were the official watchwords of the Public Schools Athletic League. To inculcate such values, the league consciously exploited the athletic interests of the students. Each year General Wingate wrote an open letter to the boys warning them of a host of dangers that might adversely affect their athletic performances. Above all, "you must keep out of bad influences of the street if you want to be strong," he wrote. While it may be doubted that Wingate's advice had much influence on the behavior of the boys while they were away from school, the teachers quickly recognized that the PSAL could be used effectively to promote discipline in the classroom. "All of the little imps in my class have become saints," wrote one teacher, "not because they want to be saints, but because they want to compete in your games." No student could compete without a certification from his teachers that his deportment and class performance had been satisfactory. Peer group pressure also encouraged student conformity. "Many a big, vigorous boy out of sympathy with his school work," reported another source, "is driven to his lessons by his mates so that he can be eligible to represent his school."[16]

Perhaps it was little wonder that the city's teachers volunteered to spend long hours after school and on weekends in planning and supervising every aspect of the league's program. The improvement by the student "on the side of ethics, school discipline, and *esprit de corps* is even greater" than in athletic proficiency, concluded a report in 1910.[17]

The Playground Movement

The early twentieth-century movement for city playgrounds furnished Gulick and his followers with even broader opportunities for implementing their evolutionary theory of play.[18] Before 1900, a few private citizens and charity groups had organized playgrounds—usually consisting of sandpiles and simple play equipment—for preadolescent children in the slums of the larger cities. A turning point came in 1903 when the voters of the Chicago South Park district approved a $5 million bond issue for the construction of ten parks. Unlike previous efforts, the Chicago system included field houses at each park with a gymnasium for both boys and girls.

The Chicago authorities hired a professional physical educator, Edward B. de Groot, as director and furnished each park with two year-round instructors to supervise play activities. The managers of the new system sponsored a host of activities ranging from organized athletic leagues to community folk dances. Inspired by the Chicago example, middle- and upper-income taxpayers around the country exhibited a remarkable enthusiasm for supervised recreation programs. Between 1906 and 1917 the number of cities with managed playgrounds grew from 41 to 504.

The same concerns and values that shaped the PSAL also guided the work of playground leaders. The evolutionary theory of play furnished them with ready-made formulas for supervising playgrounds. For example, among the questions on the standard examination administered to all candidates for employment with the New York playgrounds was "What is meant by the 'club or gregarious instinct'? How can it be developed and utilized with beneficial results on the playground? What athletic events are appropriate for boys aged 10–14?...for boys aged 14 to 16?"[19] Not only were prospective playground leaders expected to master the principles and practical implications of play theory, they were also expected to exercise the subtle psychological techniques essential for managing youth without resorting to harsh repression. The playground leaders abhorred the unsupervised, unstructured play that arose from the spontaneous impulses of children. Henry S. Curtis, in the leading textbook for playground supervisors, wrote that "scrub play," that is, play that the children themselves initiated, "can never give that training either of body or conduct, which organized play should give; for in order to develop the body, it must be vigorous, to train the intellect, it must be exciting, to train the social conscience, it must be socially organized. None of these results come from scrub play."[20]

Despite the enthusiasm of municipal governments for organized recreation, however, the playgrounds usually failed to extend their control over spare-time activities to those who presumably needed it the most—the immigrant population. According to the sweeping claims of the playground leaders, supervised recreation sharply reduced the incidence of juvenile delinquency. But even Henry Curtis, one of the movement's most prominent leaders, admitted that less than 10 percent of urban youngsters regularly used available playgrounds. The playgrounds appealed most to the children of old-stock families of the middle- and upper-income ranks, youngsters who had already been shaped by the values espoused by recreation leaders. Working class youth tended to admire physical prowess—particularly as expressed in street fighting—spontaneity, and defiance of authority rather than the values of self-restraint and cooperation so dear to the playground leaders.

Public High School Sports

The institution that wove athletics most deeply into the nation's cultural fabric was the comprehensive high school, which spread throughout the country in the first decades of the twentieth century. Between 1909 and 1920, the percentage of high school-aged youngsters enrolled in high school more than doubled, going from 14 to 31 percent. By 1930, it was approaching 50 percent.[21] The proponents of the comprehensive high school shared many of the perceptions and ideas of their predecessors in youth work. They believed that modern industrial life had eroded the traditional socializing institutions. According to *The Cardinal Principles of Secondary Education,* "In connection with the home and family life have frequently come lessened responsibility on the part of the children; the withdrawal of the father and sometimes the mother from home occupations to the factory or store; and increased urbanization resulting in less unified family life. Similarly, many important changes have taken place in community life, in the church, in the State, and in other institutions. These changes in American life call for extensive modifications in secondary education."[22]

To meet these changes, the committee recommended that high schools seek to teach students (and sometimes their parents) the social values essential for coping with modern life. By social values the committee meant "those common ideas, common ideals, and common modes of thought, feeling, and action that make for cooperation, social cohesion, and social solidarity." Like Gulick, the social educators believed that activity rather than the teaching of moral precepts was the key to developing good character. Thus, they asked that the high school give special attention to the "participation of pupils in common activities…such as athletic games, social activities, and the government of the school."[23]

As high schools started sports programs, leaders quickly saw other benefits: High school sports created broad enthusiasm and support, not only among students, but also within communities as a whole. Across the country, crowds flocked to newly built high school football fields and crowded into crackerbox gymnasiums to cheer on their youthful athletes in their defense of community honor. In 1923, a writer in *North Carolina Education* touched on the significance of sports, suggesting that a school newspaper might be used to spark interest "in any undertaking of the school," but also noting that "This is particularly true in athletics. Announcements of contests, accounts of games, stories about the individual players, will do a great deal towards arousing enthusiasm and creating school spirit which can be done through athletics as in no other way."[24]

While the leaders of the play movement had focused most of their concern on boys, the spread of sports into high schools offered new opportunities for girls. Inspired by the political and social strides they saw around them, young women stepped eagerly into the athletic fray. In 1920, the year that women gained the right to vote, a group of female students trooped to the principal's office at Central High School in Charlotte, N.C., and announced that they were forming a girls' basketball team. "We had played together; we were friends," recalled team member Mary Dalton. "So we just decided we wanted to have a basketball team and we said: 'We'll be it.' " Beneath their year-book picture, the new team proudly announced: "Man's age has been heretofore, but now woman's age is coming in, not only in politics but in athletics."[25]

At other schools, coaches started teams for their female students. Iowa coach G.L. Sanders explained his conversion to his female students' cause in a 1948 article. From 1912 to 1920, Sanders wrote, "I spent so much time with the boys…that I didn't pay much attention to girls' basketball. Then suddenly it dawned on me that less than half of my high school enrollment was being provided with the privilege of participation in any sort of supervised athletics. So I began encouraging the girls in my school to play the game." Sanders joined with a group of other coaches to found the Iowa Girls' High School Athletic Union, which became one of the strongest women's athletic associations in the country.[26]

Conclusion

In the early decades of the twentieth century, concerns about the moral development of young people in an industrializing and urbanizing society led to the creation of a wide range of youth athletic programs, ranging from YMCA development to playground building to varsity high school sports. Many of these athletic programs would face the same set of challenges as college programs, particularly regarding the drive to win at any cost. But like college programs, they would continue to expand, making organized, competitive sports an integral part of an American childhood.

Critical Thinking Questions

1. Efforts to promote youth sport often highlighted differences between the interests of the adults who organized youth sports and the young people who participated in them. Which set of interests do you think prevailed and why?
2. Based on your own experience growing up, what do you think of G. Stanley Hall's "evolutionary theory of play"?
3. What does the growth of youth sport tell us about the process by which cultural institutions such as high school sports take shape?

Notes

1. *The "H"*, 1926, n.p. For a more detailed description of the development of girls' basketball in Iowa, see Janice Beran, *From Six on Six to Full Court Press: A Century of Iowa Girls' Basketball* (Ames, Iowa: Iowa State University Press, 1993).
2. L.H. Gulick, *A Philosophy of Play* (New York: Scribner's, 1920), 219. For the larger movement to organize and manage the spare-time activities of youth, see Joseph F. Kett, *Rites of Passage: Adolescence in America, 1790 to the Present* (New York: Basic Books, 1979); and for historiography, Stephen Hardy and A.G. Ingham, "Games, Structures and Agencies: Historians and the American Play Movement," *Journal of Social History* 17 (1983), 285–301.

3. Henry S. Curtis, *The Play Movement and Its Significance* (New York: Macmillan, 1917), 119–20.

4. F.D. Bonyton, "Athletics and Collateral Activities of Secondary Schools," *Proceedings and Addresses of the National Education Association* (1904), 210.

5. L.H. Gulick, "Young Men in the Cities, II," *Athletic League Letters* (February 1899); Paul Boyer, *Urban Masses and Moral Order in America 1820–1920* (Cambridge, MA: Harvard University Press, 1978), 115–16; L.W. Fielding and C.F. Wood, "The Social Control of Indolence and Irreligion: Louisville's First YMCA Movement, 1853–1871," *Folsom Club Historical Quarterly* 58 (1984), 219–36. See also Clifford Putney, *Muscular Christianity: Manhood and Sports in Protestant America, 1880–1920* (Cambridge, MA: Harvard University Press, 2001), and Tony Ladd and James A. Mathisen, *Muscular Christianity: Evangelical Protestants and the Development of American Sport* (Grand Rapids, MI: Baker Books, 1999).

6. L.H. Gulick, "State Committees on Athletics," *Young Men's Era* 18 (1892), 1365.

7. L.H. Gulick, "Basket Ball," *Physical Education* 4 (1895), 1200. See also L.H. Gulick, "Abolish Basket Ball," *Men* 5 (1897), 687.

8. Athletic League Letters (June 1911), 1. In addition to *Athletic League Letters* (1896–1911), see W.H. Ball, "The Administration of Athletics in the Young Men's Christian Association," *American Physical Education Review* 16 (1911), 12–22.

9. L.H. Gulick, "Psychological, Pedagogical, and Religious Aspects of Group Games," *Pedagogical Seminary* 6 (1899); L.H. Gulick, "Psychical Aspects of Muscular Exercise," *Popular Science Monthly* 53 (1898), 793–805; and L.H. Gulick "The Psychology of Play," *Association Outlook* 8 (1899), 112–16.

10. G.S. Hall, *Adolescence*, 2 vols. (New York: D. Appleton, 1905), I, 202–03; Joseph Lee, *Play and Education* (New York: Macmillan, 1915); 234; Henry S. Curtis, "The Proper Relation of Organized Sports on Public Playgrounds and in Public Spaces," *Playground* 3 (1909); 14; W.B. Forbush, *The Boy Problem* (Boston: Pilgrim, 1901), 9.

11. See G.D. Pratt, "The Sunday School Athletic League," *Work with Boys* 4 (1905), 131–37, and "Recreation in the Church," *Literary Digest* 53 (1916), 256.

12. Gulick, "A Philosophy of Play," 92; Hall, *Adolescence*, I, 207.

13. L.H. Gulick, "Athletics for School Children," *Lippincott's Monthly Magazine*, 99 (1911), 201.

14. G.W. Wingate, "The Public Schools Athletic League," *Outing* 52 (1908), 166.

15. A.B. Reeve, "The World's Greatest Athletic Organization," *Outing* 57 (1910), 107–14. See also J.T. Jable, "The Public Schools Athletic League of New York City: Organized Athletics for City Schoolchildren, 1903–1914," in S.A. Riess, ed., *The American Sporting Experience* (West Point, NY: Leisure, 1984), 219–38.

16. Quotations from ibid., 169; Reeve, "The World's Greatest Athletic Organization," 110; and C.A. Perry, *Wider Use of the School Plant* (New York: Charities Pub. Com., 1910), 308.

17. Reeve, "The World's Greatest Athletic Organization," 108.

18. See the literature cited in Hardy and Ingham, "Games, Structures and Agencies."

19. "Questions for Teachers to Answer," *Gymnasia* 2 (1906), 149.

20. Curtis, *The Play Movement*, 81.

21. U.S. Department of Education, "120 Years of American Education: A Statistical Portrait" (Washington, DC: National Center for Education Statistics, 1993), 26–7.

22. *Cardinal Principles of Secondary Education* Bul., 35 (Washington, DC: GPO, 1918), 7–8.

23. Quotations in ibid., 21, 23.

24. *North Carolina Education* 18 (February 1923), 13.

25. Pamela Grundy, "From Amazons to Glamazons: The Rise and Fall of North Carolina Women's Basketball, 1920-1960," *Journal of American History* 87 (June 2000), 115–16.

26. *Iowa Girls Basketball Yearbook* 1948, 31.

CHAPTER 10

The Age of Sports Heroes

Boxer Jack Johnson spars with an opponent.

LEARNING OBJECTIVES

10.1 Explain how different sports heroes served different social needs in the first half of the twentieth century.

10.2 Summarize the principal qualities Americans admired in sports heroes of the first half of the twentieth century, and explain how those qualities related to the realities of life and work in that era.

10.3 Analyze the particular significance that Jack Johnson's boxing victories held for African Americans, the stereotype he broke, and the fears he aroused in white leaders.

10.4 Outline the sources of Babe Ruth's appeal to a broad American public, taking into account his personality, his athletic abilities, and the way his career was promoted.

10.5 Describe how the combination of Jack Dempsey's talents and Tex Rickard's promotional skills built a controversial individual into a sporting hero.

10.6 Articulate the sources of Helen Wills' appeal and the ways that her successes helped create a new version of athletic womanhood.

In the first decades of the twentieth century, as American sports expanded, popular culture began to fill with sports heroes, larger-than-life figures who sparked widespread admiration and whose actions often held a significance that reached beyond the sporting realm. From boxer Jack Johnson to baseball phenomenon George Herman "Babe" Ruth to tennis player Helen Wills, all these athletes embodied American dreams, and at times sparked sharp debates.

Why sports idols? Part of the interest sprang from savvy salesmanship. The same skill and shrewd promotion that successfully hawked automobiles, breakfast foods, and lipstick also sold athletes to the public. Behind the sport heroes stood professional pitchmen: George "Tex" Rickard, Jack "Doc" Kearns, Charles C. "Cash and Carry" Pyle, and Christy Walsh, to name a few. Then there were the journalists and radio broadcasters such as Grantland Rice and Graham McNamee who created heroic images of athletes that often overshadowed actual achievements.

Yet the public idolization of athletes went deeper than the skillful ballyhooing of the promoters and journalistic flights of fancy. Towering home runs, forceful knockout punches, and overnight athletic successes provided a tantalizing alternative to the increasingly complicated and bureaucratic world within which growing numbers of Americans passed their lives. For Americans relegated to the margins of society—most notably Americans of African descent—stars such as Jack Johnson or Joe Louis challenged demeaning stereotypes that had become an entrenched part of American culture. Female stars such as Helen Wills expanded understanding of women's capabilities.

Athletic idols were also part of a new popular culture that emerged in the early decades of the century. In an age of mass consumption and burgeoning bureaucracies, this culture presented the public with a complex set of alternative images, fantasies, and myths. Some were comic: Charlie Chaplin was the carefree little tramp who eluded cops, bullies, and pompous officials, and even outwitted machines. Some were independent: Mary Pickford played strong-willed young women who cheerfully defied both tragedy and convention. Some were dashing and romantic: Douglas Fairbanks slashed his way through hordes of villains. Still others vaulted quickly to the top. In nineteenth-century drama and fiction, the hero won the hand of the rich man's daughter through his virtuous character. Rudolph Valentino won her through his irresistible physical charm.

Images of power and instant success flourished in the world of sports. In sports—or so it seemed—one could still catapult to fame and fortune without the benefits of years of arduous training or acquiescence to the demanding requirements of bureaucracies. Achievement in the world of sports was also unambiguous, measured precisely in home runs, knockouts, touchdowns, victories, and even salaries. Those standing on the assembly lines and those sitting at their desks in the bureaucracies seem to have found the greatest satisfaction in the athletic hero who presented an image of all-conquering power. They preferred the towering home runs of Babe Ruth to the "inside" strategy of base hits, steals, and sacrifices personified by Ty Cobb; they favored the smashing knockout blows of Jack Dempsey over the "scientific" boxing skills displayed by Gene Tunney. Perhaps it was little wonder that children traded dreams of business success for those of athletic stardom.[1]

Jack Johnson: Smashing Race Stereotypes

The twentieth century's first transformative athletic hero—prizefighter Jack Johnson—also proved its most controversial. In 1908, at the heart of one of the darkest periods of African American life, Johnson smashed through the color line to take the world's most prestigious athletic title—the Heavyweight Boxing Championship. His achievements heartened African Americans, who celebrated his victories around the country. But the challenge he posed to the reigning ideology of white supremacy deeply troubled many whites.

Trouble was nothing new for Johnson, whose rough-and-tumble youth taught him the value of both toughness and persistence. Born in the port town of Galveston, Texas, he did much of his early fighting in "battles royal," in which a group of boys fought over nickels and pennies until only one was left standing. No one was tougher in a fight than Johnson. But he also developed a radiant smile and a potent charisma that would serve him well as he rose through the boxing ranks. While some fans and promoters shunned him for his color, his skill, charm—and earning potential—won others over.[2]

Johnson got a shot at the championship under unusual circumstances. Starting with John L. Sullivan, heavyweight champions had "drawn the color line," refusing to meet black challengers. Australian Tommy Burns, the reigning champion in 1908, sought to do the same, declining to schedule a match with Johnson even after Johnson had bested all other potential contenders. Unwilling to accept Burns' decision, Johnson literally pursued him around the world, issuing challenges as he went. Money finally won out. Hugh McIntosh, a wealthy Australian businessman, guaranteed Burns $30,000 to fight Johnson, win or lose. It was a purse far larger than for any previous prizefight. Johnson was to receive $5,000.

Burns also underestimated Johnson. Black fighters were dogged by a set of stereotypes that meshed neatly with the assumptions of white supremacy: Whites assumed that black fighters reasoned slowly, easily lost control of their emotions, and lacked the courage to prevail in tough contests. Earlier in 1908, Burns had dismissed Johnson and other black fighters with the flat statement: "All coons are yellow." That miscalculation proved his downfall. In front of an enormous, largely hostile crowd in Sydney, Australia, Johnson toyed easily with the much smaller fighter, keeping him at a distance for 14 rounds before closing in to knock him out.

Almost at once, ex-champions, fight promoters, and newspapermen launched a hunt for a "Great White Hope" to retake the crown from Johnson. As Johnson disposed of several second-rate contenders, the demand grew for James J. Jeffries, a popular former heavyweight champion, to come out of retirement and rid boxing of the "black menace." Finally, in 1910, Jeffries agreed to battle Johnson at Reno, Nevada. Jeffries himself interpreted the fight in racial terms. "That portion of the white race that has been looking for me to defend its athletic superiority may feel assured," he said, "that I am fit to do my very best."[3] Jeffries's very best, however, was far from enough. In a contest in which the outcome was never in doubt, Johnson knocked Jeffries out in the 15th round (in the early twentieth century, prizefights were filmed and the film rights sold, so fighters had an incentive to prolong fights in order to increase the films' earning potential).

African Americans celebrated Johnson's victories in newspaper articles, popular songs, and in the streets, where large crowds gathered to listen to reports of the contest. This pride, however, came at a price. Johnson might be able to bloody white men, but other African Americans more often found themselves on the receiving end of violence. Musician Louis Armstrong recalled being a 10-year-old on the streets of New Orleans when a group of black youngsters came running toward him and yelled "You better get started, black boy. Jack Johnson has just knocked out Jim Jeffries. The white boys are sore about it and they're going to take it out on us." Riots broke out across the country, and at least eight people lost their lives.[4]

The violence testified to the significance of Johnson's victory. To both whites and African Americans, Johnson's ascension to the heavyweight throne possessed incalculable symbolic significance. In the most primeval of American sports, the ultimate metaphor of masculine conflict, the best of the black men had defeated the best of the white men. Newspaper columnist Max Balthazer wrote of the prospective Jeffries—Johnson fight: "Can the huge white man [Jeffries]…beat down the wonderful black and restore to the Caucasians the crown of elemental greatness as measured by strength of blow, power of heart and being, and, withal, that cunning or keenness that denotes mental as well as physical superiority?"[5]

The holes that Johnson's victories punched in the idea of white superiority posed particular concern for supporters of the nation's unequal racial order. While Johnson did not participate in organized efforts for greater racial justice in America, whites worried that his feats might inspire other African Americans to challenge white supremacy. After the fight, for example, an editorial entitled "A Word to the Black Man" appeared in the *Los Angeles Times* "Do not point your nose too high," the *Times* warned. "Do not swell your chest too much. Do not boast too loudly…Remember, you have done nothing at all. You are just the same member of society today you were last week…You are on no higher plane, deserve no new consideration, and will get none…No man will think a bit higher of you because your complexion is the same as that of the victor at Reno."[6]

Johnson fanned those flames with his behavior. In an age in which racial ani-mosity had reached a fever pitch, he exacerbated deep-set white fears. In the ring, while smiling broadly, he badgered, taunted, and jeered his white opponents. He was a big spender who loved the high life—flashy dress, champagne, night clubs, fast cars, and women. Most important, he defied the nation's greatest racial taboo; he married three white women and slept with many others. As well as frightening whites, his actions also worried black leaders who believed that racial advancement rested on proving that blacks could demonstrate the self-control and moral restraint that would mark them as "civilized" rather than as "savages."

A concerted effort began to put Johnson out of the limelight. Local and state governments barred the showing of the Johnson–Jeffries fight films in American theaters; in 1912, Congress cooperated by prohibiting the transportation in inter-state commerce of all moving pictures of boxing matches. Johnson himself became the target of legal attacks. In 1912, a federal grand jury charged Johnson with vio-lating the Mann Act of 1910, which forbade transporting women across state lines for "immoral purposes." Belle Shreiber, formerly a prostitute at the fancy Everleigh Club in Chicago, testified that she had been paid by Johnson to engage in "immoral" and "unnatural" acts during the pair's travels about the country. In 1913, a Chicago jury found Johnson guilty, and the judge sentenced him to jail for one year and a day. During the stay of execution to appeal the decision, Johnson jumped bail and fled the country, first to Canada and then to Europe.[7]

While Johnson toured in Europe and then South America, the search continued in the United States for a new "Great White Hope." In 1915, with World War I raging in Europe, Johnson met Jess Willard in Havana, Cuba. Willard knocked him out in the 26th round. Johnson later claimed that he threw the match in return for $50,000 and an exemption from his prison sentence. A photograph of Johnson on the canvas during the knockout lends some credence to his claim; the champion appears to have raised his glove over his face to shield his eyes from the blinding Havana sun. However, boxing authorities present at the fight and Randy Roberts, Johnson's biographer, have concluded that Johnson was indeed the victim of a genuine knockout.[8]

In any case, American officials refused to rescind the sentence. In 1920, Johnson returned to the United States and served his time at Fort Leavenworth prison. Later he performed in vaudeville, gave temperance lectures, appeared in a few fights, and engaged in sparring exhibitions. In 1946, he died from injuries suffered in an auto-mobile accident.

Although the hostility he faced cut short his career, Johnson nonetheless worked a major transformation on American culture. Prior to Johnson's victories blacks had been considered inferior to whites in every way: physical as well as mental. A number of nineteenth-century "scientists" had in fact claimed that African Americans would prove unable to survive outside of slavery, and would die out before the century was up. While Johnson's victories did not shatter all those stereotypes, they forced whites to regroup, an effect captured in remarks by adventure novelist Rex Beach. "[Johnson] demonstrated further that his race has acquired full stature as men," Beach wrote of Johnson's victory over Jeffries, although he was careful to add: "whether they will ever breed brains to match his muscle is yet to be seen."[9]

African Americans themselves often viewed Johnson's victories more broadly, noting that it took far more than brawn to get as far as Johnson did. William Pickens, a professor at Talladega College in Alabama, summed up the Johnson–Jeffries fight, as well as the violence that followed, in expansive terms. "It was a good deal better for Johnson to win and a few negroes be killed in body for it, than for Johnson to have lost and negroes to have been killed in spirit by the preachments of inferiority from the combined white press," he wrote. "The fact of the fight will outdo a mountain peak of theory about the negro as a physical man—and as a man of self-control and courage."[10]

Babe Ruth: Extraordinary Success

As World War I ended, and the Roaring Twenties began, a far less controversial group of athletic heroes made their way onto the public stage. Chief among them stood George Herman "Babe" Ruth. No modern athletic hero exceeded Babe Ruth's capacity to project multiple images of brute power, the natural, uninhibited man, and the fulfillment of the American success dream. Ruth was living proof that the lone individual could still rise from mean, vulgar beginnings to reach not only fame and fortune, but also a position of public recognition equaled by few men in American history. With nothing but his bat, Ruth revolutionized the national game of baseball. His mighty home runs represented a dramatic finality, a total clearing of the bases with one mighty swat.[11]

Everything about Ruth was extraordinary—his size, strength and coordination, his appetite for the things of the flesh, even his salary. He transcended the world of ordinary mortals, and yet he was the most mortal of men. He loved playing baseball, swearing, playing practical jokes, eating, drinking, and having sex. Despite his gross crudities, wrote big-league umpire Billy Evans, "Ruth is a big, likeable kid. He has been well named, Babe. Ruth has never grown up and probably never will. Success on the ball field has in no way changed him. Everybody likes him. You just can't help it."[12]

Ruth saw himself as a prime example of the classic American success story. "The greatest thing about this country," he said in his ghostwritten autobiography, "is the wonderful fact that it doesn't matter which side of the tracks you were born on, or whether you're homeless or homely or friendless. The chance is still there. I know."[13] Ruth encouraged the legend that he had been an orphaned child. While the story had no basis in fact, his early years were indeed grim. His saloonkeeping father and sickly mother had no time for the boy; he received little or no parental affection. By his own admission, he became a "bad kid," who smoked, chewed tobacco, and engaged in petty thievery. At the age of seven, his parents sent him to the St. Mary's Industrial Home for Boys, an institution in Baltimore run by the Xaverian Order for orphans, young indigents, and delinquents. Except for brief interludes at home, Ruth spent the next 12 years at St. Mary's. There, as a teenager, he won a reputation for his baseball prowess. In 1914, he signed a professional contract with the Baltimore Orioles of the International League. That same year the Boston Red Sox purchased him as a left-handed pitcher.

Ruth never struggled for success in baseball. For him, both pitching and hitting were natural talents rather than acquired skills. Converted from a top pitching star to an outfielder, Ruth surprised the world of baseball in 1919 by hitting

29 home runs, two more than the existing major-league record that had been set in a crackerbox ball park in 1884. Traded to the New York Yankees in 1920, he followed with a stunning total of 54 four baggers, which was a larger number than any entire major league team had compiled. For Ruth, this was only the beginning. From 1918 through 1934 he led the American League in homers 12 times with an average of more than 40 a season; from 1926 through 1931 he averaged slightly more than 50 home runs per season. For every 11.7 times at bat, he hit a round tripper, an individual record that stood until the great hitting barrage of the 1990s. In addition, Ruth hit for an exceptionally high average. His lifetime mark of .342 has been equaled by few players in baseball history.

The public responded to Ruth's feats with overwhelming enthusiasm. Before Ruth, the Yankees' best annual attendance had been 600,000. With him, the team drew more than a million every year. Everywhere in the league, the fans poured out to the ballparks to see the Yankees play, apparently caring little whether the home team won or lost, only hoping to witness the Babe hammer a pitch out of the park. Even Ruth's mighty swings that failed to connect brought forth a chorus of awed "Oooooooohs," as the audience realized the enormous power that had gone to waste and the narrow escape that the pitcher had temporarily enjoyed. Each day, millions of Americans turned to the sports page of the newspaper to see if Ruth had hit another homer.[14]

The connotations associated with Ruth's home-run blasts ran counter to the increasingly dominant world of bureaucracies, scientific management, and "organization men." Ruth was the antithesis of science and rationality. Baseball's previous great batter, Ty Cobb, relied upon "brains rather than brawn," upon, as he put it, the "hit-and-run, the steal and double-steal, the bunt in all its varieties, the squeeze, the ball hit to the opposite field and the ball punched through openings in the defense for a single." Ruth, on the other hand, swung for the fences. According to sportswriter F. C. Lane in 1921, Ruth "throws science itself to the wind and hews out a rough path for himself by the sheer weight of his own unequaled talents."[15] No ulterior motives seemed to tarnish his pure love of the game.

The Ruthian image also ran counter to Victorian mores. Ruth's appetite for the things of the flesh was legendary. He drank heroic quantities of bootleg liquor; his hotel suite was always well stocked with beer and whiskey. People watched him eat with awe; he sometimes ate as many as 18 eggs for breakfast and washed them down with seven or eight bottles of soda pop. Ruth was not only the "Sultan of Swat," he was also a sultan of the bedroom. In each town on the spring training tours and in each big-league city Ruth always found a bevy of willing female followers.[16]

Ruth's propensity for immediate gratification had its more endearing side. He won a deserved reputation for loving children. Everywhere he went, children flocked to him, and he regularly visited them in hospitals. The public also adored Ruth for his crude egalitarianism. He deferred to no one. Introduced, for instance, to President Calvin Coolidge, he responded: "Hi, Pres. How are you?" According to one story, possibly apocryphal, while Ruth was holding out for a higher salary in 1930, someone pointed out to him that a depression existed and that he was asking for more money than President Herbert Hoover earned. "What the hell has Hoover got to do with it?" Ruth demanded. "Besides, I had a better year than he did."[17]

Ruth's huge earnings added to his heroic stature. From the time Ruth set his first homerun record in 1919, he was besieged by commercial opportunities outside of baseball. Since the early days of the game, star players had supplemented their salaries by product endorsements, vaudeville acts, and personal appearances, but no player had the opportunities that became available to Ruth. In the winter of 1921, Christy Walsh, a sports cartoonist turned business agent, convinced Ruth to permit him to handle the demand by newspapers for Ruth's "personal analysis" of each home run that he hit. For 15 years Walsh employed a stable of ghostwriters, among them Ford Frick, future commissioner of baseball, to write pieces allegedly by Ruth for newspapers and magazines. Ruth "covered" every World Series from 1921 through 1936. Eventually Walsh's syndicate provided ghostwriting services for a large number of athletes and public celebrities, including Knute Rockne, the famed Notre Dame football coach.

Walsh became the first modern athletic business agent. Beginning in 1921, he handled nearly all of Ruth's nonbaseball commercial ventures. In 1921 he signed Ruth to a vaudeville tour, the first of several, which called for Ruth to receive $3,000 per week for 20 weeks, a record-shattering sum for a vaudeville performer. He also managed Ruth's many barnstorming baseball tours in the off-season. He assembled a list of all the commercial products with which his client could be associated and set out to convince the manufacturers of the benefits to be gained by Ruth's endorsements. In time, Ruth promoted, among other products, hunting and fishing equipment, modish men's wear, alligator shoes, baseball gear, and sporty automobiles. In Boston he might trumpet the virtues of Packards, in New York, Cadillacs, and in St. Louis, Reos. He received pay to appear at banquets, grand openings, smokers, boxing events, wrestling matches, and celebrity golf tournaments. When the purchasing power and the low income tax of that era are taken into account, Ruth's earnings were phenomenal. His total baseball income ranged between $1.25 million and $1.5 million, his nonbaseball earnings between $1 million and $2 million, for a total in the neighborhood of $3 million. Although Ruth was a hopeless spendthrift, Christy Walsh convinced him to put some of his income into untouchable annuities. He thus survived the 1929 stock market crash with enough money to retire comfortably in 1935.

Jack Dempsey and Tex Rickard: Charisma and Ballyhoo

A charismatic hero, combined with careful application of the promotional arts, also helped carry boxing to a peak of popularity—its "Golden Age." Never before or since has boxing achieved such a high plateau of popularity. In the prewar years, gate receipts from a single bout never exceeded $300,000; in the 1920s, promoter Tex Rickard promoted five consecutive million-dollar gates, including two legendary contests between champion Jack Dempsey and challenger Gene Tunney. Fans paid over $2 million to see the second Dempsey–Tunney fight. In terms of purchasing power, these sums were far larger than any modern gates. Over 100,000 fans witnessed each of the Dempsey–Tunney fights—again, figures unequaled in the annals of boxing history. Day after day the major newspapers placed boxing items on the front page.[18]

World War I helped soften the traditional animosity toward prizefighting. During the war, the army used boxing as part of doughboy training. After the war, often at the instigation of the American Legion, state after state dropped legal barriers to prizefighting. Boxing acquired a new level of respectability. Clandestine fights on barges, in the backrooms of saloons, or in isolated rural spots gave way to fights held in glittering arenas and huge stadiums. No longer were fights patronized exclusively by workingmen, roughnecks, and the "sporting set." Members of "high society," "proper" women, and middle-income groups began to attend fights. Celebrities from all fields of American life turned heavyweight championship fights into glittering social events. Ordinary people may have come as much to see the celebrities as the fights themselves.

No one in the 1920s sensed the possibilities of exploiting the public hunger for heroes better than Tex Rickard. Rickard had many apt nicknames: the "King of the Ballyhoo," "King of Sport Promoters," and "Phineas T. Barnum" of the twentieth century. Long before the 1920s, he revealed a propensity for taking high risks and a talent for promotion. As a youth in the 1890s he had left a dusty cow town in Texas for the Yukon-Klondike gold fields. While in Alaska, he reputedly won and lost several fortunes as a professional gambler, gold speculator, saloon owner, and barroom fight promoter. Rickard catapulted to the national level when he staged the famous Johnson–Jeffries fight in Reno in 1910.[19]

For the next five years, Rickard pursued multiple careers as a gambling house proprietor, rancher in Paraguay, and fight promoter. In 1916, his name resurfaced when he promoted a "no-decision" bout between the heavyweight champion Jess Willard, fresh from his victory over Jack Johnson, and Frank Moran. Earning a $30,000 stake from the fight, he promptly doubled it by betting on Woodrow Wilson to win the 1916 presidential election. Having established a tacit priority for the promotion of future Willard fights, he was in a position to launch the Golden Age of American boxing. He needed only a new boxing hero to replace the uncharismatic Willard. An unknown western fighter named Jack Dempsey soon filled that need.

On the face of it, Dempsey was an unlikely prospect for a popular hero. Born into a poor, itinerant Irish American family at Manassa, Colorado, he had been little more than a saloon brawler, fighting in Western tank towns for a hundred dollars or less per bout. Dempsey's reputation as a great slugger rested as much on myth as fact. He also suffered from an even more serious liability: He had not fought in World War I, and in 1920 the federal government charged him with being a "slacker." Although he was acquitted on the grounds that he had provided financial support to his wife and mother, the issue clouded his heroic image.

Still, the right publicity could work wonders. Dempsey had the good fortune of meeting Jess Willard, the "Pottawatomie Giant," in a championship bout staged by Rickard at Toledo, Ohio, in 1919. Willard, who stood 6' 6" and weighed 245 pounds, towered over the 6' 1" Dempsey. Still, Dempsey floored the massive Willard five times in the first round. At the end of the third round, a bloody and bewildered Willard, his face swollen to twice its normal size, conceded defeat. The image of Dempsey as giant killer caught on at once. Publicity stunts, such as having Dempsey's sparring partners wear inflated chest protectors and catcher's masks, reinforced the image, encouraging the public to accept the mistaken notion that Dempsey was a small man.[20]

The Dempsey–Willard fight launched Rickard's career as the nation's premier sports impresario. In 1920, the New York legislature legalized prizefighting. Two weeks after the law was passed, Rickard, with John Ringling of circus fame as a silent partner, obtained the financial backing to lease Madison Square Garden. Under his astute management, the Garden, which had been something of a white elephant to previous managers, became a highly profitable enterprise. Rickard offered a variety of attractions unequaled by any other palace of entertainment in the world. Boxing, wrestling, circuses, horse shows, six-day bicycle races, rodeos, professional hockey—these and many other activities became regular fare on the Garden's schedule.

Rickard juggled conflicting interests with the same skill and daring that he had perfected as a professional gambler. He courted newspaper reporters with frequent "leaks," free cigars, liberal quantities of liquor, and special seating privileges. He always reserved a number of free seats for the minions of the Tammany Hall political machine. Simultaneously, he won the support of New York's superrich. In 1921, at the invitation of Anne Morgan, philanthropic sister of J. Pierpont Morgan, he held a benefit fight in the Garden to kick off a fund-raising drive for war-torn France. Such clever gestures assisted Rickard in marshaling the funds for the construction of a new $5 million Madison Square Garden in 1926.

Rickard exhibited the full arsenal of his promotional skills in the Dempsey–Georges Carpentier fight of 1921. Carpentier, the light heavyweight champion of Europe, was no match for Dempsey in the ring. But Rickard set out to highlight the many contrasts between the two fighters, giving everyone a reason to take sides. For the native-minded, it would be a "foreign foe" versus an American. For those with vivid memories of war, it was a war hero—Carpentier had twice been decorated for valor in World War I—versus a "slacker." For class-minded fans, it was the "rapier" of the skilled fencer versus the "broadsword" of the peasant; the civilized man versus the "abysmal brute." "That's you, Jack," the elated Rickard reputedly exclaimed.[21]

As Rickard had hoped, the nation took sides. The American Legion passed a resolution condemning Dempsey; the Veterans of Foreign Wars retaliated by siding with the champ. In general, the "lowbrows," workingmen and ethnics, favored Dempsey. The "highbrows," especially the nation's literati, supported Carpentier. Even George Bernard Shaw, the distinguished British playwright, enlisted his vast literary talents in Carpentier's behalf.

As a financial event, the fight was an unprecedented success. Over 80,000 fans paid nearly $2 million to see the fight. The "Who's Who of the social, financial, and entertainment world" attended the bout.[22] As an athletic contest, the bout was a farce. Dempsey had little difficulty knocking Carpentier out in the fourth round. Nonetheless, everyone seemed satisfied. Even the dignified *New York Times* announced the results of the fight in front-page headlines. Few Americans were left untouched by the spectacle at "Boyle's Thirty Acres."

After defeating Louis Firpo in another highly publicized match, Dempsey went three years without defending his title. Rickard was busy with the management of the new Garden, and Dempsey enjoyed living the life of a celebrity who earned as much as $500,000 annually from endorsements, movie contracts, and vaudeville performances. But the primary reason for Dempsey's absence from the ring may have been Harry Wills, the "Brown Panther" from New Orleans, who was clamoring for a crack at the championship.

In every respect except race, Wills was a qualified challenger. The story of his inability to get a match with Dempsey is obscured in intrigue. On several occasions the New York Athletic Commission ordered Dempsey to fight Wills—actions apparently designed to please the black voters of New York City. But according to Rickard, each time he agreed to give Wills a title shot, he received a word from high political figures in Albany that the match would be blocked. Politics aside, Rickard may well have feared a loss by Dempsey, a consequent reduction in the gates of future fights, and violent racial incidents similar to the outbreaks that had accompanied Johnson's defeat of Jim Jeffries in 1910.

Rickard settled instead on Gene Tunney, who "was almost universally regarded as a second-rater" by boxing aficionados, but who provided the same kind of promising contrast with Dempsey as had Carpentier. The insistence of the New York Athletic Commission upon a Dempsey–Wills match forced Rickard to hold the bout elsewhere. He chose Philadelphia's Sesquicentennial Stadium and scheduled the fight for September 23, 1926. The buildup followed Rickard's familiar formula. In the "Battle of the Century" it was the dark, savage-visaged, mauling Dempsey versus the smooth, "scientific" boxer Tunney. To the surprise of nearly all the 120,757 fans present and several million radio listeners, Tunney stayed with Dempsey for full 10 rounds, avoiding Dempsey's famed rushes and scoring repeatedly on solid but nonlethal blows. He won the match on points.

Undaunted, Rickard scheduled a second "Fight of the Century" between Tunney and Dempsey in 1927—a fight that brought him to the pinnacle of his promotional career. More than 104,000 customers paid more than $2 million to witness the event at Soldier Field in Chicago. Spectators on the outer perimeter of the stadium sat as far as 200 yards from the ring, making the boxers almost indiscernible. An estimated 50 million Americans heard Graham McNamee's broadcast from one of 73 stations connected to the NBC radio network.

For the first six rounds, the fight seemed to be a replay of the Philadelphia bout. Then in the seventh round, Dempsey landed a series of blows that crumpled Tunney to the mat. As the referee began to count, he waved Dempsey to a neutral corner of the ring. Dempsey ignored the motion. By the time the referee convinced Dempsey to retire to a neutral corner, several seconds had expired. The referee then began the count anew, reaching nine before Tunney came to his feet. Although the referee's action conformed to the Illinois boxing codes, the legendary "long count" furnished a source of endless debate among fight fans. Tunney survived the seventh round and outboxed Dempsey in the final three rounds to win a unanimous decision. In defeat, Dempsey's popularity soared higher than when he had held the championship. Tunney, on the other hand, never caught the public's heart.

The contrast in the popularity of Dempsey and Tunney underscored the type of heroism that most appealed to the broad American public. Dempsey's rushes proved more satisfying than Tunney's defensive finesse. Dempsey's rough scrabble image inspired more identification than the polish of a man who married a socialite, lectured on Shakespeare to a class at Yale, and was a personal friend of the writer Thornton Wilder. Tunney's victory signaled the end of the Golden Age of American boxing. The public did not respond to the new heavyweight king, and in 1928 Rickard lost some $400,000 in promoting Tunney's next title defense, against Tom Heeney of New Zealand. After winning that fight, Tunney retired from the ring, leaving the heavyweight scene in chaos. In 1929, while launching an elimina-tion series to determine a new champion, Rickard suddenly died from an attack of appendicitis. Rickard's funeral revealed that the promoter was in his own right a public celebrity. Over 15,000 persons filed past his ornate $15,000 bronze casket in the main arena of Madison Square Garden. The next day, 9,000 attended his funeral. No new impresario replaced him.

Helen Wills: "The American Girl"

At the same time that Jack Dempsey sat atop the world of boxing, a very different athlete began her climb to tennis fame. In the fall of 1922, 16-year-old Helen Wills became the talk of the U.S. tennis world. Wills had traveled from her home in California to compete in the East Coast's summer tournaments, including the National Women's Singles Championship (now the U.S. Open). To onlookers' sur-prise, the teenager with long braids and a pleated-skirt school uniform reached the finals, losing only to reigning national champion Molla Mallory. A few days later, in a different tournament, she came within points of beating Mallory. By the end of the season, she had the third-highest ranking among American women. Observers predicted a bright future.[23]

Far too often, tennis prodigies make an astonishing start, and then burn out. Not Helen Wills. She returned East in 1923 and won the national title, becoming the second-youngest player to do so. In 1927 she won her first Wimbledon, losing only a single set during the tournament. "Queen Helen" went on to dominate world women's competition so thoroughly that she did not lose another set in competition for six full years. Along the way, she helped transform the way Americans viewed female athletes.

Born in 1905, Helen Wills grew up in a culture that warmly supported many women's sports, especially tennis. Not only did the California climate make it pos-sible to play year-round, California civic leaders had built thousands of public courts in parks throughout the state. In keeping with the less tradition-bound society of the American West, men and women played on largely equal terms. By the 1910s, according to noted player Maurice McLoughlin, one could find "scarcely any place of importance in California where the ladies' events are not treated as of equal importance with those of the men." This appreciation, McLoughlin continued, "stimulates both interest and keen competition, which is so absolutely essential to the development of a high-class tennis player."[24]

In the first years of the century, a string of California women held the national championship. May Sutton took the title in 1904, and Hazel Hotchkiss won in 1909, 1910, and 1911, followed by Mary K. Browne in 1912, 1913, and 1914. Hodgkiss would win again in 1919. McLoughlin, California's first male champion, took his first title in 1912. California women became known for their hard-hitting game, developed on the state's concrete (as opposed to grass) courts, and their focused concentration. It became common for top California women to practice against men, further develop-ing their strength and speed. Young women had plenty of stars to look up to, and they started playing early. Helen Wills got her first racket when she was eight.

By the time Wills reached her teens, tennis was becoming a significant spectator sport not just in California, but also around the country. The U.S. Lawn Tennis Association increased promotion of its events, and a series of charismatic stars, including Mallory, McLoughlin, and the colorful "Big Bill" Tilden took center stage. A net of tournaments soon stretched across the country, with city championships, regional championships, and club championships, as well as divisions for adults and "juniors." In California, top players played regular exhibitions at clubs and on public courts, and Wills and her father frequently came out to see the matches. Wills was especially fond of Bill Johnston, who succeeded Maurice McLoughlin as the men's national champion, and she sought to reproduce his powerful strokes while she was on the court.[25]

Fortunately for Wills, her father was a doctor who could afford the coaching and travel needed to launch her career. Unlike baseball, boxing, or golf, tennis remained an amateur endeavor, with competitors forbidden to make money from their talents, whether in prizes or product endorsement. As with other "amateur" sports, top players could garner outside support in a variety of ways. Private clubs could "sponsor" players, and tournaments frequently "reimbursed" players for "travel expenses." Newspapers might pay players to write (or have ghostwritten) their impressions of places and people. When Wills returned to California in the fall of 1924, having won an Olympic gold medal in Paris and a second national title, the citizens of Berkeley presented her with a brand-new Buick—not for her tennis skills, they were careful to specify, but for the splendid publicity she had brought to her home state.

But even without lucrative contracts, or a professional agent such as "Cash and Carry" Pyle to keep her in the news, Helen Wills had no shortage of publicity. She played dramatic tennis—hitting harder than anyone had seen a woman hit before, and winning many of her matches by stunningly decisive margins. She also happened to have movie-star looks—one New York editor famously remarked that "all the males in America…are a little in love with her."[26] But in contrast to the often-scandalous young flappers who filled newspaper columns with their short skirts, bobbed hair, and generous use of rouge and lipstick, as well as their fondness for alcohol, cigarettes, and nightclubs, Wills wore long skirts and avoided makeup. On the court, her behavior was impeccable. The press held her up as a model of a new "American Girl" who combined the confidence and energy of the modern age with the sensible modesty of the past.

"Remember the good old days, about a year ago, when people wondered what this younger generation was coming to, and what, since parents and preachers and police had failed, would intervene to save it from perdition?" one writer asked after Wills captured her Olympic gold. "The Olympic Games are the answer to both questions. After bolshevism, a newer sanity. After the flapper, Helen Wills and the welcome young American whom she typifies."[27]

Interest in the new young star stretched around the world. In January of 1926, Wills traveled to the French Riviera in search of a match with French player Suzanne Lenglen, considered the best female player of all time. Dozens of reporters and photographers from around the world were dispatched to report on her endeavors. A month later, when the two women finally met, the match made headlines around the world, giving tennis a celebrity status that it had not previously enjoyed in the United States. Although Lenglen managed a narrow victory, Wills was clearly the player to watch.

Wills also helped to pioneer a new version of athletic womanhood, one that balanced the "masculine" qualities of force and aggression on the athletic field with thoroughly conventional femininity in every other aspect of life. Her game was often compared to that of men. She regularly practiced against men, and periodically played exhibition matches against them—matches that she often won. But a number of factors combined to spare her criticism. In general, tennis was considered a feminine sport, showcasing grace as much as force. In 1927, when Wills defeated Spain's hard-hitting Lili de Alvarez to win her first Wimbledon championship, one English writer described the players' forceful styles as "man-like strokes to which the perfect poise of feminine grace was added."[28] Wills downplayed her devotion to her sport, frequently avowing that she was more interested in the art classes she was taking at the University of California. She loved attractive clothes, and looked marvelous in them. Late in 1929, she married San Francisco stockbroker Fred Moody, who had been a frequent companion on her European tours.

As her career advanced, Wills did begin to feel some of the tensions of being such a pioneering figure. Her marriage to Moody foundered after several years, in part because Moody felt that she paid too much attention to tennis, and not enough to him. Her dominance of the sport became so complete that writers lost some of their enthusiasm for her, and began to portray her as a ruthlessly competitive machine, the "Killer of the Courts," rather than a charming girl.[29] Her winning streak finally ended in 1933, when she lost to Helen Jacobs in the U.S. National finals. She drew heavy criticism for defaulting near the end of the match, citing a back injury. She spent several weeks in the hospital, and did not play competition tennis for the next two years. She would recover enough to win Wimbledon twice more—in 1935 and 1938, but she played a limited number of tournaments and was no longer the dominant figure she had been. At the end of 1938, she retired for good. A year later she remarried, and pursued a largely private life. But tennis would remain a thriving sport for women—thanks in part to the attention she had brought to the sport, and to a new crop of young stars who had been inspired by her example.

Conclusion

With the expansion of American sports arose a panoply of sports heroes. While these heroes played a variety of games, and came from many walks of life, they had several things in common: they played with unprecedented power, they dominated their sports, and their exploits were given larger-than-life status by promoters and eager news outlets. They also logged achievements that many ordinary Americans could only dream of: a black man who beat white men bloody without being lynched; an apparent orphan who won fame and fortune with the swing of a bat; a young woman whose athletic skills took her around the world. Even as their fame reflected the specific issues and concerns of their times, the marks they made would resonate for the rest of the century.

Critical Thinking Questions

1. William Pickens summed up the Johnson–Jeffries fight and the violence that followed by saying, "It was a good deal better for Johnson to win and a few negroes be killed in body for it, than for Johnson to have lost and negroes to have been killed in spirit by the preachments of inferiority from the combined white press." Do you agree with this statement? Why or why not?
2. Compare and contrast the personalities and achievements of Babe Ruth and Jack Dempsey. What do the similarities tell you about the nature of sports heroism in the 1920s? What about the differences?
3. Which of these heroes do you think made the most significant contribution to American sports history? To American history?

Notes

1. Most efforts to explain American heroes in modern times see them as fulfilling cherished American ideals or myths. See, for example, Leo Lowenthal, *Literature, Popular Culture and Society* (Englewood Cliffs, NJ: Prentice Hall, 1961), 109–41; Leverett T. Smith Jr., *The American Dream and the American Game* (Bowling Green, OH: Bowling Green University Popular Culture Press, 1975); J.W. Ward, "The Meaning of Lindbergh's Flight," in Joseph Kwait and Mary Turpie, eds., *Studies in American Culture* (Minneapolis: University of Minnesota Press, 1960); R.W. Nash, *The Nervous Generation* (Chicago: Rand McNally, 1970), 126–37; C.L. Himes, "The Female Athlete in American Society, 1860–1940," unpub. Ph.D. diss., (University of Pennsylvania, 1984), chapter 5; Michael Oriard, *Dreaming of Heroes:* (Chicago: Nelson-Hall, 1982); B.G. Rader, "Compensatory Sport Heroes: Ruth, Grange, and Dempsey," *Journal of Popular Culture* 16 (1983), 11–22; E.J. Gorn, "The Manassa Mauler and the Fighting Marine: An Interpretation of the Dempsey-Tunney Fights," *Journal of American Studies* 19 (1983), 27–47.
2. See Randy Roberts, *Papa Jack* (New York: Free Press, 1983); Al-Tony Gilmore, *Bad Nigger: The National Impact of Jack Johnson* (New York: Kenikat Press, 1975).
3. Quoted in Finis Farr, *Black Champion* (New York: Charles Scribner's Sons, 1964), 107.
4. Quoted in Lawrence Levine, *Black Culture and Black Consciousness: Afro-American Folk Thought from Slavery to Freedom* (New York: Oxford University Press, 1977), 431.
5. Quoted in Randy Roberts, "Jack Dempsey: An American Hero in the 1920s," *Journal of Popular Culture* 8 (1974), 412.
6. *Los Angeles Times*, July 6, 1910.
7. For a fascinating account of Johnson's travels, including an assessment of the growing racism he encountered around the world, see Theresa Runstedtler, *Jack Johnson, Rebel Sojourner: Boxing in the Shadow of the Global Color Line* (Berkeley: University of California Press, 2012).
8. Roberts, *Papa Jack*, 12.
9. Gilmore, *Bad Nigger*, 46.
10. *Chicago Defender*, July 30, 1910.
11. Tom Meany, Martin Weldon, Claire Ruth with Bill Slocum, Lee Allen, Dan Daniel, and Waite Hoyt wrote early biographies. More recent books by Ken Sobel, Kal Wagenheim, Robert Creamer, and Marshall Smelser are in most respects superior, but see also especially Smith, *The American Dream and the American Game*; and Harold Seymour, *Baseball: The Golden Age* (New York: Oxford University Press, 1971).
12. Quoted in Smith, *The American Dream and the American Game*, 207.
13. Babe Ruth and Bob Considine, *The Babe Ruth Story* (New York: Scholastic Books, 1969), 9.

14. Paul Gallico, *The Golden People* (Garden City, NY: Doubleday, 1965), 36–7; and Smith, *The American Dream and the American Game,* 198.

15. Quotations from Ty Cobb with Al Stump, *My Life in Baseball* (Garden City, NY: Doubleday, 1961), 280, and Smith, *The American Dream and the American Game,* 190, 205.

16. Marshall Smelser, "The Babe on Balance," *American Scholar* 44 (1975), 299.

17. Quoted in Seymour, *Baseball,* 428.

18. See especially Allison Danzig and Peter Brandwein, eds., *Sport's Golden Age* (New York: Harper & Bros., 1948), 38–85; Randy Roberts, *Jack Dempsey* (Baton Rouge: Louisiana State University Press, 1979); Gorn, "The Manassa Mauler"; and Jeffrey T. Sammons, *Beyond the Ring: The Role of Boxing in American Society* (Urbana: University of Illinois Press, 1988), chapters 3 and 4.

19. See Charles Samuels, *The Magnificent Rube* (New York: McGraw-Hill, 1957) and Mrs. "Tex" Rickard, *Everything Happened to Him* (New York: Frederick A. Stokes, 1936).

20. Jack Dempsey, *Round by Round* (New York: McGraw-Hill, 1940), 176.

21. Jack Dempsey with C.J. McGurik, "The Golden Gates," *Saturday Evening Post* 207 (October 20, 1934), 11.

22. Jack "Doc" Kearns with Oscar Fraley, *The Million Dollar Gate* (New York: Macmillan, 1966), 147–48.

23. For a detailed account of Wills' life and career, see Larry Engelman, *The Goddess and the American Girl: The Story of Suzanne Lenglen and Helen Wills* (New York: Oxford University Press, 1988).

24. Quoted in ibid., 64.

25. See Danzig and Brandwein, eds., *Sport's Golden Age*, 208–27, and Frank Deford, *Big Bill Tilden* (New York: Simon & Schuster, 1975).

26. Quoted in Engelman, *The Goddess and the American Girl*, 293.

27. Quoted in ibid., 99.

28. Quoted in ibid., 291. For a thoughtful description of reporters' struggles with portraying female athletes as both strong and feminine, see Susan Cahn, *Coming on Strong: Gender and Sexuality in Twentieth-Century Women's Sport* (New York: The Free Press, 1994), 211–17.

29. Quoted in Cahn, *Coming on Strong*, 291, n. 6

CHAPTER 11

Baseball's Golden Age

New York's Polo Grounds, during the World Series of 1913.

LEARNING OBJECTIVES

11.1 Analyze the factors that made baseball the pre-eminent American sport in the first half of the twentieth century, as well as the variety of challenges baseball team owners faced.

11.2 Describe the diversity of characters—both comic and intense—that helped give baseball wide appeal.

11.3 Summarize the challenges that baseball team owners faced as they sought to stabilize their industry between 1900 and 1920.

11.4 Explain the antitrust exemption and its importance for baseball's development.

11.5 Detail the varying opportunities available to African American baseball players in the first decades of the twentieth century.

11.6 Explain how Latin American players complicated the racial dichotomy that prevailed in U.S. baseball.

Until the 1950s, no other sport seriously challenged baseball's supremacy as the "national pastime." Wars and economic downturns only temporarily set back steady gains in attendance at all levels of the game. Despite the often rowdy behavior of the players (and sometimes managers and owners as well), baseball gained in acceptability among all social groups. Even the president of the nation extended his endorsement; in 1910 William Howard Taft established the precedent of the president opening each season by throwing out the first ball. Baseball stars were sometimes even better known than the president of the United States; only Hollywood actors and actresses successfully competed with them for celebrity status. Minor-league professional baseball also grew, from 13 leagues in 1903 to 51 at mid-century. Every city, town, and village of any consequence had one or more amateur, semiprofessional, or professional teams. Boys everywhere grew up reading baseball fiction, learning the rudiments of the game, and dreaming of one day becoming diamond heroes themselves.[1]

As baseball came of age, promoters perpetuated the Doubleday myth of its origins; professional teams built magnificent stadiums of steel and concrete; and owners created the modern structure of the major leagues, including the annual World Series that capped regular season play. The major leagues successfully weathered a set of trials, including war, depression, scandal, and periodic disunity among owners. The game also extended its reach further into Latin America and the Caribbean, building new fan bases and new pools of talent.

Baseball's Coming of Age

During the first two decades of the twentieth century, professional baseball became the nation's most entrenched and mature professional sport. In a nation that comprised a multiplicity of ethnic, racial, and religious groups, one without a monarchy, an aristocracy, or a long, mystic past, the experience of playing, watching, and talking about baseball games became one of the great common denominators. In the perceptive words of British novelist Virginia Woolf, it provided "a centre, a meeting place for the divers activities of a people whom a vast continent isolates [and] whom no tradition controls." No other sport, it seemed to contemporaries, quite captured the essence of the nation's character as did baseball.[2]

Appropriate to baseball's embodiment of the nation's character, the custodians of the national game nurtured a creation myth. In 1907, a special commission of men of "high repute and undoubted knowledge of the Base Ball" issued a report that placed an official stamp on the legend that Army officer Abner Doubleday had invented baseball at Cooperstown, New York, in the summer of 1839. (Later scholars have discredited the claim.) The commission, appointed by the ever-entrepreneurial Albert Spalding, engaged in no firsthand research, although it did send out letters of inquiry to old-timers who had been associated with organized teams in the antebellum era.

The commission's conclusions, as Spalding so effectively put it, helped free baseball "from the trammels of English traditions, customs, conventionalities."[3] In 1939 the major leagues celebrated the "centennial" of baseball with impressive ceremonies at Cooperstown. There they dedicated a Hall of Fame, presented a pageant showing Doubleday's alleged contribution to the sport, and staged an all-star game. The U.S. government joined the festivities, issuing a commemorative stamp that marked 1839 as the official date of the national game's birth.

The Doubleday-Cooperstown myth helped give baseball a quasi-religious status. As Muslims have their Mecca and Christians have their Bethlehem, for decades to come baseball followers would have their Cooperstown. Each year, thousands of Americans would make a "pilgrimage" to the "shrine" at Cooperstown to gaze at statues and pictures of past heroes and observe the "relics" that they used—old, discolored bats, balls, and uniforms. They would visit the "hallowed ground" of Doubleday Field, where the young Doubleday "immaculately conceived" the game. Each year, sportswriters would dutifully select great players of the past for "enshrinement," after which they would become "immortals."[4]

Baseball's supporters also credited the game with a significant role in building social solidarity through the way it helped assimilate the nation's many immigrants. As Morgan Bulkeley, the National League's first president put it, "There is nothing which will help quicker and better amalgamate the foreign born, and those born of foreign parents in this country, than to give them a little good bringing up in the good old-fashioned game of Base Ball." Bulkeley went even further, arguing that the game helped prevent revolutionary conspiracies. "They don't have things [like baseball] on the other side of the ocean," declared Bulkeley, "and many spend their hours fussing around in conspiring and hatching up plots when they should be out in the open improving their lungs."[5] What Bulkeley failed to mention, however, was that baseball also mirrored American society in the limits of its vision. While a robust baseball culture developed in African American and Latino communities, as well as in the countries of the Caribbean Basin, a "gentleman's agreement" continued to exclude African Americans and other dark-skinned players from the major-league ranks.

Among the most tangible signs of baseball's coming of age was the annual World Series. Beginning in 1903, the pennant winners of the American and National leagues agreed to play a nine-game "World Championship" series. No postseason games were played in 1904, but in 1905 the World Series became a permanent feature of big-league baseball. The series furnished an exciting conclusion to the regular season; the entire nation soon became absorbed in its outcome. Fans congregated in the city streets to watch the play-by-play progress of the series as reported on the boards posted in front of newspaper offices. Reportedly, the series sometimes even delayed the proceedings of the U.S. Supreme Court.

The era's baseball games offered fans a cornucopia of drama and entertainment. Baseball had a cast of well-defined heroes and villains, familiar plots, comedy, and the unexpected. Since most of the fans had played the sport as youths and had watched plenty of games, they understood the intricacies of the plot—the purpose of bunting, the hit-and-run play, a deliberate base on balls, the removal of a struggling pitcher, the appropriate place for the insertion of a pinch hitter. Baseball was a rational sport, one in which means were manifestly related to ends. Even though one could never predict when a ground ball might strike a pebble and bounce over a fielder's outstretched glove, "baseball, year by year, [has] grown more scientific, more of a thing of accepted rules, or set routine," baseball reporter F. C. Lane noted. "This slow evolution of the sport displayed itself in batting, in the form of the bunt, the place hit and various other manifestations of skill."[6]

In contrast to the rationality of the rules, early twentieth-century baseball presented a marvelous set of stock characters. "There were a lot of characters in baseball back then," recalled Samuel "Wahoo Sam" Crawford in the 1960s. "Real individualists. Not conformists, like most ball players—and most people—are today."[7] The fans noticed and adored the special physical traits and idiosyncratic behavior of the players. Their colorful nicknames—Bugs, Babe, Rube, Wahoo Sam, Mugsy, Chief, Muddy, Kid, Hod, Dummy, Dutch, Stuffy, Gabby, and Hooks, to list only a few—suggested baseball's capacity to produce characters. And, of course, the umpire served as the chief villain.

The players seemed to take a special delight in spicing the game with comedy and the unexpected. Perhaps none equaled the feat of Herman "Germany" Schaefer, who once stole first base! With the score tied in the late innings of a game between Detroit and Cleveland, Schaefer was on first base and Davy Jones on third. Schaefer gave the sign for a double steal and broke for second. The catcher, fearing that Jones would steal home if he threw the ball, simply held it, leaving players on second and third. "Well, on the next pitch Schaefer yelled, 'Let's try it again!' " Jones recalled. "And with a bloodcurdling shout he took off like a wild Indian *back to first base*, and dove in headfirst in a cloud of dust." The move stunned both teams. "Everybody just stood there and watched Schaefer, with their mouths open, not knowing what the devil was going on," Jones continued. "Even if the catcher *had* thrown to first, I was too stunned to move....But the catcher didn't throw. He just stared!" Apparently satisfied with the effect of his antics, Schafer carried on. On the next pitch, "darned if he didn't let out another war whoop and take off *again* for second base." This time, Jones noted, the fed-up catcher threw the ball, "and when he did I took off for home and *both* of us were safe."[8]

An Age of the Pitcher

Until recently, baseball historians have labeled the first two decades of the twentieth century as the "dead ball era." However, recent research suggests that this designation is inappropriate. Although run production increased in the wake of the adoption of a cork-cushioned ball in 1910, the improvement proved temporary.

The best evidence indicates a series of other reasons behind low scores, including the enlarging of home plate (and thus the strike zone) from a 12-inch square to a five-sided figure 17 inches across; the counting of the first two foul balls as strikes; a group of bigger, stronger pitchers; and an interest in "scientific" or "inside" baseball, which championed systematic run production through bunts and singles rather than extra-base hits.[9]

John J. McGraw, the colorful, controversial, and longtime manager of the New York Giants, was a master of the nuances of one-run-at-a-time tactics. After nine years of play with the famed Baltimore Orioles in the 1890s, McGraw came to New York to take the helm of the Giants in 1902, a post he held for the next 30 years. He led the Giants to 10 National League pennants and four "world championships." Like most of the managers of the era, McGraw concentrated on acquiring good pitchers, such as Joe McGinnity, Christy Mathewson, and Rube Marquard. The Giants had no outstanding stars beyond the pitching staff, but they always had speed, aggressiveness, and the peerless McGraw.[10]

Perfectly suited to New York City—the nation's center of commerce, high finance, show business, and ethnic diversity—McGraw attracted headlines both on and off the field. The epitome of the day's martinet managers, he exercised a harsh discipline over his players. He drilled them in the game's fundamentals: covering bases, place hitting, bunting, sliding, and base running. He brawled with players, fans, umpires, and league officials. Fans in other National League cities liked nothing better than to see his hated Giants defeated. McGraw took full advantage of the excitement offered by New York City, frequently indulging in theater, horse racing, gambling, parties, and highballs. All of these things, plus his Irish charm, endeared him to New Yorkers.

Ty Cobb

Had it not been for Tyrus "Ty" Raymond Cobb, long-time star of the Detroit Tigers, the pre-1920 era would probably be remembered only for its pitching heroes. In a career that spanned 24 seasons, from 1905–1928, Cobb had the highest lifetime batting average (0.367) and won the league batting championship more seasons—12—of any player in baseball history. Statistics fail to do Cobb full justice. He had no peer as a master of inside baseball tactics. If the infield played deep, he would use his spread-handed grip to bunt; if the infield tightened up, he would slash the ball through the holes or over the fielders' heads. His dazzling speed and recklessness on the base paths terrorized opponents.

Cobb personified, in an exaggerated way, the rugged individualism of the nineteenth century. Lacking the exceptional physical attributes of a Babe Ruth, Cobb relentlessly drove himself to excel. To Cobb, baseball was a form of warfare. "When I played ball, I didn't play for fun," Cobb wrote in his autobiography in 1961. "It's no pink tea, and mollycoddles had better stay out. It's a contest and everything that implies, a struggle for supremacy, a survival of the fittest."[11] This view led Cobb to reject many of the sport's old amateur traditions. Since the 1880s, brawls between players had unfolded within a framework of understood conventions that involved a great deal of verbal warfare but limited physical contact. Cobb used every weapon at his disposal—his spikes, fists, bat, and tongue—all in an effort to intimidate and defeat his opponents. Instances of Cobb's violent disposition off the field were equally legion.

Cobb never became a popular hero in the mold of a Babe Ruth or even a Cap Anson. Almost everybody thoroughly disliked him, including his own teammates. He evoked fear and respect, but never affection; he never had a close, personal friend among the big-league players or managers. He ate alone, roomed alone, and for years at a time did not speak to certain of his teammates. The depth of the feeling against Cobb showed clearly in 1910 when he appeared to have won the American League batting championship. In the final doubleheader of the season Napoleon Lajoie, the leading contender for the title, made eight hits in eight times at bat. Six of the hits came from bunts toward third base, which the notoriously slow-footed Lajoie had somehow beaten out. It soon became clear that the St. Louis Browns had deliberately tried to deny Cobb the crown by "giving" Lajoie free access to first base. (Incidentally, the strategy failed, for Cobb was able to retain the title by a single percentage point.) But the public was drawn to villains as well as to heroes. Fans everywhere came out to see the rampaging Cobb, partly in awe of his ability, but also in hopes of seeing him stymied by the local club or of witnessing a brawl in which Cobb would be the principal victim.

The Quest for Order

Baseball also benefited from the owners' success in creating a stable order for the game. This was no easy task. On the one hand, owners were proponents of free enterprise; they wanted the freedom to operate their individual ball clubs as they saw fit. Yet, such freedom could be economically disastrous, especially for franchises located in the smaller cities. So the big leagues entered into collusive agreements, or what can be labeled an economic cartel. Specifically, they sought to devise a means of avoiding direct competition among franchises for players, to prevent the formation of rival big leagues, to restrict the total number of big-league teams, and to bring the minor leagues under their control. The resulting entity, which became known as "Organized Baseball," was large and unwieldy. It was only sporadically effective.

Baseball's quest for order in the pre-1920 era began inauspiciously. Despite the collapse of the Players' League in 1890 and the American Association in 1891, the decade of the 1890s was a grim one for the National League. Burdened by the debts accumulated from the brotherhood war and the purchase costs of four association clubs, the league also faced a general economic depression and public disillusionment with the professional game due to the players' revolt. The new 12-team loop was a near disaster. Teams with poor records, such as the Louisville and St. Louis franchises, attracted few fans. The New York and Chicago clubs, franchises vital to the success of the league, failed to field strong teams. Finally, in 1899, the league returned to eight clubs. The new circuit, composed of Boston, Brooklyn, Chicago, Cincinnati, New York, Philadelphia, Pittsburgh, and St. Louis, would remain intact until 1953, when the Boston Braves moved to Milwaukee.

The league then faced a new challenge—a rival American League, led by the indomitable Byron Bancroft "Ban" Johnson. When the National League returned to an eight-team loop, Johnson was president of a minor league known as the Western League. He convinced his followers to claim major-league status, to rename the circuit the "American League," and to raid National League player rosters. With Johnson in firm control of the American League franchises and the National League owners divided, the senior loop finally sued for peace.

The peace settlement, known as the National Agreement of 1903, became the centerpiece of professional baseball. The leagues agreed to recognize each other's reserve clauses and established a three-man National Commission. Composed of the presidents of the two leagues and a third member chosen by them, the National Commission served primarily as a judicial body to resolve disputes arising from within the cartel. In the National League, the owners retained nearly absolute power to manage their franchises as they saw fit; in the American League, Ban Johnson ruled with a firm hand until the 1920s. The 1903 agreement also recognized the territorial monopolies of minor-league teams; granted them reserve rights in players; and set up a system by which the major leagues could annually draft players from the minors for a set price.

In the pre-1920 era, the club owners confronted two major challenges: keeping salary costs under control and fighting off another contender for big-league status, called the Federal League. The reserve clause allowed the owners to limit salaries to less than the players would have received on the open market. Still, as attendance and club profits rose rapidly in the early years of the century, player salaries slowly drifted upward. Star players sometimes effectively "held out;" they refused to play until they obtained higher pay. Probably as many as 10 stars received salaries of $10,000 or more by 1910, while players with ordinary talents might earn as little as $1,900 annually. When the upstart Federal League threatened to lure players from the cartel between 1912 and 1915, the salaries of superior players jumped sharply. Ty Cobb's salary, for example, leaped from $9,000 in 1910 to $20,000 in 1915. With the demise of the Federal League at the end of the 1915 season, however, the owners were once again able to hold the line on salaries.

The Black Sox Scandal and the Reign of Kennesaw Mountain Landis

In September 1920, a shocking revelation rocked the country. The 1919 World Series had been fixed. The worst team scandal in the history of American sport, soon labeled the "Black Sox Scandal," crowded the "Red Scare" and every other major story off the front pages of the nation's newspapers. Americans were incredulous. According to baseball legend, a small boy approached "Shoeless Joe" Jackson, one of the alleged conspirators and a star outfielder with the Chicago White Sox. "Say it ain't so, Joe," begged the lad as tears welled from his eyes. "I'm afraid it is, son," Jackson responded. The hurt cut deeply. Boston newsboys condemned the "murderous blow" to the national pastime by the "Benedict Arnolds of baseball." In Joliet, Illinois, an angry fan charged Buck Herzog with being "one of those crooked Chicago ball players." A fight erupted and Herzog was stabbed, even though he was a member of the Chicago Cubs rather than the White Sox. Future novelist Nelson Algren, then a lad on Chicago's South Side, became disillusioned. "Everybody's out for The Buck," he later concluded "even the big leaguers." A character in F. Scott Fitzgerald's *The Great Gatsby* reflected: "It never occurred to me that one man could start to play with the faith of fifty million people."[12]

Although the dismay that accompanied the Black Sox Scandal of 1919 proved that baseball had finally won wide-scale public acceptability, in retrospect the scandal should not have been so surprising. Like those engaged in other forms of commercial entertainment, many of the players, managers, and owners had close links with the urban demimonde. They spent much of their spare time at race tracks, theaters, hotel lobbies, and saloons, where they consorted with publicly known gamblers. Most big-league players did not hesitate to wager upon themselves or their teams. Yet organized baseball, fearing adverse publicity and the loss of valuable property in the form of the players, attempted to cover up all reports connecting baseball with gambling and game fixing. Had it not been for an enterprising reporter, Hugh Fullerton, the 1919 Black Sox scandal might have remained a mere rumor.

Later evidence revealed that eight Chicago players had taken money from gamblers to dump the 1919 World Series. Seven of the eight alleged fixers admitted to a grand jury they had received sums varying from $5,000 to $10,000—figures that exceeded the annual salaries of most of the accused—to throw the series to Cincinnati. Somehow, however, the grand jury records disappeared before the trial. (At a later trial in which Joe Jackson sued White Sox owner Charles Comiskey over back pay, the player confessions "mysteriously" reappeared—in the possession of Comiskey's attorney.)

At the trial held in 1921, all of the players repudiated their earlier confessions, leaving the testimony of Bill Maharg, a professional gambler, as the only substantial evidence against them. After a few hours of deliberation, the jury acquitted all the players plus two gamblers. The spectators in the courtroom roared their approval, and the jurymen and players retired to a local restaurant to celebrate. But the joy of the players was short-lived, for Judge Kenesaw Mountain Landis, the newly appointed Commissioner of Baseball, banished them from organized baseball for life.

The Black Sox scandal provided an opening for those owners who were dissatisfied with the governing National Commission and with the power of Ban Johnson, imperious president of the American League.

In a new National Agreement of 1921, the owners gave sweeping powers to a new commissioner, including the power to investigate anything "suspected" of being "detrimental to the best interests of the national game." If the commissioner determined that leagues, club owners, or players had taken actions harmful to the sport, he was given the authority to suspend, fine, or banish guilty parties. In their eagerness to improve the image of baseball and bring a semblance of order to the game, the owners even agreed to waive their rights to take disputes between themselves or with the commissioner to the civil courts. The Agreement of 1921 established the model for the governmental structures of professional football and basketball in the post–World War II era as well.

The imperious Landis, whose tall, thin body and stern, craggy face gave him an aura of staunch morality, wasted little time in trying to alter baseball's image. He arbitrarily banished more than a dozen players from the game for life. He ordered Charles A. Stoneham, owner of the New York Giants, and John J. McGraw, Giant manager, to divest themselves of their stock in race tracks located in Cuba and New York. Although he treated the questionable actions of the owners far more gingerly than those of the players, his 22-year reign brought a new image of integrity to the game.

Soon after Landis was appointed Commissioner of Baseball, the U.S. Supreme Court added a legal boon. The teams of the defunct Federal League had filed antitrust suits against the major leagues, one of which reached the U.S. Supreme Court in 1922. Justice Oliver Wendell Holmes Jr., speaking for a unanimous court, declared that professional baseball games did not constitute a "trade or commerce in the commonly-accepted use of the words." In a rather tortuous definition of terms, Holmes reasoned that the "personal effort" of ballplayers was "not related to production" and therefore could not be involved in commerce. Nor was interstate movement essential to their activity, for the movement of ballplayers across state lines was simply "incidental" to their playing ball. Whatever the merits of the legal justification of professional baseball's exemption from the antitrust laws, the decision provided a legal umbrella for the agreements upon which the professional baseball cartel rested.

A final boost came from a hitting revolution, sparked in large part by the batting successes of Babe Ruth. Not only did the hitters who copied Ruth's full swings smash out more home runs, but they also seemed to strike the ball more squarely than those who had earlier taken a shortened swing. Batting averages, scoring, and home run totals soared. By 1925 the combined batting averages of the major leagues was 45 points higher than it had been in 1915. Only four hitters in the first two decades of the century had hit 0.400 or better; eight batters achieved this distinction in the twenties. By 1930, major-league teams averaged three and a half more runs per game than in 1915. The most remarkable development of all was the quantity of home runs. Major-league totals quadrupled from 384 homers in 1915 to 1,565 in 1930. While aficionados of "scientific" baseball saw the hitting revolution as abominable, fans loved it.[13]

An Age of Team Dynasties

While the major leagues argued that measures such as the draft and the reserve clause would help equalize competition among teams, and thus increase fan interest, this did not come to pass. From the start of the twentieth century, the clubs located in the largest cities enjoyed better records than those in smaller cities. From 1900 to 1952, the New York Giants, Brooklyn Dodgers, and Chicago Cubs won 30 of 52 National League pennants. Until the purchase of the New York Yankees by new owners in 1915, the size of the market area bore little relationship to team success in the American League. But after the Yankees acquired Babe Ruth in 1920, they proceeded to win 20 of the next 32 flags. Through 1980, the combined franchises in New York, Chicago, and Los Angeles won over half of the total flags of the two leagues.

The main cause for big-city success was simple: Big-city teams could draw more fans, make more money, and buy up the best players. The history of the New York dynasty vividly reveals the importance of the market area served by the club and the advantages of wealthy, freespending owners. The club had a mediocre record until 1915, when it was purchased by Jacob Ruppert Jr., a wealthy brewer, and Tillinghast Huston, a prosperous engineer. The club's performance slowly improved as the owners purchased player talent from minor-league clubs as well as other big-league clubs. The big breakthrough came between 1919 and 1923, when the Boston Red Sox virtually became the Yankee farm club. Harry Frazee, a Broadway producer and owner of the Red Sox, sought the money to finance his shows by dismantling his powerful baseball team. (The Red Sox had won pennants in 1915, 1916, and 1918.) In 1919, he sold star pitcher Carl Mays to the Yankees for $40,000, and the next year startled the baseball world by selling Babe Ruth to the Yankees for $125,000 (plus a $300,000 loan), a sum twice as high as had ever previously been paid for a player. By 1923, 11 members of the 24-man Yankee roster had formerly played with Boston. The hapless Red Sox sank to the American League cellar in 1922, where they remained for eight of the next nine seasons. The Yankees, in contrast, continued to buy up top talent and lost the American League flag only 14 times over the next 45 years.[14]

The most successful small-market franchise, the St. Louis Cardinals, succeeded because general manager Branch Rickey managed to offset some of the advantages enjoyed by big-city clubs through an ingenious method of avoiding expensive player purchases: the farm system. After joining the poverty-stricken Cardinals in 1917, Rickey slowly but methodically purchased direct ownership of minor-league clubs. By 1940, the Cardinal system contained 32 clubs and 700 players. The Rickey system produced remarkable results. The Cardinals won nine league championships between 1926 and 1946 and took second place six times. The Cardinals profited from player sales as well; in one year alone 65 players from their farm system were listed on the rosters of other big-league clubs. Initially, owners of the other clubs resisted the ownership of minor-league clubs, but as the success of the Rickey system became evident, they too began to emulate St. Louis.

The Negro Leagues

In baseball's heyday, the major leagues were only the tip of the baseball iceberg, the pinnacle of an extensive system of less exalted teams. Some of the best players competed in a shifting amalgam of teams that became collectively known as the Negro Leagues. Barred by the "gentlemen's agreement" from big-league play, and from most other predominantly white squads as well, African American players and entrepreneurs formed their own teams. As with the major leagues, the top clubs were based in major cities, where a swelling population of southern migrants was helping to build a full range of vibrant urban black institutions. In 1920, Andrew "Rube" Foster, a star pitcher and manager of the Chicago American Giants, formed the Negro National League, which had two teams in Chicago and one each in Detroit, Indianapolis, Kansas City, and St. Louis. The Great Depression temporarily killed the league in 1931, but it re-formed two years later, and eventually became the Negro American League. The Negro Leagues achieved their greatest prosperity in the 1940s, a time when the annual all-star games held in Chicago filled major-league parks to capacity and teams frequently attracted as many as 5,000 fans to regular-season weekend contests.

The Negro Leagues were never as central to black baseball as the major leagues were to white baseball. Of some 200 games played by each black team in a season, only a third were league games. African Americans simply did not have enough discretionary income to support full-fledged black leagues. To survive, black teams barnstormed, traveling throughout the United States, Canada, and the Caribbean to play each other, local semipro teams (both black and white), and the occasional major-league barnstorming team. Barnstorming demanded flexibility—facilities and equipment were frequently subpar—and it required showmanship as well as skill, keeping players on their toes.

Pitcher Satchel Paige, perhaps the quintessential Negro League player, illustrated the multifaceted talent required to thrive in such a challenging situation. Born in Mobile, Alabama, Paige became an extraordinary talented pitcher, often described by both black and white players as the best they had ever faced. In the major leagues, a player of his caliber would likely have been purchased by a big-city team and kept for an entire career. Making a living in the Negro Leagues required far more initiative. Between 1926 and 1932 Paige played for eight teams in eight different cities, including Birmingham, Nashville, New Orleans, Baltimore, Cleveland, and Pittsburgh. He then played in Mexico and the Dominican Republic before settling down to several years with the Kansas City Monarchs. He enhanced his reputation—and thus his appeal to spectators—through unparalleled showmanship. He became known for calling his outfielders to the infield and pitching without them, for promising to strike out strings of batters, and for the colorful names he developed for his blazing fastball ("bee ball," "jump ball," and "trouble ball"). "Just the sight of him strolling languorously toward the mound—an improbably figure rising high on pencil-thin legs—was enough to send waves of excitement coursing through the ballpark," historian Robert Peterson wrote.[15]

U.S.-Caribbean Connections

Baseball also thrived outside the United States, particularly in the Caribbean Basin, where the game had established itself in the late nineteenth century. Twentieth-century baseball was marked by a steady exchange of players between the United States and a number of Latin American countries. Although players from Latin America complicated the major league's racial dichotomy, light-skinned players could claim European credentials. Cuban catcher Miguel "Mike" Gonzalez, for example, was described by one supporter as "of pure Spanish blood, not of the mongrel Indian or Negro mixture." Several dozen Latin American players, most of them from Cuba, played in the major leagues in the 1930s and 1940s. Players whose African ancestry was too visible for the major leagues to risk, such as Jose Mendez, Cristobal Torrienti, and Martin Dihigo, made careers with Negro League teams. (Babe Ruth once reportedly remarked that if Mendez and Torrienti were allowed to join the Yankees, "we would win the pennant in July, and go fishing for the rest of the season.") Many Latinos played for the New York Cubans and the Cuban Stars, Negro League teams run by Alejandro "Alex" Pompez, a Florida-born son of Cuban immigrants who used multifarious connections to build teams that mixed Latinos from the Caribbean with African Americans.[16]

U.S. players also traveled south. Nations such as Cuba and the Dominican Republic played their professional season in the winter, and a number of U.S. professionals, both black and white, headed to the region in the off-season to pick up some extra money through barnstorming or playing for professional teams. The Mexican League, in contrast, had a summer season, and starting in 1937 began to compete with U.S. teams for U.S. talent. Headed up by oil tycoon Jorge Pasquel, the deep-pocketed league offered a significant incentive to U.S. players, particularly African Americans, who could often make more money playing in the Mexican League than in the Negro Leagues. In 1941, for example, Josh Gibson, the great catcher for Pittsburgh's Homestead Grays, was lured to Veracruz with a significant salary increase. Other Negro League greats moved for a time as well, including Satchel Paige, Willie Wells, James Dandridge, and James "Cool Papa" Bell. When U.S. leagues retaliated by attempting to blacklist players who signed with Mexican teams, the Mexican League responded by tightening its hold on its own players, a move that would make it difficult for U.S. teams to recruit Mexican players into the twenty-first century.[17]

Latin American baseball in fact offered a model of an integrated game, with players of all colors and backgrounds competing together. The fierce competition made it clear that the major leagues did not remain all-white through a lack of talent among dark-skinned players. White players took orders from Latin American managers, and African American catchers showed themselves thoroughly capable of working effectively with white pitchers. For African American players, life in Latin America also offered a welcome break from the segregation and discrimination that was so much a part of daily life in the United States. While Latin American countries had their own hierarchies of color, they were generally far less rigid than those found in the United States. "I am not faced with the racial problem in Mexico," explained Willie Wells, who earned the nickname "El Diabolo" from his Mexican fans. "When I travel in Vera Cruz we live in the best hotels, we eat in the best restaurants and we can go anywhere we care to." Catcher Bill Cash felt the same relief. "You would be real thirsty and see a water fountain and look above it for the 'White Only' sign and there was none," Cash recalled. "Water never tasted so good."[18]

End of an Era

Baseball's status as the top American sport would not last forever. The professional game suffered heavily during the Great Depression and then during World War II. There were great players aplenty in the thirties and forties—Hank Greenburg, Ted Williams, Joe DiMaggio, and Stan Musial, to name a few—but none had the magic of Babe Ruth. Only a few clubs prospered. Owners experimented with new ways to recoup lost fan support; they inaugurated an annual All-Star game between the best players of each league, founded the Cooperstown Hall of Fame in 1936, and relaxed restrictions on radio broadcast. Larry MacPhail, general manager of the Cincinnati Reds, daringly departed from some of the game's staid traditions, introducing night baseball, red uniforms, cigarette girls in satin pants, and usherettes as well as helping break down the resistance to radio. (Although in the 1920s the Chicago Cubs had permitted all of the club's games to be broadcast and the club had experienced a sharp increase in attendance, most clubs feared that radio broadcasts would reduce ticket-buying.)

Conclusion

In the first half of the twentieth century, baseball became the undisputed leader among American sports, solidifying its claims to be the national pastime. Shrewd economic decisions on the part of major team owners, bolstered when the Supreme Court exempted baseball from federal antitrust legislation, put the sport on a firm financial footing. Dramatic stars—most notably the inimitable Babe Ruth—kept fans involved. Baseball also made its mark at local levels, with an unmatched number of teams in every kind of community, enlivened by the periodic visits of colorful barn-stormers. But this exalted status would not last forever. Following World War II, a new set of developments that included the exodus from cities to suburbs, the advent of television broadcast, and competition from the upstart National Football League would challenge the sport's claim to be the nation's sport.

Critical Thinking Questions

1. Baseball's early promoters sought to establish baseball as the "American" game. What arguments did they use to establish that claim, and what do those arguments tell us about the nature of American identity in the early twentieth century?
2. African American baseball players faced both opportunities and challenges in the first decades of the twentieth century. Beyond playing skill, what qualities do you think that African American players such as Satchel Paige needed to succeed in this era? Were these qualities different from those needed by white players?
3. For the most part, baseball was racially segregated in the United States and integrated in Latin America. What lessons might U.S. players and coaches, both black and white, have learned from integrated Latin American play?

Notes

1. See Harold Seymour, *Baseball*, 3 vols. (New York: Oxford University Press, 1960, 1970, 1990); David Voigt, *American Baseball*, 3 vols. (Norman: University of Oklahoma Press, vols. 1 and 2, 1966, and University Park: Penn State University Press, 1983); Robert F. Burk, *Never Just a Game* and *Much More Than a Game* (Chapel Hill: University of North Carolina Press, 1994 and 2001); Benjamin G. Rader, *Baseball: A History of America's Game*, 3rd ed. (Urbana: University of Illinois Press, 2008); S.A. Riess, *Touching Base*, rev. ed (Urbana: University of Illinois Press, 1998); Leverett T. Smith Jr., *The American Dream and the National Game* (Bowling Green, OH: Bowling Green University Popular Culture Press, 1970); Richard Crepeau, *Baseball: America's Diamond Mind* (Lincoln: University of Nebraska Press, 2000); G. Edward White, *Creating the National Pastime: Baseball Transforms Itself, 1903–1953* (Princeton, NJ: Princeton University Press, 1996); and Dean A. Sullivan, ed. *Middle Innings: A Documentary History of Baseball, 1900–1948* (Lincoln: University of Nebraska Press, 1998).
2. Albert Spalding, *America's National Game* (Lincoln: University of Nebraska Press, 1992), 4.
3. Ibid.

4. For these parallels, see Seymour, *Baseball*, I, 4.

5. Quoted in Seymour, *Baseball*, II, 4.

6. Quoted in Smith, *The American Dream*, 190.

7. Lawrence S. Ritter, *The Glory of Their Times* (New York: Macmillan, 1966), 49.

8. Ibid., 44–5.

9. See Rader, *Baseball*, 96–101.

10. See especially Charles Alexander, *John McGraw* (New York: H. Holt, 1988).

11. Ty Cobb and Al Stump, *My Life in Baseball* (Garden City, NY: Doubleday, 1961), 280. See also Charles Alexander, *Ty Cobb* (New York: Oxford University Press, 1984).

12. Quotations in Seymour, *Baseball*, II, 278.

13. See Rader, *Baseball*, 124–28, and William Curran, *Big Sticks* (New York: Morrow, 1990).

14. Ray Kennedy and Nancy Williamson, "Money: The Monster Threatening Sports," *Sports Illustrated* 49 (July 1978), 80. See also Lance E. Davis, "Self-regulation in Baseball, 1909–1971," in Roger Noll, ed., *Government and the Sports Business* (Washington, DC: Carnegie Foundation, 1974), 349–86.

15. Robert Peterson, *Only the Ball Was White* (Englewood Cliffs, NJ: Prentice Hall, 1970), 129–44. See also Donn Rogosin, *Invisible Men* (New York: Atheneum, 1973); Jules Tygiel, *Baseball's Great Experiment* (New York: Oxford University Press, 1983), chapter 2; Janet Bruce, *The Kansas City Monarchs* (Lawrence: University Press of Kansas, 1985); and Rob Ruck, *Sandlot Seasons* (Urbana: University of Illinois Press, 1987).

16. Jorge Iber, et. al., *Latinos in U.S. Sport: A History of Isolation, Cultural Identity and Acceptance* (Champaign, IL: Human Kinetics, 2011), 119, 83. For an account of Alejandro Pompez's life and career, see Adrian Burgos, Jr., *Cuban Star: How One Negro League Owner Changed the Face of Baseball* (New York: Hill and Wang, 2011).

17. Adrian Burgos, Jr., *Playing America's Game: Baseball, Latinos and the Color Line* (Berkeley: University of California Press, 2007), 167–68.

18. Quoted in ibid., 164, 167.

CHAPTER 12

The Intercollegiate Football Spectacle

A Georgia Tech University player employs a relatively new football technique known as the forward pass on a Thanksgiving Day game between Georgia Tech and Auburn University, 1921.

LEARNING OBJECTIVES

12.1 Explain the factors that turned college football from an upper-class sport into a popular culture obsession, as well as the challenges that college officials faced in keeping the sport under control.

12.2 Detail the conflicts that threatened college football at the turn of the century and the different steps that colleges took to defuse them.

12.3 Analyze the significance of football's role as a new focus for identity

and community pride in the face of massive social change.

12.4 Describe some of the communities where football proved especially appealing, and explain the sources of that appeal.

12.5 Outline the factors that catapulted Notre Dame coach Knute Rockne to national hero status.

12.6 Summarize the findings of the Carnegie Report and its effects on college football programs.

In 1939, while the United States was still in the midst of the Great Depression and World War II had just commenced in Europe, the *New York Times Magazine* announced the arrival of a new football season. Author L. H. Robbins only casually mentioned the game itself. Instead, he sought to describe the atmosphere that accompanied college football games. "The cheer leaders turning cartwheels on the turf. The mascot mules, lion cubs, bulldogs and what not." The coaches on the sidelines, and on the benches, the "blanketed reserves." "The bands and the banners. The score-card scouts flashing their signal cards." In the stands, the "beauty in fox and mink and chivalry in coonskin....And below, on white-striped green, the half-dozen officials who risk their middle-aged lives and limbs to run the game, and twenty-two lusty lads who play it."[1] For nearly all the fans, it was not the game itself, but the total experience that brought them outdoors on crisp fall afternoons.

In describing the centrality of *spectacle* to college football, Robbins recognized an important fact. During the first half of the twentieth century, baseball was the national pastime. But it was football, especially the college game, that emerged as the nation's single greatest team sporting spectacle. In a society that celebrated few holidays, college football became a "time out" from normal routines, a time of pageantry and revelry in which millions let go of their emotions and had fun. With its uniforms, school colors, card sections, bands, cheerleaders, cheering spectators, hip flasks, and homecoming queens, football was, in a vital sense, America's equivalent to Europe's great carnivals and festivals. Indeed, by the 1930s journalists were calling the sport "King Football." In communities small and large across the nation, the sportive monarch offered millions a momentary release from their daily cares. King Football helped to tie them together and to provide them with a shared identity.

The Age of Crisis

The story of football's emergence as a great public spectacle began in an age of crisis. Between 1890 and 1913, the game's supporters contended with heated conflicts over injuries, deaths, eligibility, recruitment, and payments for players, all of which threatened college football's very existence.

One controversy revolved around the idea of amateurism. Many supporters, including most of the game's most articulate enthusiasts, were upper-class Anglophiles. They continued to believe that the game ought to be played in a manner similar to English upper-class sports. Football, they argued, should be an athlete-centered affair, one that was played out of a deep love for one's college and for the sheer fun of it. Athletes should never play for pay. Neither should they play too seriously or strenuously. For "gentlemen," sport should always be an avocation rather than a vocation. But while powerful upper-class traditions of restraint and convention governed English college sports, custom meant far less to American collegians, who frequently infused the gridiron with the values of the marketplace. "The spirit of the American youth, as of the American man, is to win, to 'get there,' by fair means or foul," observed a *Nation* writer in 1890, "and the lack of moral scruple which pervades the struggles of the business world meets with temptations equally irresistible in the miniature contests of the football field."[2]

One temptation was to recruit the best athletes available, regardless of their academic interests. As early as the 1860s and 1870s, Northeastern colleges hired professional rowers to strengthen their crews. As football grew in importance, college teams began to employ "tramp athletes," who made their way around the country playing college football for pay. Colleges offered other enticements as well. In 1905, *McClure's* magazine reported that James J. Hogan, the renowned 27-year old captain of the Yale team, lived in a style befitting a prince. He enjoyed free tuition, a free suite in swank Vanderbilt Hall, a $100 scholarship, a 10-day paid vacation in Cuba and a monopoly on the sale of American Tobacco Company products on Yale's campus. Apparently the students took Hogan's good fortunes in stride, for they affectionately spoke of smoking "Hogan's cigarettes."[3]

Apart from paying players to play and using nonstudents on their teams, college athletic associations also sought to enhance their prospects of winning by employing professional coaches, a decision that dramatically changed the game. "Players like to win," observed a former Yale player in 1904, "but head coaches and especially paid coaches, had to win."[4] To reach that goal, some coaches drove their players relentlessly, subjected them to countless repetitions of the same plays and regaled them with verbal harangues. "What has become of the natural, spontaneous joy of the contest?" asked Owen Johnson through a fictional character early in the century. "Instead, you have the most perfectly organized business systems for achieving the required result—success. Football is slavish work."[5]

The greatest outcry, however, came from injuries and deaths. The notorious "flying wedge" formations, in which players linked arms and sought to force their way through clusters of defenders, had been banned in 1894. But teams continued to use mass-momentum plays in which the ball was advanced largely through brute force, and which produced ample numbers of bloodied heads, broken limbs, and unconscious players, as well as a startling number of deaths. In 1897, after one such death, the Georgia legislature sought to abolish the sport, only to have the governor veto the measure.

Criticism of football reached a crescendo in 1905 and 1906 when muckraking journals such as *McClure's, Collier's,* and *Outlook* published scathing exposés of the sport. The magazines described in shocking detail how American collegians ignored the conventions of gentlemanly behavior; laid out the "insidious" role of money in the sport; and explained how teams devised tactics to "knock out" key opponents early in the contests. The outcry prompted an intervention by President Theodore Roosevelt, an ardent supporter of vigorous athletics and the father of a Harvard player. Roosevelt invited a select group to a White House conference intended "to get them to come to a gentleman's agreement not to have mucker play."[6]

A few months later, after Union College player Harold P. Moore died from injuries suffered in a game against New York University, NYU president Henry B. McCracken called together a group of college presidents who decided to convene a national college convention and form a new rules committee, wresting control of the game's rules away from Walter Camp and his allies. On December 28, 1905, the convention quickly organized the Intercollegiate Athletic Association (IAA), which became the National Collegiate Athletic Association (NCAA) five years later. The delegates gave the NCAA no power to punish colleges but allowed it to formulate standards of conduct and—most important—to create rules committees.

Reducing football brutality by changing the game's rules proved more difficult than anticipated. For the next several years, the rules committee made controversial decisions such as expanding the yardage required for a first down from five yards to 10 and allowing a limited version of a forward pass (the ball had to be thrown five yards or more to the right or left from where it had been put into play, and an incomplete pass brought a 15-yard penalty). When those changes had limited effects, the committee tried again, with changes that forbade interlocking interference, liberalized the passing regulations, and gave teams four downs, rather than three, to make a 10-yard gain.

These cumulative rule changes marked the beginning of the "modern" game of football. Coaches, particularly in the West, slowly began to exploit the potential of the forward pass. In 1913, when Notre Dame came east to play Army, passes from Gus Dorais to Knute Rockne resulted in a stunning upset for the tiny men's Catholic school. Later in the same season the cadets profited from their earlier disaster by using the "Western" passing game to defeat archrival Navy. By producing a far more exciting game, these early twentieth-century changes helped to make college football into a sporting spectacle.[7]

The Formation of Conferences

Neither changes in the way the game was played nor the formation of a national association addressed the issues of recruitment, eligibility, and financial support of college athletes. In theory, the colleges should have been able to establish a level playing field by joining together, establishing a set of common rules and imposing harsh penalties on one another's violations. But given their continuing allegiance to amateurism and their reluctance to admit that their football programs were commercial enterprises, they ultimately allowed each school to govern its sports as it saw fit. As a result, many colleges turned to regional associations or conferences to bring order to the game.

College presidents first stepped into the tricky business of governing the game in 1895 with the organization of the Intercollegiate Conference of Faculty Representatives. Later known as the Western Conference, and then as the Big Ten, the conference initially included the large Midwestern universities of Chicago, Illinois, Purdue, Michigan, Minnesota, and Northwestern. From its founding, the conference conceived of itself as the "anchor of amateur athletics in America." It pioneered eligibility rules, the prohibition of subsidies to student athletes, and the faculty supervision of athletes—measures subsequently copied by other conferences. The Conference of Faculty Representatives had one major weakness, however—it left enforcement in the hands of faculty committees of the member institutions. It soon became clear, as asserted by reporter Edward S. Jordan in 1905, that faculty control was "a myth."[8] At the typical college, the faculty shared the actual supervision of sports with coaches, presidents, trustees, and the alumni, any of which might thwart faculty control. Moreover, faculty committees were often handpicked by the college presidents, and were just as interested in the success of the football team as any other group.

"King Football"

The reign of football as the king of American sporting spectacles began in the 1920s, as attendance at college games doubled and gate receipts tripled. From Columbus, Ohio, to Los Angeles, California, colleges built colossal stadia of steel and concrete. Many colleges named their fields "Memorial Stadium," thereby explicitly linking football to patriotism and the casualties of World War I. In 1920, only one college field could seat 70,000 fans, but by 1930 seven had exceeded that capacity. By comparison, only two major-league baseball parks could hold 70,000 spectators in 1930.

Attendance was only one measure of "King Football's" success. College football became the darling of the media. During the 1920s, the sheer space devoted to football in the nation's press doubled. By the end of the decade, five different newsreel companies offered theatergoers moving pictures of the previous Saturday afternoon's action. In the 1930s, fans could hear dozens of games on radio; football was the subject of no fewer than 48 full-length movies; and the most popular mass-circulation magazines of the day, the *Saturday Evening Post* and *Colliers'*, published a total of 42 football stories.[9]

Much of the success of King Football's reign in the interwar years and afterward rested on the sport's growing capacity for evoking community pride and identity. As early as the 1890s, the game helped bind together local college communities of students, professors, alumni, and townspeople. It continued to do so throughout the twentieth century. "Through no design or deliberation on the part of any man or group of men," observed Ralph Cooper Hutchison in 1952, "football has become the emotionally integrating force of the American college."[10]

In the twentieth century, as Michael Oriard has persuasively argued, the forces of modernity increased the importance of football as a constituent of local identities. By the 1920s and 1930s, a national consumer culture; a nationalization of sights and sounds via the media; the growth of a new white-collar class that thought of itself in national rather than local terms; the shocking behavior of youth; the growing ethnic, racial, and religious pluralism of the big cities; and a growing secularization of American life all seemed to threaten those who grounded their identities in their local communities. Peoples from the countryside and smaller cities and towns tended to see themselves under siege by the modern ways of the big cities. The older middle class of small businessmen, locally oriented professionals, prosperous farmers, and skilled workingmen continued to find their identities and their values in the ways handed down from the past and in their families, their churches, and their local communities or neighborhoods rather than in their occupations or in whatever happened to be currently fashionable. Locally based athletic teams joined extended families, local churches, local civic organizations, and gossipy local newspapers in bolstering a traditional way of life.[11]

Not unexpectedly, college football was especially popular in the smaller cities and towns that hosted major state universities. Many citizens in states without a conspicuously significant history, great civic monuments, or remarkable physical scenery not only formed powerful emotional bonds to their state university's football team but also found in the team an important source of personal identity.

Many Americans also continued to see college football as an especially effective testing ground for manliness and masculinity. According to most of the media, as well as the commentary of coaches and players, football was *the* one sport in which a "sissy" could not survive. Boys with the misfortune of having falsetto voices, "angel faces," pink cheeks, curly hair, or some other explicitly female trait could, according to a popular theme found in the mass-circulation periodicals of the day, prove their manliness on the gridiron. As the separate spheres of the sexes characteristic of the nineteenth century broke down, as work required less physical prowess, and as men and women engaged increasingly in shared activities, football became one of the few arenas in which traditional manliness could be affirmed. Simultaneously, and perhaps paradoxically, it was also one in which open male bonding could be expressed without arousing suspicions.

College teams gained standing and importance to the extent that they could obtain national recognition. In the 1920s, and to a somewhat lesser extent in the 1930s, the route to prestige led to the Northeast, where the Big Three—Harvard, Yale, and Princeton—continued to rule and where the most influential sportswriters covered games. Colleges everywhere sought to schedule and win games with the Big Three. If unsuccessful in scheduling such games, they sought foes from among lesser-known schools in other regions. That four special trains brought 750 Southern Methodist University fans from Dallas to West Point for a 1928 game with Army offers a glimpse of the degree to which fans were committed to winning intersectional recognition.

Each region allegedly possessed a distinctive style of play, but during the interwar years college offensive systems were highly portable. Either Knute Rockne's famed "Notre Dame Box" or Pop Warner's equally famous single- and double-wing formations prevailed nearly everywhere. Each of these formations featured "hikes" directly from the center to the ball carrier (or passer) who stood several yards behind the line of scrimmage. Unlike the earlier mass formations, the newer systems featured sweeps outside the tackles or ends. "There are no longer any distinctive systems in football," wrote Fielding H. Yost on the eve of the 1940 season. "Nobody sees a balanced line any more except at Notre Dame, and even some of the Rockne-trained coaches are getting away from it. There is only one formation that's any good and it's the single wing."[12] In that very year, however, Clark Shaughnessey at Stanford reintroduced the T formation, which gradually replaced the single wing in popularity. All of the formations used since then essentially represent variations on the T.

Nevertheless, in the minds of fans and the media, the playing style of the college teams mirrored the cultures of the regions from which they came. The Midwest's college teams were said to feature a run-oriented, rock-'em, sock-'em style of power football, as epitomized by Jock Sutherland's University of Pittsburgh teams. Reflecting the Wild West shootout spirit of the Southwest, teams from that region were said to rely more on a wide-open passing attack, such as Southern Methodist's "aerial circus." (That these stereotypes possessed some validity was probably due more to differences in weather than regional cultural variations.) Teams from the Deep South emphasized defense and were said to play with the fervent spirit of the antebellum Old South.

The employment of football to express regional consciousness and identity was especially powerful in the South. For the South, at least in the minds of the media and many fans, every intersectional contest became a reenactment of the Civil War. The media from both sections, for example, identified Dixie running backs with DeForest's raiders or Pickett's cavalry at Gettysburg. Writers from both North and South embraced the "romance with the legendary Old South and Lost Cause."[13] In addition, Southerners saw prowess at the "modern" sport as a way to counter widespread stereotypes of Southerners as "backwards" and to advertise their region's fitness for modern life. Southerners took particular pride in the University of Alabama teams coached by Tennessee native Wallace Wade, who led the Crimson Tide to four conference championships and three national championships between 1923 and 1931. As Alabama governor Bibb Graves put it, "We have been hampered industrially by an unfair picture the world seems to have of Alabama as a state of undersized, weak people living in swamp lands full of malaria and tuberculosis." Wade's powerful teams, he continued, swept those images away. "None who have seen Wade's Tide in action, or have read the accounts of the games, will continue to embrace the idea."[14]

Not all of college football's popularity sprang from its capacity to arouse regional or local identities. Alumni of the Northeastern elite schools, who were scattered across the country, avidly followed the football exploits of their alma maters. The world wars supplied ready-made cheering sections for the two service academies. Those who had worn khakis in the wars supported Army; bellbottoms made one a Navy rooter. After World War II, when the Big Three de-emphasized football, the annual Army–Navy games attracted more national interest than the classic Yale–Princeton or Yale–Harvard matches.

No football team exceeded the "Fighting Irish" of Notre Dame in attaining a national following and fervent fan support. Beginning in the 1920s, Catholics everywhere, regardless of their ethnic origins, became rabid Irish fans, as well as devotees of Notre Dame's coach Knute Rockne. When Notre Dame met Army in their annual tilt in New York, the passions of the city's large ethnic population reached a fever pitch. "New York was never before, or since, so sweetly gay and electric as when Rock brought his boys to town," wrote Paul Gallico. "The city was wild with excitement."[15]

As a minority within a predominately Protestant culture, one that in the 1920s came under assault from the revived Ku Klux Klan, Roman Catholics found a powerful source of identity and pride in the successes of Notre Dame's football team. Regardless of any other connection with the college, Notre Dame for them became "our team." In the 1930s, according to Mary Jo Weaver, a professor of religion at Indiana University, "the custom began in primary and secondary parochial schools, each Friday in the fall, to have students pray for a Notre Dame victory the following day.... It was an important part of our 'Holy War' against the Protestant majority in America."[16]

As Notre Dame's experience made clear, football could be a means of college building. In a nation where colleges and universities engaged in keen competition for students and public support, football victories, especially victories in intersectional games, could call local and national attention to hitherto obscure and little-known schools. Indeed, tiny Centre College of Kentucky's victory over mighty Harvard in 1921 made anything seem possible. Attention gathered from such gridiron exploits, college authorities frequently believed, aided in the recruitment of students, increased support for the institution by local business and community leaders, deepened the bonds of alumni loyalty and, if a public-supported institution, might increase appropriations from state legislatures. To the extent that college leaders accepted the idea that football could be a means of institution building, they were more likely to throw their support behind their college's football team and to acquiesce to violations of the amateur spirit.

The Football Coach as Hero

Unlike baseball, in which heroes sprang from the ranks of the players, in football it was the coaches who won the greatest renown. While student athletes came and went, coaches such as Amos Alonzo Stagg (Chicago), Knute Rockne (Notre Dame), Glenn "Pop" Warner (Pittsburgh, Stanford, Carlisle, and Temple), and Dana X. Bible (Texas A & M, Nebraska, and Texas) became well-known public figures with enduring reputations. The heroic status of coaches flowed, in large part, from the belief that good coaching spelled the difference between victory and defeat. Given the stakes involved and the belief in the importance of coaching, it was not surprising that by the 1920s football coaches typically received higher salaries than the highest paid professors on campus.

Knute Rockne outdistanced all other rivals in capturing the public imagination. As with Babe Ruth, Red Grange, Jack Dempsey, and other sports-related heroes of the 1920s, Rockne's life seemed to embody the story of the self-made man. Born in Norway, Rockne had immigrated with his family to Chicago as a boy. At the age of 22, according to legend, he enrolled in Notre Dame and "went down to South Bend with a suitcase and $1,000 feeling the strangeness of being a lone Norse-Protestant invader of a Catholic stronghold."[17] (Rockne later converted to Catholicism.) After graduation, he stayed on as a chemistry assistant and assistant football coach. In 1918, at the age of 30, he landed the head coaching job.

Rockne's fame sprang mostly from what Murray Sperber has described as "Notre Dame's unique formula." The formula included a rich athletic culture, "fan identification based on ethnicity and religion, an innovative and charismatic coach, a phenomenal won-lost record, powerful media allies, and immense and increasing numbers of supporters throughout the nation."[18] Playing against the best teams with whom he could schedule games (Big Ten and Northeastern elite colleges refused to play the upstart Catholic school), Rockne's teams recorded 105 victories, 12 defeats, and 5 ties. His teams enjoyed five unbeaten and untied seasons.

No coach was more charismatic than Rockne. Both the players and the press loved him for his quick wit. He could be caustically hilarious. "The only qualification for a lineman is to be big and dumb," he reputedly said. Then turning to the smirking backs, he said: "To be a back, you only need to be dumb."[19] According to the media hype of the day, Rockne was not only a teacher but also a father figure; he, along with fellow coaches at other colleges, guided the "boys" through the difficult rites of passage that transformed them into "men."

While trailing Army by a touchdown in 1928, Rockne allegedly made the most memorable half-time speech in football history. He told of George Gipp, famed Notre Dame halfback, who had tragically died from pneumonia at the end of the 1920 season. According to Rockne, when Gipp was on his deathbed he gave his coach one final request: "When things are wrong and the breaks are beating the boys, tell them to go in there with all they've got and win one just for the Gipper."[20] In the second half, the Irish responded with two touchdowns to win 12 to 6. In 1940, Warner Brothers retold the story in the popular film *Knute Rockne—All American*, in which Pat O'Brien played Rockne and an up-and-coming young actor named Ronald Reagan played the Gipper. To answer his extensive mail and handle his endorsement opportunities, Rockne hired a personal agent (Christy Walsh). When Rockne died in a plane crash in 1931, he assured his own apotheosis.

Incomplete Democratization

As the story of the rise of Notre Dame football to national prominence suggests, in the first half of the twentieth century the sport became less exclusive than it had been in the past. It spread geographically from the elite Northeastern schools to lesser-known state universities and private schools, and helped "to put on the national map" isolated state universities such as Kansas and Nebraska, as well as hitherto unknown Southern schools such as Alabama and Georgia Tech.

The brawny stars who lured fans to the massive new stadiums in the 1920s also came increasingly from farming and working-class, ethnic families. Lower-class youth who surmounted obstacles to become college football heroes emerged as a favorite trope of the newspapers, periodicals, and movies in the interwar years. Paradoxically, the ethnic transformation of college football came at the very time that the United States developed a policy of immigration exclusion. Following the conclusions of popular pseudo-science of the day, which placed ethnic and racial groups in a rigid, hierarchical arrangement, the Immigration Act of 1924 sharply reduced immigration from Southern and Eastern Europe while completely excluding Asians. Yet, the media rarely, if ever, presented the appearance of the new ethnics in college football in negative terms.

As was so often the case, however, African Americans faced far greater obstacles than other minorities. African American colleges developed a robust football culture, and the black press covered African American teams as lavishly as the white press covered white teams. Hotly contested rivalries included Howard–Lincoln, Hampton–Morgan State, and Virginia Union–Virginia State. In the 1930s, Morgan State coach Edward Hurt, along with assistant coach Talmadge Hill, created a coaching dynasty to rival that of any white school. But unlike Catholic Notre Dame or Native American Carlisle, black college teams did not have the opportunity to prove themselves against the nation's most prominent teams, even though black newspapers frequently campaigned for interracial matchups.[21]

The handful of African Americans who played for predominantly white schools faced a different set of challenges. Northern teams regularly benched black players when playing Southern opponents. When they did take the field, black players could expect rough treatment—in the most brutal of many incidents, Jack Trice, the first black athlete at Iowa State, died from injuries suffered in a 1921 game against Minnesota. After the death of Walter Camp, selection of All-American teams shifted to Grantland Rice, who pointedly overlooked top black players such as William King of Long Island University, Kenny Washington of UCLA (who had Jackie Robinson as a teammate), and Wilmeth Sidat-Singh of Syracuse University.

Continuing Controversies

While most football fans worried little or not at all about the commercial or semi-professional character of the college game, a small but loud set of critics continued to reiterate charges similar to those that had been leveled at the game during the opening years of the twentieth century. These critics, who were usually intellectuals, focused on a fundamental contradiction at the heart of big-time college athletics: How could the colleges maintain the illusion that their athletes were student amateurs while recruiting and frequently subsidizing athletes with little or no regard for their academic qualifications or performances?

This contradiction was at the bottom of a continuing set of "crises" as well as fitful attempts at reform. The first of these erupted in 1925 when Red Grange decided to turn professional before finishing his senior year of college. The next came in 1929 when the Carnegie Foundation issued a bombshell. Based on information gathered from 112 colleges and universities, the report's chief author, Howard J. Savage, concluded that only 28 colleges operated "ethical" athletic programs. Unethical practices ran the gamut from occasional contacts with potential recruits by coaches and friends of the team to "an intensely organized, sometimes subtle, system" of recruitment.[22]

Savage also reported that the guilty colleges engaged in elaborate and ingenious systems of paying players to play. "Needy" athletes frequently received pay for nominal work such as pushing a broom, supervising intramural athletics, or dispensing towels. They might have well-paying jobs off campus; for example, in the 1930s, Ohio State University track star Jesse Owens had a job operating an elevator in the state capitol building in Columbus. Some colleges, especially those in the South and the Southwest, avoided hypocrisy simply by granting direct "athletic scholarships." Given its findings, the Carnegie report reached an obvious conclusion: "Apparently the ethical bearing of intercollegiate football contests and their scholastic aspects" were "of secondary importance to the winning of victories and financial success."[23]

After making a strong case for the importance to the colleges of having winning teams and generating money, the Carnegie report unrealistically called on college presidents and faculties to lead campaigns on behalf of institutional self-restraint. A tiny number of college presidents sought to do just that. They tried to reform their football programs by eliminating athletic scholarships, disallowing special treatment of athletes on campus, curtailing the recruitment of students solely on the basis of their athletic talents, and reducing the power of booster organizations. But, in doing so, many of the reform presidents, especially those at state universities, risked being fired. Hence, in most instances, the state university presidents retreated from reform. As Blair Cherry, the former head football coach at the University of Texas, bluntly put it: "In the final analysis the public, not the colleges, runs college football."[24]

The story of reform in private universities followed a somewhat different trajectory. Against a backdrop of growing criticism of college athletics, beginning in the mid-1930s and continuing into the postwar era, the once-powerful Ivy League schools of the Northeast began a gradual process of de-emphasizing football. Like many other intellectuals in the interwar years, Robert Maynard Hutchins, appointed president of the University of Chicago in 1929, openly rejected the time-honored argument that football was effective in building good character. In 1939, Hutchins persuaded the university's regents to abolish the sport. That the Chicago eleven failed to have a single winning season after 1924 made the decision more palatable to the university's alumni and patrons.[25] More than a dozen other schools, including once-major Catholic powers such as Fordham, St. Mary's, and Santa Clara, dropped the sport as well.

Conclusion

College football expanded enormously in the early twentieth century, becoming an institution in communities across the nation. The growing spectacle of college games could draw upward of 100,000 fans a week to newly built, often palatial stadiums. Successful teams became sources not only of excitement, but also of individual and community identity. The great popularity of college teams only heightened the dilemmas that big-time sports posed for university officials, who sought to maintain an academic tenor in a game that was increasingly a major commercial enterprise. But well-documented reports of misplaced priorities and under-the-table payments did little to dent the sport's popularity. College football would weather the Great Depression more successfully than professional baseball, in part because its higher income fans withstood the rigors of the Depression more successfully than less-well-off Americans. In the face of Nazism in the 1930s and early 1940s and Communism in the late 1940s and 1950s, college football would in fact take on greater symbolic weight, becoming a vital ingredient in what was considered by many to be "the American way of life."[26]

Critical Thinking Questions

1. In the early twentieth century, college supporters attempted to reduce violence by changing the game's rules. How successful were they, and what does the effort say about the role of rules in shaping competitive sport?
2. Both high school and college sports became important sources of community identity in the early twentieth century. What would you say was similar about those identities and what was different?
3. College football has been described as one component of the "American way of life" in the mid-twentieth century. If that is the case, what does the sport's history tell us about the strengths and drawbacks of that way of life?

Notes

1. L.H. Robbins, "As Millions Cheer or Groan," *New York Times Magazine*, October 3, 1939, 11. See Michael Oriard, *King Football: Sport and Spectacle in the Golden Age of Radio and Newsreels, Movies and Magazines, the Weekly & the Daily Press* (Chapel Hill: University of North Carolina Press, 2001), 199–200. We are deeply indebted to this book for its research and analysis of college football as spectacle. For other aspects of the chapter, see also Ronald A. Smith, *Sports and Freedom: The Rise of Big-Time College Athletics* (New York: Oxford University Press, 1988); Robin Lester, *Stagg's University: The Rise, Decline, and Fall of Big-Time Football at Chicago* (Urbana: University of Illinois Press, 1995); Murray Sperber, *Shake Down the Thunder: The Creation of Notre Dame Football* (New York: Henry Holt, 1993); John Sayle Watterson, *College Football: History, Spectacle, Controversy* (Baltimore, Md.: Johns Hopkins University Press, 2000); Patrick B. Miller, "Athletes in Academe: College Sports and American Culture, 1850–1920," unpub. Ph.D. diss., University of California, Berkeley, 1987; and Guy M. Lewis, "American Intercollegiate Football Spectacle, 1869–1917," unpub. Ph.D. diss, University of Maryland, 1964.
2. *Nation* 51 (November 20, 1890), 395.
3. H.B. Needham, "The College Athlete," *McClure's Magazine* 25 (1905), 15–28, 160–73.
4. Quoted in Smith, *Sports and Freedom*, 147.
5. Quoted in B.M. Kelley, *Yale: A History* (New Haven, CT: Yale University Press, 1974), 298.
6. For the issue of brutality, see Lewis, "American Intercollegiate Football Spectacle," 223–346; Smith, *Sports and Freedom*, chapter 14; and Watterson, *College Football*, Part 1. Watterson has found that the press grossly exaggerated the number of deaths attributable to football.
7. See Sperber, *Shake Down the Thunder*, 40.
8. E.S. Jordan, "Buying Football Victories," *Collier's* 36 (November 18, 1905), 23. For the 1920s, see Sperber, *Shake Down the Thunder*; Harold J. Savage et al., *American College Athletics* (New York: Carnegie Foundation, 1929), 100 and 101; and Watterson, *College Football*, chapters 8 and 9.
9. Oriard, *King Football*, 11–7.
10. Ralph Cooper Hutchinson, "Football: Symbol of College Unity," *Christian Century* 69 (April 16, 1952), 461.

11. See Benjamin G. Rader, *American Ways* (Fort Worth, TX: Harcourt College Publishers, 2001), chapters 8 and 9.

12. Quoted in Ron Fimrite, "A Melding of Men All Suited to a T," *Sports Illustrated* 47 (September 5, 1977), 92.

13. Oriard, *King Football,* 89. See also the essays by Patrick B. Miller and Andrew Doyle in Patrick Miller, ed., *The Sporting World of the Modern South* (Urbana: University of Illinois Press, 2002). However, also note that Ted Ownby in the same book asserts (336) that, in the South, college football "did not dominate newspapers, normal conversation, and life on Saturdays on campuses and in campus towns until the post-World War II period."

14. Andrew Doyle, "Turning the Tide: College Football and Southern Progressivism," *Southern Cultures* 3 (Fall 1997), 45.

15. Paul Gallico, *The Golden People* (New York: Doubleday, 1965), 142.

16. Quoted in Sperber, *Shake Down the Thunder,* 436–37.

17. Quoted in Edwin Pope, *Football's Greatest Coaches* (Atlanta: Tupper and Love, 1955), 195.

18. Sperber, *Shake Down the Thunder,* 185.

19. Quoted in Pope, *Football's Greatest Coaches,* 189. Sperber in *Shake Down the Thunder* subjects this legend along with others about Rockne to a systematic reexamination.

20. Quoted in Pope, *Football's Greatest Coaches,* 200.

21. Arthur Ashe, Jr., *A Hard Road to Glory: A History of the African-American Athlete, Vol. 2, 1919-1945* (New York: Amistad Press, Inc., 1993), 92–104.

22. For the impact of the report, see Oriard, *King Football,* 106–107; Watterson, *College Football,* 158–76; John R. Thelin, *Games People Play: Scandal and Reform in Intercollegiate Athletics* (Baltimore, MD: Johns Hopkins University Press, 1994), 15–37.

23. Savage, *American College Athletics,* 298.

24. Quoted in Harry Paxton, ed., *Sport U.S.A.: The Best from the Saturday Evening Post* (New York: Thomas Nelson and Sons, 1961), 405.

25. See especially Lester, *Stagg's University.*

26. See J.F. Steiner, *Americans at Play* (New York: Arno, 1933), 86–94, and *New York Times,* December 26, 1937.

CHAPTER 13

The Rise and Decline
of Organized Women's Sports

Alice Coachman, center, and other sprinters compete in the AAU 100-meter championship, 1946.

On August 6, 1926, nineteen-year-old Gertrude Ederle slathered herself with grease and entered the chilly, turbulent waters of the English Channel, the 21-mile-wide stretch of water that separated England from France. Only five men had managed to swim the full width of the Channel, and the speediest crossing had taken more than 16 hours. No one imagined a woman could do it. Ederle was determined to prove them wrong. "It was just that everybody was saying it couldn't be done," she explained many years later. "Well, every time somebody said that, I wanted to prove it could be done."[1]

Despite wind and tides that pushed her well off course, Ederle kept swimming until she reached French soil. Her time, 14 hours and 31 minutes, was nearly two hours faster than the best men's time. News of her feat flashed around the world, and when she returned home to New York, she was treated to a ticker-tape parade attended by an estimated two million people. Newspapers immediately acclaimed her as "America's Best Girl," and movie, stage, and commercial offers poured in.[2]

Gertrude Ederle emerged from a broad-based world of grassroots women's sports that took shape in the 1910s and 1920s. Working-class women in particular discovered expanded opportunities for sports in community-based programs sponsored by churches, YWCAs, settlement houses, city recreation departments, commercial or industrial concerns, and private promoters. Opportunities also arose for national and international competition. The all-male Amateur Athletic Union (AAU) inaugurated a national women's swim meet in 1916, a track championship in 1924, and a basketball tournament in 1926. A few women had participated in women's golf, tennis, and archery exhibitions at the 1900 and 1904 Olympic Games. The United States sent a team of skaters and swimmers to the 1920 Games; the American women won four of five gold medals in swimming and diving and continued to dominate those events at the 1924 and 1928 Games (Ederle won three swimming medals at the 1924 Games, a gold and two bronzes). Pressures from European track enthusiasts prompted the admission of women's track and field competition to the 1928 Games.[3]

Still, female athletes negotiated difficult terrain. Female athletic skill could be seen as intriguing, threatening, or both at the same time. Some sports, such as swimming and tennis, were cast as appropriate for women. Others, such as basketball or track, were often frowned upon. While athletic women often found acceptance within their own communities, those who stepped onto the national stage faced the more restrictive demands of middle-class womanhood, where strength and assertiveness were considered strictly "masculine" qualities. To gain acceptance in these circles, top female athletes generally had to "prove" that they were in fact normal women by contrasting their athletic accomplishments with more conventionally feminine activities. Gertrude Erdele, like tennis player Helen Wills, took this route, describing herself as an ordinary young woman who just happened to be a remarkable swimmer. According to her mother, Gertrude developed her strength from doing household chores; she was a "'plain home girl,' who preferred sewing and cooking to smoking, drinking, and going out with young men." This need to appear "normal" meant that women's sports was particularly vulnerable to social shifts—strengthening in eras that valued women's strength and independence, and falling back at times that highlighted female dependence and docility.[4]

Babe Didrikson: Triumph and Struggle

The challenges faced by female athletes showed especially clearly in the career of Babe Didrikson, the most famous and accomplished female athlete of her era. Between 1930 and 1932 Didrikson broke American, Olympic, or world records in five separate track and field events. She was a three-time All-American basketball player, and she led her team, the Dallas-based Golden Cyclones, to the AAU women's national championship in 1931. She had no peer as a golfer, winning 34 of the 88 amateur and professional tournaments she entered. She reportedly bowled a 170 average, could punt a football 75 yards, and could swim close to world record times for short distances.[5]

Growing up in a working-class culture that held female strength and assertiveness in higher esteem than did the middle and upper classes, Didrikson had no hesitation about joining the local boys in their games. At Beaumont High School, in Beaumont, Texas, she participated in all sports available to girls: volleyball, tennis, golf, basketball, and swimming. After she graduated, the Employers Casualty Company of Dallas offered her a job (ostensibly as a stenographer) and a spot on its Golden Cyclones basketball squad. The company also sent her as a one-woman team to the women's AAU track and field championships in 1932. In the space of three hours in a single afternoon, Didrikson won six gold medals and broke four world records—in the baseball throw, javelin, 80-meter hurdles, and high jump—and single-handedly amassed enough points to win the national team championship. A few weeks later, at the 1932 Olympics in Los Angeles, she shattered world records in the javelin, the 80-meter hurdles, and the high jump, though the Olympic officials disqualified her high jump because she had "dived" over the bar. Had women been permitted to enter more than three Olympic events, Didrikson would undoubtedly have won even more gold medals.

Even as Didrikson became a national sensation, however, she faced growing criticism. In the early years of her career, she emphasized her distance from conventional femininity, cutting her hair short, refusing to wear makeup, and delighting in making shocking statements about her disdain for traditional female activities. This approach put her in the news, but also prompted harsh critiques. In "The Texas Babe," published in *Vanity Fair* in 1932, noted sportswriter Paul Gallico stuck Didrikson with the label "Muscle Moll," a phrase that conjured images of a somewhat disreputable woman focused on her own strength, rather than on conventionally feminine charm ("moll" was a term generally applied to the girlfriends of the era's gangsters). Babe's tremendous skill, he went on to suggest, had not made her happy, largely because it held no attractions for men.

Such criticism had broad social effects, sending women scrambling to avoid similar censure. The term "muscle moll" became a convenient symbol for the idea of a hardened athlete, who stood no chance of finding a husband or living a normal life. In some physical education classes, signs admonished students: "DON'T BE A MUSCLE MOLL." The message was clear: Women might play sports, but taking them too seriously was perilous. "My mother used to cry when I played softball," one woman later recalled. "She'd say, 'I just don't want you to grow up to be like Babe Didrikson.'"[6]

Hazel Walker: Creating Professional Opportunities

Away from the disapproving eyes of the national press, however, thousands of other women found warm support for their athletic activities. While most women's colleges continued to discourage competition, athletically minded women found other opportunities, especially in the Midwest and the South. Women's basketball became an institution in high schools across the regions, and local businesses—especially those that employed large numbers of women—began to sponsor popular "industrial" teams such as the Golden Cyclones or the Hanes Hosiery Girls. The 1930s saw an explosion in women's softball teams, and when the Amateur Softball Association formed in 1934, it offered championship play for both men and women. In 1938, the Los Angeles area was home to nearly a thousand women's softball teams, and semiprofessional teams such as Chicago's Rockola Chicks packed stadiums with fans. The varieties of women's sports, and the zeal and creativity of participants and organizers, offer a glimpse into the vibrant and varied grassroots sporting cultures that sprang up beyond the gaze of the national press.[7]

The career of Hazel Walker, born in Arkansas in 1914, embodied the range of opportunities available to a talented and determined athlete born into the right circumstances. Walker grew up on a farm outside the tiny town of Oak Hill, Arkansas. She started playing basketball in grade school, shooting a rag-filled sock at a rain-barrel hoop. The game captivated her from the start. "My parents thought I was crazy to work so hard at basketball," she wrote. "I used to get up at five in the morning and run a mile before the school bus came. Then I'd go out to the hen house and eat two or three raw eggs, because they said that was supposed to build up your wind."[8] In her senior year, she led tiny Ashdown High to a second-place finish in the Arkansas state tournament.

Walker's next stop was Tulsa Business College, in Tulsa, Oklahoma. "Business colleges," which taught secretarial and bookkeeping skills, frequently sponsored basketball teams, and Tulsa had one of the best. Walker won a scholarship to the school, and then took the Tulsa Stenos to the 1934 AAU championship. After marrying her high school sweetheart and moving to Little Rock to work as a bookkeeper, Walker helped organize a series of AAU teams sponsored by local companies that included Lion Oil, Arkansas Motor Coaches, Dr. Pepper, and Lewis & Norwood Insurance. As the leader of the Lewis & Norwood Flyers, she captured three more AAU crowns, in 1937, 1940, and 1941.

Walker then set her sights even higher. In 1946, a few years after her husband's death, she decided to try to make a living at the game she loved. At the time, the major professional women's team was the All-American Red Heads, which had been barnstorming the country since 1936, playing exclusively against men's teams. Hazel played with the Red Heads from 1946 through 1949, before deciding to form her own team—Hazel Walker's Arkansas Travelers. Like the Red Heads, the Travelers played with men's rules against men's teams. They pursued a grueling schedule. For six-and-a-half-months out of the year they would play almost every day, driving into a town, playing an evening game, and then taking off in the morning for the next date, which might be several hundred miles away. "It was just routine—like taking a drink of water," Walker recalled. "We had a lot of doubleheaders. Sometimes we would play one game at seven and then drive forty miles and play again that same night. Then we had to get up and move the next day. We played eleven or twelve games a week sometimes."[9] For women who loved basketball, it was paradise. "Once you make up your mind, that is all there is to it," Walker wrote potential player Frances Garroutte in a recruiting letter, "I guarantee you, you will be happy, satisfied, have [the] best time you ever had or will ever have, save money, and play all the basketball you want to."[10]

Like other barnstorming teams, the Travelers played with showmanship as well as skill. The players had a repertoire of ballhandling tricks, and also developed a handful of comic, often flirtatious routines. At base, though, they were top ballplayers who kept their winning percentage high with talent, not with gimmicks. "We played it straight," Walker wrote. "We told the men to play us just like we were men. We couldn't fast break as long as they could, but we did when necessary, and we learned to conserve our energy and put it out when it counted."[11]

Walker also carefully monitored the team's appearance and behavior. Like many top-level female athletes of the time, Walker and her team members deflected potential criticism the same way that Helen Wills and Gertrude Ederle had done, through what historian Mary Jo Festle has called a "strategy of apology."[12] The Travelers competed with—and usually beat—men on the court. But once the game was over, they conformed to every requirement of conventional middle-class femininity, displaying impeccable grooming and manners as well as a definite interest in men and eventual marriage. Team members were required to curl their hair, wear makeup, and dress in skirts or tailored slacks. They avoided any hints of sexual impropriety by never dating alone. "We had to act like ladies, and when we came out of the motel room, we had to be fully dressed," Doris Coleman recalled. "Everything had to be perfect."[13] The combination worked: The Travelers toured successfully for 16 years.

Historically Black Colleges Nurture Female Athletes

African American women found their own athletic opportunities—which often included college competition. Somewhat paradoxically, these greater opportunities sprang from the difficulties of African American life: Addressing the challenges of poverty and discrimination meant that even better-off African American women frequently had to step beyond the bounds of conventional middle-class womanhood. In addition, African American communities were eager to celebrate racial excellence in any form, and they often warmly supported women's athletic accomplishments. As a result, while physical educators at white schools fashioned noncompetitive athletic programs that meshed seamlessly with ladylike ideals of gentility and order, students at black schools often developed a more complex sense of identity. Black colleges were vigilant about their female students' reputations, with long lists of rules designed to ensure that students met the highest standards of ladylike conduct. Still, there was room for basketball. "We were ladies," recalled Ruth Glover, who starred for North Carolina's Bennett College in the 1930s. "We just played basketball like boys."[14]

Black women's basketball reached its peak with the Philadelphia Tribunes, a semiprofessional squad sponsored by Philadelphia's African American newspaper. The Tribunes were led by Ora Washington, a woman of extraordinary talent whose reputation stretched across black America. Washington had left rural Virginia for Philadelphia as a teenager, joining the legion of black southerners who sought greater opportunities in northern cities. After getting work as a maid, she began to spend her free time at Germantown's black YWCA, where instructors quickly picked up on her extraordinary abilities. A few short years later, Washington became the dominant force in black women's tennis, winning eight national singles titles and 12 national doubles titles between 1925 and 1937. "Her superiority is so evident that her competitors are frequently beaten before the first ball crosses the net," the *Chicago Defender* reported in 1931. Her basketball talents won her descriptions such as "Queen Ora" and "the greatest girl player of the age."[15]

Like most of her male counterparts, Ora Washington found her opportunities limited to African American circles. Although she badly wanted to test her skills against white tennis champion Helen Wills, the U.S. Lawn Tennis Association would not admit African Americans to its events until 1948. The Amateur Athletic Union, whose basketball ranks were dominated by Southern teams, would not invite a black team to its basketball tournament until 1955. But a group of Washington's contemporaries had better luck. The AAU track championships, inaugurated in 1924, allowed both women and African Americans to compete. Two teams from historically black colleges—Alabama's Tuskegee University and Tennessee State University—won every women's title from 1937 into the 1960s.

The climb to the top started with Cleveland Abbott, the men's track coach at Tuskegee University. In 1929, the year after women's track events were added to the Olympics, Abbott formed a women's track team, and added women's events to the school's annual Tuskegee Relays. He began to scour the region around Tuskegee for talented young women. The opportunity to compete and—more important—to gain a coveted college education drew dozens of young women to the school, where they followed an intensive training program. Other African American schools followed suit. Team members loved the competition and the attention that it brought them. "I just wanted to run and win during that time," recalled sprinter Lula Hymes, who won multiple national titles and tied one world record in her years with the team. "I was out there enjoying myself."[16]

Black colleges entered women's track and field at a propitious time. While the middle-class dominated sports of tennis, golf, and swimming were generally viewed as appropriately "feminine" sporting activities, by the end of the 1920s the working-class activity of track and field came under attack as "profoundly unnatural," described as an activity that created "manly" women who were forced to sacrifice their "health, physical beauty, and social attractiveness."[17] The number of women's track teams fell dramatically, opening the field for those institutions that had a broader view of women's capabilities. Black female athletes were well aware of the racial prescriptions that circumscribed their activities—especially when they traveled. But within their supportive college communities, they felt both accepted and appreciated. "I think that a whole lot of people looked up to Tuskegee women," Leila Perry noted.[18]

Young women fortunate enough to reach Tuskegee found it an almost magical place. Abbott combed the South for talented young women, and treated them like his own daughters. Tuskegee was a magnet for black intellectuals and entertainers, the likes of which most of the young athletes had ever seen. The track team also developed close ties with one another. On sunny days, team members rubbed their legs with peanut oil made by famed Tuskegee chemist George Washington Carver and lay out behind the gym. Many black women avoided the sun, seeking to keep their skin as light as possible. But Abbott believed that sun was good for muscles, and the players had fond memories of those afternoons. "We used to rub with that peanut oil, and go down there and lay on the ground. Let the sun bake us," Lula Hymes explained. "You talk about some pretty brown," Coachman chimed in. "We had a good time out there," Leila Perry echoed. "Lay out there talking and whatnot. Those were good days. You'd be tired…but they were enjoyable."[19]

The players pushed each other to new competitive heights. In high school, Hymes recalled, her confidence often faltered. "When I would do something wrong, I would cry…I used to think I couldn't." But as soon as she got to Tuskegee: "I was told never say you can't do a thing….There were three of us, used to run together in high school, and we came to Tuskegee together. And one of the girls used to beat me. And a friend told me, 'Never say you can't do it, Lu.' And I guess that's why I pushed so hard, started running so hard." Two years later, when Coachman arrived at the school, Hymes took the teenaged star under her wing, working to instill her with "the winning mind." "They always pushed you to win," Coachman recalled.[20] Win they did. Starting in 1937, Tuskegee would win the AAU championship in 11 of 12 years, before ceding its dominance to another black team, the Tigerbelles of Tennessee State. Alice Coachman would win the high jump gold medal at the 1948 Olympics, becoming the first woman of African descent to win an Olympic event.

All-American Girls

World War II brought new opportunities for female athletes. When men went off to war, athletes helped fill their ranks. In 1944, for example, the *Sporting News* reported that only 40 percent of the major league baseball players on the rosters in 1941 were still in the starting lineups. Women stepped up to fill not only factory jobs but sports team rosters as well. The most dramatic opportunity in the Midwest came when Philip K. Wrigley, chewing gum magnate and owner of the Chicago Cubs, came up with the idea of organizing a professional women's baseball league. Familiar with the popularity of women's softball in Chicago and worried that big-league baseball might be closed down during World War II, Wrigley started a league that he originally called the All-American Girls Softball League. The league (which eventually became the All-American Girls Baseball League) began to play in 1943 with teams in four cities: Kenosha and Racine, Wisconsin, South Bend, Indiana, and Rockford, Illinois. Its 108-game schedule attracted 176,000 fans, which, according to one estimate, represented "a higher percentage of the population" in the teams' home cities "than major league baseball ever [drew] in its greatest attendance years."[21]

Arthur Meyerhoff, the league's longtime operator, dealt with the challenge of women playing a "men's" game by selling the league as a novel exhibition of feminine beauty and masculine playing skills. A league handbook put Meyerhoff's point bluntly: "The more feminine the appearance of the performer, the more dramatic the performance."[22] To ensure a more feminine look than that of typical softball players, short skirts were mandatory and the league required that the players attend a charm school conducted by Helena Rubenstein's Chicago-based beauty salon and finishing school. There they learned how to apply makeup, fix their hair, and display conventionally feminine social graces. Although the finishing school program was abandoned after two years, the league's dress code became increasingly stringent. "MASCULINE HAIR STYLING SHOES COATS SHIRTS T-SHIRTS ARE BARRED AT ALL TIMES" read the code of 1951.[23] Whereas ejection from a game by the umpire could cost a player a $10 fine, a much stiffer penalty of $50 awaited the player who appeared "unkempt" in public. The combination apparently worked: The league gave more than 500 women the opportunity to play professional baseball, and the peak of its popularity attracted nearly a million fans annually.

A War Over Turf and Principles

In the years following World War II, however, women's sports suffered major setbacks. A combination of postwar retrenchment, Cold War ideology, changing ideas about womanhood, and the declining influence of local institutions sharply reduced women's opportunities at high school, college, and professional levels. The All-American Girls Base Ball League folded in 1954, after several years of declining attendance. Many of the top industrial basketball teams disbanded, and black colleges cut a number of women's varsity programs. The number of state high school championships for girls declined.

Perhaps surprisingly, some of the most ardent and effective opponents of women's competition were women themselves—specifically, a powerful group of female physical educators who had established themselves at colleges and high schools around the country. Their role in the suppression of women's competition makes it clear that the question of whether and how women should play sports involved not a simple issue of women versus men, but rather class differences, broader questions about female and male natures, and debates over the roles that women should play in a changing American society.

Female physical educators believed strongly in using exercise to build women's strength, confidence, and independence. But they held significant reservations about high-level competition, which gave priority in resources and training to a small number of top-flight athletes, and which tended to foster both "unladylike" behavior and a win-at-all-costs attitude. In contrast to the scandal-plagued world of men's college sports, they held up a vision of a more orderly, cooperative and inclusive athletic realm. The 1923 platform of the Women's Division of the National Amateur Athletic Foundation took as its premise the democratic motto "a sport for every girl, and every girl in a game," and stated that women's athletics should "be protected from exploitation for the enjoyment of the spectator, the athletic reputation, or the commercial advantage of any school or organization...." Furthermore, "individual accomplishment and the winning of championships" should be subordinated to universal participation.[24]

To counter these dangers and assert their control over women's athletics, female physical educators launched an all-out assault on the AAU, Olympic officials, and the leaders of competitive community-based programs. Within the profession they worked through the Committee on Women's Athletics, founded in 1917. Outside the profession they found an ally in the National Amateur Athletic Foundation, founded in 1922. The Foundation's Women's Division, founded in 1923, included leaders in women's education, the Girl Scouts, YWCAs, and women's clubs. With interlocking directorships and overlapping memberships, the two groups presented a united front.

To turn their principles into practice, physical educators invented alternatives to interscholastic and intercollegiate athletics. These took four principal forms: intramurals, telegraphic meets, play days, and sports days, all of which had a player-centered orientation. A survey of 77 colleges taken in 1936 indicated that 74 percent had been involved in a telegraphic meet, 70 percent in a play day, and 41 percent in a sports day.[25] Telegraphic meets curbed the competitive spirit between schools by replacing face-to-face competition with telegraphed reports of performances. Frequently, the colleges competed in only one activity. Play days, which brought together all the girls from several schools to a single site, minimized competitiveness by arbitrarily selecting girls from several schools to form teams. The play days also featured a wide array of informal contests and placed a high emphasis on social interaction among the girls. Sport days did permit teams representing their respective colleges to play, but to ensure a player-centered orientation the directors altered the rules of games such as basketball and refused to announce winners. The Women's Division moved forcefully to spread its philosophy of restraint into high school sports, claiming credit for the discontinuation of 14 statewide high school girls' basketball tournaments between 1931 and 1939.[26]

The end of the All-American Girls Baseball League was part of a larger trend. ɛ migration from small towns to cities, and from cities to suburbs, as well as the growing popularity of television loosened community ties and increased the enticements of at-home diversions. Attendance suffered at both minor and major league baseball games, and the percentages of men and women who played on community softball teams declined. Thousands of company-sponsored teams, both men's and women's, were also eliminated.

Still, women's sports faced particular strong pressures. As the Cold War intensified, pressure mounted to conform to a homogenous "American" way of life, including a newly restrictive conception of femininity that revolved around the suburban ideals of marriage, home, and family. The era also saw a growing tide of homophobia, which raised suspicions about anyone who did not conform to a strict set of gender norms. As women devoted to a "masculine" activity, many of whom were single and some of whom did in fact love other women, physical educators felt particularly pressed. Many worked harder than ever to distinguish women's sports activities from men's.

A few programs managed to survive the decline. In 1949, for example, Babe Didrikson helped found the Ladies Professional Golf Association. Didrikson had worked her way back into public favor through her ongoing athletic excellence and through a dramatic makeover in which she married wrestler George Zaharias, changed her looks and expressed a sudden interest in cooking and housekeeping. The Ladies Professional Golf Association (LPGA) offered American women their first major opportunity to make a living through sports. Some long-standing athletic programs continued to turn out great athletes. The Tigerbelles of Tennessee State reached their apogee in 1960, the year that team member Wilma Rudolph, who had overcome a childhood bout with polio, captured three gold medals at the Rome Olympics and became the nation's most widely celebrated female athlete since the heyday of Helen Wills.[27] But for many young women, the decline had a devastating effect. Mary Alyce Clemmons, a high school basketball star who looked forward to playing at a historically black college, mourned as the teams she had hoped to play for were eliminated. "I thought I could do anything athletically that I had the opportunity to do," she later recalled. "But that was the missing thing, the opportunity. I thought I would play basketball until couldn't move anymore. But it didn't work out like that. Didn't work out that way at all."[28]

Rah, Rah, Rah

As women's sports shrank, a new role for women gained strength: cheerleading. Like schools sports, cheerleading had started as a male activity. The nation's first intercollegiate "football" game, the 1869 contest between Princeton and Rutgers, had been enlivened when "some Nassau Hall residents let fly with a throaty 'Siss, boom, Ahhh!' "[29] By the 1890s, male "yell captains," "rooter kings," "yell leaders," or "yell masters" stood along the sidelines of gridirons across the nation, exhorting fans to root for the home team. By the 1920s, colleges routinely featured two or three male cheerleaders, who wore uniforms consisting of slacks and sweaters in school colors, used megaphones, and led synchronized yells. In that decade, the yell leaders symbolized the carefree undergraduate who lived mainly for the campus's social rather than its academic life.

A few female cheerleaders joined male squads in the 1920s. Intriguingly, the first female cheerleaders faced criticisms similar to the first female athletes. Critics questioned whether women should display themselves publicly or engage in unseemly jumping and yelling. They worried that acrobatics would harm girls' reproductive systems, and that loud yelling would damage their voices. But unlike supporters of women's sports, defenders of female cheerleading were able to draw on the dominant culture's growing emphasis on female appearance. While young women might not be quite as acrobatic as young men, a Midwestern advocate of female cheerleading confessed in 1938, "girls are more magnetic in appearance and will become the center of attention for the crowd and the leading of the cheers will, therefore, be easy."[30] By the mid-1930s, female cheerleaders had established themselves in many communities, and the heroine of a 1934 young adult novel dreamed of being "eligible for the highest honor for girls in high school, the much coveted position of cheer leader."[31]

In the post–World War II era, the growing celebration of cheerleading, majorettes, and beauty queens at male athletic contests meshed with a massive effort by the media and the fashion industry to "refeminize" the American woman. During the war the popular culture had blended the glamor of Hollywood stars with the "manly" jobs of Rosie the Riveters, but once the war ended, movies, magazines, radio, and television began to feature women endowed with full figures, billowing skirts, carefully coifed hair, bountifully applied makeup, and—especially—husbands.[32] By the 1950s, the media frequently presented cheerleaders as a blend of the wholesome girl-next-door and a voluptuous starlet. Male cheerleading shrank into obscurity, and the contrasts between female cheerleaders and male athletes underscored the widening gap between "female" and "male" roles, enhancing both the "femininity" of cheerleading and the "manliness" of athletic contests. The growing popularity of tournament and homecoming beauty queens accentuated the postwar impulse to sharpen female–male distinctions, at times lending sports events an enhanced erotic tone. In 1950, for example, the queen of North Carolina's Dixie Classic basketball tournament, Tulane student Sarah French, presented Sammy Ranzino with the MVP trophy. She then kissed him with such ardor that he dropped it.

Conclusion

American female athletes took a roller-coaster ride during the first half of the twentieth century. While national attention focused mainly on men, aspiring female athletes found support in many pockets of the country, especially rural, working-class, and African American communities. That support carried a handful of women to national prominence and allowed many others to reap the benefits of athletic competition. Despite their obvious skills, however, dedicated athletes frequently had to walk a fine cultural line, devising ways to make places for themselves in an activity still generally viewed as masculine. They also faced considerable opposition, sometimes from men threatened by female athletic skill, sometimes from women who valued cooperation over competition. After World War II, when national culture took a conservative turn, women saw a sharp decline in opportunities. Not until the feminist movement of the 1970s would women's sports begin to regain its strength.

Critical Thinking Questions

1. Like Jack Johnson, Babe Didrikson was both inspiring and controversial. Compare and contrast the two athletes and the effects they had on the society around them. Which do you think had the most powerful impact and why?

2. What does the uneven development of women's sports in the United States tell us about the lives that American women led at the time? Did you find anything surprising in this story?

3. In the years after World War II, the American economy boomed and women's competitive sports declined. What do those contrasting trajectories say about the concept of historical "progress"?

Notes

1. *New York Times,* April 30, 2001.
2. *New York Times,* August 7, 1926.
3. In 1921, Alice Milliat founded the Féderative Sportive Féminine Internationale (FSFI), which sponsored the first Women's Olympic Games in Paris in 1922. The competition furnished by the new Women's Olympic Games convinced the Olympic officials to adopt a five-event track and field program for the 1928 Olympics. As part of the compromise, the FSFI then changed the title of its meets to the International Ladies' Games, which continued to be held until 1934.
4. For accounts of the era's shifts in ideas of women and their effects on women's sports, see particularly Susan Cahn, *Coming on Strong: Gender and Sexuality in Twentieth-Century Women's Sport* (New York: The Free Press, 1994); Pamela Grundy, *Learning to Win: Sports, Education and Social Change in Twentieth-Century North Carolina* (Chapel Hill: U.N.C. Press, 2001).
5. For accounts of Didrikson's life, see Susan E. Cayleff, *Babe: The Life and Legend of Babe Didrikson Zaharias* (Urbana: University of Illinois Press, 1996); Babe Didrikson Zaharias and Harry Paxton. *This Life I've Led: My Autobiography* (New York: A.S. Barnes and Company, 1955); and Pamela Grundy and Susan Shackelford, *Shattering the Glass: The Remarkable History of Women's Basketball* (New York: The New Press, 2005), chapter 2.
6. Quoted in Cahn, *Coming on Strong,* 91–92.
7. Ibid., 141.
8. Quotes and information about Hazel Walker come from Gary Newton's, unpublished compilation of material on Walker, titled "Hazel Walker: Miss Basketball." Copies can be found at the Women's Basketball Hall of Fame, Knoxville, Tenn., and the Naismith Basketball Hall of Fame, Springfield, Mass.
9. Ibid.
10. Garroutte letter from Elva Bishop, producer, *Women's Basketball: The Road to Respect* (University of North Carolina Public Television, 1997).
11. Ibid.
12. Mary Jo Festle, *Playing Nice: Politics and Apologies in Women's Sports* (New York: Columbia University Press, 1996).
13. Bishop, *Women's Basketball.*
14. Rita Liberti, "We Were Ladies, We Just Played Like Boys: African-American Womanhood and Competitive Basketball at Bennett College, 1928–1942," in Patrick B. Miller and David K. Wiggins, eds., *Sport and the Color Line: Black Athletes and Race Relations in Twentieth-Century America* (New York: Routledge, 2004), 92. Much of the resurgence of interest in this era of black women's basketball is due to Liberti's pioneering research into the subject.

15. Young, *Negro Firsts in Sports*, 195; *Chicago Defender*, March 14, 1931. See also Pamela Grundy, "Ora Washington: The First Black Female Athletic Star," in David K. Wiggins, ed., *Out of the Shadows: A Biographical History of African American Athletes* (Fayetteville: University of Arkansas Press, 2006), 79–92.

16. Quoted in Cahn, *Coming on Strong*, 123.

17. Ibid., 114–115.

18. Leila Perry Glover interview by Susan Cahn, April 8, 1992, in Cahn's possession. See also Jennifer H. Lansbury, *A Spectacular Leap: Black Women Athletes in Twentieth Century America* (Fayetteville, University of Arkansas Press, 2014), chapter 2; Cahn, *Coming on Strong*, chapter 5; Grundy and Shackelford, *Shattering the Glass*, chapter 3.

19. Leila Perry Glover interview by Susan Cahn; Alice Coachman Davis and Lula Hymes Glenn interview by Pamela Grundy, 26 February 2004, in Southern Historical Collection, Wilson Library, University of North Carolina, Chapel Hill, NC.

20. Ibid.

21. Quoted in Benjamin G. Rader, *Baseball: A History of America's Game*, 3rd ed. (Urbana: University of Illinois Press, 2008), 158.

22. Quoted in Cahn, *Coming on Strong*, 150.

23. Ibid., 151.

24. Quoted in Ellen Gerber, "The Controlled Development of Collegiate Sport for Women, 1923–1936," *Journal of Sport History* 2 (1975), 11.

25. Cited in ibid., 3.

26. A.A. Sefton, *The Women's Division* (Stanford, CA: Stanford University Press, 1941), 44. For the classic statement of a leader in women's physical education, see Mabel Lee, "The Case for and against Intercollegiate Athletics," *Research Quarterly* 2 (May 1931).

27. For an account of Rudolph's career, see Lansbury, *A Spectacular Leap*, chapter 4.

28. Pamela Grundy, *The Most Democratic Sport: Basketball and Culture in the Central Piedmont, 1893-1994* (Charlotte: Museum of the New South, 1994), 28.

29. Quoted in Mary Ellen Hanson, *Go! Fight! Win! Cheerleading in American Culture* (Bowling Green, OH: Bowling Green University Popular Press, 1995), 10. See also Grundy, *Learning to Win*, 246–55, 285–90; and Michael Oriard, *King Football: Sport and Spectacle in the Golden Age of Radio and Newsreels, Movies and Magazines, the Weekly and the Daily Press* (Chapel Hill: University of North Carolina Press, 2001), 280–8.

30. John J. Gach, "The Case for and against Girl Cheerleaders," *School Activities* 9 (1938), 301.

31. Quoted in Hanson, *Go! Fight! Win!*, 21.

32. Grundy, *Learning to Win*, 247–49.

CHAPTER 14

Globalizing Sports, Redefining Race

Jesse Owens soars to victory in the Olympic long jump competition in Berlin, Germany, 1936.

LEARNING OBJECTIVES

14.1 Analyze how American interpretations of international sports competition both reflected changing international politics and influenced race relations within the United States.

14.2 Describe the origins of the Olympic Games and the patriotic significance that American Olympic organizers ascribed to them before World War I.

14.3 Outline the debate over whether the United States should boycott the Nazi Olympics, assessing the arguments on both sides, and what each side hoped to accomplish.

14.4 Explain the varying effects that the 1936 Games had on worldwide perceptions of Aryan superiority and of the Nazi government.

14.5 Summarize the personal qualities and political context that made Jesse Owens and Joe Louis "American" heroes.

14.6 Detail the lessons that Joe Louis learned from Jack Johnson's career, and the way that he attempted to avoid Johnson's fate.

On August 3, 1936, American sprinter Jesse Owens burst out of the starting blocks of the Olympic 100-meter finals, a blur of accelerating speed. Just over 10 seconds later, his chest broke the finish line tape, making him the Olympic champion, and placing an indelible mark on athletic history. In the past, the athletic accomplishments of African Americans such as Owens had been frequently downplayed or overlooked. This time was different. Owens captured his gold medal—one of four he would win that week—in the heart of Nazi Germany, at an event that had been billed as a showcase for the Nazi ideology of Aryan superiority. By turning in a set of performances widely seen as the greatest in Olympic history, Owens turned that notion on its head, and returned home to a hero's reception. He became one of the first African American athletes widely celebrated by white as well as black Americans.

The improvements in transportation and communication that knit the globe closer together in the twentieth century increased international sporting competition in sports that ranged from golf to soccer to ping-pong. It also gave sports new meanings. International competitions were generally billed as ways to build goodwill among nations through friendly competition. But amid the shifting global politics of a contentious century, sports events quickly became political arenas, used to build patriotic fervor and to show off national "prowess" through the orchestration of impressive events or through the triumphs of a nation's athletes. This significance intensified at times of heightened international conflict—particularly in the years that led up to World War II.

Connections between sports and nationalism gave African American athletes such as Jesse Owens an additional opportunity to use sports in the ongoing effort to build racial respect, by serving as representatives of their country, in addition to their race. When Jack Johnson contended for the heavyweight championship, most Americans cast his fights in racial terms, as contests between blacks and whites over racial superiority. Three decades later, when Joe Louis fought German boxer Max Schmeling for that same championship, he was cast as a representative of American democracy opposing Nazi tyranny.

The Olympic Games

The modern Olympic Games, first held in Athens, Greece, in 1896, created an especially prominent focus for international rivalries. The Olympics were the project of Pierre de Coubertin, an aristocratic Frenchman who loved the British commitment to sport and who was also determined to inspire the youth of France to develop courage, determination, and physical abilities. Building the Games proved a challenging task. After Athens, the next three Games were essentially sideshows to other more publicized attractions: the Paris Exposition of 1900, the World's Fair held in St. Louis in 1904, and the Franco-British Exposition of 1908 held in London. Only 15 nations competed in the 1900 Games, and only 11 in the 1904 contests.[1]

The United States began to take the Games seriously in 1908. As the Olympics became more organized, the International Olympic Committee required that each country put together a national Olympic committee that would certify all its contestants. James E. Sullivan, head of the powerful Amateur Athletic Union, became the first head of the U.S. Olympic Committee, which selected top athletes and raised funds to send them to the Games.

The committee had plenty of talent to choose from, especially in track and field. The sport had migrated out of private clubs into high schools and colleges, and the quality of U.S. track and field athletes was rising rapidly. Northeastern colleges organized the Intercollegiate Association of Amateur Athletes of America (commonly known as the IC4A) in 1876, and began to conduct annual, full-scale track meets. The University of Pennsylvania (Penn) Relays, which began in 1895, introduced a colorful athletic carnival that combined intercollegiate and interscholastic track. At the Penn Relays of 1925, more than 3,000 athletes representing more than 500 colleges and secondary schools competed before 70,000 fans in the finals. The Penn Relays spawned imitators across the country, including the Drake University Relays at Des Moines, Iowa, and the Tuskegee Relays in Tuskegee, Alabama. Early in the twentieth century, several other groups joined forces with the athletic clubs, the AAU, and colleges to promote track and field.

At the 1908 Olympics, Sullivan was open about his ambitions, bluntly declaring, "We have come here to win the championship in field sports, and we are going to do it."[2] The athletes did not disappoint. While the British compiled the largest medal total, Americans dominated the track and field events, winning 15 of the 27 events. The American press devised an unofficial point system so that national achievements could easily be compared. In what the *New York Times* called "the greatest ovation in the history of athletics," 250,000 people turned out for a parade in New York City to welcome the American athletes home.

Jim Thorpe: American Olympic Legend

Four years later, the Olympics created its first American athletic legend. The 1912 Olympics were held in Stockholm, Sweden, with 28 nations and 2,500 athletes participating. The unquestioned star of the Games was Sac and Fox Indian Jim Thorpe, who captured the pentathlon and the decathlon in spectacular style.[3] Thorpe won four of the five individual events in the pentathlon and scored a 700-point margin over his nearest competitor in the decathlon. He was widely hailed as the "greatest athlete in the world."

Thorpe's tremendous athletic abilities had first been noticed when he was a teenager attending a one-room schoolhouse near his Oklahoma home. The single instructor, Walter White, quickly noticed that Thorpe loved sports and excelled at almost everything he tried. White knew that Carlisle Institute head Richard Henry Pratt was always on the hunt for athletic talent. A few years earlier, Pratt had specifically encouraged his field agents to keep their eyes out for athletes, writing the Sac and Fox agent: "Incidentally, if you should by chance have a sturdy young man anxious for an education who is especially swift of foot or qualified for athletics, send him and help Carlisle to compete with the great universities."[4] White recommended Thorpe to Carlisle, where he became part of Pop Warner's increasingly successful football teams. Thorpe proved a dazzling runner and strong all-around player. In 1911, after a remarkable season, Walter Camp named him a first-team All-American. He spent the spring of 1912 training for the Olympics, his eyes on two new events: the five-event pentathlon and the 10-event decathlon. At the Olympic trials, his pentathlon performance was so dominant that the Olympic Committee decided not to bother with a decathlon trial.

That year's Olympic Committee had made a particular effort to scour the country for talent, choosing participants from more than two dozen states. Supporters proudly hailed "the men who have been gathered from the furthermost quarters of the Union as the most fitting types of the speed and brawn of Young America."[5] (While the 1912 Olympics offered several events for women, Sullivan did not approve of women's sports, and no U.S. women were allowed to enter.) Organizers cast the team as quintessentially American: a melting pot of backgrounds united by a distinctively American drive to achieve. "Time was when we got our champions from the English, Irish, Scotch or their sons, but now look at the composition of our team," Sullivan noted. "Men whose forebears would almost take in every nation in Europe, but who have taken in and absorbed that American trait of going in to win which is the proper spirit, when coupled with fair dealing to fellow-competitors."[6] That year's Olympic Committee president, Col. Robert M. Thompson, sounded a similar theme, promising to prove to the world that "composite though we are, our forbears made no mistake in becoming a part of this great country."[7]

Rhetorically, these men overlooked the full diversity of their team, which in addition to Thorpe included Penobscot runner Andrew Sockalexis, Hopi runner Louis Tewainima, Native Hawaiian swimmer Duke Kahanamoku, and African American sprinter Howard Drew. But the athletes made their mark nonetheless: Thorpe with his two golds, Tewainima with a silver medal in the 10,000 meters, and Kahanamoku with a gold in the 100-meter freestyle (Drew was favored to win both the 100 and 200 meter dashes, but pulled a muscle in the 100-meter semifinal and was unable to continue).

Unfortunately for Thorpe, in addition to becoming the first American Olympic legend, he also became the most notable example of the perils of the amateur code. Six months after the Olympics, reports began to surface that Thorpe had played professional baseball in 1909 and 1910. Since he had accepted money to play a sport, he was not an amateur by the Olympic definition when he competed in Stockholm. During the next several months, as the affair was debated around the world, popular opinion held that Thorpe was a great athlete whose achievements should not be tarnished by what many viewed as a simple technicality. The International Olympic Committee, however, stuck firmly to its defense of amateurism. In May of 1913, it voted to strike Thorpe's victories from its official records, and demanded that he return his medals. (The decision would be reversed in 1983, 30 years after Thorpe's death.)

The Olympics as Civic Showcase

Questions about Olympic eligibility and amateur status were soon swept aside by the outbreak of World War I. The Games of 1916, scheduled to be held in Berlin, were canceled. After the war ended, the 1920 Games were awarded to Antwerp in recognition of the great sacrifices made by the Belgians during the war. The country was still recovering, and the Games were modest. But in subsequent years, the Games took on a new significance, as a way for host countries to showcase themselves to the world. The number of events continued to expand: A separate Winter Games was inaugurated in 1924 and by 1928 a group of European women had forced the IOC to institute women's track and field events, by creating a separate "Jeux Feminines," which threatened the IOC's control over worldwide sport.[8]

The 1932 Games were awarded to Los Angeles, and promoters were determined to make the Games a showcase for their city as well as the state of California. To finance the spectacle, the city floated a $1.5 million bond issue, and California voters, in a special referendum, approved the expenditure of $1 million in state funds. At Los Angeles the athletes found magnificent facilities: a 105,000-seat stadium, an indoor auditorium with seats for 10,000, a swimming structure with a seating capacity of 12,000, and the first specially constructed Olympic village. Hollywood celebrities made regular appearances in the grandstands. American standouts included Babe Didrikson, who set two world records, and Eddie Tolan, who won gold in the 100 and 200 meter dashes. The Games were declared a splendid success, and the organizers donated more than $200,000 in profits to the city and the county.

The 1936 Olympics, held in Berlin, were also designed to show off a rising corner of the world. The German government spent a huge amount of money to prepare for the Games. Many parts of Berlin were rebuilt or repainted. They constructed a huge, new sports complex, including a 100,000-seat Olympic stadium, an expansive Olympic village, and an open-air pool with seats for 18,000 viewers. They installed all the latest technology: a closed-circuit television system, a radio network that reached 41 nations, photo finish equipment, and electronic timing devices. They also commissioned Leni Riefenstahl, a brilliant producer, to make a $7 million film of the event. Her film *Olympia* subsequently became a classic in cinematography.

The Nazi Olympics

As the event drew near, however, the world focused less on the preparations than on who was making them. The Olympics had been awarded to Berlin in 1931. In 1933, Adolph Hitler and his National Socialist Party took control of the German government. Questions quickly arose about Berlin's suitability as an Olympic venue. Americans serving on the International Olympic Committee protested Nazi discrimination against Jews and the AAU voted to boycott the Games unless Germany's policy regarding Jewish athletes was "changed in fact as well as in theory."[9] The German Olympic Committee took nominal steps to reassure the Americans, but in 1935 Hitler put into place the "Nuremberg Laws," which deprived German Jews of their citizenship and prohibited German–Jewish marriage in an avowed effort to preserve the "purity" of the "Aryan race." When the IOC decided to continue with the Games, debates broke out in many countries, including the United States, about whether to send teams to Berlin.

Avery Brundage, the self-made millionaire president of the American Olympic Committee (AOC), who counted many Nazis as his friends, led the advocates of participation. AAU president Jeremiah T. Mahoney, a Catholic who was disturbed by Nazi paganism and anti-Semitism, led a boycott movement. "Germany has Violated the Olympic Code," one Mahoney pamphlet proclaimed, proceeding to document discrimination against Jewish athletes that included the expulsion of Jews from top athletic clubs and a prohibition on German–Jewish competition. A Gallup poll revealed that 43 percent of the American people favored a boycott. A showdown came at the AAU convention in 1935, where Brundage mustered a two-and-a-half vote margin to defeat a resolution that would have delayed the American decision to enter the Games pending further investigation of German behavior. The American team sailed for Germany on July 15.

The debate had raised some key questions about the role of sporting competition in international affairs. Would it have been better to ostracize the Nazis and their racial beliefs by refusing to participate in the Games? Or was it more effective to show up their claims to racial superiority by beating them? After two weeks in Berlin, those questions remained open.

Athletically, the Olympics were far from a wholesale advertisement for Aryan superiority. A Korean athlete, Kitei Son, won the prestigious marathon event. The Japanese team dominated swimming and diving. Egyptians finished atop the standings in weightlifting. A Jewish woman from Hungary took the women's high-jump competition. Most dramatically, African American men triumphed in many of the headline track and field events, including the 100, 200, 400, and 800 meter races; the broad jump; and the high jump. The star of the Games was African American Jesse Owens, who garnered gold medals in the 100 and 200 meter sprints, the long jump, and the 4 × 100 meter relay (although American track and field coach Dean Cromwell sidestepped an opportunity to make an even more dramatic racial statement with a last-minute decision to drop Jewish athletes Sam Stoller and Marty Glickman from the 400-meter relay team).

Owens dominated the Games from the start, tying the world record in the 100 meters on the first morning of competition, and winning the gold medal with another record-tying performance the next afternoon. The next day, he broke the Olympic long jump record with a dramatic final jump, and the day after that bested the Olympic record for the 200 meter dash by a full half-second. Americans rushed to celebrate these triumphs of Owens and other "decidedly non-Aryan American Negros," as well as the slap in the face they offered to Nazi ideology. Conveniently overlooking the discrimination African Americans faced in the United States, they also used black athletic achievements to underscore the ideal of American meritocracy. "In what other country would this saga of Jesse Owens come true?" the *Cleveland Plain Dealer* asked.[10]

But the ruling Nazis also had reason to be pleased. Germany topped the medal count, finishing with 33 gold medals to 24 for the second-place United States, and 89 overall medals, to 56 for the United States. The world had come to Berlin, and gone away impressed. All the anti-Jewish signs had been removed for the Games, and visitors found the city streets quiet, quaint, and orderly. Although a cold rain had fallen much of the time, the event had gone off without a hitch, showcasing Germany's formidable organizing abilities. There had been a few hints of prejudice: One German paper had referred to the African American athletes as "black auxiliaries," and many reporters noted that Hitler had stopped personally congratulating medal-winners once African Americans began to climb the victors' podium. But the German crowds had welcomed the foreign athletes eagerly, and given Jesse Owens the largest ovations of the Games. The event gave many people reason to agree with Avery Brundage's contention that the Nazis were not as bad as advertised.

The Brown Bomber

As Jesse Owens celebrated his victories, another African American athlete was busy plotting a comeback. While the Olympic athletes were making their Atlantic crossing, Joe Louis, known as the "Brown Bomber," had been knocked out by German fighter Max Schmeling, a fight that delighted Adolph Hitler and shocked the boxing world. It was a stunning setback for Louis, who had his sights set on becoming the first African American fighter since Jack Johnson to get a shot at the heavyweight title. But Louis was only 22, one year younger than Owens. His previous victories had already made him the best-known African American in the country. More than 60,000 people had paid to see his first big fight. He had plenty of time to recover.

Louis and Owens had much in common. Both had been born in rural Alabama to families who eked out a living in the South's grim sharecropping economy. Both had come North at a young age, as their families sought better opportunities— Owens landing in Cleveland and Louis in Detroit. Both were guided by experienced mentors who recognized their talent early, helped them hone their skills, and guided their career decisions. For Owens it was junior high school coach Charles Riley, who spent years helping him perfect his running technique and navigating him through high school and on to college at Ohio State. Louis was guided by an experienced trio: trainer Jack Blackburn, who taught him conditioning and technique, and managers John Roxborough and Julian Black, whose success in the Detroit numbers-running business had prepared them well for the ins and outs of running a prizefighter's career.

As a prizefighter, Louis faced both greater opportunities and greater challenges than Owens. Track and field remained an amateur sport, and Owens was never able to find a way to make a living from his talent. Prizefighting was unabashedly professional, with gate receipts that could run into the millions for big fights. But unlike Owens, Louis had to contend with the shadow of Jack Johnson. Johnson's defiance of racial norms, and the deep hostility his victories had stirred up, made many promoters leery about scheduling African Americans for major fights. When Roxborough and Black approached Blackburn about training Louis, he told them he would take their money, but it would be a waste because a black heavyweight would never have a chance at the top title.

As a result, Louis had to learn about far more than boxing. His mentors carefully schooled him in the behavior that would help him avoid stirring up memories of Johnson. He could never speak badly of an opponent, especially if that opponent were white. He could never smile while in the ring, not even when he won a match. He could not go to nightclubs alone, and he could never allow himself to be photographed with a white woman. As Louis prepared for his first major fight, against Italian Primo Carnero, promoters prepared a flood of publicity that portrayed him as a modest man who saved his money, neither drank nor smoked, who read the Bible every night, and who spent his first big paycheck on a new house for his mother. "I realize the Negro people have placed a big trust in me," Louis was quoted as saying in one publicity piece. "I can't throw my race down by abusing my position as a heavyweight challenger. It is my duty to win the championship and prove to the world that, black or white, a man can become the best fighter and still be a gentleman." Louis played the part well. Many of the stories told about him were in fact true (he did not drink or smoke) and he learned to be discrete about those that were not (such as his lavish spending, which included presents for numerous girlfriends, not all of whom were black).[11]

He was also the kind of fighter the public liked—a hard puncher who usually won by knockout. Because of his skills—and his ability to draw a large, paying crowd—he was offered a shot at the heavyweight title less than a year after losing to Schmeling. More than 45,000 paying spectators filed into Chicago's Comiskey Park to see Louis fight heavyweight champion James J. Braddock. Louis fought a carefully strategic fight, landing punch after punch. In the eighth round, Braddock went down for good. Joe Louis was heavyweight champion of the world.

Louis's victory set up one of the most storied fights in American history: a rematch with Max Schmeling. The fight was scheduled for Yankee Stadium on June 22, 1938. The political stakes of the fight escalated through that spring, as Nazi designs on Europe became increasingly clear. That March, Germany annexed Austria, and began to threaten Czechoslovakia. Pressure on Germany's Jewish residents was mounting, and political prisoners were already being sent to "concentration camps." A few days before the fight, the U.S. government charged several U.S. residents with spying for the Nazis. Casting the Louis–Schmeling contest as the United States against the Nazis fit the public mood. It also made for great publicity.

Schmeling arrived in New York to pickets and protesters. Louis assured the public that "I fight for America against the challenge of a foreign invader."[12] Seventy million people tuned into the radio broadcast. Louis came out punching hard, sending Schmeling straight into the ropes. In two quick minutes, the fight was over. Louis would go on to hold the heavyweight crown for nearly 12 years, defending the title 25 times without a loss. Both were records for any weight division.

Significance of Racial Accomplishment

The accomplishments of Louis and Owens, as well as the worldwide acclaim they won, meant a great deal to African Americans. Not only did the athletes demonstrate remarkable abilities, their presence on the world stage also indicated that some racial barriers were beginning, slowly, to fall. Maya Angelou vividly recalled the mood at her grandmother's country store in her small, Arkansas town, whenever the community gathered to listen to a broadcast of a Louis victory. "[E]ven the old Christian ladies who taught their children and tried themselves to practice turning the other cheek would buy soft drinks, and if the Brown Bomber's victory was a particularly bloody one they would order peanut patties and Baby Ruths also," Angelou wrote. "Champion of the world. A Black Boy. Some Black mother's son. He was the strongest man in the world. People drank Coca-Colas like ambrosia and ate candy bars like Christmas."[13] Louis became the focus of songs, newspaper articles, and citywide celebrations.

The impact of star African American athletes outside African American communities was more difficult to ascertain. Without question, the broad acclaim given to black athletes such as Owens and Louis produced a shift of sorts in public opinion, the kind of effect invoked by the NAACP magazine *The Crisis,* which in 1935 underscored the appeal that athletic champions held for ordinary Americans. "For these millions, who hold the solution of the race problem in their hands, the beautiful breasting of a tape by Jesse Owens and the thud of a glove on the hand of Joe Louis carry more 'interracial education' than all the erudite philosophy ever written on race."[14]

For a number of whites, however, these mid-twentieth-century African American athletic triumphs were softened by the growing idea that blacks possessed innate athletic abilities, a supposed physical advantage that carried with it a suggestion that successful black athletes did not have to be as intelligent or disciplined as whites. There was ample evidence to disprove this idea. Both Jesse Owens and Joe Louis were hard workers who had benefited from top-level training. When a Cleveland doctor took Owens' measurements to see if he indeed had any natural physical advantages, he concluded that Owens' superior performances resulted from technique and training, not from any quirks in his physique. But even admiring stories about black athletes often swung back and forth between the old competing stereotypes, referring to animals and "savagery," or to indolence and indulgence (Louis's own team at times took advantage of the latter stereotype, spreading stories of Louis's supposed reluctance to train as part of a strategy designed to make opponents underestimate the Brown Bomber).

The columnist Hugh S. Johnson clearly illustrated this rationalization in his reaction to Louis's drubbing of Max Schmeling. "These black boys are Americans," he wrote, adding, "There should be just as much pride in their progress and prowess under our system as any other American." He was careful to note, however, that the achievements he was lauding did not necessarily extend beyond the physical. "The average of white intelligence is above the average of black intelligence probably because the white race is several thousand years further away from jungle savagery," he explained in the same piece. "But, for the same reason, the average of white physical equipment is lower."[15] African American athletes would continue to confront this kind of demeaning rationalization for decades.

Conclusion

The rise of sports as a forum for showcasing national virtues and pursuing international rivalries proved a boon to African Americans who sought to use sport to win greater racial respect. When African Americans such as Jesse Owens and Joe Louis took on representatives of hostile countries, Americans of many backgrounds rallied around them with unprecedented patriotic zeal. While both national and international sport would soon take a back seat to the armed conflict of World War II, the war offered other opportunities. A month after Japanese forces attacked Pearl Harbor, Joe Louis solidified his reputation as an exemplary citizen by participating in a hastily arranged title defense, donating most of his $70,000 purse to the Naval Relief Fund. He then signed up with the Army. Millions of less prominent African Americans did likewise. Their dedicated service would help lay the groundwork for a far broader transformation in race relations, and in American sports.

Critical Thinking Questions

1. In what different ways did the Olympics give nations the opportunity to demonstrate national abilities? How accurate were these portrayals?
2. Do you think the United States should have boycotted the Nazi Olympics? Why or why not?
3. Chart the achievements and limits of efforts by Jesse Owens and Joe Louis to combat racial stereotypes? What do those achievements and limits say about the particular role sports can play in fighting racial hierarchies?

Notes

1. For material on Olympic history see Mark Dyreson, *Making the American Team: Sport, Culture, and the Olympic Experience* (Urbana: University of Illinois Press, 1998); R.D. Mandell, *The First Modern Olympics* (Berkeley: University of California Press, 1976); John MacAloon, *The Great Symbol* (Chicago: University of Chicago Press, 1981); John Lucas, *The Modern Olympic Games* (New York: A.S. Barnes, 1980); Allen Guttmann, *The Games Must Go On: Avery Brundage and the Olympic Movement* (New York: Columbia University Press, 1984); Allen Guttmann, *The Olympics: A History of the Modern Games*, 2nd ed. (Urbana: University of Illinois Press, 2002); and S.W. Pope, *Patriotic Games* (New York: Oxford University Press, 1997), chapter 3.
2. As quoted in P.J. Graham and Horst Ueberhorst, eds., *The Modern Olympics* (Cornwall, NY: Leisure, n.d.), 32.
3. See R.W. Wheeler, *Jim Thorpe*, rev. ed. (Norman: University of Oklahoma Press, 1979).
4. Kate Buford, *Native American Son: The Life and Sporting Legend of Jim Thorpe* (Alfred Knopf, 2010), 34.
5. *New York Times*, June 15, 1912.
6. *New York Times*, August 11, 1912.
7. *New York Times*, June 14, 1912.
8. Guttman, *The Olympics*, 39–48.

9. Richard D. Mandell, *The Nazi Olympics* (New York: Macmillan, 1971; Urbana: University of Illinois Press, 1987), 71. See also William J. Baker, *Jesse Owens* (New York: Free Press, 1986); Arnd Kruger, "The 1936 Olympic Games—Berlin," in Graham and Ueberhorst, ed., *Modern Olympics,* 168–82; George Eisen, "The Voices of Sanity: American Diplomatic Reports from the 1936 Berlin Olympiad," *Journal of Social History* 11 (1984), 56–78; and Duff Hart-Davis, *Hitler's Games* (London: Macmillan, 1986).

10. *New York Times*, August 4, 1936; quoted in Baker, *Jesse Owens*, 4.

11. Quoted in Chris Mead, *Champion Joe Louis: Black Hero in White America* (New York: Charles Scribner's Sons, 1985), 56.

12. Quoted in ibid., 145.

13. Quoted in Lawrence Levine, *Black Culture and Black Consciousness: Afro-American Folk Thought from Slavery to Freedom* (New York: Oxford University Press, 1977), 435.

14. Quoted in Mark Dryeson, "Jesse Owens: Leading Man in Modern American Tales of Racial Progress and Limits," in David K. Wiggins, ed., *Out of the Shadows: A Biographical History of African American Athletes* (Fayetteville: University of Arkansas Press, 2006), 118.

15. Quoted in Mead, *Champion Joe Louis*, 158.

CHAPTER 15

The Setting of Organized Sports Since World War II

Jackie Robinson integrated major league baseball in 1947, when he moved up from the minor league Montreal Royals to become a Brooklyn Dodger.

On May 19, 1947, the turnstiles at Chicago's Wrigley Field admitted the largest crowd in the storied stadium's 43-year history. Would-be spectators arrived early to assure themselves of seats, and the stadium was almost filled a full two hours before the game between the Chicago Cubs and the Brooklyn Dodgers was scheduled to begin. It was only the start of the season, and the contest meant little in terms of team standings. But the spectators who packed the stands had not come to watch a game. They had come to see Jackie Robinson, the first African American to play in the major leagues for more than half a century. Led by general manager Branch Rickey, the Dodgers had taken the step that baseball executives had been discussing for decades: They had hired a black player, and placed him on the field. Organized baseball—and American sports—would never be the same.

When the Dodgers made it to the World Series that year, they became part of another milestone. The 1947 Series was the first to be broadcast on television. The audience for the series—won by the Yankees in seven games—was relatively small. Full-scale commercial broadcast had just begun, and there were fewer than 100,000 television sets in the entire country. That number would quickly grow. A decade later, TVs could be found in more than 80 percent of American homes, and the new medium was well on its way to transforming American life. In subsequent decades, television would bring sporting events to vast new audiences, generate enormous revenues, and further expand the influence of sports on American culture.

Even as American sports expanded its reach through television and desegregation, it also took on greater prominence in the nation's vision of itself. The Cold War between the United States and the Soviet Union, which dominated international politics from the end of World War II to the dissolution of the Soviet Union in 1991, intensified American identification with competitive sports. The Cold War was a contest not only between nations, but also between political and economic systems: the competitive capitalism of the United States on one side and the planning-oriented communism practiced by the Soviets on the other. Leaders of both countries were eager to point to athletic victories as proof of national superiority. The U.S. attributed victories to the value of individual freedom and initiative; the Soviets claimed they resulted from the virtues of organization and collective endeavor. Athletes began to see themselves as surrogate warriors in the Soviet–American battle for prestige and influence. The Soviets, noted two-time Olympic decathlon champion Bob Mathias, "were in a sense the real enemies. You just loved to beat 'em. You just had to beat 'em. It wasn't like beating some friendly country like Australia."[1]

The U.S.-Soviet rivalry contributed to making sports a key component of a loosely formulated ideology that developed during this era, often summed up as "the American way of life." According to this vision, it was free competition, as well as freedom, tolerance, social inclusiveness, religiosity, and individual opportunity that distinguished the United States from its totalitarian enemies. "Our Olympic team and athletes play a significant role in preserving our way of life," President John F. Kennedy concluded in 1961. In the decades to come, as Americans contended with an ongoing series of physical, cultural, and technological transformations, sports became more deeply woven into the fabric of American life, reenacting the structures and rhythms of competition in compelling, frequently heroic fashion, week by week and season by season. At the same time, the links between sports and other components of American society meant that sports would continue to be a key forum for a wide range of debates over the strengths and weaknesses of American society.[2]

Affluence and Suburbanization

The postwar United States was a busy, bustling place, changing in many ways. As the economy expanded, incomes rose and the population boomed. The nation saw a mass migration to single-family homes in newly built suburban neighborhoods, as well as to rapidly growing cities in the South and West. Abetted by soaring automobile sales, developers with a knack for building houses en masse, the construction of countless miles of multilane freeways, and federal subsidies to new homeowners, cornfields and cow pastures became acres and acres of suburbs. In addition, manufacturers, retail outlets, corporate headquarters, and dozens of other businesses relocated along the beltways and the intersections of arterial highways. By the mid-1960s, more jobs existed in the busy suburban rings than in the inner city.

The transformation brought new opportunities for professional sports teams. Professional sports became one way to build civic spirit in expanding metropolitan areas. As cities grew and competed with one another, leaders also often determined that being "big league" required a professional team—and they were willing to open public coffers to get one. As the cathedral represented the spirit of the Middle Ages and the great railroad terminal that of the nineteenth century, publicly financed sports stadia were frequently seen as the quintessential symbol of the modern metropolis. Growing demand prompted the top professional leagues to expand their ranks. In 1950 only 42 major-league professional franchises existed, and these were located mostly in a tier of industrial states that extended from the Northeast to the upper Midwest. By 1990 the figure had swollen to more than 100, and no major metropolitan area in the nation was without at least one big-league franchise.

The Dodgers became one of the first teams to take advantage of this interest. They played their last game in Brooklyn in the fall of 1957, the year after Jackie

Robinson retired. They opened the 1958 season in a brand-new stadium in Los Angeles, California. While the Dodgers were one of the most prosperous franchises in baseball, owner Walter O'Malley was looking to the future. Eager to gain the prestige of a major league franchise, Los Angeles presented the Dodgers with Chavez Ravine, which occupied 300 downtown acres (the low-income, manly Latino families who lived there were summarily cleared out). Not only could the Dodgers build a new stadium, spectators would have plenty of room for parking as well as easy access to several freeways—key advantages in an era when families were increasingly relying on cars for transportation. In addition, at a time when television contracts were becoming an ever-larger component of big-league budgets, Los Angeles offered the Dodgers an uncontested media market in the nation's third largest metropolitan area.[3]

As competition for big-league teams grew, cities had to provide potential franchises with increasingly generous terms. Beginning in the 1960s, local governments went on a stadium-building binge. Of the 28 teams in the National Football League, for example, 26 would eventually play in city, county, or state-built facilities. In the early 1960s the price tag on a modest stadium ran to some $30 million. Houston's Astrodome, the first stadium with a roof for all-season play, upped the ante, opening in 1965 with a price tag of $45 million. More than 20 percent of the new structures were built outside the downtown area, usually in a suburban satellite city within easy access of freeways. The Patriots football team moved out of Boston to Foxboro, Massachusetts, where they renamed themselves the New England Patriots; the Dallas Cowboys encamped at Irving, Texas; the Texas Rangers located at Arlington, Texas; both the football Giants and Jets departed from New York City to northern New Jersey; and the Detroit Lions moved to Pontiac, Michigan, 25 miles from downtown Detroit. Suburban facilities permitted easier access to cars and to more affluent fans, while providing an escape from the congestion, dirt, and newly perceived perils of the inner city.

Television Transforms American Life

In addition to establishing teams across the country, big-time sports also spread its influence through television, which brought unprecedented change to the rhythms of American life. "And so the monumental change began in our lives and those of millions of other Americans," one man reminisced about his family's first television set in 1950. "More than a year passed before we again visited a movie theater. Money that previously would have been spent for books was saved for TV payments. Social evenings with friends became fewer and fewer still." By 1956 three out of four families owned television sets; those families watched television an average of 35 hours each week.

Novelty alone did not account for the new medium's magnetism. Americans persisted long afterward in spending a staggering amount of their free time watching television. A 1980 study of Muncie, Indiana, found that the median viewing time for all families was 28 hours per week. The significance of such figures could not be dismissed by the argument that families simply had their sets running in the background, as Muncie residents could recall substantial amounts of program content. "Television is the 800 pound gorilla of leisure time," concluded a study of how Americans spent their spare time.[4]

Television and the automobile, along with central heating, air conditioning, and more spacious houses and yards, contributed to a general shift in leisure from public places to the privacy of the home. Do-it-yourself projects, home repairs, and conquering the "crabgrass frontier" consumed much of the suburbanite's spare time. "No man who owns his own house and lot can be a Communist," observed one of the mass builders of suburban housing in 1948. "He has too much to do."[5] Indeed, for many, the house became a self-sufficient recreation center, or a "family playpen," as an anthropologist aptly put it. The enjoyment of children and "family togetherness," according to the popular media of the 1950s, became virtually a moral obligation. At the same time, however, television became one way to bind the myriad of individual households together, linking people across the country through a common experience of news and entertainment. Television would play a seminal role in national experiences of the civil rights movement, the Vietnam War, the assassination of President John F. Kennedy, and many other events.[6]

Television Transforms Sports

Television quickly became the most important factor in the history of post–World War II American sports. The fans at home, not those in the stadium or the arena, became the ultimate arbiters of teams' fates. To attract more television viewers and meet the demands of commercial sponsors, television directors developed a range of new techniques that included multiple cameras, replays, slow-motion shots, flashy graphics, catchy music and, charismatic announcers. Likewise, the moguls of sports changed their games to make them more compelling television spectacles. These shifts included new rules designed to speed up action, arbitrary time-outs for television commercials, and lengthy playoff systems for national championships.

Television affected American sports in other ways. It contributed to the further nationalization and eventually even the globalization of sports. When fans could regularly see sports performed at the highest plateau of excellence on television, attendance at local sporting events frequently declined. Indeed, television made the future prosperity of professional sports increasingly dependent upon the creation of a broad-based national constituency rather than relying solely on local fans. Pro football, the first sport to recognize fully the potential of the new media, deliberately downplayed the traditional attachment of teams to cities and chose to stage its Super Bowl at predetermined locations around the country, rather than in the home stadium of one of the participating teams. Finally, television pumped additional millions of dollars into sports, enriching team owners and—eventually—players while raising new questions about the impact of big-time, big-money sports on educational institutions and on the life ambitions of star-struck young fans.

Creating such profitable connections between sports and television required work and creativity. During television's pioneer stage, from the first regularly scheduled broadcasts in 1938 to the early 1960s, technology limited the potential of televised sports.[7] Primitive television cameras more effectively captured the excitement of arena spectacles such as roller derby, wrestling, and prizefighting than outdoor games such as baseball and football. Television fans could follow two men whose combat was restricted to a small ring with relative ease—and boxing enjoyed nearly a decade of television popularity, thanks in large part to the Gillette Razor Company and its Gillette Friday Night Fights. But a small white baseball was often hard to distinguish from the ever-present white dots that were commonly known as television "snow." When viewers were able to see the hit ball, they could rarely determine its precise location relative to the playing field. Football fared somewhat better because of its more concentrated action. Still, a single camera located well back from the playing field could hardly capture the essence of sophisticated football plays. Mud-covered and grass-stained uniforms sometimes made the teams indistinguishable.

Roone Arledge, ABC, and the Rise of Televised Sport

The difficulties of televising sport did not particularly trouble television executives. Business was booming: Money spent on television advertising swelled from just under $500 million in 1952 to more than $2.5 billion in 1965. No one considered sports programming critical to television's overall success; networks put far more of their resources and talent into comedies, Westerns, and popular dramas. In the early 1960s, however, ABC broke with this pattern. Having long lagged behind the two other major networks—NBC and CBS—ABC gambled that increased sports programming would give its network greater visibility, bring in new local television stations as affiliates, and improve the audience ratings for all shows. The gamble paid spectacular dividends. Sports telecasts contributed substantively to ABC's sudden rise from third place in prime-time audience ratings in the 1950s to the top in the 1970s.

No single person was more responsible for ABC's success than Roone P. Arledge. The year after he won a television Emmy for producing the best children's program of 1959 (NBC's "Hi Mom"), Arledge joined ABC to direct and produce the network's football games. Arledge was determined to do more than put on a good sports broadcast. He wanted "to get the audience involved emotionally," reasoning that "If they didn't give a damn about the game, they still might enjoy the program."[8] To obtain more audience involvement, he attempted to capture the full ambience of the game setting. He used cranes, blimps, and helicopters to obtain novel views of stadiums, towns, and campuses; employed hand-held cameras for close-up shots of cheerleaders, band members, eccentric spectators, and nervous coaches; and deployed rifle-type microphones to pick up the roar of the crowd, the thud of a punt, or the crunch of a hard tackle. Arledge also made the crowd itself part of the performance. Once the fans perceived themselves as potential performers, they began to carry banners, run onto the playing field, and enliven games in other ways.

Arledge also brought his talents to other sporting events. In addition to turning the 1968, 1972, and 1976 Olympic Games into television extravaganzas, he created *The Wide World of Sports*, which was to win more Emmys than any other sportscast. A pioneer in stop-action filming, *Wide World* consisted of a potpourri of feats and games, including boxing matches, track meets, ski races, surfing, cliff diving, barrel jumping, wrist wrestling, and demolition derbies. The program was especially effective in stimulating public interest in winter sports.

The popularity of televised sport produced an escalation in television contracts, especially for football. By 1977, the average audience for televised NFL games was

20 million. That year, NFL commissioner Pete Rozelle negotiated a $656 million contract with the major networks, which brought each team nearly $6 million a year. At the same time, ABC was paying the College Football Association, made up of 61 of the top college football programs, upward of $20 million a year. As the rewards for success escalated, so did the quality of training and play. And as broadcast time expanded and audiences grew, so did the role that sports played in American culture.

Sports and Social Change

The 1960s saw both prosperity and turmoil. The nation's economy expanded enormously, with low unemployment, large jumps in productivity, and rising wages and profits. Economic growth, combined with government programs such as Medicare, sent average incomes up by 50 percent and cut poverty rates in half. At the same time, however, Americans from many different parts of society mounted campaigns to challenge what they saw as shortcomings in national policy and culture.

African Americans took the lead, challenging the many forms of discrimination they had faced since before the Civil War. From the mid-1940s through the 1960s, the civil rights movement combined legal action with grassroots endeavors that included marches, demonstrations, boycotts, and voter registration drives, eventually toppling legal segregation and sparking federal legislation that banned unequal treatment based on race. Sports would provide one focus for those efforts. As racial barriers began to fall, growing numbers of African American athletes emerged into the national spotlight, from basketball sensation Oscar Robertson to boxer Muhammad Ali to sprinter Wilma Rudolph. As well as becoming symbols of African American achievements, many of these athletes also became prominent advocates of further change. Athletes representing other disadvantaged groups would follow their example.

As the 1960s came to a close, the women's liberation movement began to gain momentum, and growing numbers of U.S. women began to see sports as a way to build individual capabilities and advertise women's abilities. The passage of the landmark legislation known as Title IX required the nation's colleges and universities to create women's sports programs that offered college women the same athletic opportunities they offered men. Grassroots efforts pressed institutions to follow through on that requirement, vastly increasing both opportunities and incentives for young women to compete. Female tennis and golf players established successful professional leagues. More women's sports, including basketball, became part of Olympic competition. Between 1970 and 1979, the number of female college athletes doubled, and the number of female high school athletes approached two million.

Sports would also come in for its share of criticism during the era, both because of its own shortcomings and because its ties to Americanism made it into a symbol for critics of national policy. Two serious gambling scandals in college basketball, for example, sparked broader critiques of the players, the colleges that had recruited them, and the communities that had celebrated their athletic skills. "It may indeed be that the big news in this story is the disclosure of a sort of sneaking corruption of American society itself which has reached the areas in which America is supposed to be doing most to build the intellectual and moral quality of its future," editors at one North Carolina newspaper wrote in response to one of the scandals.[9] The counter-culture movement, made up largely of young people who viewed the United States as overly materialistic and aggressive, frequently criticized the intensive, seemingly warlike competition involved in sports such as football, and promoted alternatives such as freestyle Frisbee.

Athletes themselves also chimed in. In the first part of the twentieth century, sportswriters and publicists had studiously ignored the failings of the athletes they covered, limiting most of their coverage to on-field activities and the more innocuous off-field pursuits. The more critical tenor of the 1960s gave sports journalism new bite. Within a range of only a few years, a rash of books by athletes, coaches, and journalists raised questions about whether high-level sports did in fact build character or offer a valuable model for society. NBA star Bill Russell examined racism in professional basketball (1966); Dave Meggyesy, an All-Pro lineman with the St. Louis Cardinals, denounced the brutality, militarism, and inhumanity of the NFL (1970); Jim Bouton revealed the all-too-human frailties of his "heroic" New York Yankee teammates (1970); Harry Edwards recapped the plight of African American athletes in *The Revolt of the Black Athlete* (1969); and Jack Scott summed up a variety of discontents in *The Athletic Revolution* (1971).

A New Generation

By the 1970s, however, many of the social struggles of the 1960s began to fade from public view. Many Americans turned to a focus on self-sufficiency and individual well-being that led writer Tom Wolfe to dub the 1970s the "Me Decade." Sports saw a new emphasis on individual fitness during this time, especially among middle- and upper-class Americans, many of whom had become dissatisfied with the anonymity and lack of autonomy found in even highly paid white-collar work. A "running boom" among both men and women prompted the establishment of road races and marathons across the nation, particularly after American Frank Shorter won the Olympic marathon competition in 1972. By the late 1970s, the number of Americans who claimed to exercise regularly had jumped to 20 million. As more and more white-collar employees replaced two-martini lunches with jogging, swimming, and working out on exercise machines, YMCAs, YWCAs, and similar organizations experienced a sudden reversal in their long-term membership declines. The number of commercial health clubs multiplied from 350 in 1968 to more than 7,000 in 1986.[10]

Recognition of the limits of modern medicine also provided an impetus to the quest for greater self-sufficiency through fitness. The antibiotic revolution of the 1940s and 1950s brought many contagious diseases under control, but not cardiovascular disease or cancer, diseases that became the leading causes of death. Self-improvement seemed to be the most effective way of countering these dreaded killers. White-collar professionals in particular began to practice a more abstemious lifestyle—exercising more, trying to control weight, drinking less, and ending their addiction to tobacco. But this new strenuosity extended beyond a desire to achieve physical fitness. While many jogged short distances a few times weekly, an astonishing number of Americans took up regular long-distance running. In 1970, only 126 men entered the first New York marathon. By the mid-1980s the organizers accepted 20,000 "official" entries from both men and women while rejecting thousands of others. The apostles of fitness also invented the iron-man triathlon, which included a 2-mile swim, a 112-mile bicycle ride, and a 26-mile run. In 1986 more than a million Americans completed this grueling event.

Supporters attributed many benefits to running, including building and/or releasing additional sources of energy, improving sex, reducing anxieties, and inducing a mystical "runner's high," a trancelike euphoria that could become addictive. A distinctive runners' culture emerged, one that revolved not only around running, but also around clubs, magazines, special diets, and in-group behaviors. It also sparked a flourishing equipment industry, as advertisers and manufacturers quickly moved to exploit the new enthusiasm by offering new products. Sales at Blue Ribbon Sports, which began manufacturing running shoes in the late 1960s and introduced its Nike brand in 1972, jumped from $10 million in the early 1970s to $270 million in 1980 (Blue Ribbon Sports would officially become Nike, Inc. in 1981).[11]

Political Retrenchment

A focus on individual self-sufficiency and success came to the political forefront in 1980, when Ronald Reagan was elected President. Reagan's political vision combined a celebration of the striving, competitive individual with a vision of an ordered, harmonious society that harked back to the pre-1960s era. Throughout his campaign, Reagan had promised to return the nation to its "traditional values," primarily through reducing the size of government and ending many of the social programs that had been enacted in the 1960s. He also called for reducing government regulation of business, which he argued had short-circuited robust economic competition.

Sports provided an ideal metaphor for this vision, giving a heroic tenor to competitive struggles. Reagan, who had played football in college and worked as a sports announcer before becoming a movie actor, touched on the significance he saw in sports in a commencement address at Notre Dame shortly after his election. (Reagan had played George Gipp—"the Gipper"—in the iconic film *Knute Rockne: All-American*). "Knute Rockne as a boy came to America with his parents from Norway," he told the graduates. "And in the few years it took him to grow up to college age, he became so American that here at Notre Dame, he became an All American in a game that is still, to this day, uniquely American." He then held up Rockne as an ideal role model. "As a coach, he did more than teach young men how to play a game. He believed truly that the noblest work of man was building the character of man. And maybe that's why he was a living legend. No man connected with football has ever achieved the stature or occupied the singular niche in the Nation that he carved out for himself, not just in a sport, but in our entire social structure."[12] This new conservatism would have a variety of effects on sports itself, which ranged from slowing federal efforts to expand athletic opportunities for women to encouraging the growth of new and powerful sports-oriented businesses.

Cable and the Internet

Ronald Reagan became president at a time when technological developments were also contributing to a new and highly profitable expansion of televised sports. Syndicated sports shows, cable television, and direct-broadcast communication satellites added vast new dimensions to the fight between media outlets for supremacy in sports. From the earliest days of the new medium, independent producers had put together shows that would then be aired either by one of the major networks or by a special syndicated network of local stations. The launching of the first communications satellite in 1974 and the end of complex legal restrictions on cable television in 1977 paved the way for "superstations" and cable network systems. Fans of televised sports particularly rejoiced at the formation of the Entertainment and Sports Programming Network (ESPN) in 1979. As ESPN required countless games to fill its 24-hour day, the network at first telecast a mosaic of local contests, obscure college sports, and minor sports such as billiards. But in time the network went mainstream, landing contracts for college and pro football as well as big-league baseball. In the 1990s, ESPN became part of a vast Disney media conglomerate that included the ABC network.

Cable television and other technical developments helped give American athletes a worldwide audience, as companies packaged American sports and stars—most prominently the National Basketball Association—and sold them around the globe. The expansion of television and eventually Internet offerings also made it possible for U.S. sports fans to spend almost unlimited amounts of time following teams and athletes. By 2007, for example, the NCAA men's basketball tournament, later trademarked "March Madness" at the cost of $17 million, had all 63 games either televised or streamed live on the Internet. As many as 75 million Americans watched the opening rounds, and *Business Week* estimated that the tournament cost employers $1.2 billion in lost productivity. American viewers had the option of tuning into separate cable channels devoted entirely to golf, tennis, soccer, and motorsports, as well as broadcasts from stations around the world, and a 24-hour station devoted exclusively to the country's Spanish-speaking sports fans.[13]

Conclusion

The second half of the twentieth century saw a tremendous expansion in the reach and cultural significance of American sports, sparked by the wide-ranging influences of television, political activism, and demographic change. This sporting expansion meant that by the twenty-first century American sports fans could easily follow a far broader range of sports than ever before, and cheer for both male and female athletes from almost any racial, ethnic, or economic background. Sports had also become bigger business than ever, generating unprecedented profits for teams and players, as well as for many other enterprises. Still, even as the popularity of sports expanded, athletes, coaches, and communities continued to wrestle with its many challenges—both old problems such as the dilemma of balancing athletic and academic priorities, and new ones such as the proliferation of performance-enhancing drugs.

Critical Thinking Questions

1. Once television became a part of American life, was the rise of television-fueled sports inevitable?
2. In 2007, *Business Week* estimated that the NCAA men's basketball tournament cost employers $1.2 billion in lost productivity. What does this say about American society?
3. American sports has undergone several major transformations: the beginnings of commercial sport in the nineteenth century, the incorporation of sports into many American institutions in the first part of the twentieth century, and the growing economic and cultural role played by sports in the late twentieth and early twenty-first centuries, fueled both by television and by expanding opportunities for previously marginalized groups such as women and African Americans. Which of these eras do you think represented the greatest change and why?

Notes

1. Quoted in Richard Espy, *Politics of the Olympic Games* (Berkeley: University of California Press, 1979), 38.
2. Quoted in Benjamin G. Rader, *American Ways: A History of American Cultures* (Belmont, CA: Thomson/Wadsworth, 2006), 311. See also Kathryn Jay, *More Than Just a Game: Sports in American Life Since 1945* (New York: Columbia University Press, 2004), chapters 1–3.
3. Jim Caplan, "Perspective," *Sports Illustrated*, May 23, 1983, MW2. See also N.J. Sullivan, *The Dodgers Move West* (New York: Oxford University Press, 1987).
4. Benjamin G. Rader, *In Its Own Image: How Television Has Transformed Sports* (New York: Free Press, 1984), 35; Theodore Caplow et al., *Middletown Families* (Minneapolis: University of Minnesota Press, 1982); John P. Robinson, *How Americans Use Time* (New York: Institute of Social Research, 1977), especially 172–79; and Herbert J. Gans, *The Urban Villagers* (New York: Free Press, 1962), 187–96.
5. Kenneth T. Jackson, *Crabgrass Frontier* (New York: Oxford University Press, 1985), 231.
6. W.J. Levitt, as quoted in Jackson, *Crabgrass Frontier*. See also Robert Fishman, *Bourgeois Utopias* (New York: Basic Books, 1987).
7. The long-accepted date for the first American sports telecast has been 1939, but a year earlier a college football game was telecast in Philadelphia. See NCAA Football Television Committee, *Football Television Briefing Book* (Shawnee Mission, KS: NCAA, 1981), 1.
8. Quoted in William O. Johnson Jr., *Super Spectator and the Electric Lilliputians* (Boston: Little, Brown, 1971), 161.
9. *Raleigh News and Observer*, May 15, 1961.
10. See especially Benjamin G. Rader, "The Quest for Self-Sufficiency and the New Strenuosity," *Journal of Sport History* 18 (1991), 255–67; Michael S. Goldstein, *The Health Movement* (New York: Twayne, 1992); and Roberta J. Park, "A Decade of the Body: Researching and Writing about the History of Health, Fitness, Exercise and Sport, 1983–1993," *Journal of Sport History* 21 (1994), 59–82.
11. Walter LaFeber, *Michael Jordan and the New Global Capitalism* (New York: W.W. Norton and Company, 2002), 61.
12. Ronald Reagan, "Address at the Commencement Exercises at the University of Notre Dame," May 17, 1981, http://www.reagan.utexas.edu/archives/speeches/1981/51781a.htm.
13. See Del Jones, "March Madness Is Here, So Go Ahead and Goof Off," *USA Today*, March 16, 2007. For the trademark cost, see Steve Weisburg, "NCAA paid $17 million to protect 'March Madness' term," May 10, 2011. http://usatoday30.usatoday.com/sports/college/mensbasketball/2011-05-10-march-madness_N.htm.

CHAPTER 16

Professional Team Sports in the Age of Television

The Monday Night Football crew of (l-r) Howard Cosell, Don Meredith, and Frank Gifford helped make the National Football League the nation's most popular sport.

LEARNING OBJECTIVES

16.1 Describe the variety of strategies that NFL team owners used to take advantage of television broadcast, and explain the factors that made the NFL far more successful than major league baseball in the television era.

16.2 Summarize the advantages that professional football's owners brought to the postwar era.

16.3 Outline the strategies that football owners used to make professional football the most financially successful professional sport of the postwar era.

16.4 Analyze the combination of marketing and playing styles that turned professional football into a cultural phenomenon in the 1970s and 1980s.

16.5 Detail the factors that contributed to the decline of major league baseball in the television era.

16.6 Explain the factors that helped professional basketball players form the most effective players' association, as well as the results that effectiveness produced.

It was third down, with less than two minutes remaining, and the Baltimore Colts, trailing 17–14, had the ball on their own 14-yard line. Four completed passes later, however, Colts quarterback Johnny Unitas had brought his team 62 yards—close enough for Colts kicker Steve Myhra to kick a game-tying field goal and send the 1958 National Football League championship into sudden-death overtime. The New York Giants won the coin toss but got nowhere. The Colts then launched a 13-play drive, later dubbed the "thirteen steps to glory," that culminated in a one-yard touchdown run to win the championship. Nearly 65,000 fans filled the Yankee Stadium seats. An additional 30 million followed the game on television, more tuning in as the contest stretched into Sunday evening. Professional football had already become a regular attraction on television broadcast schedules. The Colts' dramatic victory, quickly termed "the greatest game every played," only increased the game's appeal. In the two decades that followed, effective management and the savvy use of television would turn the once-obscure professional league into a national obsession.

Baseball, in contrast, found the television era much rougher going. Thousands of semipro teams folded in the 1950s, and minor-league baseball became a shell of its former self. The major leagues fared only somewhat better. Average attendance at big-league games peaked in 1948, but then started to decline. It would take three full decades for attendance to climb back to its former heights, and even then it lagged population growth in metropolitan areas served by big-league franchises. By the mid-1960s, the television audiences for regular season baseball games fell to nearly half of that of regular season pro football games.[1]

The contrast between the two sports highlights many of the challenges and opportunities that American sports faced as the nation entered an era of rapid cultural and economic reconfiguration. Television was a tantalizing new source of audience and funds—if a sport could adapt to its requirements.

Early Days

Professional football grew out of the tough mine and mill towns in western Pennsylvania and Ohio. Starting in the 1890s, local clubs began to pay some men a few dollars to risk life and limb to play on Sunday afternoons. At the Panhandle Shop of the Pennsylvania Railroad in Columbus, Ohio, for example, men "worked in the shop until four Saturday afternoon, got their suppers at home, grabbed the rattlers to any point within twelve hours' ride of Columbus, played the Sunday game, took another train to Columbus, and punched the time clock at seven Monday morning."[2] No leagues existed before 1920, and each team scheduled its own matches.

Unlike college football, which was dominated by the white middle and upper classes, the pro sport was primarily ethnic, Catholic, and working class. Some rosters even included a few blacks and Native Americans. For almost a decade, Jim Thorpe, the Carlisle Indian School football great and hero of the 1912 Olympics, was the game's premier attraction. Many other aspects of the game placed it outside the bounds of conventional respectability, including the employment of collegians and sometimes high school athletes playing under aliases; the players' tendency to jump from team to team during the season to maximize their pay; and widespread wagering and charges of game fixing.

Pro football took its first steps toward greater organization in 1920, when a group of the game's supporters gathered at the Hupmobile automobile agency showroom in Canton, Ohio. Led by Joseph F. Carr, a sportswriter, minor-league baseball owner, and manager of the Columbus football team, the group formed a new pro league that they hoped would improve the game's image and profitability. In 1922, this league became the National Football League, or NFL. Stability, however, proved elusive. More than 40 franchises joined the league, struggled, and then expired. The Great Depression wiped out all the small-city franchises, with the notable exception of Green Bay, Wisconsin. Even though the NFL signed such college heroes as Red Grange and Ernie Nevers in the 1920s, most college stars passed up the pro game. Newspapers, especially outside the cities hosting pro teams, all but ignored the league.

Following World War II, pro football's fortunes began to improve. By 1950, average game attendance had doubled. More college stars began to go pro. Paul Brown, owner-coach of the Cleveland Browns, introduced a series of offensive innovations, including the invention of the modern "pocket" in which the quarterback stands to throw. Still, the sport's following remained limited. In 1952, halfback Frank Gifford traveled from California to New York to play for the New York Giants. When he returned home after that first season his friends asked: "Where have *you* been?"[3] As late as 1956, *Sports Illustrated* ran 55 feature stories on baseball and only four on pro football.

Football's rapid rise to the pinnacle of American professional sports rested on several factors. One involved management. The football owners had much in common. Nearly all of them were Irish Catholic in origin and they shared the long history of the league's financial tribulations. Unlike the savagely independent barons of baseball, they were far more willing to delegate authority to the commissioner's office. And unlike the baseball owners, they chose as commissioners men who had experience in the game's business side. In the post–World War II era, both

DeBenneville "Bert" Bell and Alvin "Pete" Rozelle provided the NFL with astute leadership. Bell, a former owner-coach of the Philadelphia Eagles, established the framework for a powerful NFL during his tenure (1946–1959). His work was carried on by Rozelle (1959–1989) and Paul Tagliabue (1989–2006). The commissioners welded the NFL owners into a united and highly effective economic cartel—an organization whose members, acting together, effectively reduced internal competition and thus maximized collective profits.[4]

Television provided the other key. Football was ideally suited to television. Apart from the sheer physicality of the sport, the central requirement of the game— that the offense must move the ball 10 yards in four plays or give it up to the opposing team—set up recurring crises, keeping the viewer's attention riveted to the screen. The pause between plays permitted the viewer to savor the drama. If the situation were third down and long yardage, would the linebackers blitz? Would the quarterback throw or call a draw play? Football was a high-speed, highly complex game, not always easy to follow. Announcers helped novice viewers understand and appreciate the intricacies of the sport, one play at a time. "You watched a game on television and, suddenly, the wool was stripped from your eyes," one fan explained. "What had appeared to be an incomprehensible tangle of milling bodies from the grandstand made sense." Television, he continued, "created a nation of instant experts in no time."[5]

Technological breakthroughs also contributed to pro football's growing popularity. As interest in sports telecasts grew, technicians began to experiment with ways to improve viewers' experience, making a televised game a different—and in many ways far richer—experience than watching from the stands. Instant replay was first used by CMS in 1963, to replay a touchdown in the annual Army–Navy game. The idea was so novel that the announcer repeatedly cautioned viewers, "This is not live!" "Army did not score again!" But instant replay—especially in slow motion—could pinpoint a receiver running a pattern, the vicious blocking of an interior lineman or the intricate steps of a running back eluding would-be tacklers. Color television, artificial playing surfaces, and bright uniforms with the names of individual players on their backs added to the visual appeal. More than one viewer shared the judgment of critic Richard Kostelanetz, who declared that compared with telecast games "live games now seem peculiarly inept, lethargic, and pedestrian." Televised football became the preferred way for many men to spend fall Sunday afternoons.[6]

Television also helped to create a rival to the NFL: the American Football League (AFL). Rebuffed in their efforts to obtain NFL franchises, two millionaire Texans, Lamar Hunt of Dallas and K. S. "Bud" Adams of Houston, announced the formation of the new league in 1959. The AFL began play in 1960 with eight teams, four of which were in cities already occupied by the NFL. The AFL nearly went down at the outset; it lost an estimated $3 million in its first year, and the undercapitalized New York franchise, essential to the AFL's potential success, threatened to drive the entire league into bankruptcy. Only a willingness to innovate and work together kept it afloat. In 1960, Harry Wismer, former sportscaster and eccentric owner of the New York team, persuaded the AFL owners to sell the league's television rights to ABC as a package, each franchise sharing equally in the receipts. The modest contract helped keep the lights on during the league's rocky early years.

In the meantime, the NFL continued to forge ahead. In October of 1959, Commissioner Bert Bell died of a sudden heart attack while watching a game between the Steelers and his beloved Eagles. After nine days of heated discussion, the NFL owners made the surprise choice of 33-year-old Pete Rozelle as their new commissioner. Rozelle, whose affable exterior masked a shrewd and steely core, had served as both chief publicity man and general manager of the Los Angeles Rams, learning the game through business and public relations rather than as a player or coach. He so won the admiration of the owners that they gave him more authority than any other professional sport commissioner.

The "Boy Czar" soon got an opportunity to test his skills. In 1961 the NFL signed a joint television pact with CBS similar to the one that the AFL had made with ABC. A federal judge ruled that the contract violated federal antitrust law, because the owners were collaborating when they should be competing. Aroused by this adverse decision, professional sports leagues turned to Congress for relief. Led by Rozelle, they argued that package or pooled contracts, in which franchises shared equally in the receipts, were essential to the existence of modern sports leagues, because they would prevent disparities in competition. (None of the witnesses got around to pointing out that the monopolistic practice of pooling contracts would also be likely to result in increased profits for all franchises.)

Responding to the appeal, Congress quickly passed and President John F. Kennedy signed the Sports Broadcasting Act of 1961. The act permitted the professional clubs to negotiate the sale of national broadcast rights as a single economic unit. As well as demonstrating the clout of professional sports on Capitol Hill, this hasty action helped lay the foundation for the golden age of pro football.

Pro Football's Golden Age

By any measure, the success of pro football from the 1960s to the early 1980s was staggering. Although the owners refused to open their financial records to public perusal, teams seem to have lost money only rarely. "Any dummy can make money operating a pro football club," declared Al Davis, managing partner of the Oakland Raiders, in 1978.[7] By the 1970s, attendance at each pro stadium regularly exceeded 90 percent of its capacity, even for preseason training games. Most of those grand sporting palaces had been built at public expense, by cities anxious to attract or retain professional franchises. The average audience for televised games leaped from 11 million in 1967 to nearly 20 million by 1977.

Two league policies virtually insured financial success for individual franchises. One was the decision to continue splitting television revenues equally among the franchises. In addition, visiting teams received 40 percent of gate receipts for individual games, allowing the NFL to avoid the gross disparities in revenues among franchises that characterized major-league baseball. The philosophy of "Think League," in which owners focused on the success of the league as a whole rather than on maximizing profits at individual franchises, proved an enduring, if somewhat ironic success. As Cleveland Browns owner Art Modell once happily quipped: "We're 28 Republicans who vote socialist."[8]

Television revenues continued to grow, thanks to the Sports Broadcasting Act of 1961 and the astute negotiations of Pete Rozelle. In 1964, Rozelle signed a

$14 million pact with CBS—nearly three times the 1962 contract—prompting Arthur Rooney Jr., veteran owner of the Pittsburgh Steelers, to exclaim: "Pete Rozelle is a gift from the hand of Providence."[9] Unwilling to be shut out of the increasingly popular game, NBC decided to gamble on the AFL by paying the new league $42 million over five years.

NBC's generosity allowed the AFL to embark on a "battle of the paychecks" with the NFL for college stars. In 1965, the AFL signed the biggest prize of all, Joe Willie Namath, a slope-shouldered quarterback out of the University of Alabama, for the (then) astonishing sum of $420,000 for three years. Art Modell of the rival NFL hooted that the signing of Namath was merely a "theatrical stunt," but the high command of the New York Jets, headed by David "Sonny" Werblin, recognized the value of a player possessing talent and charisma, both of which Namath had in abundance. In the first season with Namath at the helm, Jets ticket sales doubled. Soon other players received even higher contracts, making Namath's salary one of the best bargains in pro sports.

The rising costs of competition for player talent drove the competing leagues to the peace table in 1966. Under terms of the merger agreement, Rozelle became the sole commissioner, the combined league established a common player draft to end the bidding war, and the two leagues (or conferences as they were to be known after 1969) agreed to an NFL championship game to begin in 1967. Congress quickly passed a law exempting the merger from antitrust action. Senate Whip Russell Long and House Whip Hale Boggs, both from Louisiana, were chiefly responsible for guiding the legislation through Congress. Perhaps not coincidentally, only nine days after the Football Merger Act became law, the NFL awarded New Orleans an expansion franchise.

The American Football Conference, as it became known after the merger, soon caught up with the senior loop in the quality of play. Vince Lombardi's Green Bay Packers easily disposed of the first two AFC champions, but Super Bowl III in 1969 symbolically established the AFC's parity with the NFC. Joe Namath, whose AFC New York Jets faced the NFC's Baltimore Colts, confidently predicted: "We'll win. I'll guarantee it." And the Jets did, 16–7.

The contrast between the Packers and the Jets pointed to another aspect of football's appeal. At a time when the nation was facing political rebellion from many quarters, including African Americans fighting for greater civil rights, young people challenging their parents' politics and lifestyles, and women beginning to question their place in society, regular Sunday football games offered a point of stability, a place where men engaged in fierce competition within a carefully ordered set of rules. Many fans saw hard-nosed Packer coach Vince Lombardi as an enduring symbol of "old-fashioned" values.[10] But football also managed to incorporate new developments without changing its fundamental structure. Joe Namath might boast loudly, wear his hair long, and pursue a "swinging" lifestyle, but on the field he was as disciplined and focused as any of Lombardi's players. Growing numbers of African American players such as Jim Brown and Otis Taylor were also becoming part of the pro game, providing viewers with dramatic on-field displays of interracial teamwork. Many different kinds of fans had reason to tune in.

Marketing Professional Team Sports

The NFL also excelled at marketing. Until the age of television, the moguls of pro sports had operated from the premise that their games sold themselves. True, they might concede, spectators needed minimal comforts. Even in the nineteenth century baseball owners had provided seats (though sometimes merely of sun-bleached boards), refreshments, and player programs. Sometimes they festooned their parks with pennants or hired a brass band to play before the game and during lulls between innings. But fans, they believed with justification, came primarily to see the artistry of physical feats performed at the highest plateaus of excellence and to witness genuine, unscripted dramas. All that was needed otherwise, it seemed, was for the sports entrepreneurs to guarantee to the fans that their games were not fixed and that every team had a reasonable chance of winning.

With the introduction of television in the last half of the twentieth century, however, pro sports faced a new challenge. To obtain revenues from the new medium, they now needed to make games attractive to a new set of viewers, those sitting in the comfort of their dens or in local bars rather than in the stands. The NFL, under the tutelage of Pete Rozelle, led the way. While initially reluctant to interrupt the flow of a game for commercials, by the mid-1970s NFL referees received signals from the television crews to call no fewer than 14 timeouts while each game was in progress. Commercials added at least 30 minutes to the length of each game. Traditionally, the NFL had all but ignored the hoopla that had long surrounded college football. But in the late 1970s, pro teams urged fans to bring banners, pennants, and towels to wave during the games. By 1980, nearly every franchise hired skimpily dressed female cheerleaders to prance along the sidelines.

The NFL also became the center of a new kind of broadcasting, with a new Roone Arledge production titled *Monday Night Football*. Initiated in 1970 when the National Football League threatened to sell its rights to a Monday night game to an independent network, this prime-time sport show altered the Monday night habits of a huge number of Americans. Monday movie attendance plummeted, restaurants closed, and bowlers rescheduled their leagues. Much of *Monday Night Football's* success stemmed from Arledge's decision to hire the most controversial sportscaster in the country: Howard Cosell. (When drawing up the Monday night agreement, Arledge had refused to sign the traditional contract providing for "announcer approval" by league officials.) Cosell had been an early champion of boxer Muhammad Ali's highly controversial refusal to fight in the Vietnam War, and he was well known for his biting, irreverent commentary.

True to his reputation, Cosell treated professional football with none of the reverence that his predecessors had bestowed upon the sport, claiming to "tell it like it is" by second-guessing the wisdom of head coaches, criticizing the decisions of officials, and lampooning the owners. Caustic, unctuous, polysyllabic, and given to making even the most trivial observation sound like something profound, he became a man the audience "loved to hate." Unlike any other broadcaster, Cosell was able to get away with simultaneously promoting, reporting on, and criticizing an event packaged and merchandised by his own network. His presence helped make *Monday Night Football* a national cultural event as well as a football game.

As a part of their marketing endeavors, football's moguls were also willing to experiment with rules and structure. Although the low-scoring, power football of the 1960s and early 1970s satisfied millions of spectators both at home and in the stands, critics charged that the pro games had become too predictable and that coaches seemed determined above all else to avoid costly mistakes. In 1978, the NFL sought to bring more offense to the game by adopting a radical rule change in pass rush defense, designed to protect quarterbacks. Previously, offensive linemen could not open their hands or leave their arms extended, which forced them to hit rushing defenders, move their feet, and recoil, then again hit and recoil. In 1978, the rule makers permitted pass rush defenders to extend their arms and open their hands to protect the passer. The change soon altered the job description of offensive linemen, as teams sought even bulkier and stronger men to hold off pass rushers. The average weight of offensive linemen soared.

In the meantime, reported *Sports Illustrated,* the offenses went "wild."[11] Within three years, passing yardage nearly doubled, and quarterback sacks fell to an all-time low. Seizing on the opportunities offered by the new blocking rule, in the 1980s Bill Walsh of the San Francisco 49ers introduced the West Coast Offense, a ball-control, mostly short yardage passing game that used multiple receivers to attack every part of the field. Innovative defenses gradually slowed the offensive barrage. But with both defenses and offenses taking more chances than before, NFL football became an even more exciting spectacle than it had been in the past.

The NFL also pioneered efforts to establish a more level-playing field. Recognizing that lopsided games, runaway races for the championships, and having the same teams repeatedly in the playoffs threatened to reduce interest in the sport, the NFL expanded its playoffs to include eight teams rather than four. A "wild-card" berth, a system that admitted the non-division-winning team with the best record from each conference, added excitement to the regular season. In time both the National Basketball Association (NBA) and major-league baseball adopted similar playoff systems.

The result was a game that wove itself into American culture like none had done before. By the early 1970s, the NFL championship, dubbed the "Super Bowl," would enjoy a larger national audience than horse racing's venerable Kentucky Derby or baseball's World Series. By the 1980s, over half the nation's population watched the game on television. Super Bowl Sunday became an unofficial national holiday, one that was more rigorously observed in many circles than Washington's Birthday, Independence Day, or even tippling on New Year's Eve. "Pro football is our biggest civic tent, *our* last genuinely mass entertainment," one author claimed.[12]

The Woes of Baseball

As football thrived, baseball struggled. Major-league baseball expanded its reach to a number of new cities during the era. In the 1950s, the Brooklyn Dodgers and the New York Giants headed to California, the Boston Braves to Milwaukee, the St. Louis Browns to Baltimore, and the Philadelphia Athletics to Kansas City. Expansion and further moves brought the game to Minneapolis-St. Paul, Atlanta, Houston, San Diego, Oakland, Seattle, and Montreal. But audiences lagged, in part because of shifts in the urban leisure patterns that had helped create the games.

The exodus of families from cities to suburbs drained baseball's traditional audience. Many new suburbanites hesitated to drive into cities to attend games. In addition, they had plenty of new ways to spend their spare time. "Why should a guy with a boat in the driveway, golf clubs in the car, bowling ball and tennis racket in the closet, a trunkful of camping equipment, two boys in the Little League and a body full of energy left over from shorter working hours pay to sit and do nothing but watch a mediocre game?" asked W. Travis Walton of Abilene, Texas, in a letter to *Sports Illustrated* in 1958.[13] In addition, baseball did not lend itself to effective television broadcast. Not only was it difficult for television to capture all of baseball's dimensions, the sport's long season also meant that only a few games seemed crucial enough to attract large television audiences.

Baseball owners also struggled to devise a satisfactory television policy. In contrast to the "Think League" approach of NFL owners, big-league baseball owners generally focused on the interests of their individual teams. In part, minor-league baseball was a victim of this greed. The economic growth that followed World War II had stimulated a new boom in minor-league baseball, with annual attendance increasing from 15 to 42 million between 1939 and 1949. Then came television. Threatened by antitrust action by the Justice Department and seeking to maximize their own broadcast revenues, major-league owners repealed their ban against their games being aired in minor-league territories in 1951. Attendance at minor-league games subsequently plummeted to 15 million in 1957 and 10 million in 1969. The number of minor leagues shrank from 51 in 1949 to 20 by 1970.

Until 1961, when Congress passed the Sports Broadcasting Act, major-league baseball was also unable to develop a national television package for regular season games that included all franchises. In 1954, the majors submitted to the Department of Justice a plan for a "Game of the Week" in which the commissioner of baseball would negotiate with the networks for the sale of national television rights of the member franchises. But the Justice Department advised that the proposal would violate federal antitrust laws. Organized baseball acquiesced without taking the issue to the federal courts; apparently the owners feared the possible loss of baseball's unique legal status. Instead, individual clubs negotiated with the networks for national telecast packages. While these deals produced a bonanza of televised baseball in the late 1950s, those clubs that could not land network telecasts (usually those located in smaller population areas) suffered from both declining attendance and a reduction in potential broadcasting revenues. The passage of the Sports Broadcasting Act of 1961 brought contracts with the television networks in which all clubs shared equally in the revenues. But in contrast to the major jumps in NFL contracts, the size of baseball's network contracts drifted fairly slowly upward, generally paralleling the rate of inflation.

On the Diamond

The every-owner-for-himself approach meant than the first decades of postwar play were dominated by big-city teams. In one stretch, the New York Yankees captured an astonishing 15 flags in 17 seasons. Superior resources arising from larger attendance, more broadcast revenues, and skilled management accounted for the longevity of the Yankee dynasty. Casey Stengel, the erstwhile field manager of the Yankees from 1949 to 1960, had so many good players at his disposal that he platooned many of his hitters, using left-handed hitters against right-handed pitchers and vice versa. For similar reasons the Brooklyn-Los Angeles Dodgers franchise enjoyed almost equal success in the National League.

The 1960s were also marked by a step that proved a near disaster. In 1963, apparently to speed up games, the big leagues instructed umpires to enlarge the strike zone, calling as strikes some pitches that had formerly been balls. Offensive output dropped precipitously. At the very time when baseball faced its greatest competition, the game had transformed itself into a series of defensive contests reminiscent of the early twentieth century. To reverse the damage caused by the 1963 decision, in 1969 the rulemakers lowered the pitching mound from 15 to 10 inches (thereby making the curve and the slider less effective) and ordered the umpires to reduce the expanded strike zone. Moreover, in 1973 the American League replaced pitchers in the batting order with "designated hitters." These changes improved offensive output, though not to the levels of the pre-1960s.

The years after the 1960s also saw greater team parity. Several factors played into the shift. In 1965, the leagues implemented an amateur free agent draft. For the first time, clubs could gain the rights to negotiate with any unsigned amateur player in reverse order of their standings in the previous season. The draft decidedly reduced the advantages that the richer franchises had long enjoyed in the chase after promising college and high school players. In 1969, the leagues added four new teams, split each league into two divisions, and added a league championship play-off series before the World Series.

Finally, the 1970s and 1980s produced a new kind of game, one that featured raw power, dazzling speed, and specialized pitching. Quickness and strong arms allowed shortstops and second basemen to play far deeper than in the past. No departure from earlier managerial strategy was more striking than the use of relief pitchers. In the past, managers had been tied to "the complete game mystique." But in the two-divisional era, the number of complete games pitched plummeted to less than one in ten. By the 1980s, teams were beginning to develop relief specialists. In the eighth or ninth inning, regardless of how well the earlier pitcher had been doing, managers brought in their bullpen kings—"the closers."

Professional Basketball on the Rise

Like professional football, professional basketball languished in the long shadows cast by other teams: specifically college squads, Amateur Athletic Union fives, and the Harlem Globetrotters.[14] In the 1920s and 1930s, most professional teams operated as barnstormers, and only a few enjoyed more than short-term success. The New York Original Celtics, the most prosperous club of the 1920s, occasionally drew as many as 10,000 fans to Madison Square Garden. The 1930s saw the rise of a number of strong teams, including the all-black New York Renaissance, the Philadelphia Sphas, a largely Jewish quintet named for the South Philadelphia Hebrew Association, and the Harlem Globetrotters, who despite their name were based in Chicago.

The pro game began its rise in 1946, when a group of big-city arena owners decided to form their own league, the Basketball Association of America (BAA), as a way to fill the vacancies in winter schedules dominated by more profitable ice hockey and college basketball matches. Three years later, the BAA merged with the Midwest-based National Basketball League to form the NBA. As the league stabilized, its teams began to eclipse the Amateur Athletic Union and barnstorming teams that had drawn much of basketball's talent. The emergence of the powerful Minneapolis Lakers, led by towering George Mikan, strengthened the NBA's claim that the league featured the "best of basketball." In the 1950s, the NBA began to recruit top black stars and to outbid the AAU teams for players. It also benefited from the point-shaving scandal that rocked college basketball in the 1950–1951 season. In the wake of the scandal, most top colleges reduced their support for basketball and stopped playing in big-city arenas. In these cities, fans either had to forego their hunger for basketball or attend pro games.

Although early teams stumbled, especially in New York City, the pro game continued to improve. The 24-second rule, implemented in 1954, increased both speed and scoring. Bob Cousy, of the Boston Celtics, introduced a razzle-dazzle style of guard play that featured expert dribbling, pinpoint passing, and occasional behind-the-back throws. Bill Russell, also of the Celtics, revolutionized the center position. Russell, who was exceptionally quick and agile, not only reduced the effectiveness of opposing centers, but also essentially played a one-man zone (zone defenses were technically illegal in the NBA), by clogging driving lanes and preventing easy lay-ins. With Russell in the middle, Boston's other four players could gamble by pressing the ball everywhere, causing numerous turnovers without being victimized by easy shots. Russell's rebounding and precise outlet passes also ignited Boston's vaunted fastbreak offense. With Russell leading the way, and Arnold "Red" Auerbach coaching, the Celtics captured nine NBA championships between 1957 and 1966. Russell became the Celtics' player-coach in the fall of 1966, and led the team to two additional championships before retiring in 1969.

Pro basketball shared in the largesse of the sports boom of the 1960s, though by no means as spectacularly as pro football. NBA attendance increased from less than two million in 1960 to 10 million in the late 1970s. Network television, however, remained lukewarm toward the NBA. In 1962, NBC dropped its coverage of regular season games, and in 1964 ABC paid a mere $750,000 for a package of Sunday afternoon regular season telecasts. While the NBA's media fortunes slowly improved, the American Basketball Association, founded in 1967 with hopes of capitalizing on television to ensure its success, was unable to land a network contract, and folded in 1976. Not until the 1980s, with the advent of cable television, new marketing techniques, and the rise of major stars such as Earvin "Magic" Johnson, Larry Bird, and Michael Jordan could the NBA become a true powerhouse league.

Players Get Involved

As the money involved in professional sports grew, players sought to share in the bounty. Professional football, baseball, and basketball players all organized player associations, or unions, in the 1950s. While players continued to negotiate individual salary contracts, the players' associations dealt with broader issues such as minimum/maximum salaries, league-wide salary caps, grievance procedures, salary

TABLE 16.1 Salary Average of Professional Athletes, Selected Years					
	1967	**1980**	**1990**	**2000**	**2006**
Major-League Baseball	$19,000	$144,000	$598,000	$1.9 million	$2.7 million
Basketball	$20,000	$170,000	$817,000	$4.2 million	$5.2 million
Football	$25,000	$79,000	$352,000	$1.1 million	$1.4 million

Source: Data from U.S. Census, Statistical Abstract of the United States, annual editions; Major League Baseball Players Association; National Basketball Players Association; and National Football League Players Association.

arbitration, pensions, and healthcare issues. But the associations had limited effect until the 1960s, when players became more united and assertive.

Thanks to a long season, a small number of players, and the able leadership of Oscar Robertson, who served as association president from 1965 to 1974, NBA players developed an especially cohesive and effective organization. Baseball players also saw considerable success, especially after they took the historic step of hiring a full-time executive director, Marvin J. Miller, who was a veteran employee of the hard-bitten United Steelworkers union. ("To a disinterested observer," concluded Robert H. Boyle in 1974, "Miller comes on like a David with an ICBM in his sling while the owners stumble around like so many befuddled Goliaths."[15]) Football players had a harder time, partly because football teams could more easily replace players without damaging team performance and partly because of the disciplined unity of NFL owners. In 1967, football players had the highest average salaries in professional sports, largely as a result of pre-merger salary competition between the NFL and the AFL. But in subsequent years, their pay grew far more slowly than that of their baseball and basketball counterparts.

As with other unions, the strike was the major weapon of the players' associations. The first major professional strike/lockout took place in 1968, when NFL players successfully battled to have their association recognized by league owners. In subsequent years, athletes and owners in all three major professional sports took part in periodic strikes and lockouts over contract disputes. The strikes highlighted the athletes' complicated situation: They were at once highly paid celebrities and employees of powerful corporations. As athletes at the top of their profession, players had the advantage of being difficult to replace. But as their salaries escalated, they also faced criticism from fans who had trouble relating to grievances of men who played games for a living, and whose salaries were already at levels that ordinary Americans could never hope to reach.[16]

Conclusion

The rise of television radically transformed American professional sports, from the way that games were played to the number of people who watched to the salaries that players received. Most dramatically, effective use of television helped professional football move out of relative obscurity and become an integral component of

American culture. Ironically, while professional sports promoted all-out competition, both players and team owners learned that the best way to prosper in the television era was to cooperate—negotiating for broadcast contracts or salary conditions as a group rather than as individuals. As professional sports entered the 1970s, the sporting boom showed no signs of ending. New technological developments would vastly increase both the number and the value of televised sports events, further expanding the role of sports in American society.

Critical Thinking Questions

1. What roles did off-field competition play in the NFL's rise to prominence?
2. Cleveland Browns owner Art Modell once described NFL owners as "28 Republicans who vote socialist." Why is this funny and what does it say about the nature of competition?
3. Just as college football changed football's rules at the beginning of the century, the NFL changed football's rules at the end. Compare and contrast these two efforts, looking at both the motivations for the changes and their effects. Which was the more successful effort?

Notes

1. See Benjamin G. Rader, *Baseball: A History of America's Game*, 3rd ed. (Urbana: University of Illinois Press, 2008). On television audiences, see A.C. Nielson, *Televised Sports*, published annually. For the relative popularity of professional sports, see also Research & Forecasts, Inc., *The Miller Lite Report on American Attitudes Toward Sports* (Milwaukee, WI: Research & Forecasts, 1983).
2. Harry A. March, *Pro Football*, 2nd ed. (New York: Lyon, 1934), 65. For early pro football history, see Marc S. Maltby, *The Origins and Early Development of Professional Football* (New York: Garland, 1997); Robert W. Peterson, *Pigskin: The Early Years of Pro Football* (New York: Oxford University Press, 1997); Michael Oriard, *King Football: Sport and Spectacle in the Golden Age of Radio and Newsreels, Movies and Magazines, the Weekly & the Daily Press* (Chapel Hill: University of North Carolina Press, 2001), chapter 6; John M. Carroll, *Fritz Pollard* (Urbana: University of Illinois Press, 1992); John M. Carroll, *Red Grange and the Rise of Modern Football* (Urbana: University of Illinois Press, 1999); George Halas et al., *Halas by Halas* (New York: McGraw-Hill, 1979); and Paul Brown with Jack Clary, *PB: The Paul Brown Story* (New York: Atheneum, 1979). For pro football in the age of television, see Michael MacCambridge, *America's Game: The Epic Story of How Pro Football Captured a Nation* (New York: Random House, 2004), which is rich in detail but also an unending pageant of praise for the NFL's leadership, and the more balanced and analytical Michael Oriard, *Brand NFL: Making and Selling America's Favorite Game* (Chapel Hill: University of North Carolina Press, 2007). Oriard's book, in particular, has shaped our understanding of both the NFL's recent history as well as that of the other pro team sports.
3. Quoted in Benjamin G. Rader, *In Its Own Image: How Television Has Transformed Sports* (New York: Free Press, 1984), 83.
4. See ibid., chapter 8; Frank Deford, "Long Live the King," *Sports Illustrated*, January 21, 1980, 100ff; and for a detailed analysis of the business side of the NFL up to the mid-1980s, David Harris, *The League* (New York: Macmillan, 1986).
5. Quoted in Associated Press, *A Century of American Sports* (Maplewood, NJ: Hamond, 1975), 17–18.

6. Richard Kostelanetz, "Fanfare of TV Football," *Intellectual Digest* 3 (August 1973), 54. See also Joan Chandler, "TV and Sports: Wedded with a Golden Hoop," *Psychology Today* 10 (April 1977), 64–76; and Joan Chandler, *Television and National Sport* (Urbana: University of Illinois Press, 1988), chapter 3.

7. *Sports Illustrated*, July 24, 1978, 56.

8. *Sports Illustrated*, October 15, 1979, 24.

9. Quoted in Joseph Durso, *The All-American Dollar* (Boston: Houghton Mifflin, 1971), 58–59.

10. Oriard, *Brand NFL*, 11.

11. *Sports Illustrated*, November 19, 1979, 26ff.

12. MacCambridge, *America's Game*, 458.

13. *Sports Illustrated*, September 1, 1958, 26.

14. For the early years, see Robert W. Peterson, *Cages to Jumpshots* (New York: Oxford University Press, 1990), and for later ones Leonard Koppett, *24 Seconds to Shoot* (New York: Macmillan, 1968). For the Harlem Globetrotters, see Randy Roberts and James Olson, *Winning Is the Only Thing* (Baltimore, MD: Johns Hopkins University Press, 1989), chapter 2.

15. *Sports Illustrated*, March 11, 1974, 23.

16. Research & Forecasts, Inc. *The Miller Lite Report on American Attitudes toward Sports*, 140. See also Rader, *In Its Own Image*, chapter 11.

CHAPTER 17

College Sports in the Age of Television

A 1969 *Sports Illustrated* cover captures some of the enduringly iconic images that made college football such a popular sport.

LEARNING OBJECTIVES

17.1 Analyze the factors that turned college football into big-time entertainment, and then detail the many new conflicts that arose when the desire to win clashed with the NCAA's efforts to oversee player recruitment.

17.2 Detail the advantages and disadvantages that college sports had over professional sports.

17.3 Outline the series of events that led colleges and universities to institute official athletic scholarships and turn enforcement of scholarship and recruitment rules over to the NCAA.

17.4 Summarize the developments in college football that sharply boosted the sport's popularity in the 1960s.

17.5 Describe the dilemma that recruiting posed in big-time college football, and the variety of ways—both legal and illegal—that colleges and coaches sought to appeal to top prospects.

17.6 Explain how college basketball's 1950s point-shaving scandal contributed to a broader suspicion of American institutions, and detail the effect the scandal had on college basketball as a whole.

It was New Year's Day, 1969, and more than 100,000 spectators rose to their feet as college football's greatest running back, University of Southern California senior Orenthal James Simpson, broke two tackles, cut sharply to his right, and raced down the sideline of Pasadena's Rose Bowl, well beyond the reach of Ohio State defenders. The Heisman Trophy winner's 80-yard run, followed by a successful kick, put the number-two-ranked Trojans ahead of the number-one-ranked Buckeyes, 10–0. A carefully neutral president-elect Richard Nixon looked on, as did millions of television viewers, many of whom had taken in that morning's Tournament of Roses parade and kept their televisions on for the highly anticipated matchup between two undefeated teams. They saw a fine show. O.J. Simpson would rush for 171 yards, but coach Woody Hayes' "hard-bitten" Buckeyes would come from behind to take the game, 28–16, and finish number one in virtually all the national championship polls.[1]

Throughout the 1960s, amid marches and protests, war and assassinations, college football thrived. Game attendance doubled from 10 million a year to 20 million. Strategic innovations brought new excitement to the game, as did the race for the Heisman Trophy, the week-by-week reassessment of which teams were the nation's best, and the growing anticipation that surrounded the end-of-season bowl matchups. The growth in interest brought a sizeable jump in television viewers, which translated into a sharp rise in the price that institutions received for television contracts. The enormous growth in revenue turned big-time college sports—primarily football and basketball—into a powerful economic engine that delighted a broadening range of fans. It also magnified the power of the NCAA and intensified debates over the relationship between sports programs and colleges' broader educational missions.

The Economics of College Athletics

When big-time college sports became a major commercial enterprise, college athletic programs enjoyed three distinct advantages over their professional counterparts. First, nearly all of them received some financial support from the institutions that sponsored them, whether in the form of free facilities such as a stadium or arena, direct grants from the institution's budget, and/or student "activity" fees that were transferred to athletic departments. Second, as "non-profit" educational enterprises, the athletic programs did not have to pay taxes on the money they received from admissions, sponsorships, licensing fees, and media contracts. Third, they did not have to pay their performers, the "amateur" athletes, what the market would bear.[2] Instead, through collusive agreements that first developed in the 1950s, colleges agreed to pay their athletes only the basic costs of college: tuition, room and board, and a few incidental expenses.

Colleges and universities did, however, struggle with one distinct disadvantage. They had no draft system for the recruitment of new talent. A hundred or more schools might compete for the same blue-chip football or basketball player. To avoid ugly public squabbles and to level the playing field, the schools collectively drew up rules that sought to prevent all-out bidding wars among themselves for athletes. In time they also joined together to negotiate television packages. To supervise and enforce these complex agreements among themselves, they extended greater authority to the NCAA, transforming it from an athletic association into a sprawling, frequently unwieldy, and not always effective economic cartel. As with most cartels, the NCAA faced grave difficulties in policing its membership, especially when it came to recruiting.[3]

Evolution of a Cartel

The years from 1940 through 1956 marked a watershed in the NCAA's evolution into an economic cartel. Prior to 1940, colleges had limited the NCAA's authority to the creation and modification of rules for various sports, the supervision of national tournaments in a few of the minor sports, and the assertion of amateur principles. While the NCAA frequently issued statements condemning financial subsidies to players and unseemly recruiting, the organization could only resort to moral suasion to enforce its scruples. The colleges initially operated on the premise that, being honorable institutions, they should police themselves. But the great football debates of the 1920s and 1930s revealed the utter inadequacy of self-imposed restraints. Giving more power to the NCAA seemed the best alternative.

The first major step in transforming the NCAA into a cartel came in 1948, with the adoption of the so-called "sanity code." The code decisively broke with the amateur ideal by permitting the offer of scholarships and campus jobs to college athletes. It did, however, contain one major restriction: the grants or jobs had to be awarded solely on the basis of the athlete's demonstrated financial need. From one perspective, the code seemed to be a commendable effort to treat athletes the same as other students. From another, however, the institutions in effect colluded to set rules that limited the price they would have to pay to the athletes if they openly competed with one another for new recruits.[4]

Soon after the adoption of the sanity code, the schools confronted a series of shocking revelations that forced them to reconsider all phases of intercollegiate sports. In 1950, the U.S. Military Academy acknowledged that all but two members of its varsity football team had been dismissed for cheating on examinations. The guilty cadets had stained the image of the mighty Army teams that had dominated college football for a decade. The next year, in 1951, the public learned that college basketball was the victim of perhaps the biggest scandal in the history of American sports. The New York District Attorney's office accused more than 30 players from seven colleges of taking payoffs from gamblers to manipulate game scores.

Still, neither scandals nor widespread revelations of illegal recruiting and under-the-table payoffs by alumni, booster groups, and schools themselves spurred the NCAA's members to take action. The 1950 NCAA convention saw a motion to suspend seven schools for noncompliance with the sanity code. It fell short of the necessary two-thirds vote. As a result, in 1952 the colleges granted the NCAA even greater power, charging the organization with the task of investigating and imposing sanctions upon colleges that violated the association's legislation. For the 1952–1953 seasons, the NCAA for the first time placed two schools, Kentucky and Bradley, on probation. The 1952 convention also adopted legislation governing postseason bowls, named a full-time executive director (Walter Byers, who held the post until 1988), and established a national headquarters in Kansas City, Missouri (later moved to a suburb of Kansas City and still later to Indianapolis). [5]

The virtual collapse of the sanity code led schools to take another major step away from tradition. In 1956, they approved what became known as athletic scholarships. This meant that a college or university could pay for an athlete's tuition, fees, room, board, and books, as well as a small monthly allowance for laundry and like expenses, without regard to the athlete's academic promise or performance. In short, the athlete was paid first and foremost for athletic services—not because the money would provide a promising student with the opportunity to gain an education. As the author of the NCAA's official history put it many years later: "the NCAA's founders could perhaps have been permitted a synchronized rolling over in their graves at this turn of events."[6] Responsibility for enforcement of scholarship and recruitment rules shifted away from individual schools and conferences to the NCAA.

Control of television emerged as the second major source of the NCAA's growing power in college sports. Eager to obtain the publicity of television exposure, schools at first placed no restrictions on telecasts. Each institution negotiated its own contracts with television stations or networks. But like baseball executives, college and university officials found that having games on television caused their attendance to plummet. Across the country, 1950 attendance at college games was 1.4 million below 1948 totals.

Alarmed, officials responded in 1951 by authorizing the telecast of only seven regular season games in each region and signing a national network football package for its schools with the Westinghouse Broadcasting Company. Although reports of possible Justice Department action against the NCAA for violation of the federal antitrust laws appeared in the press, the department took no action to prevent this form of economic collusion. Still, several schools threatened to ignore the NCAA. Notre Dame suffered the most from NCAA restrictions. Given its large national following, if Notre Dame had signed a separate television pact with a national net-work it could have earned much more than it did through the NCAA package.

Although every school eventually complied with the agreement, it did little to improve the situation. Football attendance continued to lag behind 1948 figures for a decade. Since only those colleges or conferences that appeared on television received funds from the networks, the medium contributed to a larger financial dis-parity among schools in their athletic budgets. In addition, the decision to grant to the NCAA control of television negotiations strengthened that organization's hege-mony over college sports.

College Football Goes Big-Time

As the 1960s dawned, however, several factors combined to send the popularity of college football soaring. The first involved changes in the game itself. Coaches intro-duced a new, wide-open style of offense. Clock-stopping rule changes allowed col-lege teams to execute 27 more plays per game in 1968 than in 1964, and a study of the 1970 season found that colleges averaged 40 more plays per game than their pro counterparts. The adoption of two-platoon football in the 1960s permitted coaches to perfect more complicated offensive systems. It also resulted in the disappearance of one of the last pretensions of player centeredness in the sport—the tradition that the players rather than the coaches call offensive and defensive signals during play.

The 1960s produced record highs in scoring, passing, rushing, receiving, and kick-ing. Quarterbacks sometimes filled the air with 50 or more passes per game, figures that would have astonished football fans of the 1920s and 1930s. The "I formation," a popular offensive system developed by Tom Nugent at Maryland in the 1950s, permit-ted a team to combine potent running and passing attacks. Perhaps even more remark-able were the triple-option formations that featured quarterbacks as an integral part of the running attack. Oklahoma's wishbone (invented by a Texas high school coach and adopted first at the college level by Darrell Royal at Texas) and Bill Yeoman's veer at Houston regularly produced more than 400 yards rushing per game. Many fans found the college game, with its explosive action, more exciting than the pros.

To accompany their games, schools added more elaborate half-time shows that featured marching bands, baton twirlers, and card sections. Animated card sections—apparently an invention of University of Southern California student Lindley Bothwell—first appeared in the early 1920s but did not become standard fare until the 1950s. The most remarkable change came in cheerleading. Starting in the 1950s, fans were regularly regaled with the spectacle of briefly clad coeds leading cheers, doing fast, leggy can-cans, and performing Broadway-like chorus-line routines.[7]

"Pseudoevents"—those created largely or solely by the media—also generated interest in the college game. Walter Camp had named mythical "All American" teams as early as the 1890s, but in the 1960s the selection of all-star teams of college foot-ball players became something of a national ritual. Press services, magazines, broad-casters, and organizations of football fans chose not only all-American teams and all-conference teams, but also participants for East–West, North–South, Blue–Grey, and other all-star bowl games. The biggest individual prize became the Heisman

Trophy, which had been awarded each year since 1936 by the Downtown Athletic Club of New York City in honor of a former coach and athletic director. After being subjected to an intensive sales campaign by sports information offices of the various colleges who put forth Heisman candidates, a group of sportswriters and sportscasters chose the "outstanding" intercollegiate football player of the year for the award.

The weekly press polls for determining the top teams in the nation furnished an additional source of excitement. Individual journalists had named national champions since the 1890s, but it was not until 1936 that Alan Gould, sports editor of the Associated Press, invented the weekly press poll. To determine the top 20 teams, the Associated Press polled about 50 writers and broadcasters nationwide. By establishing a board of college coaches to name the top teams in 1950, United Press International joined the polling game (the UPI poll was later replaced with the USA Today/ESPN coaches' poll). The absence of a system for determining the relative strength of teams or a national champion made the polls a powerful symbolic substitute.

Bowl games, though late arrivals to the college scene, furnished an exciting climax to the regular season. The parent of college bowls, the Tournament of Roses (Rose Bowl), traced its origins back to 1902. In the depressed 1930s, boosters in Southern cities hoped to attract tourists and outside investors by founding the Orange (1933), Sugar (1935), Sun (1936), and Cotton (1937) bowls. Initially, the bowls offered little financial inducement to the top football-playing schools; the inaugural Orange Bowl, for example, paid each team a mere $1,000 to make the trek to Miami on New Year's Day. Television changed that. In 1960, NBC paid the Rose Bowl half a million dollars for rights. By 1983, the figure had escalated to $7 million. That the bowl games often determined the national champions added immensely to fan interest in the contests.

As audiences grew, schools with the most prominent football programs grew increasingly unhappy about their share of the revenues earned from the NCAA's package television contract. Led by the Big Eight Conference and Notre Dame, 61 of the big-time schools formed the College Football Association (CFA) in 1976. "The major football playing universities are opposed to financing a welfare system for intercollegiate athletics," explained Charles Neinas, the Big Eight commissioner, while Notre Dame's Edmund Joyce reminded the CFA schools that "we must never forget that we are in competition with the pros for the entertainment dollar."[8] The NCAA responded to the demands of the CFA by signing ever-larger television packages and allowing the big-time schools to appear more frequently on television. ABC, which held the regular season package from 1964 through 1981, increased its payments from $3 million to $29 million annually.

Recruiting Big-Time Teams

Raising the stakes for victory brought significant benefits for coaches. Many colleges sought a quick entry to the big-time by hiring a coach with a proven record as a winner. Salaries of winning coaches soared. In 1982, Texas A&M stunned the college football world by luring Jackie Sherrill away from the University of Pittsburgh for $1.7 million over six years. A television show and boosters footed all but $95,000 of Sherrill's salary annually. To seize the new opportunities, coaches broke existing contracts with impunity. Still, such limited loyalty was more than matched by the speed with which many colleges dismissed coaches whose teams failed to live up to expectations.

The drive to win at a national level put coaches under tremendous pressure, particularly in terms of recruiting the top players who were essential to building winning teams. "Recruiting, not coaching, is the name of the game," explained Oklahoma's Barry Switzer, the nation's most successful coach in the 1970s and 1980s.[9] Effective recruiting required a systematic, well-coordinated effort that considered players from across the nation. Coaches spent hours poring over high school game films and some three months each year jetting about the country visiting high school athletes and their parents. Recruiters relied heavily upon personal contacts. Local alumni, especially if they were celebrities, often lent assistance to their alma maters. Colleges tried to appeal to rising consciousness about ethnic, religious, racial, and regional ties. Big-time football powers usually hired at least one African American coach, someone from a Catholic ethnic group, and one or more individuals identified with a region outside the state in which the university was located.[10]

Recruiters could also promise prospective team members legal or illegal benefits. All major institutions could only guarantee an athletic scholarship that consisted of room, board, and tuition. But without violating NCAA rules, a recruiter could emphasize to a potential recruit the likelihood of joining the pro ranks or landing a good job after graduation, and also trumpet the quality of the school's coaching staff, the number of past bowl or television appearances, or even the quality of education offered at the school. Until the 1990s, prospects could be shown special athletic dormitories (complete with recreation rooms, special dining halls, swimming pools, and television sets in each room), carpeted locker and shower rooms, the latest weight-training equipment, and a staff of private tutors to assist players with their studies. In addition, once prospective athletes arrived on campus, they might be greeted by the Bengal Babes, Hawk Hunters, Hurricane Honeys, or Gator Getters, all recruited by athletic departments to act as official hostesses.

Illegal inducement took a variety of often-creative forms. Alumni and booster groups, often with the tacit approval or at least the knowledge of the coaching staff, might grant cash, cars, clothes, rent-free apartments, use of charge accounts, or high-paying jobs. To obtain the admission of an athlete with a poor academic record, coaches might tamper with transcripts. To make up deficiencies in college credits or grades, coaches might arrange for snap courses offered by regular faculty, by correspondence, or by college extension divisions.

Given the intense competition among colleges for top-flight athletes, the NCAA faced formidable enforcement problems. A thin line sometimes separated legal from illegal practices. Coaches often complained that minor infractions were impossible to avoid. Some of the rules seemed petty; for example, a coach could not technically treat his players to ice cream cones from a local Dairy Queen. The rules also seemed to weigh heaviest against low-income players. A coach or a booster could not legally buy a player even basic "extras" such as airline tickets to return home for vacations.

The NCAA acted, in effect, as both police and prosecution, with an enforcement squad that grew to 15 full-time employees by 1988. But it was trying to police the complicated athletic operations of more than 900 colleges, and it had no subpoena powers. Close observers of the college athletic scene, including coaches and athletes, estimated that only a small fraction of violations resulted in punishment. Even at that, more than half of the some 140 colleges playing big-time football in the post-1950 era were placed on probation at one time or another.

Although in principle the NCAA equalized the conditions of athletic recruitment and retention, glaring disparities in playing strength appeared throughout the era of televised sports. Year after year, many of the same teams dominated conferences and appeared regularly in postseason bowls. In the last half of the twentieth century, the same 15 schools held more than 50 percent of the "Top Ten" positions in the Associated Press season-ending poll. Oklahoma and Nebraska led the parade by being chosen in the Top Ten 27 times, followed by Michigan (22), Alabama and Ohio State (21), Notre Dame (20), and Penn State (19). The Top Ten also increasingly mirrored the massive population shifts to the Sunbelt. Whereas 44 percent of Top Ten schools in the 1930s hailed from the Sunbelt, the figure exceeded 60 percent in the 1980s and 1990s. Further reflective of the shift was the enormous success of Florida's major universities—Miami, Florida State, and Florida—which collectively won or tied for seven national championships during the last two decades of the twentieth century.

College Basketball Enters the National Spotlight

As college football boomed, college basketball also began to confront the advantages and drawbacks of growing national recognition. In a few places, notably Kentucky, Indiana, and Illinois, high school and college basketball became a popular spectator sport as early as the 1920s. Yet football remained the king of campus sports. College gymnasiums usually held only a few thousand spectators, colleges scheduled few if any intersectional games, and coaching turnovers were frequent.

Perhaps architecture more than anything else converted college basketball into a sport that attained national attention. To capitalize on the boxing craze of the 1920s, entrepreneurs in about a dozen Northeastern cities built large indoor arenas seating several thousand spectators. With the onset of the Great Depression and the decline in boxing's popularity, arena owners desperately sought other ways to make their venues profitable. Intersectional college basketball games caught their eye in 1931 when New York Mayor Jimmy Walker asked a group of sportswriters to organize tripleheaders in Madison Square Garden for the benefit of the city's relief fund. Despite the Depression, the "Relief Games" of 1931, 1932, and 1933 drew full houses.

One of the sportswriters who had organized the relief games, Edward S. "Ned" Irish, decided to stage his own college games in 1934. He rented the Garden, which held over 16,000 fans, paid the fees to visiting teams, and kept whatever was left over as a profit. To maximize interest among New York residents, Irish usually pitted strong local college fives against the most powerful rivals he could attract from other parts of the nation. The Garden games promoted by Irish served as a catalyst for the transformation of college basketball into a national spectator-centered sport.

Irish's games became basketball history legends. In 1936 he matched Long Island University, winner of 43 consecutive games, and Stanford University, led by Angelo "Hank" Luisetti. Stanford won 45–31, but Luisetti was the bigger story. Showcasing his unorthodox one-handed shot, he scored 15 points and became the nation's first basketball hero. His one-handed innovation defied years of conventional coaching. "That's not basketball," sneered veteran City College coach Nat Holman. "If my boys ever shot one-handed, I'd quit coaching."[11] Yet the one-handed shot and its derivative, the jump shot, could be shot as accurately, more quickly, and with less danger of being blocked than the standard two-handed set shot. The new shooting styles, along with the elimination of the center jump after each goal in 1937, increased scoring and won the plaudits of fans.

From the late 1930s through the 1940s—World War II notwithstanding—New York was the hub of big-time college basketball. In 1938, the Metropolitan Basketball Writers' Association of New York organized the National Invitational Tournament (NIT) designed to determine the national championship team at the end of each season. The following year, the NCAA founded its own postseason invitational tournament, though the NIT would remain the premier college tourney until 1951. After World War II, Ned Irish extended his promotion beyond the Garden to Philadelphia and Buffalo, thereby offering at least a three-game package to college teams venturing to the East. Irish also increased the number of doubleheaders to 25 or more per season. By 1950, when the Garden college program drew over 600,000 spectators, it had become every schoolboy's dream to play there one day. For both financial and publicity purposes, appearances at the Garden were obligatory for those college teams striving for national status. Never had the promise of basketball as a spectator sport looked more promising.

Then disaster struck. In 1951, New York District Attorney Frank Hogan revealed that nearly three dozen players from seven colleges, including players from the strongest teams in the nation, had been involved in fixing games. It turned out that the Garden was not only the Mecca of college basketball, it was also the "clearinghouse" for New York's sports gambling establishment. In the early 1940s, when former math teacher Charles K. McNeil invented a betting strategy known as the "point spread,"[12] basketball had become a hot attraction for bettors. In point spread betting, a bettor was offered the chance not to pick a winner or to take odds on a favored team, but to bet on whether a particular team would win by more than a certain number of points. The point spread system quickly led to a gambling strategy that became known as "point-shaving." In point-shaving, gamblers paid players not to lose games, but to win by less than the quoted point spread.

The revelations of the fixes shocked the entire country. Coinciding with the "fall" of China to communism, the commencement of the Korean War, the Soviet detonation of an atomic bomb, and Joseph McCarthy's spectacular charges of treason in high governmental places, the basketball scandal contributed to a general climate of suspicion and mistrust of many American institutions. Some observers sought to dismiss the accused players as "bad apples" who lacked personal moral scruples, and called for more judicious recruitment. But others pointed fingers at what they saw as the skewed priorities that educational institutions had developed while chasing athletic glory. Presiding over a case involving players at the University of Kentucky, Judge Saul Streit proclaimed that the university's program was "the acme of commercialism and overemphasis," which included "undeniable evidence of covert subsidization of players, illegal recruiting, a reckless disregard for the players' physical welfare, matriculation of unqualified students, [and] demoralization of the athletes by the coaches, the alumni, and the townspeople."[13]

The scandal ended the Garden's pivotal role in the financial structure of big-time college basketball. Irish's famed Garden doubleheaders collapsed. College and university officials announced that they would no longer permit their teams to compete in the big-city arenas. The scandal also wiped out the powerful basketball programs of New York's metropolitan schools. After the scandal, the local schools no longer attracted the best talent in the city. But, somewhat ironically, the popularity of college basketball continued to grow. The New York exodus contributed to the sport's rise in new areas, such as North Carolina. In the 1950s and 1960s, state universities around the country began to build their own large field houses to host tournaments.

Like college football, college basketball was also becoming a more exciting game, with new strategies and markedly superior player skills, especially where big men were concerned. In the 1940s, Robert Kurland of Oklahoma A&M, a towering defensive specialist, and DePaul's George Mikan, a prolific scorer, initiated the revolution in height. The next decade produced two more outstanding big men. Bill Russell of San Francisco demonstrated that the tall center could be a dominating force as a rebounder and defender, and Wilton Chamberlain, a University of Kansas center who stood over seven feet tall, showed that a big man could be almost unstoppable as a scorer. By the 1970s, dozens of big men had reached higher levels of coordination and dexterity than most of the shorter men of the pre-1940 era. Rule changes to restrict the impact of these dominant players (defensive goal tending in 1944 and widening the free-throw lane in 1955) failed.

As an enterprise involved in the business of entertainment, college basketball increasingly resembled a scaled-down version of college football. Like football, a high rating in the national press polls helped ensure a team a berth in the NCAA or NIT tourneys, a profitable season, and "free" publicity for the college. And while basketball did not generate as much revenue from spectators or television as college football, it cost much less to field a team. Until the 1990s, basketball could offer a relatively simple and inexpensive means by which an otherwise unknown smaller college could attract national attention. LaSalle, San Francisco, Cincinnati, Loyola Illinois, Texas Western, Georgetown, and Villanova all won national titles. In the post–World War II era, more than a score of smaller Catholic-affiliated colleges dropped football and placed the lion's share of their athletic resources into basketball. Between 1939 and 1987, 17 different Catholic institutions reached the semifinals of the NCAA play-offs.[14]

As with football, the key to a successful team was the recruitment of blue-chip athletes. Unlike football, however, one or two outstanding players might reverse the fortunes of an otherwise mediocre basketball team. As a result, scores of coaches, many of whom were hired more for their recruiting ability than their coaching skills, ventured out each year to seek the services of a dozen or so of the nation's most talented high school seniors. In order to make a special pitch to African Americans, nearly all big-time programs hired at least one black assistant coach. Given the intensity of competition for the more promising prospects, the basketball coaches tended to be even more flagrant in violating or ignoring NCAA rules than their football counterparts.

Despite the possibility for small schools to shine, however, institutions with well-established basketball traditions and well-known coaches dominated conference championships and the top ten in the national polls. In fact, between 1964 and 1975, the preeminence of UCLA far exceeded the performances of any college football squad of the modern era. John Wooden's UCLA team won 10 NCAA championships in 12 years, including seven titles in a row. Inasmuch as the NCAA tourney format (where a single defeat eliminated a team) and the limit on the eligibility of a player to three years (four years after 1972) made such a feat seem virtually impossible, UCLA's success may have represented the most remarkable achievement in sport history. Wooden's first two championships seemed to be simply the products of astute coaching combined with superior athletes. After 1965, however, UCLA was the beneficiary of several of the most promising players in the country. Two of the most spectacular big men to ever play the game—Lew Alcindor (1967–1969, who later became Kareem Abdul Jabbar) and Bill Walton (1971–1974)—contributed directly to five of UCLA's 10 championships.

Conclusion

College sports in the post-1950 era combined aspects of both the old and the new. As in the past, college football (and later basketball) continued to offer entertainment to millions of Americans, to strengthen the ties of local communities, and to act as a counterweight to the forces of modernity. Yet, much was also new. Television itself encouraged a growing nationalization and commercialization of college athletic programs. To oversee the business side of sports and equalize the conditions of competition among themselves, schools relinquished some of their power to the NCAA. But, with the stakes so high, temptations to cheat on NCAA rules seemed almost irresistible. Colleges and universities would continue to wrestle with these challenges for the rest of the twentieth century, and into the twenty-first.

Critical Thinking Questions

1. Why were colleges unable to control their competition for recruits without resorting to the NCAA?
2. Despite efforts to level the playing field for athletic recruits, a handful of programs from major schools consistently dominated national play in both football and basketball. Did this dominance help or harm college sports? Why?
3. Interpretations of scandals such as the college basketball point-shaving scandal tended to fall into two camps: one side arguing that the problem could be traced to the moral weakness of the individuals involved; another contending that the problem lay in a broader distortion of values created by the college athletic system. Which argument do you find most convincing and why?

Notes

1. *New York Times*, January 2, 1969.
2. Whereas the financial aid packages might have cost a leading basketball or football program as much as $30,000 per annum per player in the 1990s, economist Robert Brown estimated that top college football players generated more than $500,000 and top basketball players between $870,000 and $1 million in revenues per annum for their college athletic programs. See Brown, "An Estimate of the Rent Generated by a Premium College Football Player," *Economic Inquiry* 31 (October 1993), 671–84; and Brown, "Measuring Cartel

Rents in the College Basketball Market," *Applied Economics* (January 1994), 27–34. So, strictly in terms of the marketplace (not in returns the athlete might receive in the form of an education), star college athletes were grossly underpaid. For this reason, many of the outstanding basketball players entered the pros directly or played college ball for only a season or so before going pro.

3. For an official history of the NCAA, see Jack Falla, *The NCAA* (Mission, KS: NCAA, 1981), and for an updated history, see Joseph N. Crowley, *In the Arena: The NCAA's First Century* (Indianapolis, IN: NCAA, 2006). For a remarkably candid account of the NCAA's history, see Walter Byers (its long-time director) with Charles Hammer, *Unsportsmanlike Conduct: Exploiting College Athletes* (Ann Arbor: University of Michigan Press, 1995). For the most part, this chapter focuses on what became the NCAA's Division I-A schools, which sponsored what might be called "semiprofessional" or "unpaid professional" athletes. See for example, A.A. Fleischer III et al., *The National Collegiate Athletic Association: A Study in Cartel Behavior* (Chicago: University of Chicago Press, 1992) and its bibliography and Andrew Zimbalist, *Unpaid Professionals: Commercialism and Conflict in Big-Time College Athletics* (Princeton: Princeton University Press, 1999).

4. Zimbalist, *Unpaid Professionals*, 10.

5. On Byers, see *Sports Illustrated*, October 6, 1986; and especially Byers with Hammer, *Unsportsmanlike Conduct*.

6. Crowley, *In the Arena*, 91.

7. Michael Oriard, *King Football: Sport and Spectacle in the Golden Age of Radio and Newsreels, Movies and Magazines, the Weekly & the Daily Press* (Chapel Hill: University of North Carolina Press, 2001), 185. See also Mary Ellen Hanson, *Go! Fight! Win! Cheerleading in American Culture* (Bowling Green, OH: Bowling Green University Popular Press, 1995); and *Newsweek*, May 21, 2001.

8. Quoted in Kathryn Jay, *More Than Just a Game* (New York: Columbia University Press, 2004), 191.

9. *Lincoln* (Nebraska) *Star*, August 30, 1979.

10. See John J. Rooney, *The Recruiting Game* (Lincoln: University of Nebraska Press, 1980); *Sports Illustrated*, August 31, 1987.

11. Quoted in Zander Hollander, ed., *Madison Square Garden* (New York: Hawthorne, 1973), 76.

12. *Sports Illustrated*, March 10, 1986.

13. Quoted in Murray Sperber, *Onward to Victory* (New York: Henry Holt, 1998), 340.

14. See James Michner, *Sports in America* (New York: Random House 1976), 231–4, and *Sports Illustrated*, March 3, 1986.

CHAPTER 18

Racial Revolution

Tommie Smith (center), John Carlos (right), and Peter Norman on the Olympic medal podium, 1968. The image may well be the most famous sports image ever created.

LEARNING OBJECTIVES

18.1 Outline the evolution of efforts to use sports to improve conditions for African Americans and other minorities in the 1950s and 1960s, taking into account the nature of the problems that athletes and coaches sought to address as well as the strategies they chose.

18.2 Describe the challenge of winning "acceptance in major-league baseball," and the strategies that Jackie Robinson and his supporters used to meet those challenges.

18.3 Explain how Muhammad Ali differed from Robinson in both goals and strategies.

18.4 Analyze the strategies of the Olympic Project for Human Rights, assessing which were most successful and why.

18.5 Explain the origins and effects of the different social change strategies adopted by baseball player Roberto Clemente and boxer Corky Gonzales.

18.6 Detail the efforts made by Native Americans to end the practice of Native American mascots, and assess their achievements.

18.7 Summarize the ways that Curt Flood's decision to challenge the Major League Baseball "reserve clause" were linked to the broader activism of the 1960s.

The two men stood on the victory platform, heads down, medals around their necks, raised fists frozen in perhaps the most indelible sports gesture ever made. Tommie Smith and John Carlos had just finished first and third in the 200-meter-dash at the 1968 Olympics in Mexico City. Australian Peter Norman, who had won the silver medal, stood quietly in front. All three men wore small, white badges that bore the letters OPHR—"Olympic Project for Human Rights."

The gesture the two sprinters made that day marked a new direction in the effort to use sports as a way to advance the fortunes of African Americans, and other Americans as well. Back in the days of Jesse Owens, Joe Louis, and Jackie Robinson, black athletes had served primarily as prominent examples of racial abilities and as inspiration to African American communities. The athletes who made up the Olympic Project for Human Rights sought to use their prominence to draw worldwide attention to the persisting inequalities in U.S. society, and thus pressure the country's leaders to address problems that ranged from poverty to police brutality. This shift, which reflected wider developments in the direction of the civil rights movement, highlighted new possibilities and new dilemmas for those who sought to use sport to promote social change, including African Americans, Latinos, Native Americans, and professional athletes themselves.

In the 1950s and 1960s, racial politics saw the same kind of rapid, unpredictable transformations found in other aspects of American life. A changing legal structure, the expansion of black political power, a degree of decline in racial prejudice, and the nation's growing concern about its international image opened the way for African Americans to challenge white supremacy more directly and forcefully than had been possible for decades. The black freedom struggle began with challenges to the legal barriers that prevented African Americans from fully participating in American life. As those barriers began to fall, many activists turned to a broader critique of American society. Participants in the growing "Black Power" movement challenged economic structures that were not spreading the benefits of prosperity to all Americans, and turned away from mainstream cultural institutions to celebrate African and African American culture. The spirit of revolt leaped to other groups of Americans as well, inspiring Latinos, Asians, Native Americans, women, and others to challenge political, economic, and cultural barriers to their full participation in American society. As these varying struggles unfolded, athletes looked for ways to do their part.[1]

Jackie Robinson and the Politics of Restraint

In the 1940s, in the wake of the pioneering endeavors of Jesse Owens and Joe Louis, the power of the ballot helped open new opportunities for African American athletes. While voting rights remained tightly restricted in the South, many cities outside the region lay in highly competitive, two-party states, and a solid bloc of black votes could often tip the balance of elections. Black leaders used this leverage to press for a range of anti-discrimination policies. In 1941, for example, President Franklin Roosevelt responded to African American lobbying by issuing an executive order that banned discrimination in hiring "because of race, creed, color, or national origins" by the federal government and its war-related contractors. The New York state legislature, its own eye on black votes, passed the Quinn-Ives Act, which banned state discrimination in hiring, in 1942. Subsequently, New York City Mayor Fiorello LaGuardia established a special committee to study race relations. Tellingly, the commission's mandate included an examination of discrimination against African Americans by New York's major-league baseball clubs.[2]

For some baseball executives, this outside pressure provided an opportunity to take steps they had been contemplating for years. One of those was Branch Rickey, general manager of the Brooklyn Dodgers. In addition to disliking segregation, the spending-conscious Rickey saw Negro League players as a huge pool of potential talent that could be recruited at far lower cost than players tied to existing major-league teams. But Rickey also knew that the high profile of baseball would put any decision to desegregate squarely in the national spotlight. He began a search for a player who would not only perform well but would also be capable of perfect self-control, able to don a "cloak of humility" in the face of expected abuse from white players and fans.

Eventually, Rickey settled on a young Negro League rookie named Jackie Robinson. Robinson, who had grown up in Pasadena, California, was used to dealing with whites. He had a stellar background: He attended UCLA for nearly four years, had been an army officer in World War II, and was an active churchgoer who did not smoke, drink, or womanize. Finally, he was a gifted athlete. He had starred in football, basketball, golf, track, and swimming at UCLA, and played his first season of Negro League baseball for the well-regarded Kansas City Monarchs.

For his part, Robinson was eager to take the opportunity. He thoroughly understood the limits that white supremacy placed on even the most talented African

Americans, and had done what he could to combat them. Pasadena had been far from a racial paradise, and when Robinson was growing up, he and his brothers fought repeated battles over racial insults. He lettered in four sports at UCLA, and drew huge crowds to his performances, but ended up dropping out to help his family with its financial struggles. After being drafted in 1942, he had been barred from a segregated baseball team, denied admission to Officers' Candidate School—a refusal he successfully contested with the help of fellow soldier Joe Louis—and confronted with a court martial for refusing to go to the back of a military bus (he was acquitted). When Rickey told him that he was looking for "a player with guts enough not to fight back" against insults and harassment, Robinson was ready. "If you want to take this gamble," he told Rickey, "I will promise you there will be no incident."[3] Rickey signed him to play for Montreal, a Dodger farm club, in 1946, with plans to move him up to the Dodgers in 1947.

Robinson became an instant hero in African American communities. "I own and operate a rural general store, and right now the farmers are gathering for your game," Bernice Franklin wrote to Robinson from Tyronza, Arkansas. "There is no greater thrill than a broadcast of a Dodgers' ball game....We are so proud of you."[4] Black fans came out in droves to see him play. Thanks to this surge in interest, which also brought out more white fans, five National League teams set new season attendance records in 1947.

Reaction from white fans and players was mixed, highlighting the uneasy racial transition the nation was undergoing. Before Robinson arrived in Brooklyn, for example, a group of Dodgers who hailed from the South circulated a petition demanding that he not be promoted to the majors. Still, Rickey and major-league management stood firm. Organized opposition on the Dodgers dissipated when Harold "Pee Wee" Reese, a southerner and the team captain, refused to sign the anti-Robinson petition, and when Rickey agreed to trade discontented players to other clubs. A threat of wholesale suspensions by National League president Ford Frick stopped a rumor that the St. Louis Cardinals players planned to boycott games with the Dodgers.

Robinson played his part to perfection. At the personal cost of persistent headaches, bouts of depression, and smoldering anger, he ignored an onslaught of racial threats and slurs and channeled his energies into magnificent play. His efforts on and off the field won him widespread admiration. He was named Rookie of the Year, and shortly afterward finished second to popular singer Bing Crosby in an annual poll to select the most admired man in the nation. He also remained his own person. After completing the 1948 season, he decided that the "cloak of humility" was no longer needed, and abandoned it. From then to the end of his career in 1956, he was as outspoken and as aggressive as other players, quick to speak out when he thought he had been wronged. As one historian noted, his determination to stand up for himself reflected his recognition that "acceptance in organized baseball marked the beginning, not the conclusion, of the struggle for equality."[5]

The role of racial representative was a difficult one, and not all African American athletes of the era were ready to assume it. Many early black stars kept their heads down and their energies focused on their play, avoiding controversy whenever possible. In 1950, for example, the United States Lawn Tennis Association (USLTA) bowed to an intensive lobbying effort and invited Althea Gibson to be the first African American to play in the U.S. National Tennis Championship (now the U.S. Open). Gibson would go on to become the greatest female player of her era, with a career that culminated with back-to-back Wimbledon and U.S. championship titles in 1957 and 1958.

But when Gibson's achievements garnered her the title of "female Jackie Robinson," she struggled with the expectations that came with such exalted status. Her situation was compounded by her gender, as strictures for "proper" female behavior were even narrower than those for men, and she was a forceful, independent person who often stepped beyond those bounds. "It was a strain, always trying to say and do the right thing, so that I wouldn't give people the wrong idea of what Negroes were like," she once explained. Even as she reached the top of her game, she tried to separate herself from the racial implications of her achievements, telling one reporter that while she was not "opposed to the fight for integration of the schools or other movements like that," she tried to "steer clear of political involvements and make my way as Althea Gibson, private individual."[6]

Widening Opportunities

By the end of the 1950s, more and more black athletes were contending with the meaning of new opportunities for athletic success, both for themselves and for African Americans as a whole. Although many teams did not open their doors as quickly or as widely as many African Americans—Jackie Robinson among them—thought they should, the number of prominent black athletes was rapidly multiplying, both in the nation's colleges and in professional leagues. In 1955 and 1956, center Bill Russell led the University of San Francisco Dons to a 55-game win streak and two national championships. He then moved on to the Boston Celtics, where his vaunted defensive skills brought the team 11 NBA titles and transformed the way the game was played. Running back Jim Brown joined the Cleveland Browns in 1957 as a top draft choice, and proceeded to lead the NFL in rushing eight out of the nine seasons he played, winning the league MVP award in 1958 and 1965.

College scholarship opportunities for black athletes multiplied throughout the 1950s and 1960s. As the growth of money and prestige in both college and professional sports made winning ever more important, informal "quotas" that had once limited the number of black players that teams felt comfortable with fielding began to fade. In the spring of 1966, the Texas Western Miners won the NCAA basketball championship with an all-black starting five. In 1971, on their way to a World Series championship, the Pittsburgh Pirates frequently fielded a starting lineup where all the players were either African American or Latino.

At the same time, however, it was also clear that progress off the field was not proceeding as rapidly as progress on the field. Along with the heartening example of courageous black activists standing up for civil rights came the disconcerting spectacle of violent white reactions, from which even the most prominent black Americans were not immune. Change often came at a snail's pace, and college and professional athletes continued to confront discrimination in myriad ways, from being forced to stay in separate hotels while playing in southern towns to being steered away from leadership positions.

Many black athletes also began to realize that sports was not necessarily the ticket to a better life that so many of them had assumed. Harry Edwards, a sociologist who would become one of the era's most outspoken black intellectuals, grew up in East St. Louis, where both black and white communities lionized talented black athletes. "Among my teachers, there prevailed an almost religious litany in praise of sports as the route to Black Salvation," Edwards later wrote. "Sports were seen as an escalator up and out of poverty and nobodiness, as a way for Blacks to make it *now*." Eventually, however, Edwards realized that such dreams were not only illusory, but dangerous. Professional opportunities were few and far between. Although the number of college scholarships was growing, far too often schools took advantage of African Americans' athletic skills while failing to push them forward in their studies. African Americans who focused on athletics as a ticket out of poverty often found themselves right back where they started.[7]

Muhammad Ali

Some prominent black athletes, among them Jackie Robinson, Bill Russell, and Jim Brown, publicly voiced their dissatisfaction with the pace and scope of racial change. But the most dramatic gesture came from a young boxer who had been born in Louisville, Ky., and given the name Cassius Clay. In February of 1963, the 21-year-old boxer stunned the world of sports by defeating Sonny Liston to win the heavyweight title. He sent out an even greater shock when he announced that he had joined the Nation of Islam and had traded his "slave name" for a new one: Muhammad Ali.

Ali's career had shown few indications that he would become a focal point of the social and cultural unrest that marked the 1960s. He had won the light heavyweight gold medal at the 1960 Rome Olympic Games by defeating a more experienced Russian boxer. Asked by a Soviet reporter about racial prejudice in the United States, he responded with remarks that could have been authored by the State Department's press secretary. "Tell your readers we got qualified people working on that, and I'm not worried about the outcome," he said. "To me, the U.S.A. is still the best country in the world, counting yours." As Ali began his climb to the championship, his good looks, enthusiasm, and loquacity made him a media favorite. But behind the playful facade lay a man who was keenly aware of the reach and tenacity of American white supremacy.[8]

Ali's announcement of his conversion prompted outrage and concern. The Nation of Islam was an all-black American branch of Islam, founded in the 1930s, which sought to build a center of African American cultural and economic strength that operated independently from mainstream society. The Nation came into public view in the late 1950s with a series of press and television reports that depicted its members as disciplined believers in black racial superiority, sparking alarm among many white Americans. The Nation's intense young spokesman, Malcolm X, espoused the philosophy of racial self-reliance with charismatic eloquence, inspiring growing admiration among young African Americans. At a time when civil rights conflicts were intensifying, the idea of a prominent black athlete openly embracing such a radical philosophy was deeply disturbing. Many reporters and news organizations refused to use Ali's new name, continuing to refer to him as Cassius Clay. Pressure mounted to strip him of his newly won title.

As had happened with Jack Johnson, an aging former champion—Floyd Patterson—was called out of retirement to take on the challenge. Patterson, a recent convert to Roman Catholicism, proclaimed that he would "give the title back to America." But, like Johnson, Ali dashed all such hopes. He outclassed Patterson, mocking and humiliating him before the referee finally called a halt to the mismatch in the twelfth round. While some African Americans continued to worry that Ali's outspoken independence would do more harm than good to race relations, others rejoiced. For writer and future Black Panther Party leader Eldridge Cleaver, Patterson had been the "leader of the mythical legions of faithful darkies who inhabit the white imagination." Ali, in contrast, was a "genuine revolutionary, the black Fidel Castro of boxing," who had inflicted "a psychological chastisement on 'white' America similar in shock value to Fidel Castro's at the Bay of Pigs."[9]

Ali's most dramatic gesture, however, was yet to come. Early in 1966, the world champion received word that he had been declared eligible for the military draft, which was enlisting a growing number of American soldiers to fight the escalating Vietnam War. Stars of Ali's magnitude faced little risk from military service, generally serving as touring morale-builders rather than front-line fighters. But Ali refused to go, officially stating that his religion did not allow him to participate in a war waged by a Christian country. His more off-the-cuff reaction, "I ain't got no quarrel with them Vietcong," summed up how many young people in the country were beginning to feel about the expanding war. It had particular resonance for young people of color, who once again were being asked to fight a war by a nation that did not treat them equally at home.

In April of 1967, after Ali officially refused Army induction, he cast his decision in sporting terms. "I am proud of the title 'World Heavyweight Champion,'" he noted. "The holder of it should at all times have the courage of his convictions and carry out those convictions, not only in the ring but through all phases of life. It is in light of my own personal convictions that I take my stand in rejecting the call to be inducted into the armed services." Ali's decision to place principle over athletic goals—boxing officials quickly stripped him of his boxing license, his world title, and his means for making a living—turned him into a symbol whose significance stretched far beyond the ring. When Martin Luther King, Jr. announced his own opposition to the war, he gave the fighter his due. "As Muhammad Ali has said," King noted, "we are all victims of the same system of oppression."[10]

The Olympic Project for Human Rights

Ali's actions placed other black athletes in a challenging position, as coaches and reporters repeatedly questioned them about the fighter. While Ali's aggressive anti-Christianity, his opposition to the war, and his pronouncements against "race-mixing" bothered many black athletes, his bravery gave many added courage. His actions also made clear that the fame that came with athletic success could be turned in a more revolutionary direction, along the lines of the developing Black Power movement. Seeking to capitalize on this new direction, a group of athletes and coaches formed the Olympic Project for Human Rights and set their sights on the 1968 Olympics.

Typically, the Olympics were a forum where nations sought to showcase their virtues. Members of the OPHR, however, threatened to use the prominent event to highlight their country's failings. It was a bold move. Amid the tensions of the Cold War, U.S. officials were profoundly sensitive to the nation's international image, especially when it came to race relations. The United States and the Soviet Union were fiercely competing for allies in Africa, Asia, and South America, and Soviet officials regularly pointed to American racial segregation as evidence that Americans did not consider dark-skinned people equal to whites. Concerns about international perceptions of American racial realities had helped drive the Kennedy administration's support for the civil rights movement. The OPHR sought to use those concerns to press for further changes. "What Black Power people are saying is that those of us who have made it, star athletes or whatever, have a responsibility to bring all our people along with us," one supporter explained. The Olympic effort, he continued, "expresses our concern for the plight of most of our people in this country. And it gives the problem international visibility."[11]

The movement began at San Jose State University, which enrolled several top Olympic prospects, and where Harry Edwards was a graduate student and sociology instructor. But interest quickly spread around the country. The organization's first event, a youth conference, featured UCLA basketball star Lew Alcindor, who would later convert to Islam himself and become Kareem Abdul-Jabbar. Alcindor pointedly expressed the anger he felt over the dual worlds he inhabited. "I'm the big basketball star, the weekend hero, everybody's All-American," he told participants. "Well, last summer I was almost killed by a racist cop shooting at a black cat in Harlem. He was shooting on the street—where masses of people were standing around or just taking a walk. But he didn't care. After all we were just niggers."[12]

The first tool that the OPHR deployed was the boycott, and its first target was the annual track championships held at the New York Athletic Club (NYAC). It was an opportune choice: The NYAC allowed black and Jewish athletes to participate in competitions, but would not accept them as club members. The boycott brought no shortage of attention. When almost none of the nation's top black competitors showed up for the meet, and many others (including the Soviets) stayed away as well, reporters from a range of major publications set out to determine why African American athletes were so dissatisfied. National publications soon filled with detailed descriptions of the many ways that persisting prejudice and discrimination continued to create obstacles for even the most successful black Americans.[13]

One of the most prominent results was a five-part series penned by veteran *Sports Illustrated* writer Jack Olson. In addition to detailing the challenges that black athletes continued to face, Olson also highlighted the dark side of black athletic stardom. Not only did many prominent college programs graduate fewer than half their black athletes, Olsen contended, dreams of athletic glory kept many young African Americans from devoting their time and energy to pursuits more likely to produce a steady living. "At the most, sports has led a few thousand Negroes into a better life while substituting a meaningless dream for hundreds of thousands of other Negroes," he concluded.[14] OPHR organizers took that divide a step further, charging that U.S. leaders used the success of a few African Americans to suggest that those who continued to struggle had no one to blame but themselves. "We must no longer allow this country to use black individuals of whatever level to rationalize its treatment of the black masses...to use a few 'Negroes' to point out to the world how much progress she has made in solving her racial problems when the oppression of Afro-Americans is greater than it ever was," read one OPHR pamphlet.[15]

Still, athletes continued to disagree over whether an Olympic boycott was the best way to address their concerns. A number of college basketball players, most notably Lew Alcindor, decided not to try out for the Olympic team. But while top basketball players saw the Olympics as an enjoyable stop on the way to the NBA, giving up the Games was a far bigger sacrifice for track athletes, who had no other showcase of similar caliber. As the Olympics drew closer, the OPHR was unable to muster a majority vote for a boycott. Instead, organizers announced, athletes would find a way to express their concerns while there.

Tommie Smith and John Carlos, San Jose State students who had been with the OPHR since its inception, were especially determined to make their position known. Their opportunity came at the end of the 200-meter race. Tommie Smith won the race in spectacular style, clocking a time of 19.83 seconds that set a new world record and made him the first runner to officially break the 20-second barrier. John Carlos and Australian Peter Norman finished in 20 seconds, Norman just edging Carlos for the silver. A few minutes later, Smith and Carlos mounted the medal podium wearing black socks and no shoes. Smith had a black glove on his right hand; Carlos had one on his left. As the U.S. and Australian flags flew, and the Star Spangled Banner began, Smith and Carlos bowed their heads and raised their fists.

The striking image appeared across the world, sparking curiosity, admiration, and tremendous controversy. Embarrassed by the scene, and under pressure from the International Olympic Committee, the USOC revoked Smith and Carlos's Olympic credentials and expelled them from the Olympic Village. Arguments about the meaning of the two athletes' gesture, as well as over the USOC's decision, quickly eclipsed the athletic events that continued to unfold in Mexico City. San Jose State President Robert Clark expressed pride in Smith and Carlos's medals, adding "I regret that our treatment of our black athletes has been such as to prompt them to feel they must use the Olympic Games to communicate their real concern for the condition of blacks in America." Others condemned the gesture as "disgraceful, insulting and embarrassing." Few were able to ignore it.[16]

Across the country, hundreds of other black athletes looked for their own ways to make a larger mark on the society around them. Between 1967 and 1971 athletes initiated or participated in racial protests on at least 37 campuses. At the University of Wyoming, for example, black football players sought to protest the Mormon Church's refusal to ordain black lay ministers by wearing black armbands in a game against Brigham Young University. After the head coach reacted by dismissing all his black players, black athletes formulated a long list of more general grievances that included a lack of black coaches, white coaches who focused on black athletic performances while neglecting academics, and expressions of racial prejudice by coaches and white teammates. In other situations, African American students actively recruited black athletes—by far the most prominent African Americans on most campuses—to lend their support to efforts that ranged from campaigns to establish black studies programs to efforts to raise wage rates for campus jobs that were generally filled by African American workers.

Latino Athletes Step Up

Latino athletes also took on greater public roles during the era, particularly in major-league baseball. Jackie Robinson's major-league debut had opened the doors not only for African Americans, but also for Latinos of African descent whose skin had previously been considered too dark for the big leagues. Many teams stepped up their Latin American scouting efforts. The New York (soon to be San Francisco) Giants were out in front, hiring longtime Negro League baseball owner and Cuban baseball expert Alex Pompez as a Latin American scout. The talent that Pompez recruited helped lift the Giants to the top ranks of baseball, and in 1960 more than half the team's starting lineup hailed from Latin America.[17]

Pathbreaker Roberto Clemente took the lead both on and off the field. Born in Puerto Rico, the centerfielder signed with the Brooklyn Dodgers in 1954, and then moved to the Pittsburgh Pirates, making his major-league debut with the Pirates in the spring of 1955. He became one of the dominant major leaguers of the 1960s, winning four National League batting titles and 12 straight Gold Gloves for his stellar fielding. He was named the National League MVP in 1966, and played a central role in the Pirates' World Series triumphs in 1960 and 1971. His 1971 World Series performance was especially spectacular; despite an injury-plagued season he batted .414, and everyone on both teams marveled at his fierce determination. The following season, he collected his 3,000th hit.

Like African American athletes of the 1960s, Clemente quickly learned that his tremendous skills did not insulate him from prejudice or discrimination. He faced particularly significant obstacles; as a Puerto Rican with significant African heritage he had to face Jim Crow segregation in addition to the challenges of language and culture that came with migrating from his Latin American home to the mainland United States. But like many of his African American contemporaries, he was not satisfied with simply overcoming his own obstacles. He began to work on plans to build sports programs for underprivileged Puerto Rican children. Throughout the 1960s, he spoke proudly about his cultural heritage, and repeatedly challenged the many stereotypes about Latino players that appeared in press reports and in the decisions of coaches, managers, and owners—decisions that in one instance involved forbidding players to speak Spanish in a team clubhouse. The first interview he granted after the 1971 World Series victory was in Spanish, addressed directly to his family and community.

Ironically, Clemente's achievements gained their widest recognition after his tragic death. In December of 1972, following a massive earthquake in Nicaragua, he boarded a small plane overloaded with relief supplies. It crashed shortly after taking off, killing everyone on board. Clemente's death prompted an outpouring of support for the people of Nicaragua—efforts spearheaded by President Richard Nixon. It also highlighted Clemente's work as a humanitarian as well as a baseball star. He was quickly inducted into baseball's Hall of Fame—the first Latino player to be so honored—and Major League Baseball's Commissioner's Award, awarded for humanitarian efforts, was renamed the Roberto Clemente Award.

Like Jackie Robinson, Roberto Clemente challenged stereotypes, but raised few questions about the fundamental structure of American society. A different Latino athlete, boxer Rodolfo "Corky" Gonzales, pursued a more radical path. Born in

Denver, Colorado in 1928, Gonzales was the son of Mexican migrants, and he spent a good part of his early life traveling with his family to pick crops. His path out of poverty came through boxing, where his skills took him "from stinking barrios/to the glamour of the ring," as he later recounted in his influential epic poem, "I Am Joaquín." Gonzales became an excellent fighter, winning the AAU bantamweight championship in 1947, and compiling a winning record as a professional featherweight while staying well clear of the corruption that so often tainted his sport. Denver's newspapers hailed him as a "classy" fighter who brought honor to his city. Boxing was an especially popular sport among Mexicans and Mexican Americans, and Gonzales's successes, along with his charismatic personality, made him an admired figure in Colorado's Mexican-American communities.[18]

Gonzales proved to be far more than an athlete. Before he retired, he became involved in local politics and used the money he had earned to open first a neighborhood bar, "Corky's Corner," and then a bail bond business. He joined civic and political organizations, worked to win Latino votes for John F. Kennedy, and was chosen chair of Denver's "War on Poverty" committee. But he became increasingly disillusioned with both local and federal efforts to improve circumstances for low-income Mexican-American communities, as well as evidence of ongoing discrimination, particularly in the ways that police dealt with Latino youth. By the late 1960s, he had become a key national organizer in what became known as the Chicano (an alternate term for Mexican-American)—movement, which pressed for Chicano autonomy and celebrated the complex legacy of Chicano culture.

Gonzales and his allies had few difficulties reconciling the fighting spirit that characterized his boxing career with the spirit that animated his battle for Chicano rights. "I've been taught that five loose fingers by themselves are nothing," Gonzales once said. "Bring them together and you have a fist."[19] For others, such as the newspapers that covered Gonzales through both his athletic and political careers, coming to terms with the shift proved a greater challenge. As a boxer, Gonzales had taken pains to follow the rules of his sport to the letter, maintaining an impeccable reputation within an often-corrupt sport. Newspapers lauded his efforts, frequently portraying him as an idealistic immigrant whose commitment to honesty and hard work stood out among his corrupt Caucasian peers. But when he joined with other Latinos to challenge the rules by which the society around him operated, those activities seemed, somehow, less sporting.[20]

Native Americans Protest "Indian" Mascots

Native Americans launched their own political and cultural movements during the era, sometimes dubbing their efforts "Red Power." In addition to efforts to enforce old treaty rights and improve life for struggling native communities, native activists advanced a distinctive criticism of American athletics, targeting the many sports teams that used Indians as mascots. Native Americans had begun to express concerns about Indian mascots back in the 1940s. This dissatisfaction grew during the 1950s and 60s, in part because of the era's activism, in part because the growing spectacle associated with college and professional sports led to more exaggerated and stereotypical portrayals (the Cleveland Indians' controversial "Chief Wahoo," for example, was created in the late 1940s, and was joined by the Milwaukee Braves' "Chief Noc-a-Homa" in the 1950s). "In almost every game of hockey, basketball, baseball, and football—whether high school, college, or professional leagues—I see some form of degrading activity being conducted by non Indians of Indian culture!" wrote Dennis Banks, a member of the Anishinabe nation who helped to found the American Indian Movement (AIM) in 1968. "We Indian people never looked the way these characters portray us," Banks continued. "It is painful to see a mockery of our ways."[21]

Organizations such as AIM, the National Congress of American Indians (NCAI), and the National Indian Youth Council, as well as Native American students themselves, began to target Indian mascots at institutions across the country. One such discussion was set off by Native American students at Stanford University, who in 1968 began to challenge the portrayal of Indians at Stanford athletic events (Stanford's football team had been known as "the Stanford Indians" since the 1920s, and the school officially adopted the symbol in 1930). In 1972, after being presented with a formal petition from students and staff that urged the university to discontinue the symbol as well as improve its Native American studies program, Stanford dropped the name. The school teams became known instead as the Stanford Cardinals (later changed to the singular "Cardinal" to indicate that it stood for the color rather than the bird).

AIM and the NCAI continued to press the issue, as did tribal governments and Native Americans in communities around the country. But while some other colleges also abandoned Indian names and mascots, among them the University of Oklahoma, Dickenson State University, and Dartmouth University, professional teams put up far more resistance. Major professional teams stopped adding new Indian names in the mid-1960s—the last one to do so was the Kansas City Chiefs, who took the name after moving to Kansas City from Dallas in 1963. But owners of existing Indian-named teams were concerned about abandoning well-established brands and about offending fans. AIM members filed a complaint with the Cleveland Indians in 1970, and in 1971 representatives from a number of organizations met with William Bennett, the then owner of the Washington Redskins football team. Little resulted.

Activism for Athletes: The End of the Reserve Clause

The activism of the 1960s also set the stage for a major transformation in professional sports—the end of the system that gave professional team owners complete control over their players' movements. In the mid-1960s, when major-league baseball players hired Marvin Miller to head up their relatively weak players' union, one of Miller's early goals was finding a player willing to mount a legal challenge to baseball's infamous "reserve clause." The player who eventually stood up, All-Star centerfielder Curt Flood, saw his action as part of the civil rights struggles of the time. As an African American player, Flood was keenly aware of the inequalities that continued to pervade American life. He had traveled to Mississippi to support civil rights workers in 1962. In 1964, after helping the Cardinals win the World Series, he had returned home to California only to be threatened with a shotgun by a man who had rented a house to the Flood family without realizing they were black.

In 1969, when the Cardinals traded Flood to Philadelphia, he decided that the time had come to take his own stand. Although he knew that the action would probably end his career, he refused to go, and filed a lawsuit. Perhaps tellingly, the letter he wrote to commissioner Bowie Kuhn noted, "I do not feel I am a piece of property to be bought and sold irrespective of my wishes." Flood lost both the lawsuit and his job, but he gained much of the credit when the reserve system was toppled four years later, giving not only baseball players but also all professional athletes the opportunity to become "free agents."[22]

Conclusion

An era of sports-related activism not only showcased the skills of black, Latino, and other nonwhite athletes as never before, but also gave sports a meaningful role in the push for greater social equality. In the decades to come, both athletes and ordinary citizens would benefit from the era's actions. But they would also find that old problems were hard to banish. The graduation rates of black college athletes remained stubbornly low, and concerns continued to grow about star-struck youngsters pursuing their athletic dreams at the expense of their studies. Plenty of stereotypes also proved hard to dispel. In 1971, for example, *Sports Illustrated* published an article that offered an updated version of old stereotypes about black physical prowess, asserting that "there is an increasing body of scientific opinion which suggests that physical differences in the races might well have enhanced the athletic potential of the Negro in certain events."[23] There was still a long way to go.

Critical Thinking Questions

1. In the 1950s and 1960s, minority athletes were viewed as "racial representatives," whether they embraced that role or not. Is that still the case today? What contemporary examples support your position?
2. As U.S. society changed, the racial goals of African American athletes changed. Was the nature of athletic competition more suited to some of these goals than others? Why or why not?
3. Dennis Banks of the Anishinabe nation has written of Native American mascots: "We Indian people never looked the way these characters portray us. It is painful to see a mockery of our ways." Do you think Native American mascots honor or demean Native American culture? Why?

Notes

1. A classic account of the changing tenor of the civil rights movement is Clayborne Carson, *In Struggle: SNCC and the Black Awakening of the 1960s* (Cambridge: Harvard University Press, 1981). For a detailed account of the Olympic Project for Human Rights, see Amy Bass, *Not the Triumph but the Struggle: The 1968 Olympics and the Making of the Black Athlete* (Minneapolis: University of Minnesota Press, 2002). For other overviews of race and sports in this era, see Patrick B. Miller and David K. Wiggins, eds. *Sports and the Color Line: Black Athletes and Race Relations in Twentieth-Century America* (New York: Routledge, 2004); Michael Lomax, ed., *Sports and the Racial Divide: African American and Latino Sport Experience in an Era of Change* (Oxford, MI: University

of Mississippi Press, 2008); and David Wiggins, *Glory Bound: Black Athletes in White America* (Syracuse, NY: Syracuse University Press, 1997), especially 279–87 for a bibliographical essay.

2. For a comprehensive account of Robinson's experiences and the early history of baseball integration, see Jules Tygiel, *Baseball's Great Experiment* (New York: Oxford University Press, 1983).

3. Quoted in ibid., 67.

4. Quoted in ibid., 197.

5. Quoted in ibid., 327.

6. Quoted in Mary Jo Festle, " 'Jackie Robinson Without the Charm': The Challenges of Being Althea Gibson," in David K. Wiggins, ed., *Out of the Shadows: A Biographical History of African American Athletes* (Fayetteville: University of Arkansas Press, 2006), 201–2. See also Jennifer H. Lansbury, *A Spectacular Leap: Black Women Athletes in Twentieth Century America* (Fayetteville, University of Arkansas Press, 2014), chapter 3.

7. Quoted in Bass, *Not the Triumph But the Struggle*, 83.

8. For the Ali quotations, see *Sports Illustrated*, December 20–27, 1976. For other assessments of Ali's cultural significance, see Elliott J. Gorn, ed., *Muhammad Ali* (Urbana: University of Illinois Press, 1995); Gerald Early, ed., *The Muhammad Ali Reader* (New York: Rob Weisbach Books, 1998); and David W. Zang, *Sports Wars: Athletes in the Age of Aquarius* (Fayetteville: University of Arkansas Press, 2001), chapter 5.

9. Quoted in Gerard O'Connor, "Where Have You Gone, Joe DiMaggio?" in R.B. Browne et al., *Heroes in Popular Culture* (Bowling Green, OH: Bowling Green University Press, 1972), 87.

10. Quoted in Dave Zirin, *People's History of Sports in the United States: 25 Years of Politics, Protest, People and Play* (New York: The New Press, 2009), 148, 146.

11. Quoted in Bass, *Not the Triumph but the Struggle*, 205.

12. Quoted in Zirin, *People's History of Sports in the United States*, 163.

13. See Harry Edwards, *The Revolt of the Black Athlete* (New York: Macmillan, 1969), 64–70; Donald Spivey, "Black Consciousness and the Olympic Protest Movement," in Donald Spivey, ed. *Sport in America* (Westport, CT: Greenwood, 1985), 239–62; and Wiggins, *Glory Bound*, chapters 6 and 7.

14. *Sports Illustrated*, July 1, 1968.

15. Quoted in Bass, *Not the Triumph but the Struggle*, 206–7.

16. Quoted in ibid., 272, 288.

17. Adrian Burgos, Jr., *Playing America's Game: Baseball, Latinos and the Color Line* (Berkeley: University of California Press, 2007), 200–12.

18. Tom I. Romero II, "Wearing the Red, White and Blue of Aztlán: Rodolfo 'Corky' Gonzales and the Convergence of American and Chicano Nationalism," in Jorge Iber and Samuel O. Regalado, eds., *Mexican Americans and Sports: A Reader in Athletics and Barrio Life* (College Station: Texas A&M University Press, 2007), 89–120.

19. Ernesto B. Vigil, *The Crusade for Justice: Chicano Militancy and the Government's War on Dissent* (Madison: University of Wisconsin Press, 1999), 10.

20. Romero, "Wearing the Red, White and Blue of Aztlán," 114–15.

21. Dennis J. Banks, "Tribal Names and Mascots in Sports," *Journal of Sport and Social Issues* 17 (April 1993), 5. See also National Congress of American Indians Report, *Ending the Legacy of Racism in Sports and the Era of Harmful "Indian" Sports Mascots*, October, 2013.

22. Quoted in Zirin, *People's History of Sports*, 206.

23. *Sports Illustrated*, January 18, 1971.

CHAPTER 19

Women's Liberation

Carol "Blaze" Blazejowski in action for Montclair State, where she scored a career 3,199 points, second only to "Pistol Pete" Maravich in all-time college scoring. In 1974, when Blazejowski entered college, women's college sports was in its infancy, and she did not receive a single scholarship offer.

It was March of 1975, and pandemonium reigned at the James Madison University arena, host of the women's national college basketball championship. Supporters of the two-time champion "Mighty Macs" of Immaculata College had brought along their famous galvanized buckets, which they pounded with drumsticks. Not to be outdone, the loyal followers of Delta State University's undefeated Lady Statesmen had headed out to local hardware stores, purchased wooden blocks, and were loudly rapping them together. For decades, the physical educators who governed college women's sport had sought to downplay competition, focusing on games and sports that emphasized the self-controlled decorum that they saw as building proper womanhood. That era had come to a decisive end. Although the tournament organizers eventually banned all noisemakers, the Lady Statesmen went on to upset the Mighty Macs, in a free-flowing, high-scoring game that ended with the score of 90–81.

The fierce competition and festive atmosphere highlighted the extent to which female athletes were becoming part of the sporting expansion that marked the last decades of the twentieth century. The day was especially sweet for Delta State coach Margaret Wade. A star high school player, Wade had played on Delta State's first women's basketball team back in the 1930s. Her career had been cut short when school leaders determined that the sport was "too strenuous for young ladies," and abolished the team. Now she was back in the fray, coaching her squad to even greater success.[1]

This new generation of female athletes faced a range of obstacles, including the cost of establishing women's athletic teams, lingering concerns about women's physical and emotional stamina, and reluctance to allow women into what many saw as men's rightful domain. Efforts to cross those bounds could provoke dramatic reactions. Women were barred from running the Boston Marathon until 1972. When Syracuse University student Katharine Switzer snuck into the contest by registering with her initials, the race director and another official tried to grab her and remove her number (their effort was thwarted by a group of her Syracuse teammates who blocked the outraged officials). Expanding athletic opportunities for women would thus prove a long struggle, one that required federal legislation, legal action, and myriad grass-roots endeavors.

Still, women pressed ahead. "[The] issue of gender equity in sports is about female strength and independence," feminist and author Gloria Steinem would later note, in words that echoed those of Senda Berenson and other early advocates of women's sports. "Society's acceptance of healthy, muscular women—usually most visible in women playing sports—may be one of the most intimate, visceral measures of change. An increase in our physical strength could have more impact on the daily lives of most women than the occasional role model in the boardroom or in the White House." Young women eagerly seized on new opportunities. Between 1970 and 1997, the number of girls who played high school sports increased nearly ten-fold, reaching nearly 2.5 million. In that same period, the number of women playing college sports approached 100,000. Tournaments and championships multiplied, and professional opportunities expanded.[2]

Small Steps

Women's competitive sports began to make gains during the 1960s, driven in part by Cold War pressures to stay ahead of the Soviet Union in Olympic competition. Because the Soviets invested more resources in their women's sports programs, Soviet women contributed far more to the all-important Olympic medal totals than did their U.S. counterparts. Facing a national call to improve U.S. women's athletic performance, as well as growing AAU investments in women's athletics, female physical educators began a gradual retreat from their rigid opposition to high-level competition. In 1958, the USOC created the Women's Advisory Board (WAB) consisting of representatives from the AAU, former female Olympic athletes, and sympathetic physical educators. In 1960, Doris Duke Cromwell, heiress of the Duke tobacco fortune, donated half a million dollars to the USOC to promote women's athletics. With these funds, the WAB and the Division of Girls' and Women's Sports (DGWS) of the national physical education association set up a series of national institutes for training female athletes.

In 1963, the DGWS reversed the stand against intercollegiate competition that it had adopted four decades earlier. "For the college woman and high school girl who seek and need additional challenges in competition and skills, a sound, carefully planned, and well-directed program of extramural sports is recommended," the new statement read.[3] In 1966, a group of women within the DGWS formed the Commission of Intercollegiate Athletics for Women, which scheduled its first two national championships—basketball and softball—in 1969. In 1971, the organization was renamed the Association of Intercollegiate Athletics for Women (AIAW). But while the AIAW was more open to competition, its leaders still sought to limit the significance of competitive athletics in their students' education, most notably through a ban on athletic scholarships.

Colleges devoted little money to those early teams, presenting coaches with significant challenges. In 1971, Vivian Stringer was hired by Cheyney State University to teach physical education and coach the women's team. She was delighted by the opportunity. Although she had been one of the best athletes in her small Pennsylvania town, the closest thing her high school had to a women's sports team was the cheer-leading squad. Stringer had joined the squad in order to be near the games. Her coaching career started in that unlikely situation, with the whispered advice she offered her male friends whenever they came off the field. But like most early teams, Stringer's Cheney State squad got minimal support from the school's administration. Stringer was not paid to coach. She had no scholarships to offer. Her team had a total of five basketballs for practice and games, and traveled in an old, highly unreli-able former prison bus. Stringer drove the bus herself and later recalled that when she reached an intersection, "I'd slow down but not enough to stop because we weren't sure we were going to start again, so my assistant would crane her neck out the window and yell, 'Vivian, keep going, no one's coming.' "[4]

Women's Liberation and Title IX

The major impetus for transforming women's sport came from outside athletic institutions, as part of the broader movement for what became known as "women's liberation." Few female activists had sports in mind when they set out to challenge the legal, cultural, and institutional structures that limited the roles women could play in U.S. society. But their push for a broader view of women's capabilities, as well as greater rights and opportunities, set the stage for an extraordinary athletic transformation.

The women's movement of the 1970s was rooted in the struggles and analysis of the civil rights movement. As the actions of civil rights activists continued to draw attention to racial inequality, their efforts spurred consideration of other injustices. In the fall of 1964, a group of female civil rights activists gave voice to a new set of concerns. "Assumptions of male superiority are as widespread and deep rooted...as the assumptions of white supremacy," they asserted. In addition to fighting for civil rights, they continued, activists should begin "the slow process of changing values and ideas so that all of us gradually come to understand that this is no more a man's world than it is a white world." As more women began to examine their own lives, they too began to call for change, both in laws that restricted women's activities and in the more far-reaching realm of custom.[5]

Education became one arena for activism. Although women were attending college in greater numbers, many still found themselves barred from some classes and majors, while others had difficulty getting university jobs. A federal class-action lawsuit filed by the newly created Women's Equity Action League led to a move-ment to pass federal legislation that would require colleges and secondary schools to end discrimination based on sex. Indiana senator Birch Bayh, who shepherded the legislation through the Senate, described it as providing "the women of America something that is rightfully theirs—an equal chance to attend the schools of their choice, to develop the skills they want."[6] The legislation, which became Title IX of the 1972 Omnibus Education Bill, used equally direct language. "No person in the United States shall, on the basis of sex, be excluded from participation in, be denied the benefits of, or be subjected to discrimination under any education program or activity receiving Federal financial assistance...."[7] President Richard Nixon signed it into law in June of 1972.

At the time, few people had any idea that Title IX would transform women's athletics. The legislation's profound impact on college sports would eventually lead many to believe it focused specifically on athletics. It did not. The initial lack of attention to the legislation's effect on sports highlighted how deeply the notion of athletics as a male realm was rooted in American culture. The gaps between opportunities for men and women in college sports had always been enormous, and had grown far greater as television boosted the budgets of college sports teams. One fairly typical large university, for example, spent $2 million on its men's sports programs and $1,900 on its women. Given the situation, Title IX had revolutionary implications.

It soon became clear that Title IX would in fact require changes in college sports. After Nixon signed the legislation, it was sent to the Department of Health, Education and Welfare (HEW) to be transformed into official regulations. As with much federal legislation, the devil was in the details: the process by which sweeping policy statements were translated into nuts-and-bolts requirements. Regulators started by making two key decisions. They ruled that Title IX would indeed cover school athletics. And rather than simply allowing women to try out for existing men's teams, they ruled that colleges and universities would have to create women's squads.

Athletic departments immediately began planning for a fight. Few sought to argue that women should not play competitive sports. But they did not want to take money from their own budgets to pay for women's teams. "Sharing money is tough," noted Donna Lopiano, who became director of women's athletics at the University of Texas in 1974. "Opening the door and saying, 'Come on, play' is easier." The NCAA, predicting the "possible doom of intercollegiate sports," set aside $1 million to fund a lobbying effort aimed at gutting the Title IX regulations. Lobbyists focused particular energy on attempting to get legislators to exempt the budgets of major revenue sports—primarily football and basketball—from the equal opportunity requirements. But supporters of women's sports, including the AIAW, launched their own counter-lobbying effort. In the end, they won. In the summer of 1975, when the official regulations were issued, they clearly called for equal athletic opportunities, and granted no exceptions.[8]

Still, supporters of women's sports faced an uphill battle. It remained extremely difficult for many athletic departments to come to terms with giving women's sports the same support that they provided men. Some saw the legislation as "giving" women opportunities that men's coaches and athletic directors had spent decades building. Similarly, many felt that young women did not possess the same levels of athletic skill, interest, or determination as young men, and thus had not proved themselves worthy of the same opportunities. Many women's programs had to fight for every dollar, and frustrated athletes often took matters into their own hands.

At Stanford, members of the women's basketball team made regular pilgrimages to the athletic director's office to demand uniforms, a paid coach, and space in the men's gym. At Yale, members of the women's rowing team became fed up with waiting on a bus, cold and wet, while the men's team took hot showers (the women's locker room, located in a trailer, had no hot water, so the women did not take showers until they got back to campus). One afternoon, team members walked into the office of the women's athletic director and took off all their clothes, revealing the words Title IX written on their chests and backs. They then read a statement detailing their concerns about the effects that waiting in the cold was having on their bodies. Their action was reported around the country, inspiring other female athletes to stand up for better treatment.

Pushed by athletes, coaches, and the federal government, programs began to build. Many of the early leaders were at small schools that were able to draw on female sporting traditions that had persisted at local levels in pockets of the country. The first three AIAW basketball championship tournaments, 1972–1974, were won by the "Mighty Macs" of Immaculata College, who got much of their talent from the highly competitive women's basketball programs in Philadelphia's Catholic schools. The next three were captured by Delta State, where Margaret Wade built her squad around players from Mississippi's strong high school squads. Wade's recruits included Lusia Harris, who became the first African American female cager to win national acclaim. Harris's recruitment typified the relaxed approach of the time. Her high school made regular appearances in Mississippi's state championship tournament, and the 6'3" Harris was hard to overlook. But she did not even think about college ball until her senior year, when a Delta State admissions counselor drove the 24 miles to her high school "and asked me did I want to play basketball in college?" The offer came with no athletic scholarship assistance. But after a campus visit, she said yes.[9]

At other schools, students took matters into their own hands. In the mid-1970s, at the University of North Carolina, a group of soccer players organized a club team and then petitioned the university for varsity status, even though there were no other women's soccer varsities in the region, and the AIAW did not sponsor a women's soccer championship. The school recruited men's soccer coach Anson Dorrance to coach the newly established team. By 1981, coaches of rising teams around the country had persuaded the AIAW to create a women's soccer program. Although the state of North Carolina did not have a women's soccer tradition, the team's early start, combined with high-level coaching, astute recruiting and inspired play, would help UNC to build a women's soccer dynasty.

Losing the Fight for Independence

As women's programs grew, however, it became more difficult for the AIAW to maintain its independence from the male-dominated college sports establishment. Part of the pressure to replicate the male athletic model came from young female players who wanted the same opportunities as men. The AIAW, for example, was forced to end its scholarship ban when a group of female college athletes challenged it in a lawsuit. Men's athletic departments also began to look for ways to exercise greater control over women's sports. College administrators began to merge traditionally independent women's physical education departments into men's departments. The NCAA, having failed to gut Title IX, also began to develop an interest in overseeing women's games.

The conflict over the direction of women's college sport came to a head in 1982, when the NCAA scheduled a set of Division I women's tournaments designed to directly compete with AIAW events. Each school had to decide which tournaments to enter and which organization to support. In many ways, it was an agonizing choice. The AIAW had been a major player in the fight for Title IX, and had nurtured women's college sports through its hard, early years. The organization was run largely by women, and women's sports were its prime concern. The NCAA, on the other hand, was a men's organization in every way, from its leadership to its athletic priorities.

But the NCAA had two things the AIAW could not hope to match: money and status. The AIAW had a $1 million budget. The NCAA, with its lucrative television contracts, had $20 million. As well as organizing and paying for women's tournaments, it offered to help pay travel expenses for schools that reached post-season play. Despite widespread concerns about the NCAA's motives, the organization also seemed to offer a more direct path to the funding and acclaim that top men's teams enjoyed. For many college presidents—in whose hands the final decision rested—the lure of the big time proved irresistible. In 1982, when the NCAA held its Division I tournament, almost half the country's schools chose the NCAA competition over the AIAW counterpart, including 18 of the previous year's top-20 programs. The loss of members—and thus of dues—doomed the AIAW. Shortly after holding its 1982 championships, the organization closed its doors.

Billie Jean King and the Women's Tennis Association

While college coaches and physical educators were working to build up women's college sports, another group of women focused on promoting professional competition. In 1970, two years before Title IX reached Richard Nixon's desk, female professional tennis players took the bold move of launching an independent series of women's professional tournaments. Those efforts would eventually help women's tennis become one of the nation's most significant spectator sports.

Tennis went professional in the 1960s, after the major tennis organizations realized that the growing amount of money in sports made professional competition inevitable. But although most tournaments had both men's and women's divisions, none of them offered women anything like the same amount of prize money that they bestowed on men. Female players became particularly angry when the Pacific Southwest championship announced that the men's champion would get a $12,500 first prize and the women's champion would get $1,500.

When women complained about the disparities in prize money, they were generally met with two arguments. The first was that since male tennis players were better than female players, they deserved more money. The second, and perhaps more germane, was that the paying spectators came to see the men. In essence, tournament organizers argued that they were really doing women a favor by allowing them to participate in the tournaments. Southwest tournament organizer Jack Kramer put it bluntly: "people get up and go get a hotdog or go to the bathroom when the women come on." As women were not helping to generate tournament receipts, Kramer and others argued, they had no right to ask to share equally in the prize money.

This was a different set of issues than those faced by college players. Title IX essentially asserted that since school athletics were part of a broader educational program, women and men deserved equal access to that educational opportunity. Professional sports was another matter entirely. A successful professional league depended on the ability to draw fans and attract corporate sponsors. To succeed as professionals, female tennis players had to prove that people would pay to sponsor them, and to watch them play.

For a sport trying to put itself on the map, corporate sponsorship was especially important. In order to build an audience, athletes had to find ways to get themselves before the public. Corporate sponsors made that possible by providing up-front dollars for organization and promotion. Through an intriguing confluence of historical circumstances that point to the many factors that have influenced the growth of U.S. sports, the female tennis players found their key sponsor in the Phillip Morris tobacco company, maker of Virginia Slims cigarettes.

Given the health risks of smoking, having a cigarette company sponsor women's professional tennis was laden with irony. But tobacco companies had money to spend. In 1964, U.S. Surgeon General Luther Terry had issued a landmark report warning of the dangers posed by cigarettes. In 1970, Richard Nixon had signed a long-anticipated law that banned the broadcast of cigarette ads on radio and television. Looking for other ways to promote their products, tobacco companies turned to sponsorships that would keep their name before the public. Some of these sponsorships went to arts programs. Many went to sports. Cigarette logos soon became a familiar sight in the background of major events in golf, tennis, car racing, and bowling, as well as on the clothes that athletes wore (Phillip Morris at one point paid a top designer to design women's "Slims Wear" for tennis players and their fans). Women's tennis was especially attractive to Phillip Morris, which had responded to the growing interest in women's liberation by creating the "Virginia Slims" brand specifically for women, and marketing it with the energetic slogan "You've Come A Long Way, Baby."[10]

The Phillip Morris money gave female players the chance to show what they could do. Led by Billie Jean King and Rosie Casals, female players worked with promoter Gladys Heldman to create and promote the Virginia Slims tour. The USLTA promptly suspended the participating players, which meant they would not be able to play in USLTA-sponsored tournaments, including the U.S. National Championship. But the women persisted. They did everything possible to draw people to their tournaments, from making personal appearances at shopping malls to standing alongside roadsides holding up signs. They wore colorful outfits and played with emotion, breaking many of the rules for conduct in an "elite" sport. Spectators and sponsors responded. In 1971, Billie Jean King became the first female athlete to win over $100,000 in prize money. Once it became clear that women could make their own way without the USLTA, the organization began to negotiate to bring them back.

The women's rebellion made an important point. The excitement of sports was as much about drama and close matches and human emotion as it was about pure athletic skill. Fans of boxing had known this for a long time. Sugar Ray Robinson, who ruled the welterweight boxing category from 1940 until his retirement in 1952, could not beat a heavyweight boxer. But that did not stop him from becoming the most popular boxer of his era, often called "pound for pound" the greatest boxer of all time. A top female tennis player might not be able to beat a top male player. But a closely fought match that featured two top-flight women players could be as compelling as one between two top men players. A charismatic woman could draw as large an audience as a charismatic man.

Billie Jean King was just that kind of athlete. While tennis remained largely an elite sport, King was the daughter of a firefighter who learned her game on public courts and played with a fast, flashy attacking style that was unusual for women at the time. She danced and pumped her fists and brought the crowd into her games. All these qualities served her well when she was offered the biggest stage in her career—a chance to take on former Wimbledon champion Bobby Riggs in a 1973 ABCTV extravaganza advertised as the "Battle of the Sexes."

The King–Riggs match, broadcast in prime time with great fanfare, furnished a dramatic focal point for women's struggle for greater opportunity in sport, for gender role conflicts and for the larger women's movement. The 55-year-old Bobby Riggs, who had won the "triple-crown" (singles, doubles, and mixed doubles) at Wimbledon in 1939, set the event in motion by loudly and publicly claiming that women players were far inferior to even lower-level male players. Proudly claiming the title of "male chauvinist pig," he boasted that despite his age he could defeat even the best female players. After Riggs made good on his word, beating highly ranked Margaret Court in a match that became known as the "Mother's Day Massacre," he promptly challenged King, who felt obliged to stand up for her sex.

ABC went all-out to promote the match, and choreographed it with extravagance. King entered the Houston Astrodome carried on a litter born by four muscular young men. Riggs arrived in a rickshaw drawn by a group of well-endowed young women. Riggs gave King a giant candy sucker; she presented him with a small, live pig. Then they got down to business. Before a crowd of 30,472, the largest audience ever to attend a tennis match, and with millions more watching on prime-time television, King routed Riggs, 6–4, 6–3, 6–3. Ironically, though Riggs claimed to represent men and King women, King played the more aggressive game. She served and volleyed while Riggs employed a stereotypical "women's style" of staying in the backcourt and hitting chips and lobs. Everyone watching knew that King could not have beaten a top male player. But her poise, confidence, and skill made it abundantly clear that women could be superb athletes, well worth watching and supporting.

Women's professional tennis continued to grow as a younger generation of talented players joined the circuit, creating new rivalries and matchups. Chris Evert, who blended powerful backcourt strokes and a fierce competitive drive with a girl-next-door demeanor, offered a particularly dramatic contrast to King's outspoken feminism. Evert streaked her blonde hair and favored ribbons, nail polish, and ruffled panties, leading one reporter to refer to her as "Miss America in a tennis dress." She had a string of boyfriends, and downplayed her commitment to tennis, talking often about her wish to eventually get married and settle down with a family. Still, neither her makeup nor her relationships kept her from becoming the sport's dominant player from the late 1970s through the early 1980s, both contributing to and benefiting from its considerable growth. By 1983, women could play in professional tournaments 49 weeks a year, and prize money for those tournaments totaled $11 million. Corporate sponsorships were plentiful and press coverage increased. In 1982, the winnings of the year's standout performer, Martina Navratilova, topped $1 million.

Public Image

As Evert's popularity suggested, even in this new era the most reliable way for a female athlete to vault to national celebrity was to combine skill with conventional, nonthreatening versions of femininity. This formula also held true with the Olympic women's sports that leapt to popularity in the television era—gymnastics and figure skating. The gymnasts who caught the public eye, starting with Russian Olga Korbut in 1972, packed extraordinary talent and grace into tiny, girlish bodies, and were generally directed by "father-figure" male coaches. Figure skating—one of the few sports where the women's competition was more popular than the men's—stressed the traditionally "feminine" qualities of grace and elegance along with strength and skill.[11]

In the 1980s, sprinter Florence Griffith-Joyner brought a new look to this mix. As Griffith-Joyner raced down the track, she projected a striking, confident version of womanhood through her long, streaming hair, elaborately painted nails, and form-fitting bodysuits that covered one leg and left the other provocatively bare. Her athletic accomplishments were equally dramatic, capped by a stunning series of performances at the 1988 Olympics in Seoul, South Korea, which brought her three gold medals and one silver. The combination of blazing speed and provocative style made Griffith-Joyner the best-known female track athlete since Wilma Rudolph, a regular presence in news, features, and advertisements. Her endorsement income soared into the millions.[12]

Still, women who did not exude this kind of heterosexual appeal—whether girlish or assertive—continued to face challenges that resembled those of their predecessors, including challenges to their womanhood. Despite women's growing list of athletic achievements, sports retained a fundamental association with masculinity. For example, starting in 1968 the International Olympic Committee began mandatory genetic testing of all female athletes, in order to ensure that no male athlete attempted to pose as a woman (testing of male athletes was not considered necessary). Top female athletes who did not stress their femininity, or were not clearly attached to boyfriends or husbands, also learned that it remained easy for journalists and the public to make the jump from the "mannish" realm of athletic skill to the assumption that women's sports was dominated by "mannish" lesbians.

Female athletes who happened to be lesbian or bisexual faced especially difficult decisions. The gay rights movement gained its own momentum in the 1970s. Like many other American minorities, gay activists saw sports as one way to gain visibility and acceptance, and a group of activists in San Francisco started the Gay Games in 1982, inviting not only gay athletes but also all others to participate. But like the civil rights movement and the women's liberation movement, greater visibility brought not only increased opportunity but also increased criticism. Female athletes felt much of the weight. Women's athletics had won greater acceptance in part because the expanding role of women in other areas of American life had reduced the gap between athletic skill and popular visions of "normal" womanhood. Sexuality, though, remained a controversial issue. At a time when women's sports remained on shaky ground, lesbian athletes and coaches carefully weighed the effect of coming out both on their individual careers and on the future of their sport.

Professional women's tennis, the sport most often in the public eye, saw the most dramatic developments. In 1981 Billie Jean King was "outed" when her former companion, Marilyn Barnett, sued her for financial support. Billie Jean had married Larry King in 1965, and he managed her career for many years. But the couple had drifted apart and Billie Jean began a decade-long involvement with Barnett. Still uneasy with her own sexuality, King worried both for herself and for her sport when Barnett's suit became public. "Nothing seems to titillate the press and the public more than homosexuality—and particularly if it relates in any form to a female athlete, because we're all supposed to be gay," she later wrote.[13]

In the end, King received far more support than criticism from tennis fans. Rising star Martina Navratilova, who chose to come out as a lesbian that same year, met with a similar reaction. But corporate sponsors, who sought to avoid controversy at all costs, were another matter. King's managers estimated that the revelation lost her $1.5 million in endorsements over the next three years. Avon, which had been sponsoring the WTA tour, did not renew its contract. The WTA began to urge players to be especially careful about their images. "Whether you are glamorous, athletic, businesslike or intellectual, make sure your image is one that the press will latch on to in a positive way," the organization advised its players in 1986.[14]

Conservative Retrenchment

The 1980s, which saw a sharp conservative turn, proved a rocky decade for women's sports. Not only did newly ascendant conservatives challenge the expansive vision of womanhood that had paved the way for expanding women's sports, they also sought to roll back the role the federal government played in fighting social inequities. The turn became clear in the fall of 1980, when Ronald Reagan was elected president. Among the "traditional" values that Reagan had promised to restore were conventional gender relationships. One of his supporters' core arguments claimed that American society had suffered when women stepped beyond the roles of wife and mother.

For many Reagan-style conservatives, inequities in the social order reflected not problems with social institutions, but rather fundamental differences in human beings. In their assessment, poverty existed largely because some people simply did not work hard enough, and government assistance only encouraged them to remain sluggish and dependent. Correspondingly, athletic imbalances sprang from basic differences between men and women. If there were no college women's sports teams, the argument ran, women must not have wanted or needed them. For the federal government to step in with a mandate for equality was "social engineering," a misguided effort to impose a false equity on institutions and society. A few months after Reagan took office, Vice President George Bush was tasked with reviewing what the administration termed "burdensome, unnecessary or counterproductive Federal regulations." Title IX was on the list.[15]

Under Reagan, enforcement of Title IX ground to a halt, which hampered efforts to increase support for women's college teams. Progress slowed even more in 1984, when the Supreme Court ruled in *Grove City College v. Bell* that because school sports teams received no direct federal funding, they did not have to meet Title IX's equal opportunity requirements. Other efforts to expand women's athletic opportunities faltered as well. American women's basketball got a significant boost in 1976, when a popular Olympic team captured the silver medal in the Olympics' first-ever women's basketball competition. Promoters sought to capitalize on that success by starting the Women's Professional Basketball League. Despite a burst of initial enthusiasm, however, the league was unable to attract enough spectators to pay the bills, and lasted only three seasons.

Still, the setbacks did not have the devastating effect of the cultural shift that gutted women's sports in the 1950s. While some Americans looked longingly back at the past, many others were determined to keep fighting for the gains that they had won. Once federal pressure slackened, some university administrations lost all interest in women's sports. Others, however, continued to support women's teams. Female athletes continued to grow more talented by the year—the result of the increased training and encouragement that the women's movement had sparked at all levels of women's sport. And many of the coaches who had won those early jobs did not slacken their efforts. They continued to recruit and train young athletes, making careful calculations about when to lobby for resources and when to hold back.

Pat Summitt, who became the head women's basketball coach at the University of Tennessee in 1974, offered one example. The 22-year-old Summitt was handed the head coaching job after the team's coach unexpectedly departed. The first practice she conducted showed that she had a lot to learn. "I worked those prospects up and down the court, at full speed, for two solid hours," she later wrote. "At the end of that, I ordered them to run a bunch of conditioning drills. I ran [them] in suicide drill after suicide drill. A group of four young ladies were running together. When they got to the end of the line, they just kept on running. They ran out the door and up the steps, and I never saw them again." But Summitt had no plans to give up. Not only did she love basketball, she also believed strongly in the value of sports for young women's development. "I knew I wanted to make a difference for women," she noted.[16] Step by step, Summitt built her program into a national power, one that would win eight national championships and more than a thousand games, giving her more victories than any other coach in NCAA basketball history, men's or women's. She was regularly cited as one of the greatest ever to coach the game.

Men as well as women lent their talents to the cause. Pat Summitt's great rival was Geno Auriemma, coach of the University of Connecticut Huskies, and the long-running Tennessee–Connecticut rivalry brought tremendous attention and excitement to the women's game in the 1990s and 2000s. At the University of North Carolina, Anson Dorrance guided his female soccer players to unprecedented success in a sport that grew more competitive by the year. The team won its 20th NCAA title in 2009, making Dorrance the first NCAA coach to win 20 national titles in a single sport. Male coaches of women's teams in fact became so prevalent that their presence sparked concerns about opportunities for women to move into coaching. Because women were rarely considered for coaching slots with men's teams, competition between men and women to coach women's teams meant that most colleges employed far fewer female than male coaches. In 1996–1997 men held 72 percent of NCAA head coaching positions, including 98 percent for men's teams and 45 percent for women's teams.[17]

The pendulum would shift back in the 1990s. Part of the shift came from a political change—Bill Clinton, elected president in 1992, was far more interested in pushing for athletic equality than either of his predecessors. Help also came from another significant force for social change—a court ruling. In 1993, Howard University women's basketball coach Sanya Tyler was awarded $2.4 million in damages in a Title IX-based suit she filed over inequalities in men's and women's basketball programs at the school. Soon, many universities found themselves the targets of actual or threatened legal action, and funding for women's college sports began to move upward.

Conclusion

Expanding athletic opportunities for American women required work on many fronts, including federal legislation, grassroots endeavors within individual schools and communities, efforts to shift both popular culture and public opinion, and at times legal action. By the twenty-first century, these efforts had accomplished an enormous amount. Female athletes were supported and celebrated as never before. By 2011, more than three million women played high school sports, 41 percent of the total (in 1972, women had been a mere 7 percent of high school athletes). According to the NCAA, in the 2011-2012 season nearly 200,000 women played college sports. They made up 43 percent of all NCAA athletes (as opposed to 28 percent in 1981-1982) and received 45 percent of all scholarship dollars.[18] But as those figures indicated, full equality remained elusive, even in institutions where it was mandated by the federal government. Efforts to establish women's professional leagues would continue to face significant obstacles. Much lay ahead.

Critical Thinking Questions

1. The growth of women's college sports got a significant boost from Title IX, a major piece of federal legislation. What do you think women's college sports would look like today, if Title IX had not been passed? Why?
2. Did the passage of federal legislation alone make the difference for women's sports? What other kinds of actions were required? What does that history say about the role of federal legislation in American society and culture?
3. The history of women's sports is marked by high and low points: periods of expansion followed by periods of decline. How do you account for this up-and-down historical trajectory? Which direction does women's sports seem to be going today?

Notes

1. Quoted in Pamela Grundy and Susan Shackelford, *Shattering the Glass: The Remarkable History of Women's Basketball* (New York: The New Press, 2005), 163. Detailed accounts of the development of women's sports in this era can be found in ibid.; Susan Cahn, *Coming on Strong: Gender and Sexuality in Twentieth-Century Women's Sport* (New York: The Free Press, 1994); and Mary Jo Festle, *Playing Nice: Politics and Apologies in Women's Sports* (New York: Columbia University Press, 1996).
2. Don Sabo, Ph.D. (1997). *The Women's Sports Foundation® Gender Equity Report Card: A Survey Of Athletic Opportunity In American Higher Education*. East Meadow, NY: Women's Sports Foundation.

3. Quoted in Festle, *Playing Nice*, 82.

4. Vivian Stringer interview by Pamela Grundy, November 3, 2004, in Grundy's possession. When Stringer tried out for the cheerleading team, she ran into one of the complications of the desegregation era: While school sports teams often welcomed African American athletes, black women often found it especially different to make cheerleading squads. Although Stringer was an excellent performer, it took the involvement of the local NAACP to get her on the squad.

5. Quoted in Festle, *Playing Nice*, 105–7. For an account of the development of the women's liberation movement, see Sarah M. Evans, *Personal Politics: The Roots of Women's Liberation in the Civil Rights Movement and the New Left* (New York: Knopf, 1979).

6. *Chronicle of Higher Education*, June 21, 2002.

7. Title IX of the Education Amendments of 1972 (discrimination based on sex or blindness), 20 U.S. Code, §§1681-1688 (1994).

8. Donna Lopiano interview by Susan Shackelford, July 18, 2003, in Shackelford's possession; Cahn, *Coming on Strong*, 254.

9. Lusia Harris-Stewart interview by Georgine Clark, December 18, 1999, Center for Oral History and Cultural Heritage, University of Southern Mississippi.

10. Robert Proctor, *Golden Holocaust: Origins of the Cigarette Catastrophe and the Case for Abolition* (Berkeley: University of California Press, 2012).

11. See Joan Ryan, *Little Girls in Pretty Boxes: The Making and Breaking of Elite Gymnasts and Figure Skaters* (New York: Doubleday, 1995).

12. Cahn, *Coming on Strong*, 269–71; Jennifer H. Lansbury, *A Spectacular Leap: Black Women Athletes in Twentieth Century America* (Fayetteville, University of Arkansas Press, 2014), chapter 6.

13. Quoted in Festle, *Playing Nice*, 236.

14. Quoted in ibid., 243.

15. Ibid., 216–19.

16. Pat Head Summitt with Sally Jenkins, *Reach for the Summit* (New York: Three Rivers Press, 1999), 21–23.

17. *The Women's Sports Foundation's Gender Equity Report Card.*

18. 2010-2011 High School Athletics Participation Survey (National Federation of State High School Associations, 2012); NCAA Sports Sponsorship and Participation Rates Report, 1981-1982–2011-2012 (NCAA, 2012).

CHAPTER 20

All Sports All the Time

Chris Senn of Costa Mesa, California competes in the first-ever Extreme Games in 1996.

The first-ever Extreme Games opened in Providence, Rhode Island, on June 24, 1995. Over the next week, spectators and cable television viewers were treated to a series of daring and frequently dangerous performances by skateboarders, sky surfers, street lugers, and other teen-aged daredevils, competing for gold, silver, and bronze medals. Many seasoned observers initially scoffed at the motley array of events, one columnist dubbing the Games the "Look Ma, No Hands Olympics."[1] They were wrong. Originally planned as a biennial event, the renamed X-Games quickly became an annual affair. In 1997, the first Winter X-Games was held in Big Bear Lake, California, with events that ranged from the aerial acrobatics of snowboarders to competitors racing down hills on modified snow shovels. Snowboarders gained even greater notice the following year, when they made their official debut at the 1998 Winter Olympics in Nagano, Japan. A handful of X-Gamers, most notably skateboarder Tony Hawk and snowboarder Shaun White (also known as the "Flying Tomato"), became household names and signed lucrative deals to promote equipment, clothing, video games, and other products.

The X-Games were the product of what had become one of the most powerful forces in American sports: cable television. Broadcasters at ESPN and ESPN II, with plenty of airtime to fill, had been looking for ways to attract young viewers who had little interest in sports such as football or baseball. They seized on the growing popularity of so-called "extreme sports"—sports in which young people tested the limits of equipment and themselves in fast-moving competitions that often involved stunning levels of expressive acrobatics. The X-Games sought to bring those events to a larger audience and, by extension, a larger audience to the ESPN networks.

The growing television exposure, in turn, increased the visibility of sponsors and the market for products that ranged from shoes to equipment to video games. The X-Games were far from alone. Sporting events had entangled athletic, commercial, and institutional priorities ever since the nineteenth century. But starting in the 1970s, a growing availability of television time created new, lucrative possibilities for advertising and sponsorships and sparked a commercial explosion that funneled startling amounts of money into a variety of sports. Sporting entrepreneurs of many stripes turned this new support in a number of directions, increasing both the visibility and the diversity of popular sports. The shift brought remarkable riches to a top range of elite athletes, and created new opportunities for many others. But it also unfolded within definite cultural limits, working most effectively when telling a familiar, non-controversial story, one that featured male athletes who fit into a standard formula of hard work, overcoming obstacles and head-to-head competition.

Cable Television

ESPN, founded in the wake of cable television deregulation, played a major role in this commercial juggernaut. While the three "major" networks had to fit sports in around a range of other programming, ESPN required countless games to fill its 24-hour day. All those empty hours gave the channel room to experiment with broadcasting a range of sports that would not have made a network cut. They also made it possible to give far greater coverage to sports that previously only graced the nation's television screens during marquee events such as horse-racing's Kentucky Derby, auto racing's Indianapolis 500, or college basketball's most high-profile matchups.

One ESPN show, *SportsCenter*, quickly jumped to the forefront of cutting-edge sports television. Introduced in 1979, *SportsCenter* soon replaced the daily newspaper as a source of scores and game reports for most fans. It even challenged *Sports Illustrated*'s near-monopoly on in-depth analysis. The program pioneered a combination of loose, hipster humor, razor-sharp commentary, nicknaming, and the invention of infectious catchphrases such as "Booyah!" "Back, Back, Back, Back, Gone!," "All the Way!," and "Touchdown!" The pace was rapid-fire and sometime furious. By reducing an entire day of sporting action to a one-hour telecast of highlights, *SportsCenter* was able to delete all the lag time that the players spent, in the words of one observer, "spitting and scratching."

SportsCenter also embodied multiple perspectives on the games it covered, regularly combining hype with skepticism. By in effect almost deifying those who hit the home runs, executed the slam dunks, and completed the long touchdown passes, *SportsCenter* elevated the game highlights into an experience bigger and frequently more compelling than the games themselves. Yet at the same time the commentators deflated the athletes and their performances with hip irony. *SportsCenter* soon spawned spinoffs not only on other American networks but also all over the world. It was said to have even influenced the presentation of television news. ESPN did not take long to build an audience. Within a decade of its founding, the channel's annual earnings topped $100 million. It became particularly popular among younger viewers.

In the 1980s, cable channels such as ESPN became a key component of a synergy of developments that transformed American sports into a commodity sold not only around the country, but also around the world. Satellite and fiber-optic cable technology had made it easy for broadcasting companies to send their products around the globe, and they scrambled to secure a share in the global marketplace. Barely a month after the first X-Games ended, the Walt Disney Company purchased ESPN's parent company, Capital Cities/ABC. Analysts touted ESPN as the big prize. The network reached more than 66 million homes in the United States and nearly 100 million worldwide. As "the premier provider of sports programming, a commodity that is marketable anywhere in the world and cannot be duplicated," it also held tremendous potential. The combination of Disney and ESPN was especially promising for international markets, one analyst noted, because children's programming and sports broadcasts "have universal appeal and offend no political position."[3]

The growth of broadcasting and international markets created an era of unprecedented wealth in American sports. Not only were Americans playing more sports than before, team jerseys and high-tech sneakers became everyday fashion, whether or not the wearers had ever bought a game ticket or stepped onto a court. This was true not only in the United States, but also in many of the other countries where sports was an obsession. Teams and sponsors were able to reach out to carefully targeted audiences such as teenaged boys or Spanish-speakers, and draw them into the sporting orbit, both expanding and diversifying the audience for sports events.

The variety of sports and athletes that expanded their appeal during this era—from the hip, inventive young people of the X-games to the "good ol' boy" drivers of the National Association of Stock Car Auto Racing to the growing number of Hispanic baseball icons to the urban, primarily African American stars of the National Basketball Association—highlighted a growing popular culture acknowledgement of the nation's cultural diversity, and also drew a broader audience into the sporting orbit. The most visible beneficiaries of this expansion were male. Outside of major events such as the Olympics, the NCAA basketball championships, and the Women's World Cup of soccer, women's sports still had to fight for regular broadcast time. But women also began to gain more attention—especially when it became clear that women were major buyers of athletic shoes and workout gear.

NASCAR

The rise of stock car racing became a key example of the way that the growing attention paid to sports, along with expanded broadcast opportunities, made it possible for a sport to expand out of a regional base to gain a national or even international following. American stock car racing had taken shape in the Southeastern states, drawing both its drivers and its fans from the southern white working class. The colorful drivers, the dramatic and often dangerous races, and the do-it-yourself quality of racing "stock" factory cars rather than custom-built open-wheel racers, proved a powerfully appealing combination for white southerners, who prized independence and self-reliance and who relished the opportunity to go to the track and have a good time. The adept promotion of William "Big Bill" France, who started his own racing career in the 1930s on the sands of Daytona Beach, Florida, built the sport into a regional sensation. By the 1970s, NASCAR held dozens of races at tracks around the south, and a top contest could draw nearly 100,000 fans.[4]

Major corporations such as Coca-Cola and STP also began to discover the benefits of sponsoring cars and drivers. Not only did sponsorship mean a popular driver for a spokesman, it also meant having a car brightly painted with company logos on prominent display for several hours every Sunday afternoon. Like women's tennis, NASCAR got an especially significant boost from the tobacco industry. In the wake of the federal ban on broadcast of cigarette ads, R.J. Reynolds agreed to become the title sponsor of the top NASCAR circuit, which was renamed the Winston Cup after the company's most famous product. Reynolds sank millions into advertising the Winston Cup series and its races, further boosting audiences.[5]

In 1979, the sport also caught a huge television break. CBS had agreed to an unprecedented broadcast—a live telecast of the entirety of the Daytona 500. It was the first time a 500-mile race had been allotted a live television slot—even the vaunted Indianapolis 500 was generally broadcast on tape delay, often in shortened form. The day of the race, the Northeast was hit with a major snowstorm that trapped people across the region in their homes. The 10 million viewers who tuned into the Daytona race were treated to NASCAR at its most exciting, with spins, crashes, come-from-behind runs, and multiple cars fighting for the lead throughout the race. On the final lap, as leaders Donnie Allison and Cale Yarborough jostled for advantage, Yarborough's tires hit the infield grass. The two cars collided several times, then locked together and crashed into the outside wall. As Richard Petty crossed the finish line to take the surprise win, Allison and Yarborough climbed out of their cars and started to fight. Donnie's brother, Bobby, stopped his own car and joined in. For the next few days, the race was the talk of the sports world, leaving viewers eager for more.

As NASCAR's national profile rose, promoters also worked hard to portray the sport in terms of what they called traditional American values, which included religion, friendliness, civility, trust, honor, and patriotism. Drivers adopted colorful names such as Richard "The King" Petty, "Awesome Bill" Elliot, and Dale "the Intimidator" Earnhardt. They tangled fiercely with each other on the track and sometimes off. But when the races ended they always paid homage to their crews and thanked fans and sponsors with polite, soft-spoken appreciation. Despite the huge attendance, and a good deal of drinking and associated rowdy conduct, races generally had a small-town feel of friendly cordiality. Many opened with public prayers and military jet fly-overs. American flags festooned every possible surface. Although promoters did not dwell on demographics, the drivers were all white, as were the vast majority of the fans who showed up at the tracks. The sport's public image meshed neatly with the conservative politics that marked much of the era, exemplified by President Ronald Reagan and his appeal to "traditional" values. In 1984, during his campaign for reelection, Reagan became the first sitting American president to start a NASCAR race.

NASCAR continued to grow at a remarkable rate. By the mid-1980s, every Winston Cup race enjoyed some version of national television broadcast, and by the end of the decade most of the races were shown live. In 1994, NASCAR inaugurated the Brickyard 400 at the famed Indianapolis Motor Speedway, and a quarter-million fans turned out to see the race. As the century drew to a close, executives signed a television contract with a consortium of networks that paid the sport $2.6 billion over eight years. Companies paid up to $20 million to sponsor a top car for a year. The sport also moved well beyond its southern base in physical terms. In 2003, races were scheduled for two different California tracks, as well as in Michigan, Delaware, Nevada, Pennsylvania, Illinois, Arizona, New Hampshire, Kansas, Indiana, and New York. In 2005, NASCAR executives claimed that their circuit was second only to the NFL in sports television ratings. While this claim was hotly disputed by major league baseball, it was clear that stock car racing had established itself in the top levels of American sport.[6]

Baseball Reaches Out to Latinos

As NASCAR executives worked to expand their sport's appeal around the country, moves made by major league baseball highlighted a different facet of a changing American society: the rapidly growing numbers of U.S. Latinos. Starting in the mid-1960s, changing immigration laws sparked a surge in immigration from Latin American countries. According to the U.S. Census, the U.S. Hispanic population multiplied more than fivefold between 1960 and 2010, topping 50 million and reaching past African Americans to become the largest minority group in the country. In addition, growing numbers of Latinos—especially those whose families had been in the United States for multiple generations—began to move into the middle class. Baseball's longtime popularity throughout Latin America, combined with decades of cross-border visits by both U.S. and Latin American players, made Latinos an obvious target audience. The expansion of media outlets—particularly Spanish-language radio and television—made it possible to tailor appeals to Spanish-speaking audiences. By the turn of the century, the Spanish-speaking audience became so important that ESPN created a Spanish-language sports brand aimed specifically at Latinos living in the United States. *ESPN Deportes* would soon move to 24-hour broadcast.

As had often been the case, the Dodgers pioneered this shift. As soon as the team moved to Los Angeles, it started radio broadcasts of its games in Spanish as well as English, the Spanish version featuring play-by-play wizard Jaime Jarrin. When the rise of cable television sparked the establishment of Spanish-language television stations—stations that seized eagerly on programming and stories to fill their airtime— teams also began to produce Spanish-language television broadcasts. The growing ease of international broadcasting meant that many of these games were broadcast in Latin America, as well as the United States.[7]

The tone for this expansion was set by the emergence of the most celebrated Latino major leaguer since Roberto Clemente. On April 9, 1981, a short, chubby rookie pitcher named Fernando Valenzuela took the mound for the Dodgers against the Houston Astros. It was opening day, an unusual time to start a rookie, but starter Jerry Reuss, runner-up for the 1980 Cy Young award, had been scratched because of injury. In an auspicious start, Valenzuela gave up only five hits in a complete-game shutout. He then won each of his next seven games, completing all of them while giving up only four runs in all eight games. A mid-year strike cancelled more than a third of the season's games, but the World Series was held as scheduled, and the Dodgers won. Valenzuela was awarded both Rookie of the Year honors and the Cy Young Award, the first time in history that a rookie had been named the best pitcher in baseball.

As the season progressed, Valenzuela's successes produced an ongoing, joyous celebration that became known as Fernandomania. While Latinos had been playing key roles on major league teams for decades, Valenzuela was the first to become an overnight, coast-to-coast sensation. A dramatic windup and tricky, reverse-spin screwball kept fans delighted and batters confused, as Valenzuela pitched his way to a 13–7 record in the strike-shortened season, leading the league in strikeouts, innings pitched and complete games. He would go on to numerous other honors in a 17-year major league career. "He makes me feel proud," noted one longtime resident of Latino East Los Angeles. "When he looks good, we all look good."[8]

Valenzuela was followed by a long line of Latino superstars. A few, such as Alex Rodriguez, had been born in the United States. Most, however, had been recruited from their home countries. This rise, as with most sporting developments, reflected both culture and economics. As the twentieth century waned, baseball dropped in popularity among young Americans, who found themselves more captivated by the rising profiles of football and basketball, or by new sports such as skateboarding and snowboarding. (Major league baseball became especially concerned about a precipitous drop in interest among African American players and fans, and launched a number of measures to try to boost baseball in black communities.[9]) But the game remained an obsession in the Caribbean Islands, as well as in other parts of Latin America. Perhaps more important, players from many Latin American countries could be signed far more cheaply than comparably talented Americans.

Fernando Valenzuela's route to the majors was unusual: Most Mexican baseball talent was carefully channeled into well-established Mexican leagues that kept a tight contractual hold on their talent and demanded high prices for their players. But in countries with a less-established baseball infrastructure, such as Venezuela and the Dominican Republic, the major leagues could have their pick of players at far lower cost. In the 1980s, to take advantage of this talent pool, numerous teams established training "academies" in Latin American countries where they brought in promising young players, worked on their skills, and provided a degree of guidance on speaking English and adjusting to U.S. life. The pipelines proved remarkably effective. By the late 1990s, nearly a quarter of major league players hailed from Latin American countries, and the numbers were even higher in the minor leagues.[10]

Newly arrived Latino players still faced many challenges, particularly in terms of language. But their situation had improved considerably. Players from earlier eras, such as Roberto Clemente and Felipe Alou, were often isolated or overlooked—despite his remarkable career, Clemente did not become a major national figure until his untimely death. The new generation of players had more Spanish-speaking teammates and coaches, enthusiastic coverage in Spanish-language media, and many more Latino fans, especially after major league teams began active efforts to attract Latinos to their ballparks. Spanish-language Web sites, changes in ballpark food offerings, and special events such as Latino heritage celebrations and dance parties all became a standard part of teams' fan outreach. Fans responded. In 2006, major league baseball estimated that Latinos made up 13 percent of overall ballpark attendance, a figure similar to their numbers in the overall population. Attendance ran far higher in areas with large Latino populations. In 2013, the Dodgers estimated that they sold just over half their tickets to Latino fans.[11]

Nike and the NBA

In the final decades of the twentieth century, however, no American sport could match the global rise of the National Basketball Association (NBA). Thanks to astute management and tremendous on-court talent, the NBA achieved a remarkable degree of worldwide fame. In the process, it highlighted interest in yet another kind of athlete, and another facet of American culture. The NBA, along with its growing bevy of sponsors and advertisers, fashioned a hip, urban atmosphere that was dominated by charismatic African American stars such as "Magic" Johnson, Michael Jordan, and Karl Malone. In the 1970s, links between the NBA and black urban youth, as well as the widespread cocaine use that marked the era, had given the league a "thuggish" reputation in some quarters, limiting both its popularity and the interest of sponsors. The new generation of stars, in contrast, combined the expressive style associated with black urban America with the clean-cut image that warmed advertisers' hearts.

The upward trend began in March of 1979, when the NCAA championship featured two extraordinary players: Earvin "Magic" Johnson of Michigan State University and Larry Bird of Indiana State. Michigan State defeated Indiana State, 75–64, in a final that was watched by 40 million viewers, and garnered the highest ratings in NCAA championship history. That summer, the two players were drafted by cross-country rivals, Bird going to the Boston Celtics and Johnson to the Los Angeles Lakers. Both players went on to Hall of Fame careers, reigniting the historic Celtic–Lakers rivalry and leading their teams to multiple NBA championships. Their contrasting images—Bird as the dogged, hardworking white player and Johnson as the flashier, more laid-back African American—gave their rivalry a cultural edge. Their tremendous respect for one another also helped to bridge that gap.[12]

As Johnson and Bird were reaching their peaks, a convergence of other developments helped propel the NBA to even greater heights. In 1984, the league elevated David Stern to be its new commissioner. Stern began his tenure determined to take advantage of the global expansion of trade and communication to promote the NBA not only within the United States but also around the globe. Then, that spring, University of North Carolina junior Michael Jordan decided to skip his senior year and enter the NBA draft. Jordan was an ideal player at an ideal time, a stellar performer with one of the nation's most respected college teams, who had secured an NCAA title with a game-winning buzzer shot. He had also developed one of the most dramatic games around, displaying remarkable scoring ability and breathtakingly graceful moves. "His adventures in Newtonian revisionism," *Sports Illustrated* observed, "keep the sports producers on late-night news programs awash in videotape." In addition, his agent proclaimed, his "striking good looks and fashionable wardrobe make him a natural corporate ambassador."[13]

Among the eyes that Jordan caught were those of Phil Knight, the chairman of Nike, Inc. Founded in the 1960s, Nike had ridden to prosperity during the fitness boom of the 1970s and 1980s, taking advantage of low-cost Asian labor to manufacture running shoes and apparel that it sold at a premium in the U.S. market. After hitting hard times in the early 1980s, Nike executives were eager to solidify their hold on other sports, and to reach out to the global marketplace. The fresh-faced, up-and-coming Jordan, who had just led the United States to basketball gold in the 1984 Olympics, seemed an ideal representative. He did not disappoint. In the next few years he would vault across boundaries of race and nationality to become a model crossover star.

Nike was only one of hundreds of corporations sinking new money into advertising and promotion. By 1990, most Americans came in contact with nearly three thousand advertisements a day—almost the twice the number they had encountered a decade earlier. Amid the growing din, Nike created a series of stylishly produced ads that stood out from the pack, and propelled Michael Jordan and his "Air Jordan" Nike shoes to worldwide stardom. In 1991, when Jordan and his Chicago Bulls defeated Magic Johnson and the Los Angeles Lakers to win Jordan's first NBA title, the finals were broadcast to more than 70 countries. Jordan became one of the most recognized figures in the world.

The next year, the first in which professional basketball players were allowed to compete in the Olympics, Jordan headed up a U.S. "Dream Team," made up of 12 of the NBA's greatest players, including Bird and Johnson. While some questioned the decision to send a team of superstars that no other team could hope to match (the average margin of victory was more than 30 points), the team's reception underscored the worldwide popularity of the NBA and its stars. "The Dream Team ran onto the court and the players on the other team began shooting," reporter Jack McCallum later recalled. "Not basketballs. Cameras. They stopped their warmups and asked the Dream Team members to pose."[14]

The highly visible ties between Dream Team members and their corporate sponsors raised a number of eyebrows, as well as questions about the relationship between Olympic ideals and corporate profits. The complications came clear when the members of the Dream Team mounted the podium to receive their gold medals. The U.S. Olympic Team was sponsored by the sporting goods company Reebok, which had spent millions for the privilege, and the official Olympic sweat suits bore the Reebok logo. But several of the Dream Team members, including Michael Jordan, had contracts with rival Nike, and did not wish to be photographed wearing a competitors' logo. After much tense negotiation, the players in question appeared on the podium draped in American flags, which added to the patriotic atmosphere and also conveniently covered the Reebok logo. "Now everyone looks at the Olympics as Nike vs. Reebok," one observer later commented.[15]

Still, despite the lopsided nature of their victories and the overt loyalty to their corporate backers, the Dream Team sparked considerable national pride. The most famous athletes in the world, the focus of unparalleled adulation, were Americans, playing an American game with a combination of creative virtuosity and hard-nosed, get-it-done competitive drive that offered a highly appealing portrait of American national character. While the 1988 team had managed only the bronze medal, the Dream Team steamrolled a starstruck competition, dramatically underscoring American superiority in the sport.

Selling Women's Sports

Riding high on their worldwide successes, corporate sponsors and NBA executives set their sights on a vast new potential audience: women. If young women could be persuaded to idolize female basketball stars, to flock to their games and buy their shoes and jerseys with anything like the enthusiasm with which young men snapped up Air Jordans, basketball's potential markets would expand enormously. Talent was not a problem. Thanks to Title IX, women's college basketball had made tremendous strides through the 1980s and into the 1990s, producing dynamic stars such as Nancy Lieberman, Cheryl Miller, Sheryl Swoopes, and Rebecca Lobo. In 1993, the year that Swoopes led the Texas Tech Lady Raiders to the national title, she made such an impression that Nike created the Air Swoopes for her—the first time a female player had her name on a shoe. The logical next step was a professional league.

A broad range of individuals and institutions were interested in promoting women's basketball. A number of these interests eventually coalesced around the creation of a female "Dream Team" for the 1996 Olympics. The USOC, the NBA, and a number of corporate sponsors agreed to bankroll a full year of practice, combined with exhibitions around the country. The USOC was determined to recoup national pride: After bringing home Olympic gold in 1984 and 1988, the U.S. women had won only the bronze in 1992. But sponsors also had grander ambitions, seeking to spread the message about the improving women's game.

The team came complete with a publicity staff that launched a blitz of promotions, placing players in television commercials, on talk shows, in the pages of fashion magazines, and in autograph-signing sessions at local shopping malls. Games were scheduled against all the top college teams in the country, as well as most of the best international teams. Most of the budget had been raised by the NBA from corporate sponsors such as Kraft, Champion, State Farm, Sears, and Nike. "We had thoughts that this could become something much bigger for women's basketball," recalled Val Ackerman, then an NBA vice president of business affairs.[16] The players did not disappoint. Despite a demanding schedule, they arrived at the Atlanta Olympics with a remarkable, 52–0 record. In the championship game, in front of 33,000 spectators and millions of television viewers, they defeated defending champion Brazil, 111–87. Announcers called the game the best they had ever seen.[17]

The game's potential seemed enormous. "We were sitting on something that had the potential to be of great appeal to corporate America," Ackerman noted, "particularly because our target audience was so different. We were seeing in this a way to reach women that the NBA and men's college basketball didn't have. It opens up the sport to a different base." The excitement the team generated sparked the formation of not one but two women's professional leagues: the independently owned ABL and the NBA-sponsored WNBA.[18]

U.S. female soccer players also sought to seize the moment. Although they had not attracted the levels of corporate sponsorship enjoyed by the basketball players, they had won their own gold medal in Atlanta. Women's soccer had become one of the nation's most popular participation sports, with 7.5 million girls and women playing on teams at different levels. The soccer players could also take advantage of an unprecedented opportunity: The United States was the host for the 1999 Women's World Cup, the top tournament in women's soccer. Played in stadiums across the nation, the World Cup's games drew more than 650,000 spectators in three weeks, making it the largest women's sports event in history. The final, in which the United States defeated China in a penalty-kick tiebreaker, drew 90,000 fans to the Rose Bowl, and a television audience of 40 million.

The soccer players were cast as a refreshing contrast to men's professional sports, a group of athletes to which fans could more directly relate. Supporters of women's sports were thrilled by the World Cup's success. "Little girls could see successful women athletes as role models," noted longtime women's sports writer Mariah Burton Nelson. "Little boys could see how talented the women were and how they were taken seriously by other adults.... I think female athletes are in the forefront of the feminist movement, although almost none of them use the word. They demonstrate strength, courage and freedom, and they are going where no women have gone before." Richard Lapchick, director of the Center for the Study of Sport in Society, speculated that "we are moving toward unlimited possibility for women in sport."[19] As soon as the tournament was over, players announced plans for their own professional league, the Women's United Soccer Association (WUSA).

Still, both basketball and soccer players quickly ran into the challenge of transforming the excitement of an Olympic or World Cup run to the week-to-week enthusiasm for a professional squad. The ABL lasted only two years, unable to compete with the WNBA for major sponsors and for television contracts. WNBA game attendance peaked at 11,000 spectators a game in 1998, and fell to 8,500 by 2004. The WUSA soccer league faced the same problems. Game attendance fell well below that for World Cup and top college games. Low attendance made it hard to attract sponsors, and the league lasted only three seasons.

While the deep pockets of the NBA helped keep the WNBA going, the difference between the men's game and the women's remained vast. Plainspoken Diana Taurasi said it clearly. Taurasi, who started with the WNBA in 2004, had done everything that could be expected of a basketball player. She was named national high school player of the year, and national college player of the year twice. In her four years playing for the University of Connecticut Huskies, the team won three straight national championships, and she was twice named the championship MVP. Nike put her name on the second signature shoe created for a female basketball player. She was the top draft choice of the WNBA. But at a time when the minimum NBA salary fell just under $400,000, and the NBA's top pick, Dwight Howard, earned more than $4 million for his rookie season, the maximum WNBA salary was $87,000. While Taurasi did not waste much time complaining about her fate, she remained fully aware of the enormous gulf that separated her from her male counterparts. "If you're a woman, you're screwed," she matter-of-factly remarked to one reporter. "It's the world we live in."[20]

Conclusion

The challenges faced by female basketball and soccer players highlighted some of the contours of the new sporting world created by the new global mix of culture, commerce, and communication. The growing space for sports created by the expansion of the public sphere brought new groups of people into the sporting orbit, and gave a far wider range of sports the opportunity to contend for public attention. "Sports has become the dominant entertainment of the world," Phil Knight proclaimed in 1996, a year in which one estimate put worldwide corporate sports sponsorship at $13.5 billion, and ESPN announced plans for a third 24-hour sports station, ESPN-3. But the expansion also had definite limits. Corporate sponsors frequently promoted the idea of diversity and inclusion—especially of people who might become new customers—but generally avoided significant political or economic controversy. Black tennis champion Arthur Ashe, a veteran of the struggles of the 1960s, was frequently frustrated by the challenges of getting younger African American stars involved in political causes, commenting at one point that "advertisers generally want somebody who's politically neutered."[21] The money that poured into sports both challenged and supported the social status quo.

Critical Thinking Questions

1. What do you see as the key qualities that were required for a sport to gain new prominence in the cable era?
2. How do you account for the simultaneous rise of NASCAR and the NBA, two very different sports with very different stars? What does the popularity of the two sports say about U.S. society and culture in the late twentieth century?
3. In the nineteenth century, popular sporting activities such as prizefighting were part of an "oppositional" culture that challenged the dominant Victorian cultural norms. Do any U.S. sports play that oppositional role today?

Notes

1. *Time*, January 22, 2009. For a history of extreme sports, see David Browne, *Amped: How Big Air, Big Dollars, and a New Generation Took Sports to the Extreme* (New York: Bloomsbury, 2004).
2. *New York Times*, August 6, 1995.
3. See Daniel S. Pierce, *Real NASCAR: White Lightning, Red Clay, and Big Bill France* (Chapel Hill: University of North Carolina Press, 2010).
4. Robert Proctor, *Golden Holocaust: Origins of the Cigarette Catastrophe and the Case for Abolition* (Berkeley: University of California Press, 2012), 98.
5. Chris Jenkins, "Baseball says NASCAR's TV claims are off track," September 22, 2005, http://usatoday30.usatoday.com/sports/baseball/2005-09-22-nascar-baseball-ratings-claim_x.htm?POE=SPOISVA.
6. See Jorge Iber, et. al., *Latinos in U.S. Sport: A History of Isolation, Cultural Identity and Acceptance* (Champaign, IL: Human Kinetics, 2011), 225–27.
7. Quoted in ibid., 226.
8. Mark Hyman, "The racial gap in the grandstands," October 1, 2006. http://www.business-week.com/stories/2006-10-01/the-racial-gap-in-the-grandstands.
9. Adrian Burgos, Jr., *Playing America's Game: Baseball, Latinos and the Color Line* (Berkeley: University of California Press, 2007), 227–42.
10. Hyman, "The racial gap in the grandstands."
11. For an excellent discussion of Johnson and Bird, see Daniel A. Nathan, " 'We Were About Winning: Larry Bird, Magic Johnson, and the Rivalry That Remade the NBA," in David K. Wiggins and R. Pierre Rodgers, eds., *Rivals: Legendary Matchups That Made Sports History* (Fayetteville: University of Arkansas Press, 2010).

12. Quotes from *Sports Illustrated*, December 10, 1984. For the rise of Michael Jordan see Walter LaFeber, *Michael Jordan and the New Global Capitalism* (New York: W.W. Norton and Company, 2002).
13. Jack McCallum, "The Best Team I Ever Covered," http://sportsillustrated.cnn.com/2011/writers/best_team_i_ever_covered/07/10/mccallum.dream.team/.
14. Quoted in LaFeber, *Michael Jordan*, 101.
15. Val Ackerman interview by Susan Shackelford, March 10, 2004.
16. Pamela Grundy and Susan Shackelford, *Shattering the Glass: The Remarkable History of Women's Basketball* (New York: The New Press, 2005), 219. Detailed and insightful accounts of the Olympic team's organization, as well as its year of competition, can be found in Sara Corbett, *Venus to the Hoop: A Gold Medal Year in Women's Basketball* (New York: Anchor Books, 1998).
17. Val Ackerman interview by Susan Shackelford.
18. Both quoted in Jere Longman, *The Girls of Summer: The U.S. Women's Soccer Team and How It Changed the World* (New York: Harper, 2000), 21–23.
19. Diana Taurasi interview by Susan Shackelford, July 1, 2004.
20. *Business Week*, July 29, 1996; LaFeber, *Michael Jordan*, 94.

CHAPTER 21

Sports in the Twenty-First Century

Sisters Venus and Serena Williams broke through numerous stereotypes as they ascended to the top of the tennis world.

LEARNING OBJECTIVES

21.1 Describe the old and new challenges faced by athletes, coaches, and communities in the twenty-first century, as well as aspects of American life that the study of sports can illuminate.

21.2 Summarize the forces driving the college "arms race" and the ongoing challenges they created for colleges.

21.3 Outline the forces driving the increased use of Performance Enhancing Drugs (PEDs) and the debates they sparked.

21.4 Explain the dilemmas that the discovery of CTE posed for the NFL, as well as for the nation's football fans.

21.5 Detail the ways that twentieth-century sports continued to engage questions about ethnic and national identities.

21.6 Analyze the variety of challenges, both real and metaphorical, created by the male–female separation in most athletic events.

Steve Cash, goalie for the U.S. sled hockey team, edged back and forth on his aluminum blades, eyes scanning the ice, waiting for the puck to come his way. He had made five saves already, including a dazzling stop of a penalty shot, but it was now the final period of the gold medal game, and his team held a slim 1–0 lead. The U.S. sled hockey team had not won gold at the Paralympics since 2002, and Cash, who had not allowed a goal throughout the Games, was determined to take home the top prize. Then, with barely a minute left, players suddenly converged at the far end of the rink. The puck shot toward the opposing goal, and teammate Taylor Lipset tapped it in, clinching the victory. As the final seconds ticked away, Cash threw up his hands in joy, only to be knocked to the ice as his team piled on him in celebration. As television cameras surveyed the rink, and announcers started to recap the game, Taylor Chace and Nikko Landeros rebalanced their sleds and carried an American flag across the ice to loud applause. Discipline, training, and determination had brought the United States gold, and the joy and confidence that the accomplishment brought the players showed in every move they made. "The only disability in life is a bad attitude," Cash later told his college paper.[1]

Growing out of a movement that began in 1948 with 16 wheelchair-bound veterans of World War II, the 2010 Winter Paralympics featured 502 athletes who competed in 64 events, sold 230,000 tickets, and claimed a cumulative online television audience of 1.6 billion worldwide. Its tremendous growth embodied the expansion in participation and in the opportunities for high-level competition for a broad variety of individuals in a remarkable range of sports.

As the U.S. moved into the twenty-first century, more of its residents played sports than ever before—many of them at far higher levels than in the past. While inequities continued to exist, many of the most obvious obstacles to athletic participation had been breached. Women made up 43 percent of college athletes, outnumbered men on the 2012 U.S. Summer Olympic team, and took home more Olympic medals. African

Americans stood among the most visible, talented, and highly promoted stars not only in football, basketball, and track, but also in the "country club" sports of men's golf (Tiger Woods) and women's tennis (Venus and Serena Williams). Along with Latinos, Asians, and other people of color, they had ably filled almost every sports-related position imaginable, from quarterbacks and goalies to coaches, managers, general managers, and team owners (although the ranks of college coaches and administrators in particular remained overwhelmingly white).

A growing number of efforts also sought to strengthen support for gay and lesbian athletes, endeavors that ranged from antidiscrimination videos made by top-ranked college teams to a new, successful line of gay-friendly clothing launched by Nike, Inc. When controversy arose around antigay policies in Russia, site of the 2014 Olympics, U.S. president Barack Obama responded by appointing Billie Jean King an official U.S. delegate to the Sochi Games. Soon after the Sochi Games ended, Michael Sam, Defensive Player of the Year for the powerhouse Southeastern Conference and a sure-fire National Football League (NFL) draft pick, became the first top-level football player to declare that he was gay.[2]

Despite this progress, however, twentieth-century athletes, coaches, institutions, and communities still face a broad range of sports-related issues. Some, such as the need to balance college sports with academics, are long-standing challenges, intensified by a rising public profile and a huge influx of money. Others, such as the strengthening link between football concussions and permanent brain damage, are new. And, in addition to directly sports-related issues, the structure, emotions, and public impact of athletic events mean that they continue to offer telling windows into many facets of American culture, helping to clarify issues and dilemmas that range from the depiction of Native Americans in popular culture to questions about differences between men and women.

Youth Sports

In youth sports, twenty-first century challenges came from different directions. One involved participation. While few overt barriers to sports participation remained, many young people still faced structural barriers—especially in low-income urban communities of color. Despite the prominence of the small number of low-income athletes of color who made marks in high-profile sports such as basketball and football, most urban youth had fewer opportunities to participate in organized sports than suburban youth, for reasons that included limited recreation facilities in schools and communities, violent neighborhoods, lack of money for travel and equipment, and other factors. The gaps were particularly evident for young women; a 2008 study indicated that only 45 percent of urban girls participated in organized athletics, as opposed to 68 percent of suburban girls. This difference showed up in college sports. In 2009, whites made up 62 percent of the U.S. college-age population, and 63 percent of freshman enrollments. They made up approximately 70 percent of the male student-athletes, and 77 percent of the female student-athletes.[3]

Young people who had more access to athletic opportunities could face a different problem: an unhealthy overemphasis on performance, especially at an early age. While many young people thrived in youth sports programs, during the first decade of the twenty-first century, dreams of college scholarship, financial rewards, and stardom also touched off what Gloria Goodale of *The Christian Science Monitor* described in 2006 as a "new arms (and legs) race."[4] Rich and poor families alike, Goodale found, were as never before "in a dead heat for the ultimate free-market prize: wealth and status" through the nurturing of star athletes. By 2006, an estimated 52 million preadolescents participated in organized sports programs managed by adults. Many well-off families took over essentially all of the spare-time activities of their child athletes, hiring pro coaches, purchasing the latest technology, and encouraging their children to train three to four hours daily.

Critics, especially recreation professionals, complained of the excessive emphasis placed on performance and winning, from the use of performance-enhancing drugs (PEDs) to the adoption of a win-at-all-costs mentality for even teams of the youngest children. The experience of coaching sometimes turned otherwise humane and reasonable adults into angry, violent tyrants. "They want to win at any cost," reported Charles Ortmann, a former Michigan All-American, after he quit as chairman of a midget football program at Glen Ellyn, Illinois. "They tell their players, 'Go out there and break that guy's arm.' They won't even let all their kids play."[5] In terms of public attention, out-of-control parents reached a tragic climax in 2000 when an angry hockey father in a Boston suburb assaulted and killed the father of another child athlete. According to the National Alliance for Youth Sports, the incidence of sports rage involving players, coaches, officials, and parents was rising.[6]

The College "Arms Race"

For colleges and universities, the rising levels of status and money associated with college athletes only intensified the tensions that had always existed between athletic and academic goals. As the potential rewards of national stardom rose, big-time programs embarked on what became known as a financial "arms race." Between 1998 and 2007, according to an estimate of *The Chronicle of Higher Education,* spending on sports programs grew three times faster than spending on academic programs. To lure and retain recruits, the colleges built ever-more lavish practice facilities, locker rooms, cafeterias, and weight rooms. Stadiums across the country were rebuilt or upgraded with luxury skyboxes and enormous scoreboards. The $8 million "Godzillatron" at the University of Texas, a 55 feet high by 134 feet wide video scoreboard that towered over the south end zone of Royal Memorial Stadium, required the university to upgrade its utility capacity, and to install a new 405-ton air conditioning unit to keep the massive board from overheating. Between 2003 and 2007, Texas doubled its expenditures per athlete, from $113,000 to $210,000 per year. Coaching salaries also escalated: Nick Saban became the highest paid college coach in history in 2007, when the University of Alabama agreed to pay him a total of $93.2 million over eight years.[7]

For most colleges, finding enough money to keep up with competitors in the arms race was not an easy matter. Despite much talk of "revenue sports," fewer than a dozen colleges earned enough directly from sports to cover basic costs, let alone expenditures for the improvements of facilities. Nearly all the big-time programs sought to offset part of their escalating costs by raising ticket prices, especially by charging more for luxury seating. Schools also put more effort into hawking merchandise; for example, the University of Texas received $8.2 million in licensing royalties from sneaker and apparel companies. Yet, to be sure of steady income year in and year out, a school needed to consistently field winning teams, which meant constant engagement in the murky realm of athletic recruiting.[8]

Critics charged that the money spent on sports contributed to a growing chasm between campus academic and athletic cultures. According to one report, "What we have now is a separate culture of performers and trainers, there to provide bread and circuses but otherwise unconnected to the institution that supports them."[9] That major college football players, according to a 2008 NCAA survey, spent an average of 44.8 hours a week practicing, playing, or training for their sport lent support to this conclusion. In the time given to their sports, varsity athletes in golf, baseball, and softball were not far behind the football players.[10] A close study of athletes at several selected colleges raised questions about athletes and academics that went well beyond the spotlight sports, arguing that "Academic underperformance among athletes is a pervasive phenomenon," regardless of sport or division.[11]

More dramatically, an ongoing series of studies and scandals underscored the difficulties that colleges continued to face in keeping other aspects of their programs in line. In 2011, the legendary football program at Pennsylvania State University was shaken to its core when longtime assistant coach Jerry Sandusky was accused and eventually convicted of sexually abusing numerous boys, some of them in the Penn State locker room. Once it became clear that fear of tainting the university and the program's reputation had led members of the athletic department to cover up evidence of the abuse for years—thus allowing it to continue—Penn State's revered coach, Joe Paterno, was fired. University president Graham Spanier resigned, and was later charged with perjury (Paterno died in January of 2012, two months after his firing). The entire country was forced to ask what kind of loyalty could lead officials to overlook crimes of such magnitude.[12]

Academic scandals continued to abound as well. In 2013, despite widely trumpeted progress in athlete graduation rates, the federally calculated six-year graduation rate for African American male athletes remained at barely 50 percent. A separately calculated analysis of graduation rates of football players at major football schools—schools whose football programs took in substantial revenue—showed football players graduating at substantially lower rates than the general population, with the gap especially large for African American players.[13] Even when athletes graduated, they had not necessarily received a quality education in return for their services. At the generally well-regarded University of North Carolina, for example, a 2011 investigation indicated that a large number of athletes had received credit for classes that were either never given, or that they never attended.

"We've been told a million times that it's OK for athletic departments, bowls and television networks to make billions of dollars on the backs of these kids, primarily basketball and football players, because 'they get a free education,'" fumed Raleigh sports columnist Luke deCock early in 2014. "Well, what if they don't? What if they're admitted unprepared for college, given just enough help to stay eligible, and then given the boot when their time is up, no better prepared for real life, no better educated than they were when they first arrived on campus? That's not compensation. That is, as [UNC former player Michael] McAdoo put it, 'a scam.'"[14]

Professionals and Performance-Enhancing Drugs

While professional sports do not have to contend with the challenge of balancing athletic prowess with educational priorities, numerous professional sports still fight public and problematic battles with PEDs, especially anabolic steroids, chemically created derivatives of testosterone that promote tissue and muscle growth (as opposed to cortical steroids, which reduce inflammation). Originally developed in the 1930s, anabolic steroids became an issue after World War II, as both the financial and political stakes of athletic success skyrocketed. At the 1968 Olympics, the world may have focused on Tommie Smith and John Carlos, but according to *Sports Illustrated*, "Shoe money and drugs were the two hottest conversational topics in the Olympic Village." As early as 1969, a former Los Angeles Dodgers team doctor predicted that "The excessive and secretive use of drugs is likely to become a major athletic scandal, one that will shake public confidence in many sports just as the gambling scandal tarnished the reputation of basketball."[15]

After considerable discussion (why, some asked, was it all right to use cortical steroids to help heal muscles but not anabolic steroids to help build them?), PEDs were widely banned. Still, enforcement remained relatively weak, in part because an ever-changing array of substances was difficult to detect, and in part because leaders of sporting institutions (not unlike leaders of educational institutions) did not want to taint the reputation of their games. But eventually, athletes began to get caught, often in dramatic fashion. In the 1988 Seoul Olympics, Canadian sprinter Ben Johnson ran a startlingly fast world record time to take the gold medal in the marquee 100-meter dash. Two days later, he was stripped of the medal after testing positive for an anabolic steroid.

Although high-profile sprinter and long jumper Marion Jones never failed a steroid test, she lost three gold and two bronze medals from the 2000 Olympics when she confessed to steroid use in 2007. In 2006, after U.S. cyclist Floyd Landis won a dramatic, come-from-behind victory in the Tour de France, tests showed him with high levels of testosterone. Four years later, he confessed to systematic use of a variety of PEDs. Shortly afterward, Lance Armstrong, whose comeback from virulent testicular cancer to win seven straight Tour de France races had become a part of American sporting legend, admitted to using a stunning range of drugs throughout his career.

Of the major American sports, steroid use became most visible in baseball, most notably in the continuing assault on every offensive mark in the game by Barry Bonds of the San Francisco Giants. Starting in 1999, Bonds went on a hitting spree never before equaled in baseball history. He struck a seasonal average of 49 home runs, had an on-base percentage of .517, and set the record for home runs in a single season (73) as well as an entire career (762). He won the NL's MVP award for a record-shattering four consecutive seasons (2001–2004). Massive changes in Bond's physical appearance—from 185 to 230 pounds in weight, from a 42 to a 52 jersey, from $10^1/_2$ to 13-size cleats, and from a size $7^1/_8$ to a $7^1/_4$-size cap—accompanied his hitting rampage. The visible changes in Bonds, and in numerous other players, sent reporters digging for answers.

Under pressure from the U.S. Senate, as well as from growing revelations about steroid use, Bud Selig, baseball's commissioner, and Donald Fehr, head of the players union, announced a new, stricter drug policy that included random tests for steroids.

A combination of investigations and confessions eventually implicated a number of the game's biggest stars, including Bonds, Red Sox pitching legend Roger Clemens, both Mark McGwire and Sammy Sosa, whose battle for home run supremacy helped revitalize baseball's popularity in 1998, and three-time American League MVP Alex Rodriguez, who was suspended from baseball for the entire 2014 season. The era from the late 1980s through the late 2000s became known as the "steroids era."

The use of steroids and other PEDs raised a range of questions about the era in which they were most in vogue, as well as about the future. Some athletes—such as Lance Armstrong—claimed that victories or records obtained while using PEDs should be honored, because drug use was so widespread that it was impossible to win without them. Baseball, a sport dominated by statistics, was faced with the question of what to do with numbers that were achieved with the help of PEDs. Significant controversy also broke out over whether steroid-using players should be inducted into the Baseball Hall of Fame. After the steroid revelations, the baseball writers who voted on membership steadfastly refused to induct players who admitted to or were suspected of using steroids, including Sosa, Bonds, and McGwire. Critics, on the other hand, charged that plenty of the players already in the hall had broken rules of many kinds, but were still elected based on their on-field performance. The debate showed no signs of ending.[16]

The NFL and CTE

While major league baseball was coping with revelations about player steroid use, the National Football League was dealing with a different, potentially more serious issue—the growing prominence of a brain disease called chronic traumatic encephalopathy (CTE). Evidence of CTE first surfaced in 2002, when Dr. Bennet Omalu of the Alleghenyh County Coroner's office conducted an autopsy of "Iron Mike" Webster, longtime star center for the Pittsburgh Steelers. Webster had died of a heart attack at age 50 after years of well-documented mental instability. Omalu saw a startling level of deterioration in Webster's brain tissue, for which he coined the term CTE. Four years later, Omalu saw similar deterioration in the brain of a second Steeler, Terry Long, who committed suicide at age 45. It also showed up in the brain of Andre Waters, a 44-year-old former Philadelphia Eagle who shot himself the next fall. Even more disturbing, in 2010, the disease was found in the brain of Owen Thomas, a college football player who hanged himself in his apartment.[17]

By then a range of studies indicated that former NFL players, especially those with a history of concussions, had unusual rates of depression and other mental illnesses. Like the heads of baseball, however, NFL executives did not address the problem immediately, and instead spent many years denying that strong evidence linked CTE with football-related concussions. In August of 2011, a group of former players filed a lawsuit against the NFL, charging that the league had covered up evidence that on-field injuries were linked to lasting brain damage. Nearly 4,500 former NFL players joined the lawsuit. One of the original plaintiffs, Ray Easterling, shot himself in April of 2012, and an autopsy revealed CTE damage to his brain. In August of 2013, the NFL reached a $765 million settlement with the former players, offering payments of up to $5 million for affected players, although the settlement remained in doubt after a federal judge questioned whether it was enough money to deal with the full extent of the problem.[18]

An agreement to deal with potential past injuries, however, did not address the games that were still played every Sunday. Football had always celebrated toughness, the willingness to take hard hits, and to get back in the game as soon as possible after being injured. Now it was becoming clear that such decisions, instead of building or revealing character, might be sabotaging players' futures. Comparisons of professional football players to gladiators—who not only fought but also died in the ring—might have been more accurate than they once appeared. "It reminds me of ancient Rome," Dr. Omalu once noted.[19]

Especially disturbing were a handful of cases of CTE in college and high school players, which indicated that even levels of contact and injury well below that experienced in the NFL could be dangerous. Parents were quick to react. Between 2010 and 2012 participation in Pop Warner football dropped nearly 10 percent, and one poll showed 40 percent of Americans supported a ban on tackle football for preteens. If football regularly caused brain damage, what would that do to the game's audience? How would it affect younger players and their families? Would better-off families pull their sons out of the game, while young men from struggling circumstances decided the potential payoffs warranted the risk? What kind of a game would football be then?[20]

Away from the Field

Sports also continues to offer an arena for exploring cultural issues not directly related to tackles, home runs, or tournament trophies. The pageantry that accompanies sports events, the broad and often deeply emotional public engagement in high-profile contests, and the rules that govern participation, all offer insights into fundamental cultural conceptions. While it would be impossible to detail all of them, considering a handful helps to suggest the range of issues that sports continue to engage.

Who Should Be a Mascot?

In the spring of 2013, more than four decades after Native Americans first met with the Washington Redskins to request that the team drop a name that many considered deeply offensive, Native American activists continued to pursue those efforts, in part through a (second) lawsuit that challenged the trademark protection on the Redskins' name (trademarking racist or offensive speech became illegal shortly after World War II). This time, pressure to change the name began to gain national momentum. While a poll showed widespread public support for keeping the name, sportscasters and newspapers began to stop using it. President Barack Obama called on the Redskins to change the name, as did a number of other Congressional representatives from both parties. Leaders of the NFL met with leaders of the Oneida Nation to discuss the Oneidas' call for league sanctions against the team. In a poll of Washington-area residents, only 25 percent said that their enthusiasm for the team would drop if the name were changed.[21]

Some of the ramifications of using Indian names and mascots were explored by journalist and historian Dave Zirin in January of 2014, shortly after the Florida State Seminoles defeated the Auburn Tigers at the Rose Bowl to win the 2013 national football championship. Zirin described the highly stereotyped pregame scene, in which the Florida State mascot, Chief Osceola, rode his horse to the center of Rose Bowl and planted his "traditional" flaming, feather-bedecked spear in the turf. Zirin then contrasted the scene with the actions of the historical Osceola, a savvy political leader who fought efforts by the United States to take Seminole land with words as well as with arms, and who was arrested by the United States at a meeting that had purportedly been called to negotiate peace. Zirin offered a suggestive comparison. "Osceola was nothing less than the American Mandela," he wrote. "Imagine before a South African soccer game, a white person in black face, dressed like Mandela, running out to midfield to psyche up the crowd." In response to claims that Indian team names kept Native American history in the public eye, Zirin responded, "No one is getting educated about Osceola or the Seminole Wars. Instead their heroic resistance has been translated for football purposes to being 'tough.' This 'respect' for their toughness not only reduces a rich and varied Seminole culture to a savage culture of war, it is also an unspoken way to praise our own ability to engineer their conquest."[22]

Who Is an American?

The high profile of sports, and the tight connections many Americans draw between sports and patriotism, also help highlight a particular set of challenges faced by Latino athletes, as well as by Latinos in general. Throughout American history, public views of specific groups of immigrants have frequently shifted based on both national and international politics. As promoters of nineteenth-century prizefighting events well knew, the massive influx of Irish immigrants in the middle of the nineteenth century created sharp tensions between Irish immigrants and native-born workers. Similarly, in the twenty-first century the swelling numbers of U.S. Latinos gave rise to a virulent anti-immigrant politics that included widespread condemnations of Latinos. These tensions surfaced dramatically at the third game of the 2013 NBA finals, held in San Antonio, Texas. Eleven-year-old San Antonio native Sebastien de la Cruz, son of a U.S. Navy veteran, took the floor before the game to sing the national anthem, clad in a mariachi outfit that sported the Spurs' black, white, and silver colors. The racist chatter that broke out on Twitter, with comments such as "Is this the American National Anthem or the Mexican Hat Dance?" and "Can't believe they have the nerve to have a beaner singing the national anthem of America," underscored long-standing assumptions that Latinos—even those who had been citizens for generations—were not "genuine" Americans.[23]

The extensive publicity and broad condemnation that accompanied the incident made it clear that the hostility directed toward de la Cruz (and, a few months later, toward Brooklyn-born Latino pop star Marc Anthony's performance of the national anthem at baseball's All-Star game) came from only one segment of the American population. But even people who bore no hostility toward Latinos did not necessarily see them as integral parts of American history or culture. Cuban-born star pitcher Luis

Tiant ran into this challenge when he asked to be included in the Black Aces Project, an endeavor to research and promote the careers of all the African American pitchers who have had 20-game winning seasons in the major leagues. One of the game's top pitchers of African descent, Tiant became an American citizen in 1969, the year after he completed the first of his four 20-game winning seasons. Canadian native Ferguson Jenkins, who came to the United States with a major league contract in the same year as Tiant did, made the cut. Tiant was turned down.[24]

Who Is a Woman?

Even as disputes continue over who is or is not an American, the rising stakes in women's competition, combined with scientific advances, have raised an even more fundamental question: who is or is not a man or a woman. The hard-and-fast divide between men's and women's competition in most sporting events assumes a similarly hard-and-fast biological division. But athletes have become some of the most visible examples that this is not always the case. In 1980, for example, Stella Walsh, one of the track and field greats of the 1930s, was murdered in a robbery attempt at the age of 69. An autopsy revealed that biologically, Walsh belonged to a group of people now commonly known as intersex—she had been born with an unusual mix of chromosomes that left her without female reproductive organs and with underdeveloped male ones. Walsh had been raised as a girl, and identified as female all her life. In the 1930s, her sex was never officially questioned. By the mid-1960s, however, women who participated in international athletic competition were required to prove that they were in fact female.[25]

These definitions, however, proved problematic from the beginning—called into question by a handful of athletes for whom, like Stella Walsh, reality was not so clear cut. In 2009, for example, runner Caster Semenya emerged from rural South Africa to win the 800-meter race at the World Championships. After other runners raised questions about Semenya's sex, tests determined that although she appeared female, and had thus been brought up as a girl, she too had an intersex chromosomal mix. Official efforts to determine whether Semenya was eligible to compete in women's events (she did compete in the 2012 Olympics, and won a silver medal) highlighted the difficulty of looking at any single factor to determine whether someone should be considered a man or a woman. "This is not a solvable problem," medical historian Alice Dreger told a reporter investigating the situation. "People always press me: 'Isn't there one marker we can use?' No. We couldn't [in the past] and we can't now, and science is making it more difficult and not less."[26]

The strict divisions between men's and women's sports also raises an additional question, particularly given the ubiquity of sport in American culture and the frequent use of sports as a metaphor for national life. Nearly a half-century after the women's movement began, sports remains one of only a very few American arenas where men and women almost never compete together or against each other. It remains one of very few arenas where men are automatically assumed to perform, on average, better than women (while top female competitors for many years were required to prove that they were in fact women, sports officials saw no need to require male athletes to prove that they were men). And it remains one of the few arenas of popular culture that at its most celebrated levels focuses almost completely on men's activities and achievements. The mismatch between sports and the rest of American society in terms of male and female roles raises one set of questions about the limits of sports as metaphor, as well as the broader consequences of the enormous role that it has come to play in American popular culture.

The limits of sports as a model for relationships between men and women also points to questions about the role that sports can play in social change in present-day American society. Sport has at times reinforced social divisions and at times challenged them. How it functions has depended on the nature of the challenges that individuals or communities face. At a time when overt legal and institutional measures barred both women and people of color from full participation in arenas of American life that ranged from voting booths to university swimming pools, achievement in the highly symbolic realm of athletic competition was one way to demonstrate that such discriminatory measures had no basis in any fundamental differences between races or genders. But as the activists of the 1960s learned, athletics does not offer an equally compelling metaphor for more structural changes in American society—changes that would require shifting not simply who is allowed to enter a competitive arena, whether economic, political, or athletic, but the rules by which any given game is played. In this context, the ubiquity of sports in American popular culture, which tends to focus attention on victory and loss within an existing system, and which celebrates its victors in heroic fashion, has often served a more conservative social function.

Conclusion

In the fall of 1997, two squads from Wolftown, North Carolina, made their way to the nearby town of Cherokee to play a game of anetso. The sport had become a regular feature of the annual Cherokee Indian Fair, which marked its 85th anniversary that year. The 1997 game in many ways resembled the contest described by James Mooney a century before—an exuberant clashing of bodies and sticks followed by a ritual, postgame visit to the river that ran alongside the field. Despite numerous changes in Cherokee life, and numerous predictions of anetso's demise, North Carolina Cherokee continue to play the game, and it continues to serve as both a public and a private affirmation of Cherokee identity and Cherokee values.[27]

In the polyglot world of the twenty-first-century United States, sports play a kaleidoscopic range of roles, embodying layers of history, the multifaceted demands of the present, and a shifting array of dreams about the future. Across the country, Americans engage in a remarkable range of games, sometimes as informal, pickup contests on streets or playgrounds, sometimes as highly choreographed rituals seen by people around the world. Some games are centuries old, others recently invented. Sports bind communities together, and sometimes divide them. Athletes swell the ranks of popular culture celebrities, revered and reviled, providing both inspirational and cautionary tales. Sports serve nationalistic interests and fill the coffers of mammoth businesses, sometimes both at the same time. They highlight some of the deepest dilemmas of American life and culture. It would be impossible to understand this nation's history, its present—or its future—without them.

Critical Thinking Questions

1. At the start of the twenty-first century, competitive athletics played a far greater role in American society and culture than it did at the start of the nineteenth century. Do you see this as a positive development? Why or why not?
2. This chapter outlines a number of present-day challenges faced by U.S. athletes, coaches, and sporting institutions. Which of these challenges do you find most compelling, and why?
3. As you look toward the future, what role do you see competitive athletics playing in American history? What additional issues do you think it can illuminate?

Notes

1. Ryan Crull, "Steve Cash Proves Himself to Be One of the Best," August 30, 2010, http://thecurrent-online.com/sports/steve-cash-proves-himself-to-be-one-of-the-best-umsl-sophomore%E2%80%99s-gold-medal-is-the-latest-in-his-inspiring-career/.
2. *Washington Post*, January 9, 2014. In 2008, approximately 89 percent of college head coaches were white. "2008 Racial and Gender Report Card: College Sport" (The Institute for Diversity and Ethics in Sport, 2009), 4.
3. "Go Out and Play: Youth Sports in America" (Women's Sports Foundation, 2008), 27. For figures on college enrollment, see Anthony P. Carnevale and Jeff Strohl, "Separate and Unequal: How Higher Education Reinforces the Intergenerational Reproduction of White Racial Privilege" (Georgetown Public Policy Institute, July 2013), 17; "2010 Racial and Gender Report Card: College Sport" (The Institute for Diversity and Ethics in Sport, 2011), 3. The NCAA did not compile figures for 2009.
4. For quotations and content in this paragraph, see *Christian Science Monitor*, October 6, 2006.
5. *Sports Illustrated*, November 17, 1975.
6. *Newsweek*, July 24, 2000; *Sports Illustrated*, July 24, 2000.
7. For a summary, see Knight Foundation Commission on Intercollegiate Athletics, *A Call to Action: Ten Years Later*, 2001; Rick Harrow, "College Football 2006: Bigger Business Than Ever," August 29, 2006, www.sportsline.com; *Journal Star* (Lincoln, Neb.), August 26, 2006.
8. Based on NCAA data, Andrew Zimbalist found in 2007 that 95 of the 117 I-A schools lost money on their athletic programs when subsidies from student fees and monies from their institutions were excluded. But, as Zimbalist noted, this figure did not include any deductions for capital expenditures such as stadium renovation. See his "College Athletic Budgets Are Bulging But Their Profits Are Slim to None," *Sports Business Journal*, June 18, 2007. In 2006, according to figures from the U.S. Department of Education, the top five universities received more than $82 million each (topped by Ohio State with $104.7 million), while the bottom five received less than $10.2 million. See *Sports Illustrated*, March 5, 2007.
9. Quoted in Knight Foundation, *A Call to Action.* In the early years of the new century, the Knight Commission, the reformed NCAA under the presidency of Myles Brandt, faculty senates at some 50 colleges, and the Association of Governing Boards of Universities and Colleges joined in a fitful, largely unsuccessful effort to close the chasm between athletic and academic cultures. See, for example, *BusinessWeek*, October 20, 2003; *New York Times*, January 17, 2003.
10. Brad Wolverton, "Athletes' Hours Renew Debate Over College Sports," *Chronicle of Higher Education* 64 (January 25, 2008).

11. James L. Shulman and William G. Bowen, *The Game of Life: College Sports and Educational Values* (Princeton: Princeton University Press, 2001), 262; 271. See also the lengthy analysis of possible ramifications of broad-based athletic recruitment in ibid., 268–88.

12. *Sports Illustrated*, November 16, 2011.

13. "Black Male Student-Athletes and Racial Inequities in NCAA Division I College Sports" (Graduate School of Education, University of Pennsylvania, 2013); "2013 Adjusted Graduation Gap Report, NCAA Division-I Football" (College Sports Research Institute, University of South Carolina, 2013).

14. *New York Times*, December 31, 2013; *Raleigh News & Observer*, January 16, 2014.

15. *Sports Illustrated*, June 23, 1969.

16. *New York Times*, January 12, 2014.

17. Mark Fainaru-Wada and Steve Fainaru, *League of Denial: The NFL, Concussions, and the Battle for Truth* (New York: Crown Archetype, 2013).

18. *New York Times*, January 15, 2014.

19. Madison Park and Stephanie Smith: "Player's text: send my brain to NFL research bank," February 21, 2011. http://thechart.blogs.cnn.com/2011/02/21/anxiety-about-brain-damage-pervades-football/

20. Bob Cook, "Why is football participation declining?" November 26, 2013. http://www.forbes.com/sites/bobcook/2013/11/26/why-is-football-participation-declining-the-answer-isnt-concussions/

21. Erik Brady, "New generation of American Indians challenges Redskins," May 10, 2013. http://www.usatoday.com/story/sports/nfl/redskins/2013/05/09/native-americans-washington-mascot-fight/2148877/; Associated Press, "Poll reveals overwhelming support for Redskins name," May 2, 2013. http://www.usatoday.com/story/sports/nfl/2013/05/02/washington-redskins-name-poll-associated-press-gfk/2131223/; Dave Zirin, "Open Letter to Redskins Owner Dan Snyder," November 4, 2013. http://www.thenation.com/blog/176980/open-letter-rdskins-owner-dan-snyder-dear-dan-you-cant-say-you-werent-warned; Survey USA News Poll #20802, October 2013. http://www.surveyusa.com/client/PollReport.aspx?g=b41b9bde-1b19-40f7-af86-0b585eb8df03.

22. Dave Zirin, "The Florida State Seminoles: The Champions of Racist Mascots," January 7, 2014. http://www.thenation.com/blog/177800/florida-state-seminoles-champions-racist-mascots.

23. Ruben Navarette, "The Mariachi Singer Is More American Than His Critics," June 17, 2013. http://www.cnn.com/2013/06/17/opinion/navarrette-mexican-american-singer/.

24. Adrian Burgos, Jr., *Playing America's Game: Baseball, Latinos and the Color Line* (Berkeley: University of California Press, 2007), 257–58.

25. *Washington Post*, August 22, 2008. For a historical account of the requirement that female athletes prove they are women, see Susan Cahn, *Coming on Strong: Gender and Sexuality in Twentieth-Century Women's Sport* (New York: The Free Press, 1994), 263–65.

26. *New Yorker*, November 30, 2009.

27. Michael J. Zogry, *Anetso, the Cherokee Ball Game: At the Center of Ceremony and Identity* (Chapel Hill: University of North Carolina Press, 2010), 5–15; 227–36.

CREDITS

Text Credits

Chapter 1: pg. 2, James Mooney, "The Cherokee Ball Play," The American Anthropologist III (April 1890), 130–31. See also Thomas Vennum, Jr., American Indian Lacrosse: Little Brother of War (Washington, Smithsonian Institution Press, 1994); Joseph B. Oxendine, American Indian Sports Heritage (Lincoln: University of Nebraska Press, 1995); and Michael J. Zogry, Anetso, the Cherokee Ball Game: At the Center of Ceremony and Identity (Chapel Hill: University of North Carolina Press, 2010.; pg. 4, Quoted in The Jesuit Relations and Allied Documents, vol. 13, (Cleveland: The Burrows Brothers, 1897), 130; pg. 6, Richard Holt, Sport and the British (Oxford: Oxford University Press, 1989). 4.; pg. 7, Quoted in R.W. Malcolmson, Popular Recreations in British Society, 1700–1850 (Cambridge: Cambridge University Press, 1975), 83.; pg. 8, For recreation in the southern colonies, see T.H. Breen, "Horses and Gentlemen: The Cultural Significance of Gambling among the Gentry in Virginia," William and Mary Quarterly 34 (1977), 239–57; Jane Carson, Colonial Virginians at Play (Williamsburg, Va.: Colonial Williamsburg, 1965); and C.R. Barnett, "Recreational Patterns of the Colonial Virginia Aristocrat," Journal of the West Virginia Historical Association 2 (1978), 1–11. For the contrast between southern and northern life, see C. Van Woodward's classic essay, "The Southern Ethic in a Puritan World," in his American Counterpoint (Boston: Little, Brown, 1971). Quote is from Breen, "Horses and Gentlemen," 250.; pg. 8, Quoted in David H. Fischer, Albion's Seed: Four British Folkways in America (New York: Oxford University Press, 1989), 361.; pg. 9, Quoted in Edmund S. Morgan, Virginians at Home (New York: Holt, Rinehart and Winston, 1962), 88.; pg. 10, Quoted in Rhys Isaac, The Transformation of Virginia (Chapel Hill: University of North Carolina Press, 1982), 102.; pg. 10, William Bradford, Of Plymouth Plantation, 1620–1647 (New York: Alfred A. Knopf, 1952), 97. For an indispensable collection of primary sources for early American sports, see Thomas L. Altherr, ed. Sports in North America: A Documentary History Vols. I & II (Gulf Breeze, FL: Academic International Press, 1997). The most analytical treatment of sports in early Anglo-America is Nancy Struna, People of Prowess: Sport, Leisure, and Labor in Early Anglo-America (Urbana: University of Illinois Press, 1996).; pg. 11, Quoted in John C. Miller, The First Frontier (New York: Dell, 1966), 87.; pg. 11, Hans-Peter Wagner, Puritan Attitudes Towards Recreation in Early Seventeenth-Century New England (Frankfurt am Main, Germany: Lang, 1982), 48; Perry Miller and T.H. Johnson, eds., The Puritans, 2 vols. (New York: Harper, 1963), I, 392. See also Bruce C. Daniels, Puritans at Play: Leisure and Recreation in Colonial New England (New York: St. Martin's, 1995).; pg. 11, David H. Fischer, Albion's Seed: Four British Folkways in America

(New York: Oxford University Press, 1989), 148.; pg. 12, Hans-Peter Wagner, Puritan Attitudes Towards Recreation in Early Seventeenth-Century New England (Frankfurt am Main, Germany: Lang, 1982), 34; and A.B. Hart, Commonwealth History of Massachusetts, 5 vols. (New York: Historical Society, 1927–30), II, 280.; pg. 12, Quotations in Fischer, Albion's Seed, 552, 555. See J.T. Jable, "Pennsylvania's Blue Laws: A Quaker Experiment in the Suppression of Sport and Amusements," Journal of Sport History 1 (1974), 107–21.; pg. 12, John Adams, The Work of John Adams, 5 vols. (Boston: Charles C. Little and James Brown, 1840), II, 125–26.; pg. 13, Quoted in Philip Greven, The Protestant Temperament (New York: A.A. Knopf, 1977), 145.; pg. 13, H.D. Farish, ed., Journal & Letters of Philip Vickers Fithian, (Williamsburg, VA: Colonial Williamsburg, 1943), 96.; pg. 13, H.S. Commager, ed., Documents in American History, 2 vols. (Englewood Cliffs, NJ: Prentice Hall, 1973), I, 86.; pg. 13, Quotations in Thomas L. Altherr, ed. Sports in North America: A Documentary History Vols. I & II (Gulf Breeze, FL: Academic International Press, 1997). Part II, 75, and H.S. Commager, ed., Living Ideas in America, new ed. (New York: Harper & Row, 1964), 555–56.; pg. 14, George Washington; pg. 14, See especially Struna, People of Prowess, chap. 8, and the data in Struna, "Gender and Sporting Practices in Early America, 1750–1810," Journal of Sport History 18 (1991), 13ff, as well as R.E. Powell, "Sport, Social Relations and Animal Husbandry: Early Cock-fighting in North America," International Journal of Sport History 5 (1993), 361–81.

Chapter 2: pg. 21, Alexis de Tocqueville, Democracy in America, 2 vols. (New York: Vintage Books, 1951), I, 51.; pg. 21, Quoted in Lewis Perry, Intellectual Life in America (Chicago: University of Chicago Press, 1989), 230.; pg. 23, Stephen Hardy, How Boston Played (Boston: Northeastern University Press, 1982) 50.; pg. 23, Quoted in Lois Banner, American Beauty (New York: Knopf, 1983), 54.; pg. 24, Harper's Weekly 3 (October 15, 1859), 658.; pg. 25, Porter's Spirit of the Times 2 (May 30, 1857), 10.; pg. 25, Quotations from Porter's Spirit of the Times 5 (October 9, 1858), 84; and Bryan D. Palmer, A Culture of Conflict (Montreal: Queens University Press, 1979), 26.; pg. 26, O.W. Holmes, "The Autocrat at the Breakfast Table," Atlantic Monthly 1 (1858), 881.; pg. 26, T.W. Higginson, "Saints and Their Bodies," Atlantic Monthly 1 (1858), 585–86.; pg. 27, Quotations in Gerald Redmond, The Caledonian Games (Rutherford, NJ: Fairleigh Dickinson University Press, 1971), 39, 45.

Chapter 3: pg. 33, Quoted in John R. Betts, America's Sporting Heritage (Reading, MA: Addison-Wesley, 1974), 162.; pg. 34, Quoted in Melvin L. Adelman's A Sporting

Time: New York City and the Rise of Modern Athletics, 1820–70 (Urbana: University of Illinois Press, 1986) 242.; pg. 35, Allan Nevins, ed., The Diary of Philip Hone, 1828–1851, 2 vols. (New York: Dodd, Mead, 1927), II, 861.; pg. 36, Quoted in Melvin L. Adelman's A Sporting Time: New York City and the Rise of Modern Athletics, 1820–70 (Urbana: University of Illinois Press, 1986) 213, 214.; pg. 36, Quoted in Melvin Leonard Adelman, "The Development of Modern Athletics in New York City, 1820–1870," unpub. Ph.D. diss., University of Illinois, 1980, 535.; pg. 39, Elliott J. Gorn, "The Wicked World: The National Police Gazette and Gilded Age Culture," Media Studies Journal 6 (Winter 1992), 14.; pg. 39, Quotations from Elliott J. Gorn, The Manly Art (Ithaca, NY: Cornell University Press, 1986) 183.; pg. 39, D.B. Chidsey, John the Great (Garden City, NY: Doubleday, 1942), 13.; pg. 40, Quoted in Elliott J. Gorn, The Manly Art (Ithaca, NY: Cornell University Press, 1986) 199.; pg. 41, Quoted in Elliott J. Gorn, The Manly Art (Ithaca, NY: Cornell University Press, 1986) 235.; pg. 41, Quoted in Dale A. Somers, The Rise of Sports in New Orleans (Baton Rouge: Louisiana State University Press, 1972), 184.; pg. 41, William Lyons Phelps, Autobiography with Letters (New York: Oxford University Press, 1939), 356.

Chapter 4: pg. 46, Quoted in George Kirsch, The Creation of American Team Sports (Urbana: University of Illinois Press, 1989), 116.; pg. 46, Quoted in Harold Seymour, Baseball, 3 vols (New York: Oxford University Press, 1960, 1970, 1990); I, 21.; pg. 47, Porter's Spirit of the Times, 1 (January 31, 1857), 357.; pg. 47, Quoted in Melvin L. Adelman's A Sporting Time: New York City and the Rise of Modern Athletics, 1820–70 (Urbana: University of Illinois Press, 1986) 151.; pg. 48, Quoted in Melvin L. Adelman's A Sporting Time: New York City and the Rise of Modern Athletics, 1820–70 (Urbana: University of Illinois Press, 1986) 173.; pg. 48, From Baseball: A History of America's Game. Copyright 2008 Board of Trustees by the University of Illinois. Used with permission of the University of Illinois Press.; pg. 48, Harper's Weekly, October 26, 1867.; pg. 48, New York Times, March 8, 1872.; pg. 49, From Baseball: A History of America's Game. Copyright 2008 Board of Trustees by the University of Illinois. Used with permission of the University of Illinois Press.; pg. 49, From Baseball: A History of America's Game. Copyright 2008 Board of Trustees by the University of Illinois. Used with permission of the University of Illinois Press.; pg. 49, akeside Monthly in 1870; pg. 49, From Baseball: A History of America's Game. Copyright 2008 Board of Trustees by the University of Illinois. Used with permission of the University of Illinois Press.; pg. 50, Quoted in Harold Seymour, Baseball, 3 vols (New York: Oxford University Press, 1960, 1970, 1990); I, 270.; pg. 51, Tristram P. Coffin, The Old Ballgame (New York: Herder and Herder, 1971), 36–37.; pg. 52, Albert Spalding's America's National Game (Lincoln: University of Nebraska Press, 1992). 184.; pg. 52, Albert Spalding's America's National Game (Lincoln: University of Nebraska Press, 1992). 297.; pg. 53, Quoted

in Harold Seymour, Baseball, 3 vols (New York: Oxford University Press, 1960, 1970, 1990); I, 270.; pg. 53, From Baseball: A History of America's Game. Copyright 2008 Board of Trustees by the University of Illinois. Used with permission of the University of Illinois Press.; pg. 54, From Baseball: A History of America's Game. Copyright 2008 Board of Trustees by the University of Illinois. Used with permission of the University of Illinois Press.; pg. 54, From Baseball: A History of America's Game. Copyright 2008 Board of Trustees by the University of Illinois. Used with permission of the University of Illinois Press.; pg. 55, Quoted in Adrian Burgos, Jr., Playing America's Game: Baseball, Latinos and the Color Line (Berkeley: University of Caifornia Press, 2007), 71.

Chapter 5: pg. 59, Robert H. Wiebe, Self-Rule: A Cultural History of American Democracy (Chicago: University of Chicago Press, 1995), 87. For the making of an American upper class, see especially E. Digby Baltzell, Philadelphia Gentlemen (New York: Free Press, 1958); E. Digby Baltzell, The Protestant Establishment (New York: Random House, 1964); Frederic Cople Jaher, The Urban Establishment (Urbana: University of Illinois Press, 1982); Ronald Story, The Forging of an Aristocracy: Harvard & the Boston Upper Class, 1800–1870 (Middletown, CT: Wesleyan University Press, 1980); and Sven Beckert, The Monied Metropolis: New York City and the Consolidation of the American Bourgeoisie, 1850–1896 (New York: Cambridge University Press, 2001). Beckert equates "bourgeoisie" with what we have here described as the upper class.; pg. 60, F.C. Jaher, "Style and Status: High Society in the Late Nineteenth Century New York," in F.C. Jaher, ed., The Rich, the Well Born, and the Powerful (Urbana: University of Illinois Press, 1973), 259.; pg. 60, Charles Peverelly, The Book of American Pastimes (New York: author, 1866), 19.; pg. 62, Quoted in Allen Guttmann, Sports Spectators (New York: Columbia University Press, 1986), 99.; pg. 63, F.W. Janssen, History of Amateur Athletics (New York: Charles R. Bourne, 1885), 35. See also Bob Considine and F.R. Jarvis, The First Hundred Years: A Portrait of NYAC (London: Macmillan, 1969); and J.D. Willis and R.G. Wettan, "Social Stratification in New York City Athletic Clubs, 1865–1915," Journal of Sport History 3 (1976), 45–63.; pg. 63, M.W. Ford, "The New York Athletic Club," Outing 33 (December 1898), 251.; pg. 63, Bob Considine and F.R. Jarvis, The First Hundred Years: A Portrait of NYAC (London: Macmillan, 1969) 43.; pg. 64, Henry Hall, ed., The Tribune Book of Open-Air Sports (New York: Tribune, 1888), 332.; pg. 64, Spirit of the Times, September 2, 1876.; pg. 65, F.W. Janssen, History of Amateur Athletics (New York: Charles R. Bourne, 1885), 103; pg. 65, Outing 6 (May 1885), 251.; pg. 66, Quoted in J.A. Lester, ed., A Century of Philadelphia Cricket (Philadelphia: University of Pennsylvania Press, 1951), 31.; pg. 67, F.H. Curtis and John Heard, The Country Club (Brookline, MA: The Country Club, 1932), 4. See Richard J. Moss, Golf and the American

Country Club (Urbana: University of Illinois Press, 2001), chap. 1.; pg. 67, F.H. Curtis and John Heard, The Country Club (Brookline, MA: The Country Club, 1932), 139. The question mark appears in the original quotation.; pg. 68, H.L. Fitz Patrick, "Golf and the American Girl," Outing 32 (December 1898), 294–95.

Chapter 6: pg. 71, John Higham, "The Reorientation of American Culture in the 1890s," in John Higham, ed., Writing American History (Bloomington: Indiana University Press, 1970), 79. For all intercollegiate sports in this era, see especially Ronald A. Smith, Sports and Freedom: The Rise of Big Time College Athletics (New York: Oxford University Press, 1988), and Patrick B. Miller, "Athletes in Academe: College Sports and American Culture, 1850–1920," unpub. Ph.D. diss., University of California, Berkeley, 1987. For football, see also Parke H. Davis, Football (New York: Scribner's, 1912); Michael Oriard, Reading Football: How the Popular Press Created an American Sporting Spectacle (Chapel Hill: University of North Carolina Press, 1993); John Sayle Watterson, College Football: History, Spectacle, Controversy (Baltimore, MD: Johns Hopkins University Press, 2000); Gerald R. Gems, For Pride, Profit, and Patriarchy: Football and the Incorporation of American Cultural Values (Lanham, MD: Scarecrow, 2000); Mark F. Bernstein, Football: The Ivy League Origins of an American Obsession (Philadelphia: University of Pennsylvania Press, 2001); Guy M. Lewis, "The American Intercollegiate Football Spectacle, 1869–1917," unpub. Ph.D. diss, University of Maryland, 1965; and the provocative interpretation offered by A.S. Markovits in "The Other 'American Exceptionalism'; Why Is There No Soccer in the United States?" International Journal of the History of Sport 7 (1990), 230–64. Also see the review essay by John Nauright, "Writing and Reading American Football: Culture, Identities, and Sports Studies," Sporting Traditions 13 (November 1996), 109–27.; pg. 72, Gerald R. Gems, For Pride, Profit, and Patriarchy: Football and the Incorporation of American Cultural Values (Lanham, MD: Scarecrow, 2000); 112.; pg. 72, Mens Sana," Harvard Magazine 4 (1858), 178.; pg. 72, J.R.W. Hitchcock, "The Harvard-Yale Races," Outing 6 (1885), 393.; pg. 75, Mark F. Bernstein, Football: The Ivy League Origins of an American Obsession (Philadelphia: University of Pennsylvania Press, 2001); pg. 75, Theodore Roosevelt, American Ideals and Other Essays (New York: Review of Reviews, 1897), 11.; pg. 76, Alfred Mahan, The Interest of America in Sea Power (Boston: Little, Brown, 1903), 121.; pg. 76, G.M. Frederickson, The Inner Civil War (New York: Harper & Row, 1965), 223–24.; pg. 76, Roosevelt, "What We Can Expect of the American Boy," St. Nicholas 27 (1900), 574. The other book recommended by Roosevelt was Nelson Aldrich's Story of a Bad Boy.; pg. 77, Caspar Whitney, A Sporting Pilgrimage (New York: Harper & Bros., 1895), 90.; pg. 77, E.L. Richards, "Athletic Sports at Yale," Outing 6 (1885), 453.; pg. 77, A.T. Hadley, "Wealth and Democracy in American Colleges," Harper's Weekly 93 (1906), 452.; pg. 78, University of North Carolina Alumni Quarterly 1

(October 1894), 28.; pg. 78, Quoted in Frederick Rudolph, The American College and University (New York: Vintage Books, 1962), 385.; pg. 78, Guy M. Lewis, "The American Intercollegiate Football Spectacle, 1869–1917," unpub. Ph.D. diss, University of Maryland, 1965; 158–59.; pg. 78, Guy M. Lewis, "The American Intercollegiate Football Spectacle, 1869–1917," unpub. Ph.D. diss, University of Maryland, 1965; 141.; pg. 78, As cited in Kooman Boycheff, "Intercollegiate Athletics and Physical Education at the University of Chicago, 1892–1952," unpub. Ph.D. diss., University of Michigan, 1954, 19. For football at the University of Chicago, see Robin Lester, Stagg's University (Urbana: University of Illinois Press, 1995).; pg. 78, A.A. Stagg and W.W. Sterit, Touchdown! (New York: Longmen's Green, 1927), 203.; pg. 78, W.H. Taft, "College Athletics," Proceedings of the Tenth Annual Convention of the National Collegiate Athletic Association (1915), 67; pg. 79, Ronald A. Smith, Sports and Freedom: The Rise of Big Time College Athletics (New York: Oxford University Press, 1988), 181. For the estimates that follow, See Oriard, Reading Football, chapter 2.; pg. 80, Quoted in Andrew Zimbalist, Unpaid Professionals: Commercialism and Conflict in Big-Time College Sports (Princeton: Princeton University Press, 1999), 7.

Chapter 7: pg. 84, William F. Foneville, Reminiscences of College Days, (Raleigh, N.C.: privately printed, 1904), 67. For more about the development of early athletic programs at Livingstone, Biddle and other historically black colleges, see Grundy, Learning to Win, chapter 1.; pg. 84, San Francisco Chronicle, 5 April 1896, 25. For more details on the game and on Mabel Craft, see Pamela Grundy and Susan Shackelford, Shattering the Glass: The Remarkable History of Women's Basketball (New York: The New Press, 2005), 19–23.; pg. 84, San Francisco Chronicle, 5 April 1896, 25. For more details on the game and on Mabel Craft, see Pamela Grundy and Susan Shackelford, Shattering the Glass: The Remarkable History of Women's Basketball (New York: The New Press, 2005), 19–23.; pg. 85, Richard Henry Pratt, Battlefield and Classroom: Four Decades with the American Indian, 1867–1904 (New Haven: Yale University Press, 1964), 317–18.; pg. 85, David Wallace Adams, Education for Extinction: American Indians and the Boarding School Experience, 1875–1928 (Lawrence: University Press of Kansas, 1995), 181–190.; pg. 86, Quoted in Kate Buford, Native American Son: The Life and Sporting Legend of Jim Thorpe (New York: Alfred A. Knopf, 2010), 61–2; pg. 87, Robert Peterson, Only the Ball Was White: A History of Legendary Black Players and All-Black Professional Teams (New York: Oxford University Press, 1991), 23, 28, 31–2; pg. 87, M.F. Walker, Our Home Colony: A Treatise on the Past, Present and Future of the Negro Race in America (Steubenville, Ohio: Herald Printing Company, 1908, 31.; pg. 88, A.M.E. Zion Quarterly Review 10 (October-December 1900), 64–65. For more about William Henry Lewis, see Gregory Bond, "The Strange Career of William Henry Lewis," in Wiggins, ed., Out of the Shadows. For an account of the career of another pioneering African American college football player, see John M. Carroll, Fritz Pollard: Pioneer in Racial Advancement (Urbana: University of Illinois Press, 1998).; pg. 90, Edith Naomi Hill, "Senda Berenson: Director of Physical Education at Smith College, 1892–1911," in "Pioneer Women in Physical Education," supplement to The Research Quarterly. (American Association for Health, Physical Education, and Recreation, October 1941), 659.; pg. 90, Frances E. Willard, A Wheel Within a Wheel: How I Learned to Ride the Bicycle (Bedford, Mass., Applewood Books, 1997), 25–26.; pg. 90, Based on Pamela Grundy and Susan Shackelford, Shattering the Glass: The Remarkable History of Women's Basketball (New York: The New Press, 2005), 16.; pg. 91, Susan Cahn, Coming on Strong: Gender and Sexuality in Twentieth-Century Women's Sport (New York: The Free Press, 1994), 20–21.; pg. 91, Quoted in Barbara Gregorich, Women at Play: The Story of Women in Baseball (New York: Harcourt, 1993), 36, 7.; pg. 91, William F. Foneville, The Taint of the Bicycle (Goldsboro, N.C.: privately printed, 1902), 10–11.; pg. 92, Charlotte Observer, April 7 and 9, 1907.; pg. 93, Berenson, "Basketball for Women," draft 1 [transcript], 98. Smith College Archives, Senda Berenson Papers, Series 6, "Speeches." URL: http://clio.fivecolleges.edu/smith/berenson/6speeches/.

Chapter 8: pg. 98, H.S. Williams, "The Educational Value and Health-Giving Value of Athletics," Harper's Weekly 39 (February 16, 1895), 165. For a similar conclusion, see Charles D. Lanier, "The World's Sporting Impulse," Review of Reviews 14 (July 1896), 58. For overviews of several of the subjects covered in this chapter, see Riess, City Games, and Gerald M. Gems, Windy City Wars: Labor, Leisure, and Sport in the Making of Chicago (Lanham, MD: Scarecrow, 1997).; pg. 100, S. W. Pope, Patriotic Games (New York: Oxford University Press, 1997), chaps. 7 and 8, and Wanda Ellen Wakefield, Playing to Win: Sports and the American Military, 1898–1945 (Albany: State University of New York Press, 1997), chapters 1 and 2.; pg. 100, Grantland Rice; pg. 100, Grantland Rice, "The Four Horsemen", New York Herald Tribune, October 19, 1924.; pg. 101, Quoted in B.G. Rader, In Its Own Image: How Television Has Transformed Sports (New York: Free Press, 1984), 28. On radio sports, see esp. Curt Smith, Voices of the Game (South Bend, IN: Diamond Communications, 1987).; pg. 103, Bruce Barton, "Ill-Gotten Gains" Collier's 77, March 6 1926, 27.; pg. 103, Quoted in R.W. Fox and T.J.J. Lears, eds., The Culture of Consumption (New York: Pantheon, 1983), 32.; pg. 103, BASEBALL: THE GOLDEN AGE, VOLUME 2 by Seymour (1971) 163w from pp. 4, 46, 278 © Harold Seymour. By permission of Oxford University Press, USA.; pg. 104, Quoted in "Decidedly Unconquerable is Mlle. Lenglen Tennis Champion," Literary Digest 62 (September 13, 1919), 80.; pg. 104, Vanity Fair, October 1932, 71.

Chapter 9: pg. 110, Based on Quoted in Pamela Grundy and Susan Shackelford, Shattering the Glass: The Remarkable History of Women's Basketball (New York: The New Press,

2005), 19–23. For a more detailed description of the development of girls' basketball in Iowa, see Janice Beran, From Six on Six to Full Court Press: A Century of Iowa Girls' Basketball. (Ames, Iowa: Iowa State University Press, 1993); pg. 111, L.H. Gulick, A Philosophy of Play (New York: Scribner's, 1920), 219. For the larger movement to organize and manage the spare-time activities of youth, see Joseph F. Kett, Rites of Passage: Adolescence in America, 1790 to the Present (New York: Basic Books, 1979); and for historiography, Stephen Hardy and A.G. Ingham, "Games, Structures and Agencies: Historians and the American Play Movement," Journal of Social History 17 (1983), 285–301.; pg. 111, H.S. Curtis, The Play Movement and Its Significance (New York: Macmillan, 1917), 119–20.; pg. 111, F.D. Bonyton, "Athletics and Collateral Activities of Secondary Schools," Proceedings and Addresses of the National Education Association (1904), 210.; pg. 113, L.H. Gulick, "State Committees on Athletics," Young Men's Era 18 (1892), 1365.; pg. 113, L.H. Gulick, "Basket Ball," Physical Education 4 (1895), 1200. See also L.H. Gulick, "Abolish Basket Ball," Men 5 (1897), 687.; pg. 114, Athletic League Letters (June 1911), 1. In addition to Athletic League Letters (1896–1911), see W.H. Ball, "The Administration of Athletics in the Young Men's Christian Association," American Physical Education Review 16 (1911), 12–22.; pg. 115, G.S. Hall, Adolescence, 2 vols. (New York: D. Appleton, 1905), I, 202–03; Joseph Lee, Play and Education (New York: Macmillan, 1915), 234; Henry S. Curtis, "The Proper Relation of Organized Sports on Public Playgrounds and in Public Spaces," Playground 3 (1909), 14; W.B. Forbush, The Boy Problem (Boston: Pilgrim, 1901), 9.; pg. 116, L.H. Gulick, A Philosophy of Play (New York: Scribner's, 1920), 92.; pg. 116, G.S. Hall, Adolescence, 2 vols. (New York: D. Appleton, 1905), I, 207.; pg. 116, L.H. Gulick, "Athletics for School Children," Lippincott's Monthly Magazine, 99 (1911), 201.; pg. 116, G.W. Wingate, "The Public Schools-Athletic League," Outing 52 (1908), 166.; pg. 116, G.W. Wingate, "The Public Schools-Athletic League," Outing 52 (1908), 166.; pg. 117, A.B. Reeve, "The World's Greatest Athletic Organization," Outing 57 (1910), 107–14. See also J.T. Jable, "The Public Schools Athletic League of New York City: Organized Athletics for City Schoolchildren, 1903–1914," in S.A. Riess, ed., The American Sporting Experience (West Point, NY: Leisure, 1984), 219–38. Reeve, "The World's Greatest," 110; and C.A. Perry, Wider Use of the School Plant (New York: Charities Pub. Com., 1910), 308.; pg. 117, A.B. Reeve, "The World's Greatest Athletic Organization," Outing 57 (1910), 108.; pg. 117, "Questions for Teachers to Answer," Gymnasia 2 (1906), 149.; pg. 117, H.S. Curtis, The Play Movement and Its Significance (New York: Macmillan, 1917), 81.; pg. 118, Cardinal Principles of Secondary Education Bul., no. 35 (Washington, DC: GPO, 1918), 7–8.; pg. 118, Quotations in Cardinal Principles of Secondary Education Bul., no. 35 (Washington, DC: GPO, 1918), 21, 23.; pg. 118, North Carolina Education 18 (February 1923), 13.; pg. 119, Based on Pamela Grundy and

Susan Shackelford, Shattering the Glass: The Remarkable History of Women's Basketball (New York: The New Press, 2005), 48–49.

Chapter 10: pg. 124, Quoted in Finis Farr, Black Champion (New York: Charles Scribner's Sons, 1964), 107.; pg. 124, Quoted in Lawrence Levine, Black Culture and Black Consciousness: Afro-American Folk Thought from Slavery to Freedom (New York: Oxford University Press, 1977), 431.; pg. 124, Quoted in Randy Roberts, "Jack Dempsey: An American Hero in the 1920s," Journal of Popular Culture 8 (1974), 412.; pg. 124, Los Angeles Times, July 6, 1910.; pg. 125, Al-Tony Gilmore, Bad Nigger: The National Impact of Jack Johnson (New York: Kenikat Press, 1975). 46.; pg. 126, Chicago Defender, July 30, 1910.; pg. 126, Leverett T. Smith Jr., The American Dream and the American Game (Bowling Green, OH: Bowling Green University Popular Culture Press, 1975), 207.; pg. 126, Babe Ruth and Bob Considine, The Babe Ruth Story (New York: Scholastic Books, 1969), 9.; pg. 127, Quotations from Ty Cobb with Al Stump, My Life in Baseball (Garden City, NY: Doubleday, 1961), 280.; pg. 127, F. C. Lane, "The Home Run Epidemic," Baseball Magazine, July 1921; pg. 127, Quoted in Harold Seymour, Baseball, 3 vols (New York: Oxford University Press, 1960, 1970, 1990); I, 21.; pg. 130, Jack "Doc" Kearns with Oscar Fraley, The Million Dollar Gate (New York: Macmillan, 1966), 147–48.; pg. 132, Larry Engelman, The Goddess and the American Girl: The Story of Suzanne Lenglen and Helen Wills (New York: Oxford University Press, 1988). 64.; pg. 133, Larry Engelman, The Goddess and the American Girl: The Story of Suzanne Lenglen and Helen Wills (New York: Oxford University Press, 1988). 293.; pg. 133, Larry Engelman, The Goddess and the American Girl: The Story of Suzanne Lenglen and Helen Wills (New York: Oxford University Press, 1988). 99.; pg. 134, Larry Engelman, The Goddess and the American Girl: The Story of Suzanne Lenglen and Helen Wills (New York: Oxford University Press, 1988). 291. For a thoughtful description of reporters' struggles with portraying female athletes as both strong and feminine see Cahn, Coming on Strong, 211–17.

Chapter 11: pg. 139. Virginia Woolf, "American Fiction," Saturday Review of Literature 1925.; pg. 139, Albert Spalding, America's National Game (Lincoln: University of Nebraska Press, 1992), 4.; pg. 139, BASEBALL: THE GOLDEN AGE, VOLUME 2 by Seymour (1971) 163w from pp. 4, 46, 278 © Harold Seymour. By permission of Oxford University Press, USA.; pg. 140, Leverett T. Smith Jr., The American Dream and the American Game (Bowling Green, OH: Bowling Green University Popular Culture Press, 1975), 190.; pg. 140, L.S. Ritter, The Glory of Their Times (New York: Macmillan, 1966), 49.; pg. 140, L.S. Ritter, The Glory of Their Times (New York: Macmillan, 1966), 49.; pg. 141, Ty Cobb and Al Stump, My Life in Baseball (Garden City, NY: Doubleday, 1961), 280. See also Charles Alexander, Ty Cobb (New York: Oxford University Press, 1984).; pg. 144,

BASEBALL: THE GOLDEN AGE, VOLUME 2 by Seymour (1971) 163w from pp. 4, 46, 278 © Harold Seymour. By permission of Oxford University Press, USA.; pg. 145, Justice Oliver Wendell Holmes Jr., Federal Baseball Club v. National League, 259 U.S. 200 (1922); pg. 147, Robert Peterson, Only the Ball Was White (Englewood Cliffs, NJ: Prentice Hall, 1970), 129–44. See also Donn Rogosin, Invisible Men (New York: Atheneum, 1973); Jules Tygiel, Baseball's Great Experiment (New York: Oxford University Press, 1983), chap. 2; Janet Bruce, The Kansas City Monarchs (Lawrence: University Press of Kansas, 1985); and Rob Ruck, Sandlot Seasons (Urbana: University of Illinois Press, 1987).; pg. 148, Quoted in Adrian Burgos, Jr., Playing America's Game: Baseball, Latinos and the Color Line (Berkeley: University of Caifornia Press, 2007), 164, 167.

Chapter 12: pg. 153, Nation 51 (November 20, 1890), 395.; pg. 153, H.B. Needham, "The College Athlete," McClure's Magazine 25 (1905), 15–28, 160–73.; pg. 153, Ronald A. Smith, Sports and Freedom: The Rise of Big-Time College Athletics (New York: Oxford University Press, 1988); 147.; pg. 153, Quoted in B.M. Kelley, Yale: A History (New Haven, CT: Yale University Press, 1974), 298.; pg. 154, Theodore Roosevelt, letter, Oct. 9, 1905; pg. 155, E.S. Jordan, "Buying Football Victories," Collier's 36 (November 18, 1905), 23. For the 1920s, see Sperber, Shake Down the Thunder; Harold J. Savage et al., American College Athletics (New York: Carnegie Foundation, 1929), 100–101; and Watterson, College Football, chaps 8 and 9.; pg. 157, Quoted in Ron Fimrite, "A Melding of Men All Suited to a T," Sports Illustrated 47 (September 5, 1977), 92.; pg. 157, Andrew Doyle, "Turning the Tide: College Football and Southern Progressivism, Southern Cultures 3 (Fall 1997), 45.; pg. 158, Paul Gallico, The Golden People (New York: Doubleday, 1965), 142.; pg. 158, Quoted in Murray Sperber, Shake Down the Thunder: The Creation of Notre Dame Football (New York: Henry Holt, 1993); 436–37.; pg. 158, Quoted in Edwin Pope, Football's Greatest Coaches (Atlanta: Tupper and Love, 1955), 195.; pg. 159, Murray Sperber, Shake Down the Thunder: The Creation of Notre Dame Football (New York: Henry Holt, 1993); 185.; pg. 159, Quoted in Pope, Football's Greatest Coaches, 189. Sperber in Shake Down the Thunder subjects this legend along with others about Rockne to a systematic reexamination.; pg. Quoted in Edwin Pope, Football's Greatest Coaches (Atlanta: Tupper and Love, 1955), 200.; pg. 160, Harold J. Savage et al., American College Athletics (New York: Carnegie Foundation, 1929), 298.; pg. 161, Harold J. Savage et al., American College Athletics (New York: Carnegie Foundation, 1929), 298; pg. 161, Quoted in Harry Paxton, ed., Sport U.S.A.: The Best from the Saturday Evening Post (New York: Thomas Nelson and Sons, 1961), 405.; pg. 162, See J.F. Steiner, Americans at Play (New York: Arno, 1933), 86–94, and New York Times, December 26, 1937.

Chapter 13: pg. 165, Elliott Denman, SWIMMING; A Pioneer Looks Back on Her Unforgettable Feat, New York Times, April 30, 2001.; pg. 167, Susan Cahn, Coming on Strong: Gender and Sexuality in Twentieth-Century Women's Sport (New York: The Free Press, 1994), 91–92.; pg. 167, Based on All of Hazel Walker's quotes, and much of the information about her comes from Gary Newton's painstaking compilation of material on Walker, titled "Hazel Walker: Miss Basketball." Copies are located at the Women's Basketball Hall of Fame, Knoxville, Tenn., and the Naismith Basketball Hall of Fame, Springfield, Mass. Much of the material can also be found in Grundy and Shackelford, Shattering the Glass, 102–108.; pg. 168, Based on All of Hazel Walker's quotes, and much of the information about her comes from Gary Newton's painstaking compilation of material on Walker, titled "Hazel Walker: Miss Basketball." Copies are located at the Women's Basketball Hall of Fame, Knoxville, Tenn., and the Naismith Basketball Hall of Fame, Springfield, Mass. Much of the material can also be found in Grundy and Shackelford, Shattering the Glass, 102–108.; pg. 168, Garroutte letter from Elva Bishop, producer, Women's Basketball: The Road to Respect (University of North Carolina Public Television, 1997).; pg. 168, : Based on All of Hazel Walker's quotes, and much of the information about her comes from Gary Newton's painstaking compilation of material on Walker, titled "Hazel Walker: Miss Basketball." Copies are located at the Women's Basketball Hall of Fame, Knoxville, Tenn., and the Naismith Basketball Hall of Fame, Springfield, Mass. Much of the material can also be found in Grundy and Shackelford, Shattering the Glass, 102–108.; pg. 168, Mary Jo Festle, Playing Nice: Politics and Apologies in Women's Sports (New York: Columbia University Press, 1996).; pg. 168, Elva Bishop, producer, Women's Basketball: The Road to Respect (University of North Carolina Public Television, 1997).; pg. Rita Liberti, "We Were Ladies, We Just Played Like Boys: African-American Womanhood and Competitive Basketball at Bennett College, 1928–1942," in Patrick B. Miller and David K. Wiggins, eds., Sport and the Color Line: Black Athletes and Race Relations in Twentieth-Century America, (New York: Routledge, 2004), 92. Much of the resurgence of interest in this era of black women's basketball is due to Liberti's pioneering research into the subject.; pg. 169, Chicago Defender, March 14, 1931.; pg. Young, Negro Firsts in Sports, 195; Chicago Defender, March 14, 1931. See also Pamela Grundy, "Ora Washington: The First Black Female Athletic Star," in Wiggins, ed. Out of the Shadows, 79–92.; pg. Susan Cahn, Coming on Strong: Gender and Sexuality in Twentieth-Century Women's Sport (New York: The Free Press, 1994), 123.; pg. 170, Susan Cahn, Coming on Strong: Gender and Sexuality in Twentieth-Century Women's Sport (New York: The Free Press, 1994), 114–15: pg. 170, Based on A more detailed account of the Tuskegee team, which includes the quotes used here, can be found in Grundy and Shackelford, Shattering the Glass, 76–80. See also Jennifer H. Lansbury, A Spectacular Leap: Black Women Athletes in Twentieth Century America (Fayetteville, University of Arkansas Press, 2014), chapter 2.; pg. 170, Grundy and Shackelford, Shattering the Glass, 79.; pg. Based on A more detailed account of the Tuskegee team, which includes the quotes used here, can be found in Grundy and Shackelford, Shattering the Glass, 76–80. See also Jennifer H. Lansbury, A Spectacular Leap: Black Women Athletes in Twentieth Century America (Fayetteville, University of Arkansas Press, 2014), chapter 2.; pg. 170, Based on All of Hazel Walker's quotes, and much of the information about her comes from Gary Newton's painstaking compilation of material on Walker, titled "Hazel Walker: Miss Basketball." Copies are located at the Women's Basketball Hall of Fame, Knoxville, Tenn., and the Naismith Basketball Hall of Fame, Springfield, Mass. Much of the material can also be found in Grundy and Shackelford, Shattering the Glass, 102–108.: pg. 171, From Baseball: A History of America's Game. Copyright 2008 Board of Trustees by the University of Illinois. Used with permission of the University of Illinois Press.; pg. 171, Susan Cahn, Coming on Strong: Gender and Sexuality in Twentieth-Century Women's Sport (New York: The Free Press, 1994), 150.; pg. 171, Susan Cahn, Coming on Strong: Gender and Sexuality in Twentieth-Century Women's Sport (New York: The Free Press, 1994), 151.; pg. 172, Quoted in Ellen Gerber, "The Controlled Development of Collegiate Sport for Women, 1923–1936," Journal of Sport History 2 (1975), 11.; pg. 173, Quoted in Mary Ellen Hanson, Go! Fight! Win! Cheerleading in American Culture (Bowling Green, OH: Bowling Green University Popular Press, 1995), 10. See also Grundy, Learning to Win, 246–55, 285–90; and Michael Oriard, King Football: Sport and Spectacle in the Golden Age of Radio and Newsreels, Movies and Magazines, the Weekly and the Daily Press (Chapel Hill: University of North Carolina Press, 2001), 280–88.; pg. 174, Quoted in Mary Ellen Hanson, Go! Fight! Win! Cheerleading in American Culture (Bowling Green, OH: Bowling Green University Popular Press, 1995), 21.

Chapter 14: pg. 179, As quoted in P.J. Graham and Horst Ueberhorst, eds., The Modern Olympics (Cornwall, NY: Leisure, n.d.), 32.; pg. 180, Kate Buford, Native American Son: The Life and Sporting Legend of Jim Thorpe (Alfred Knopf, 2010), 34.; pg. 180, New York Times, June 15, 1912.; pg. 180, New York Times, August 11, 1912.; pg. 180, New York Times, June 14, 1912.; pg. 182, Richard D. Mandell, The Nazi Olympics (New York: Macmillan, 1971; Urbana: University of Illinois Press, 1987), 71. See also William J. Baker, Jesse Owens (New York: Free Press, 1986); Arnd Kruger, "The 1936 Olympic Games—Berlin," in Graham and Ueberhorst, Modern Olympics, 168–82; George Eisen, "The Voices of Sanity: American Diplomatic Reports from the 1936 Berlin Olympiad," Journal of Social History 11 (1984), 56–78; and Duff Hart-Davis, Hitler's Games (London: Macmillan, 1986).; pg. 183, New York Times, 4 August 1936; quoted in William J. Baker, Jesse Owens (New York: Free Press, 1986); 4.; pg. 184, Quoted in Chris Mead, Champion

Joe Louis: Black Hero in White America (New York: Charles Scribner's Sons, 1985), 56.; pg. 184, Quoted in Chris Mead, Champion Joe Louis: Black Hero in White America (New York: Charles Scribner's Sons, 1985), 145.; pg. 185, Lawrence Levine, Black Culture and Black Consciousness: Afro-American Folk Thought from Slavery to Freedom (New York: Oxford University Press, 1977), 435.; pg. 185, Quoted in Mark Dryeson, "Jesse Owens: Leading Man in Modern American Tales of Racial Progress and Limits," in David K. Wiggins, ed., Out of the Shadows: A Biographical History of African American Athletes (Fayetteville: University of Arkansas Press, 2006). 118.; pg. 185, Quoted in Chris Mead, Champion Joe Louis: Black Hero in White America (New York: Charles Scribner's Sons, 1985), 158.

Chapter 15: pg. 190, Quoted in Espy, Politics of the Olympic Games, 38.; pg. 190, President John F. Kennedy; pg. 191, B.G. Rader, In Its Own Image: How Television Has Transformed Sports (New York: Free Press, 1984), 35; Theodore Caplow et al., Middletown Families (Minneapolis: University of Minnesota Press, 1982); J.P. Robinson, How Americans Use Time (New York: Institute of Social Research, 1977), esp.172–79; and H.J. Gans, The Urban Villagers (New York: Free Press, 1962), 187–96.; pg. 192, Source: K.T. Jackson, Crabgrass Frontier (New York: Oxford University Press, 1985), 231.; pg. 193, Quoted in W.O. Johnson Jr., Super Spectator and the Electric Lilliputians (Boston: Little, Brown, 1971), 161.; pg. 196, Ronald Reagan, "Address at the Commencement Exercises at the University of Notre Dame," May 17, 1981, http://www.reagan.utexas.edu/archives/speeches/1981/51781a.htm.

Chapter 16: pg. 201, H.A. March, Pro Football, 2d ed. (New York: Lyon, 1934), 65. For early pro football history, see Marc S. Maltby, The Origins and Early Development of Professional Football (New York: Garland, 1997); Robert W. Peterson, Pigskin: The Early Years of Pro Football (New York: Oxford University Press, 1997); Michael Oriard, King Football: Sport and Spectacle in the Golden Age of Radio and Newsreels, Movies and Magazines, the Weekly & the Daily Press (Chapel Hill: University of North Carolina Press, 2001), chap. 6; John M. Carroll, Fritz Pollard (Urbana: University of Illinois Press, 1992); John M. Carroll, Red Grange and the Rise of Modern Football (Urbana: University of Illinois Press, 1999); George Halas et al., Halas by Halas (New York: McGraw-Hill, 1979); and Paul Brown with Jack Clary, PB: The Paul Brown Story (New York: Atheneum, 1979). For pro football in the age of television, see MacCambridge, America's Game, which is rich in detail but also an unending pageant of praise for the NFL's leadership, and the more balanced and analytical Michael Oriard, Brand NFL: Making and Selling America's Favorite Game (Chapel Hill, NC: University of North Carolina Press, 2007). Oriard's book, in particular, has shaped my understanding of both the NFL's recent history as well as that of the other pro team sports.; pg. 201, Quoted in B.G. Rader, In Its Own Image (New York: Free Press, 1984), 83.; pg. 202, Quoted in Associated Press, A Century of American Sports (Maplewood, NJ: Hamond, 1975), 17–18.; pg. 202, Richard Kostelanetz, "Fanfare of TV Football," Intellectual Digest 3 (August 1973), 54. See also Joan Chandler, "TV and Sports: Wedded with a Golden Hoop," Psychology Today 10 (April 1977), 64–76; and Joan Chandler, Television and National Sport (Urbana: University of Illinois Press, 1988), chap. 3.; pg. 203, 5 The Buck Lateral Series, Quoted Sports Illustrated 49 (July 24, 1978), 56.; pg. 203, They Said It, Quoted in Sports Illustrated 51 (October 15, 1979), 24.; pg. 204, Quoted in Joseph Durso, The All-American Dollar (Boston: Houghton Mifflin, 1971), 58–59.; pg. 206, Michael MacCambridge, America's Game: The Epic Story of How Pro Football Captured a Nation (New York: Random House, 2004), 458.; pg. 207, Events & Discoveries, Sports Illustrated 9 (September 1, 1958), 26.; pg. 210, R.H. Boyle, "This Miller Admits He's a Grind," Sports Illustrated 40 (March 11, 1974), 23.; pg. 210, Data from U.S. Census, Statistical Abstract of the United States, annual editions; Major League Baseball Players Association; National Basketball Players Association; and National Football League Players Association.

Chapter 17: pg. 216, Joseph N. Crowley, In the Arena: The NCAA's First Century (Indianapolis, IN: NCAA, 2006) 91.; pg. 218, Quoted in Kathryn Jay, More Than Just a Game (New York: Columbia University Press, 2004), 191.; pg. 219, Quoted in Lincoln (Nebraska) Star, August 30, 1979.; pg. 221, Quoted in Zander Hollander, ed., Madison Square Garden (New York: Hawthorne, 1973), 76.; pg. 221, Quoted in Murray Sperber, Onward to Victory (New York: Henry Holt, 1998), 340.

Chapter 18: pg. 228, Jules Tygiel, Baseball's Great Experiment (New York: Oxford University Press, 1983) 67.; pg. Jules Tygiel, Baseball's Great Experiment (New York: Oxford University Press, 1983) 197.; pg. 228, Jules Tygiel, Baseball's Great Experiment (New York: Oxford University Press, 1983) 327; pg. 229, Quoted in Mary Jo Festle, "'Jackie Robinson Without the Charm:' The Challenges of Being Althea Gibson," in David K. Wiggins, ed., Out of the Shadows: A Biographical History of African American Athletes (Fayetteville: University of Arkansas Press, 2006). 201–202. See also Lansbury, A Spectacular Leap, chapter 3.; pg. 230, Quoted in Amy Bass, Not the Triumph but the Struggle: The 1968 Olympics and the Making of the Black Athlete (Minneapolis: University of Minnesota Press, 2002). 83.; pg. 230, For the Ali quotations, see "Through the Years with Ali," Sports Illustrated 45 (December 20–27, 1976), 111, 113. For other assessments of Ali's cultural significance, see Elliott J. Gorn, ed., Muhammad Ali (Urbana: University of Illinois Press, 1995); Gerald Early, ed., The Muhammad Ali Reader (New York: Rob Weisbach Books, 1998); and David W. Zang, Sports Wars: Athletes in the Age of Aquarius (Fayetteville: University of Arkansas Press, 2001), chapter 5.; pg. 231, Quoted in Gerard O'Connor, "Where Have You Gone, Joe DiMaggio?" in R.B. Browne et al., Heroes in Popular Culture (Bowling Green, OH: Bowling Green University Press, 1972), 87.; pg. 231, Quoted in Dave

Zirin, People's History of Sports in the United States: 25 Years of Politics, Protest, People and Play (New York: The New Press, 2009), 148, 146.; pg. 232, Quoted in Amy Bass, Not the Triumph but the Struggle: The 1968 Olympics and the Making of the Black Athlete (Minneapolis: University of Minnesota Press, 2002). 205.; pg. 232, Quoted in Dave Zirin, People's History of Sports in the United States: 25 Years of Politics, Protest, People and Play (New York: The New Press, 2009), 163.; pg. 232, The Black Athlete—a Shameful Story, Sports Illustrated, July 1, 1968.; pg. 232, Quoted in Amy Bass, Not the Triumph but the Struggle: The 1968 Olympics and the Making of the Black Athlete (Minneapolis: University of Minnesota Press, 2002). 206–7.; pg. 233, Quoted in Amy Bass, Not the Triumph but the Struggle: The 1968 Olympics and the Making of the Black Athlete (Minneapolis: University of Minnesota Press, 2002). 272, 288.; pg. 235, Ernesto B. Vigil, The Crusade for Justice: Chicano Militancy and the Government's War on Dissent (Madison, Wisc.: University of Wisconsin Press, 1999), 10.; pg. 236, Dennis J. Banks, "Tribal Names and Mascots in Sports," Journal of Sport and Social Issues 17 (April 1993), 5. See also National Congress of American Indians Report, Ending the Legacy of Racism in Sports and the Era of Harmful "Indian" Sports Mascots, October, 2013.; pg. 237, Quoted in Dave Zirin, People's History of Sports in the United States: 25 Years of Politics, Protest, People and Play (New York: The New Press, 2009), 206.; pg. 237, An Assessment Of 'black Is Best', Sports Illustrated, January 18, 1971.

Chapter 19: pg. 241, Quoted in The Women's Sports Foundation's Gender Equity Report Card (Women's Sports Foundation, 1997), 4. For the marathon story, see Charlie Lovett, Olympic Marathon: A Centennial History of the Game's Most Storied Race, (Westport, Conn.: Praeger, 1997), Chapter 25.; pg. 241, Quoted in Mary Jo Festle, Playing Nice: Politics and Apologies in Women's Sports (New York: Columbia University Press, 1996)., 82.; pg. 242, Based on Quoted in Grundy and Shackelford, Shattering the Glass, 139. When Stringer tried out for the cheerleading team, she ran into one of the complications of the desegregation era: while school sports teams often welcomed African American athletes, black women often found it especially different to make cheerleading squads. Although Stringer was an excellent performer, it took the involvement of the local NAACP to get her on the squad.; pg. 242, Based on Quoted in Grundy and Shackelford, Shattering the Glass, 137. For an account of the development of the women's liberation movement, see Sarah M. Evans, Personal Politics: The Roots of Women's Liberation in the Civil Rights Movement and the New Left (New York: Knopf, 1979).; pg. 242, Based on Quoted in Grundy and Shackelford, Shattering the Glass, 143.; pg. 244, Lusia Harris-Stewart interview by Georgine Clark, December 18, 1999, Center for Oral History and Cultural Heritage, University of Southern Mississippi.; pg. 245, Jack Kramer, The Game: My 40 years in Tennis; pg. 246, Robert Proctor, Golden Holocaust: Origins of the Cigarette Catastrophe and the Case for Abolition (Berkeley: University of California Press, 2012).; pg. 249, Quoted in Mary Jo Festle, Playing Nice: Politics and Apologies in Women's Sports (New York: Columbia University Press, 1996)., 236.; pg. 249, Quoted in Mary Jo Festle, Playing Nice: Politics and Apologies in Women's Sports (New York: Columbia University Press, 1996)., 243.; pg. 249, Quoted in Mary Jo Festle, Playing Nice: Politics and Apologies in Women's Sports (New York: Columbia University Press, 1996)., 216–19.; pg. 250, Pat Head Summitt with Sally Jenkins, Reach for the Summit (New York: Three Rivers Press, 1999) 21–23.

Chapter 20: pg. 254, Kate Pickert, A Brief History of The X Games, Time, January 22, 2009. For a history of extreme sports, see David Browne, Amped: How Big Air, Big Dollars, and a New Generation Took Sports to the Extreme (New York: Bloomsbury, 2004).; pg. 256, The Trophy In Eisner's Big Deal, New York Times, August 6, 1995.; pg. 259, Jorge Iber, et. al., Latinos in U.S. Sport: A History of Isolation, Cultural Identity and Acceptance (Champaign, Ill.: Human Kinetics, 2011), 226.; pg. 260, Quotes from In The Driver's Seat, Sports Illustrated, December 10, 1984. For the rise of Michael Jordan see LaFeber, Michael Jordan.; pg. 261, Jack McCallum, "The Best Team I Ever Covered," http://sportsillustrated.cnn.com/2011/writers/best_team_i_ever_covered/07/10/mccallum.dream.team/; pg. 261, Quoted in Walter LaFeber, Michael Jordan and the New Global Capitalism (New York: W.W. Norton and Company, 2002), 101.; pg. 262, Based on Grundy and Shackelford, Shattering the Glass, 219. Detailed and insightful accounts of the Olympic team's organization, as well as its year of competition can be found in Sara Corbett, Venus to the Hoop: A Gold Medal Year in Women's Basketball (New York: Anchor Books, 1998).; pg. 262, Based on Quoted in Grundy and Shackelford, Shattering the Glass, 224.; pg. 263, Both quoted in Jere Longman, The Girls of Summer: The U.S. Women's Soccer Team and How It Changed the World (New York: Harper, 2000), 21–23.; pg. 263, Based on Quoted in Grundy and Shackelford, Shattering the Glass, 254–55.; pg. 264, LaFeber, Michael Jordan and the New Global Capitalism (New York: W.W. Norton and Company, 2002), 94.

Chapter 21: pg. 267, Ryan Crull, "Steve Cash proves himself to be one of the best," August 30, 2010, http://thecurrent-online.com/sports/steve-cash-proves-himself-to-be-one-of-the-best-umsl-sophomore%E2%80%99s-gold-medal-is-the-latest-in-his-inspiring-career/.; pg. 269, Taking The Fun Out Of A Game, Sports Illustrated, November 17, 1975.; pg. 270, Quoted in Knight Foundation, A Call to Action. In the early years of the new century, the Knight Commission, the reformed NCAA under the presidency of Myles Brandt, faculty senates at some fifty colleges, and the Association of Governing Boards of Universities and Colleges joined in a fitful, largely unsuccessful effort to close the chasm between athletic and academic cultures. See, for example, BusinessWeek, October 20, 2003; New York Times, Jan. 17, 2003.; pg. 270, James L. Shulman and William G. Bowen, The Game of Life: College Sports and Educational Values (Princeton: Princeton University Press, 2001), 262; 271. See also the lengthy analysis of possible ramifications of broad-based athletic recruitment in ibid., 268–88.; pg. 270, Raleigh News & Observer, January 16, 2014.; pg. 271, Problems In A Turned-on World, Sports Illustrated, June 23, 1969.; pg. 273, Madison Park and Stephanie Smith: "Player's text: send my brain to NFL research bank," February 21, 2011. http://thechart.blogs.cnn.com/2011/02/21/anxiety-about-brain-damage-pervades-football/; pg. 274, Dave Zirin, The Florida State Seminoles; The Champions of Racist Mascots," January 7, 2014. http://www.thenation.com/blog/177800/florida-state-seminoles-champions-racist-mascots; pg. 274, Ruben Navarrette, "The mariachi singer is more American than his critics," June 17, 2013, http://www.cnn.com/2013/06/17/opinion/navarrette-mexican-american-singer/.; pg. 275,: Either/Or, New Yorker, November 30, 2009.

Photo Credits

Chapter 1: pg. 1, akg-images/British Library/Newscom. **Chapter 2:** pg. 17, Library of Congress Prints and Photographs Division[LC-USZ62-843]. **Chapter 3:** pg. 31, Baillie, James S. (fl.1838-55)/Free Library, Philadelphia, PA, USA/The Bridgeman Art Library. **Chapter 4:** pg. 44, Library of Congress Prints and Photographs Division[LC-DIG-pga-02288]. **Chapter 5:** pg. 57, Library of Congress Prints and Photographs Division[LC-DIG-pga-04042]. **Chapter 6:** pg. 70, Yale athletics photographs (RU 691). Manuscripts & Archives, Yale University. **Chapter 7:** pg. 83, Johnson C. Smith University.; pg. 83, College Archives, Smith College (Northampton, Massachusetts). **Chapter 8:** pg. 97, Bettmann/CORBIS. **Chapter 9:** pg. 109, Public Library of Charlotte and Mecklenburg County. **Chapter 10:** pg. 121, Library of Congress Prints and Photographs Division[LC-DIG-ggbain-12203]. **Chapter 11:** pg. 137, Library of Congress Prints and Photographs Division [LC-USZ62-69242]. **Chapter 12:** pg. 151, Permission of the Georgia Institute of Technology Library and Information Center, Archives and Records Management Department. **Chapter 13:** pg. 164, AP Images. **Chapter 14:** pg. 177, Hulton-Deutsch Collection/Historical/Corbis. **Chapter 15:** pg. 188, Charles Hoff/New York Daily News Archive/Getty Images. **Chapter 16:** pg. 199, The Denver Post/Getty Images. **Chapter 17:** pg. 213, SI Cover/Getty Images. **Chapter 18:** pg. 225, AP Images. **Chapter 19:** pg. 239, Manny Millan/Sports Illustrated/Getty Images. **Chapter 20:** pg. 253, Dave Hansen/Newport Daily News/AP Images. **Chapter 21:** pg. 266, Popperfoto/Getty Images.

INDEX